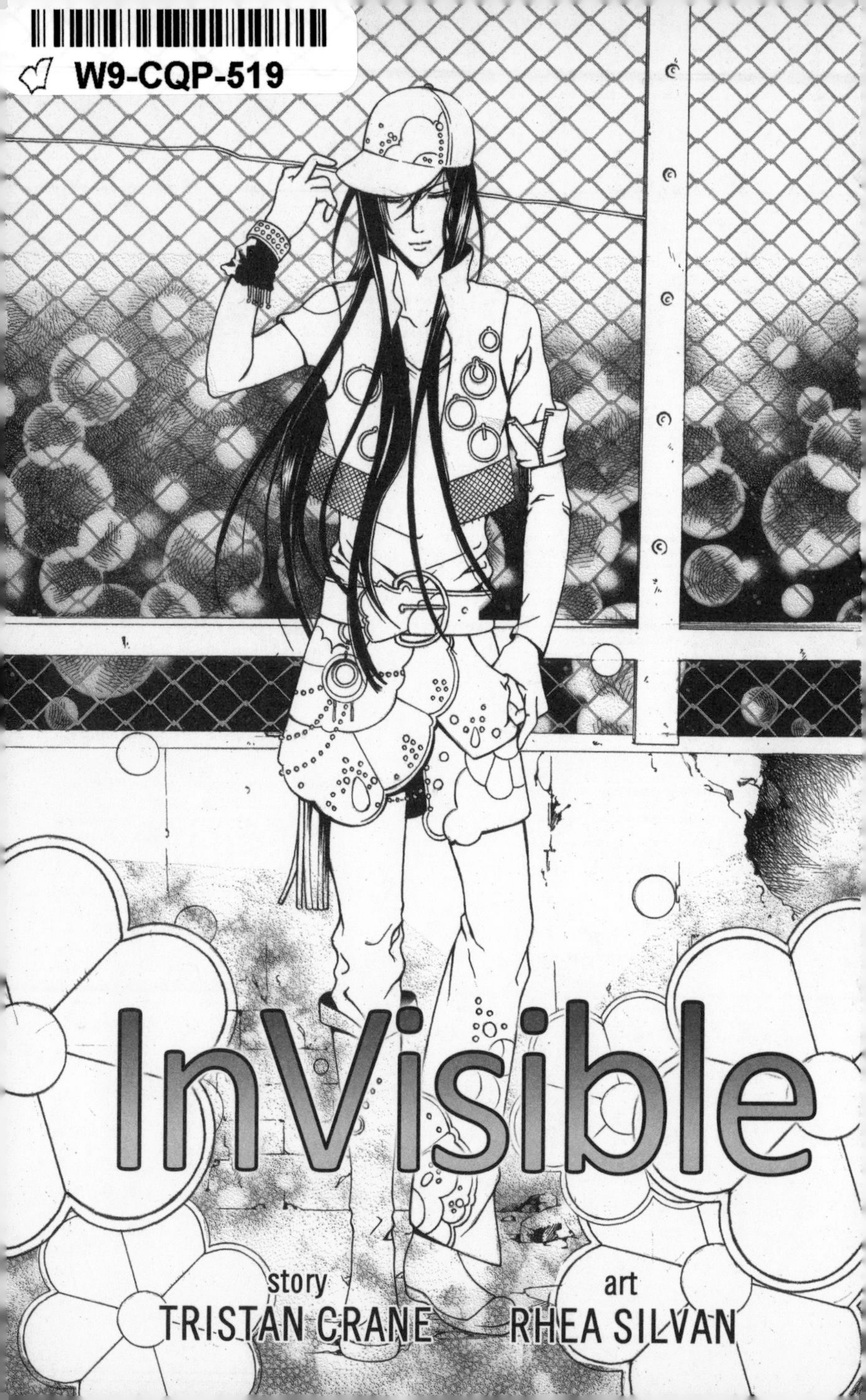

InVisible

story
TRISTAN CRANE

art
RHEA SILVAN

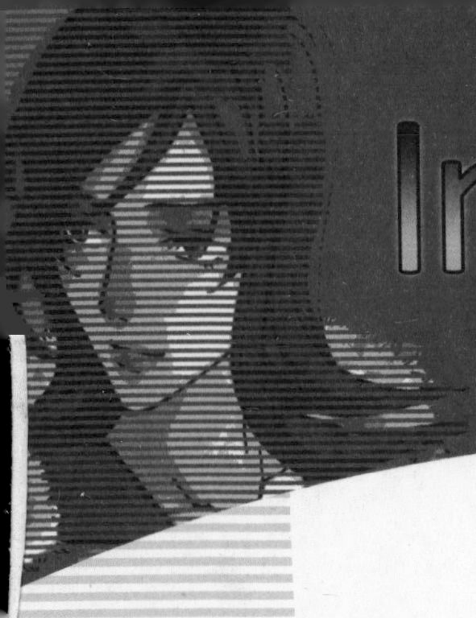

InVisible

story
TRISTAN CRANE

art
RHEA SILVAN

STAFF CREDITS

lettering **Nicky Lim**
toning **Rhea Silvan**
graphic design **Nicky Lim**
layout **Adam Arnold**
assistant editor **Jason DeAngelis**
editor **Adam Arnold**

publisher **Seven Seas Entertainment**

Visit us online at www.gomanga.com.

ISBN: 978-1-934876-19-0

Printed in Canada

First Printing: January 2009

10 9 8 7 6 5 4 3 2 1

"Alchemy is the science of life, of consciousness. The alchemist knows that there is a very solid link between matter, life, and consciousness. Alchemy is the art of manipulating life and consciousness in matter to help it evolve or solve the problems of inner disharmony."

—*Dubuis*

InVisible

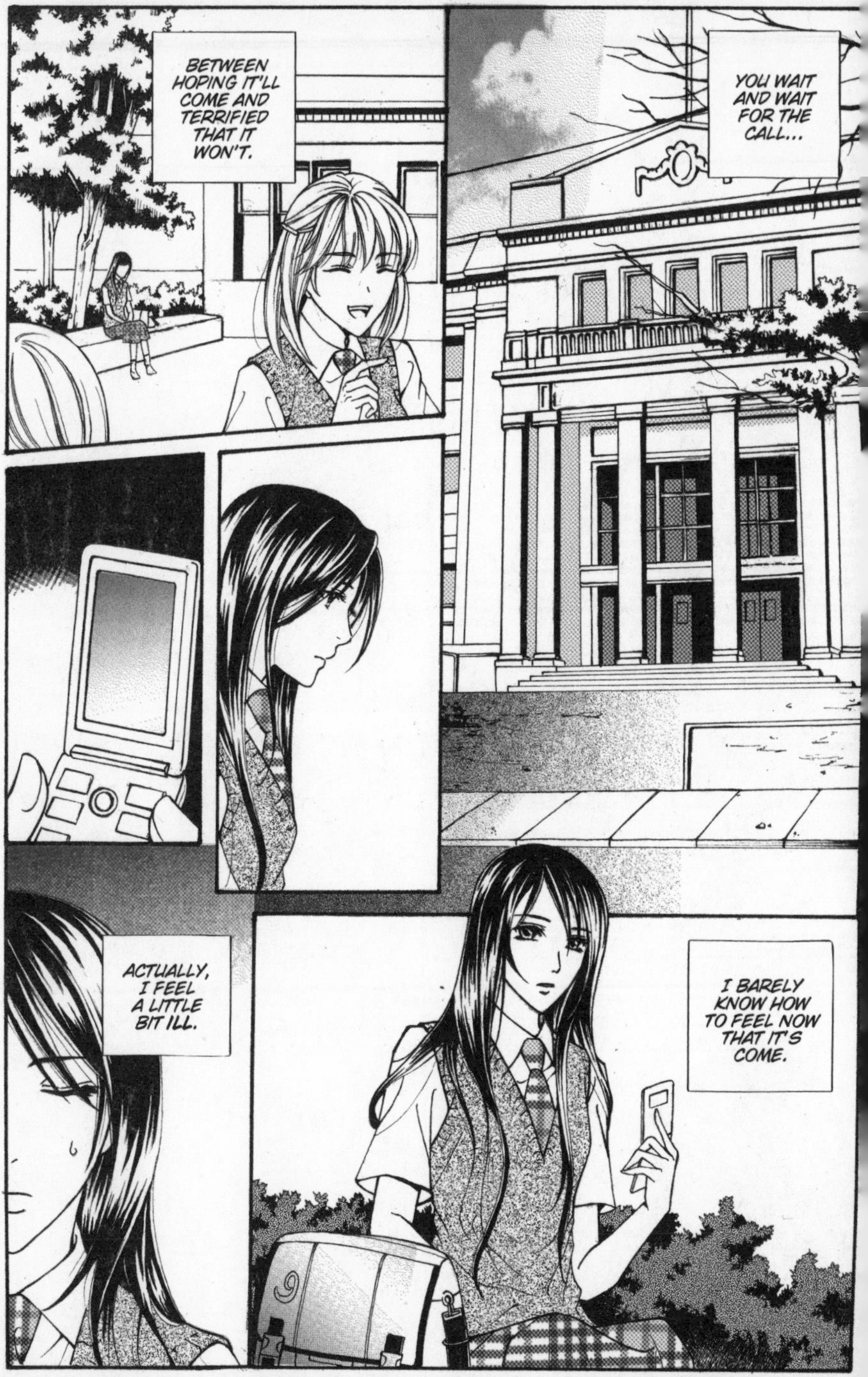
YOU WAIT AND WAIT FOR THE CALL...
BETWEEN HOPING IT'LL COME AND TERRIFIED THAT IT WON'T.
I BARELY KNOW HOW TO FEEL NOW THAT IT'S COME.
ACTUALLY, I FEEL A LITTLE BIT ILL.

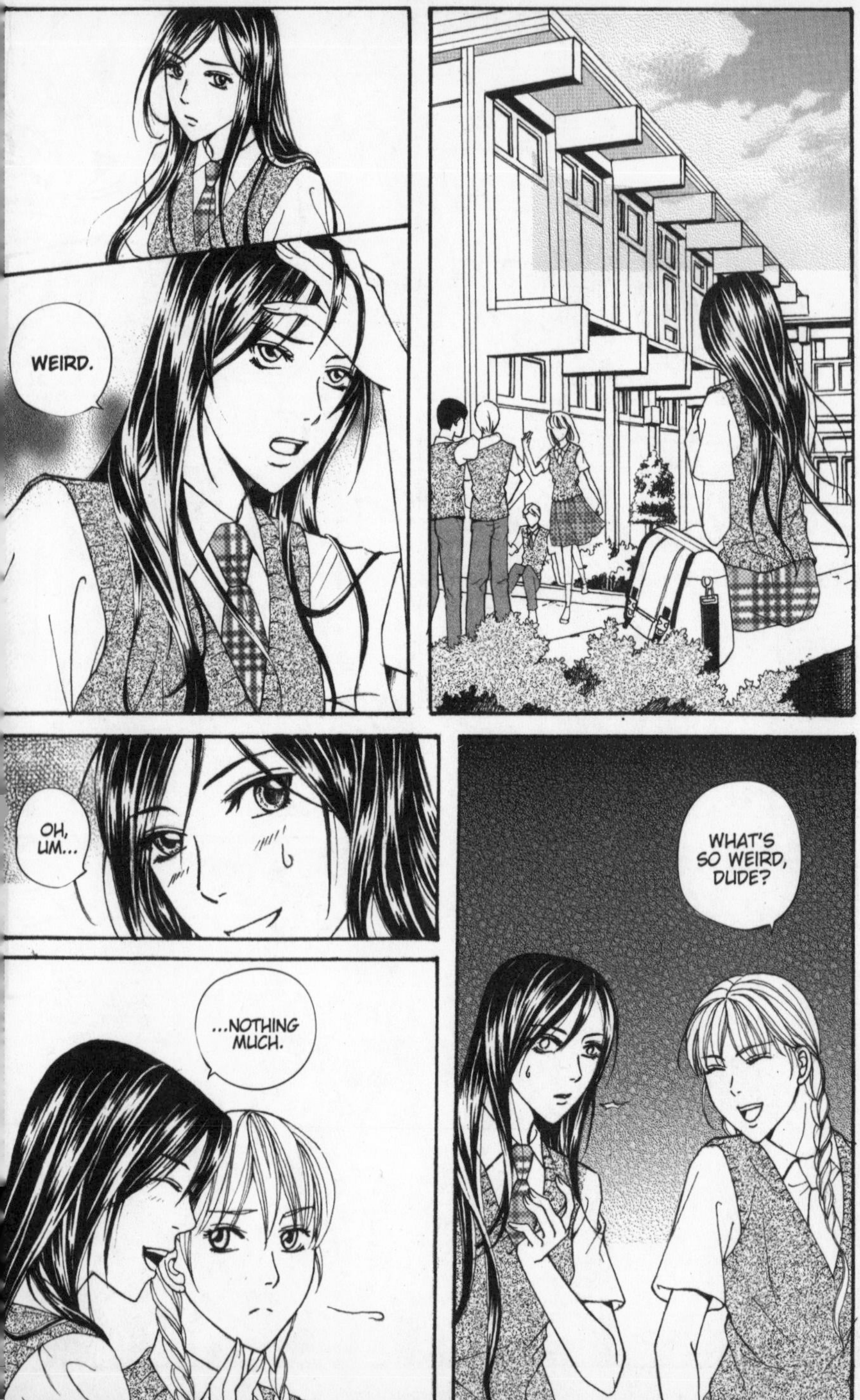
WEIRD.
WHAT'S SO WEIRD, DUDE?
OH, UM...
...NOTHING MUCH.

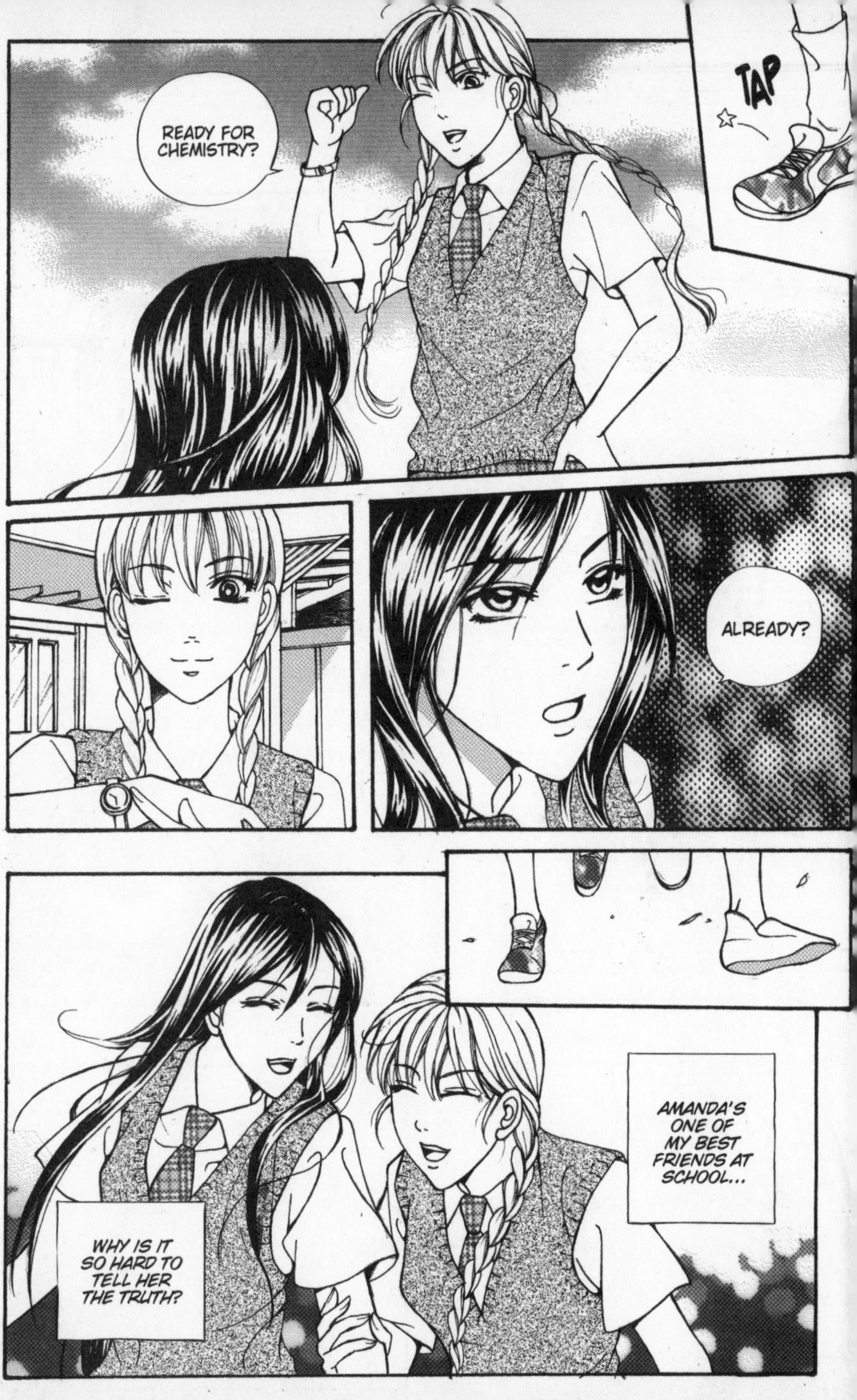
TAP
READY FOR CHEMISTRY?
ALREADY?
AMANDA'S ONE OF MY BEST FRIENDS AT SCHOOL...
WHY IS IT SO HARD TO TELL HER THE TRUTH?

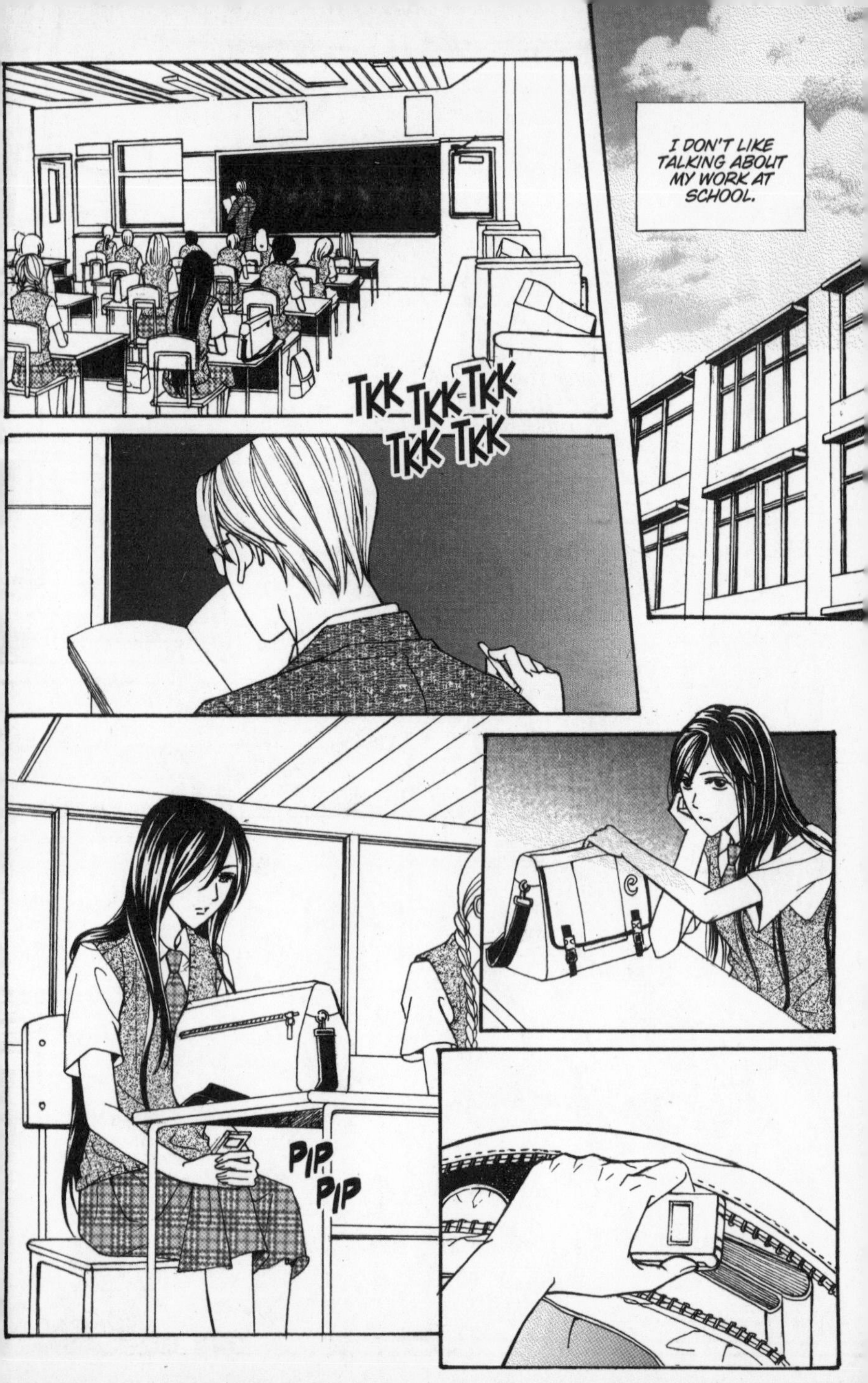
I DON'T LIKE TALKING ABOUT MY WORK AT SCHOOL.
TKK TKK TKK
TKK TKK
PIP PIP

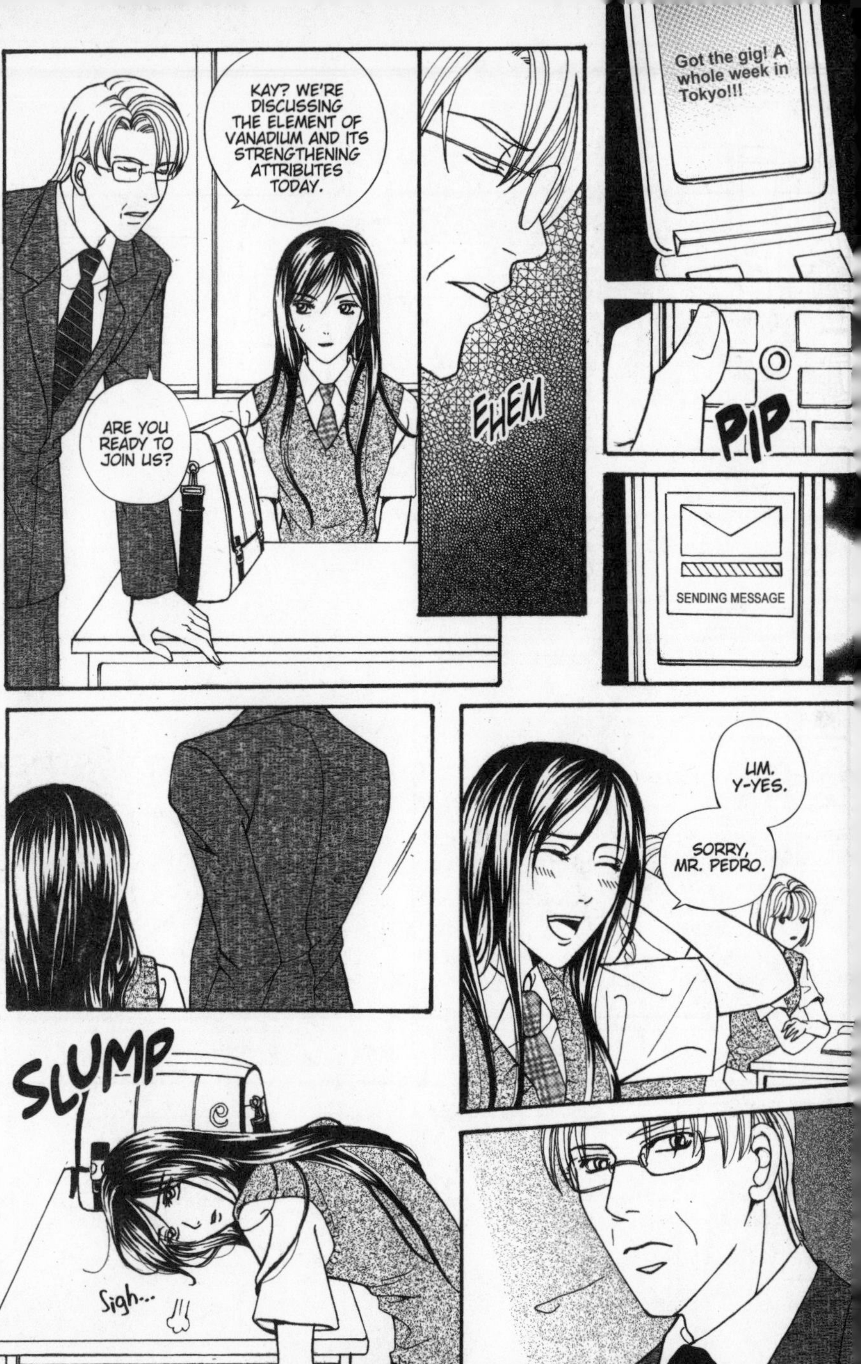
Got the gig! A whole week in Tokyo!!!
PIP
SENDING MESSAGE
EHEM
KAY? WE'RE DISCUSSING THE ELEMENT OF VANADIUM AND ITS STRENGTHENING ATTRIBUTES TODAY.
ARE YOU READY TO JOIN US?
UM. Y-YES.
SORRY, MR. PEDRO.
SLUMP
Sigh...

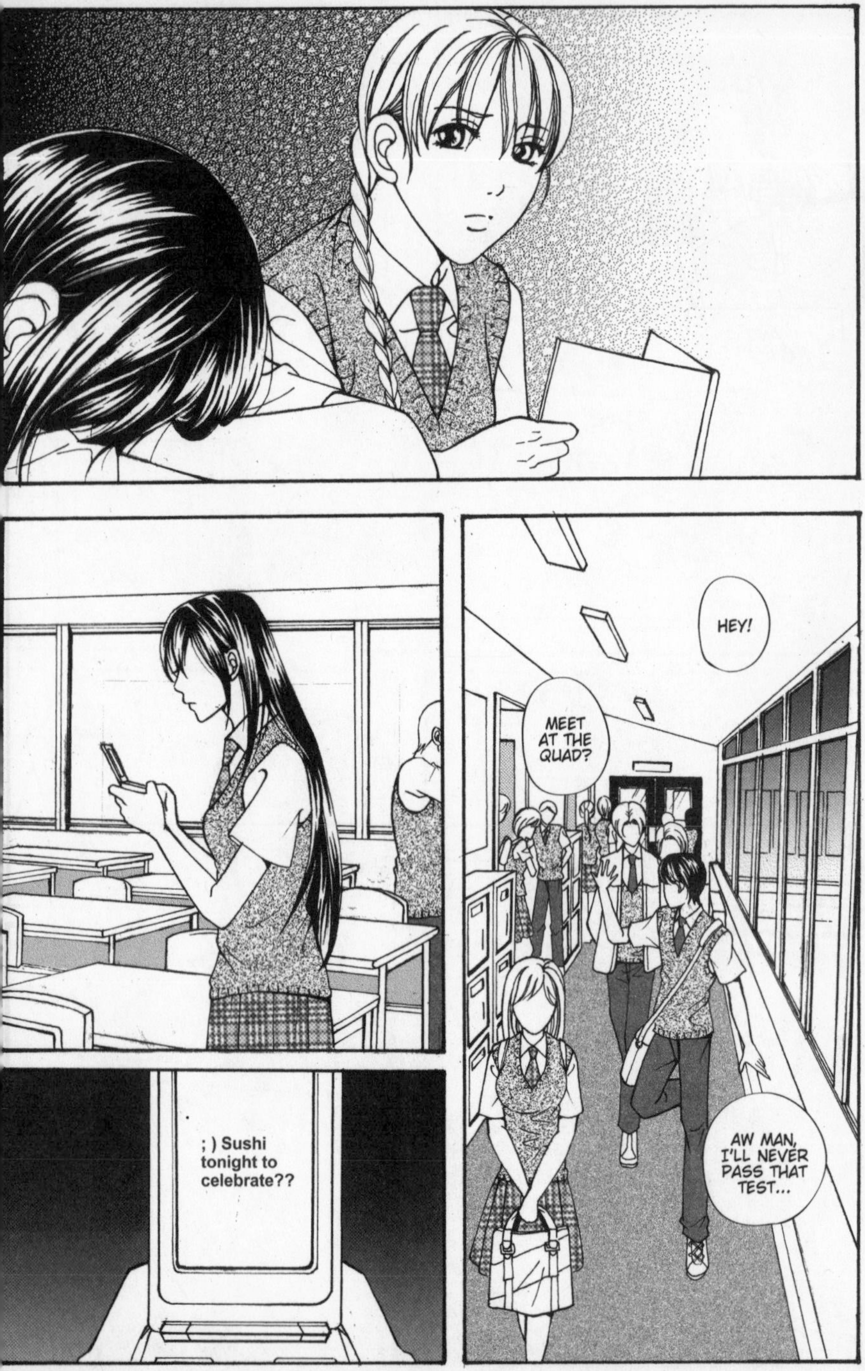
HEY!
MEET AT THE QUAD?
AW MAN, I'LL NEVER PASS THAT TEST...
;) Sushi tonight to celebrate??

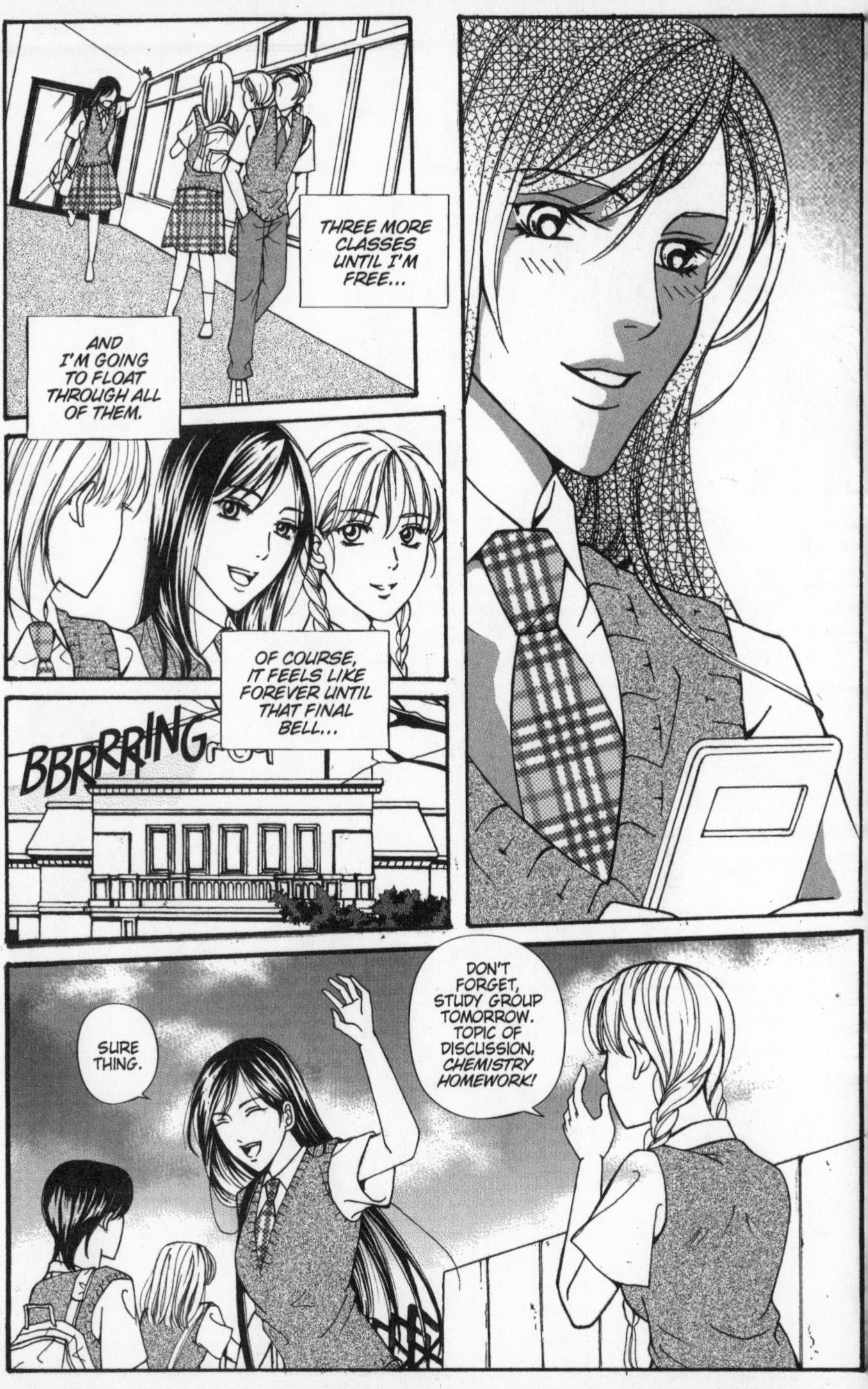
THREE MORE CLASSES UNTIL I'M FREE...
AND I'M GOING TO FLOAT THROUGH ALL OF THEM.
OF COURSE, IT FEELS LIKE FOREVER UNTIL THAT FINAL BELL...
BBRRRRING
DON'T FORGET, STUDY GROUP TOMORROW. TOPIC OF DISCUSSION, CHEMISTRY HOMEWORK!
SURE THING.

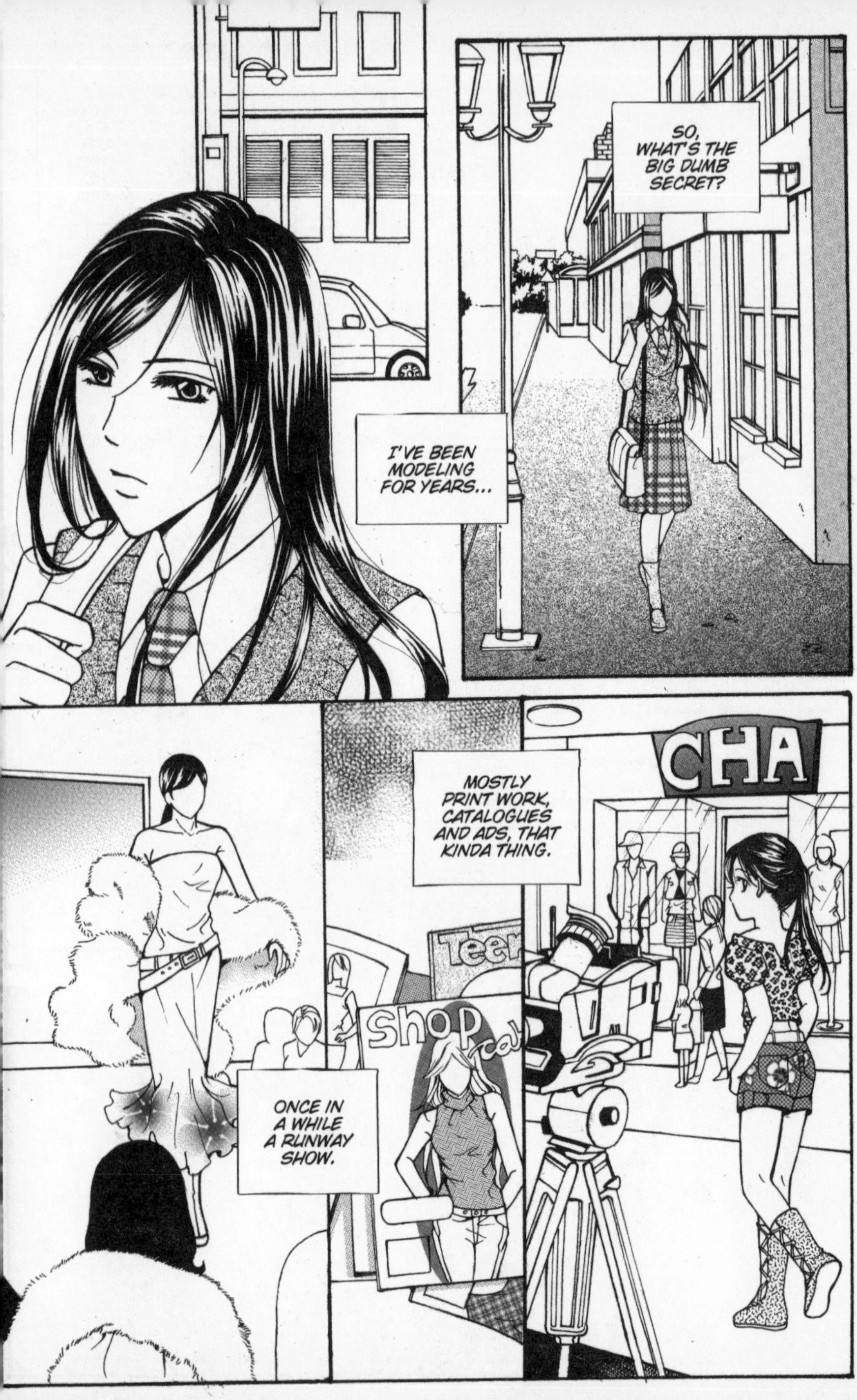
SO, WHAT'S THE BIG DUMB SECRET?
I'VE BEEN MODELING FOR YEARS...
CHA
MOSTLY PRINT WORK, CATALOGUES AND ADS, THAT KINDA THING.
Teen
shop
ONCE IN A WHILE A RUNWAY SHOW.

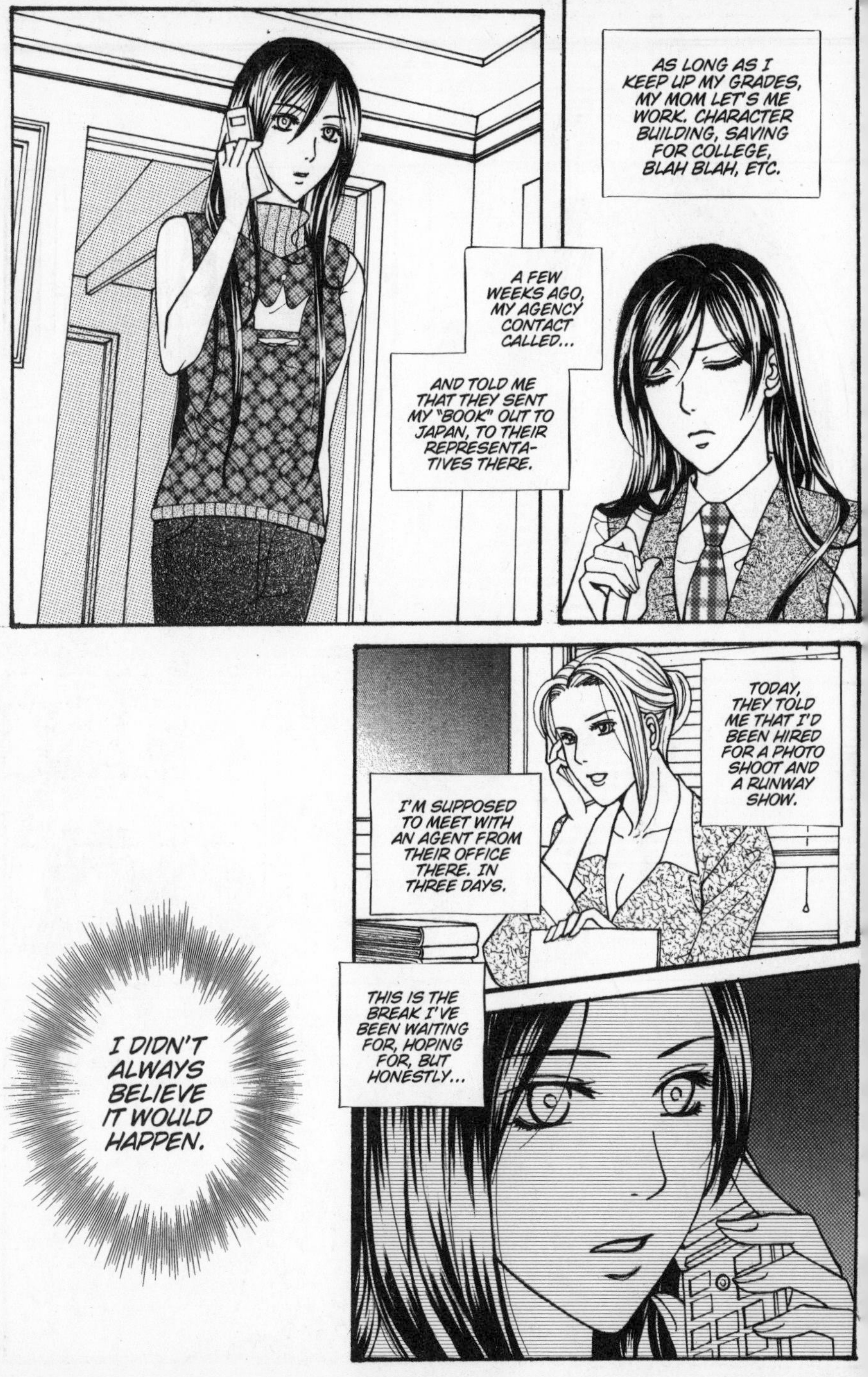
AS LONG AS I KEEP UP MY GRADES, MY MOM LET'S ME WORK. CHARACTER BUILDING, SAVING FOR COLLEGE, BLAH BLAH, ETC.
A FEW WEEKS AGO, MY AGENCY CONTACT CALLED...
AND TOLD ME THAT THEY SENT MY "BOOK" OUT TO JAPAN, TO THEIR REPRESENTA-TIVES THERE.
TODAY, THEY TOLD ME THAT I'D BEEN HIRED FOR A PHOTO SHOOT AND A RUNWAY SHOW.
I'M SUPPOSED TO MEET WITH AN AGENT FROM THEIR OFFICE THERE. IN THREE DAYS.
THIS IS THE BREAK I'VE BEEN WAITING FOR, HOPING FOR, BUT HONESTLY...
I DIDN'T ALWAYS BELIEVE IT WOULD HAPPEN.

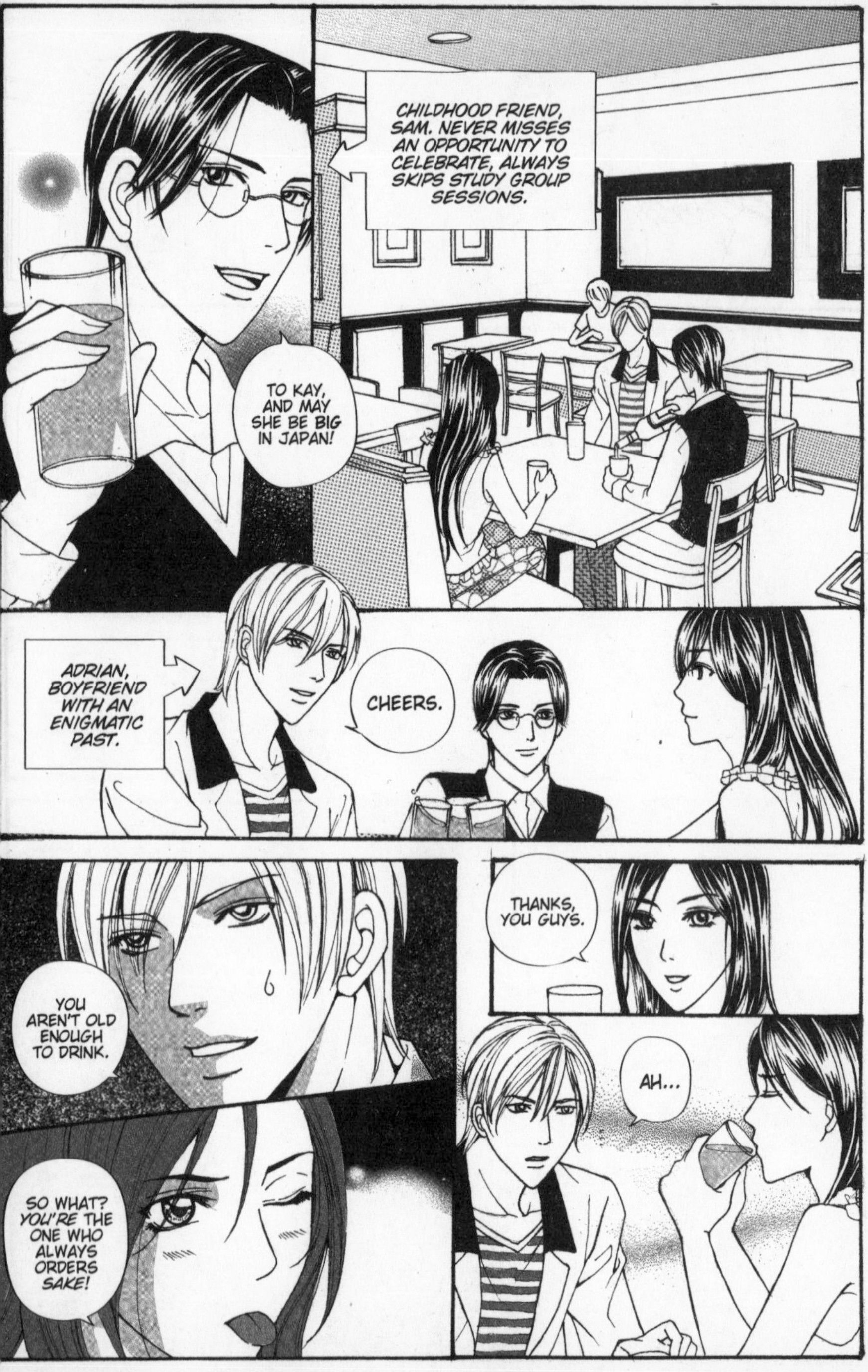
CHILDHOOD FRIEND, SAM. NEVER MISSES AN OPPORTUNITY TO CELEBRATE, ALWAYS SKIPS STUDY GROUP SESSIONS.
TO KAY, AND MAY SHE BE BIG IN JAPAN!
CHEERS.
ADRIAN, BOYFRIEND WITH AN ENIGMATIC PAST.
THANKS, YOU GUYS.
AH...
YOU AREN'T OLD ENOUGH TO DRINK.
SO WHAT? YOU'RE THE ONE WHO ALWAYS ORDERS SAKE!

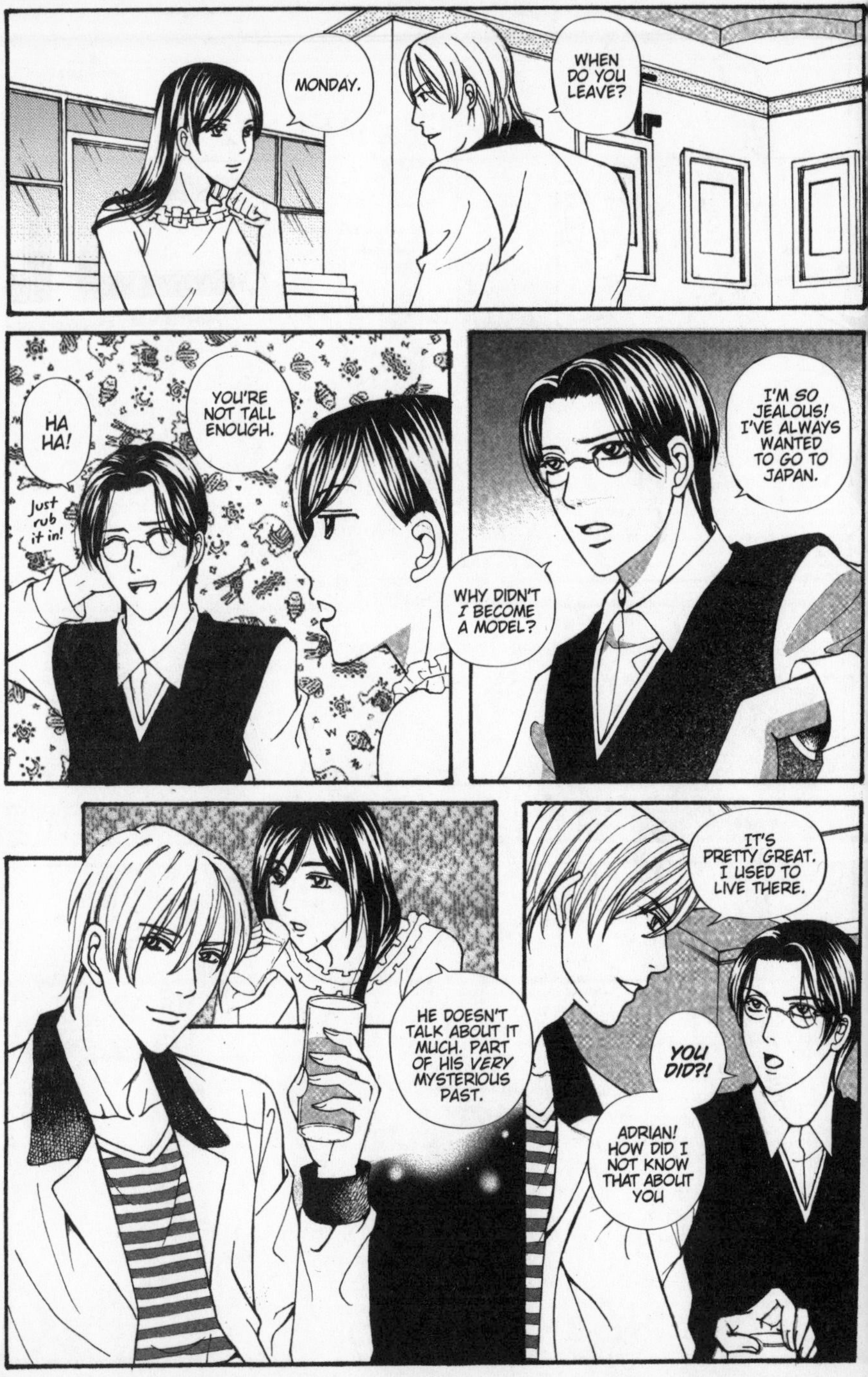
WHEN DO YOU LEAVE?
MONDAY.
I'M *SO* JEALOUS! I'VE ALWAYS WANTED TO GO TO JAPAN.
WHY DIDN'T *I* BECOME A MODEL?
YOU'RE NOT TALL ENOUGH.
HA HA!
Just rub it in!
IT'S PRETTY GREAT. I USED TO LIVE THERE.
YOU DID?!
ADRIAN! HOW DID I NOT KNOW THAT ABOUT YOU
HE DOESN'T TALK ABOUT IT MUCH. PART OF HIS *VERY* MYSTERIOUS PAST.

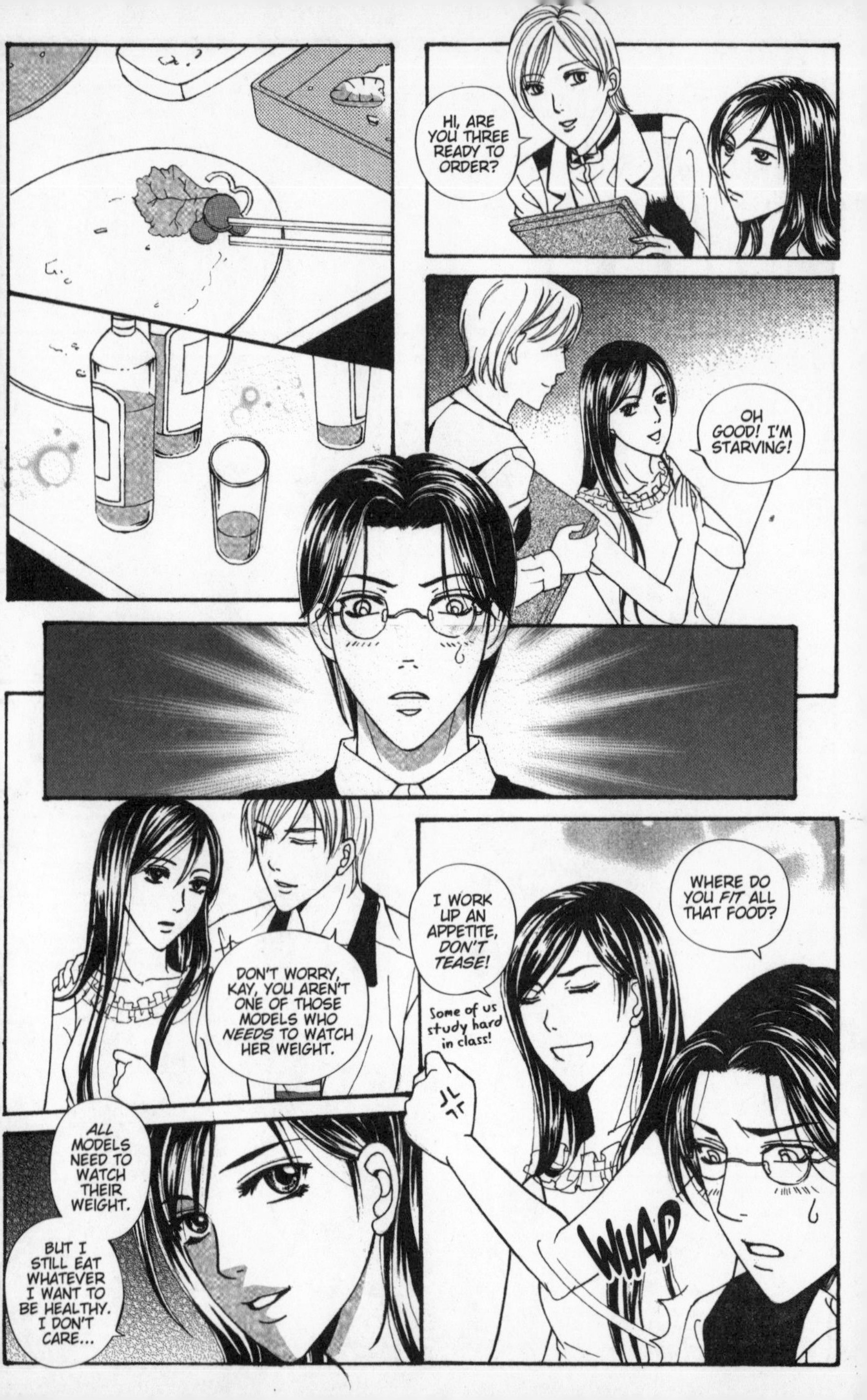
HI, ARE YOU THREE READY TO ORDER?
OH GOOD! I'M STARVING!
WHERE DO YOU *FIT* ALL THAT FOOD?
I WORK UP AN APPETITE, *DON'T TEASE!*
Some of us study hard in class!
WHAP
DON'T WORRY, KAY, YOU AREN'T ONE OF THOSE MODELS WHO *NEEDS* TO WATCH HER WEIGHT.
ALL MODELS NEED TO WATCH THEIR WEIGHT.
BUT I STILL EAT WHATEVER I WANT TO BE HEALTHY. I DON'T CARE...

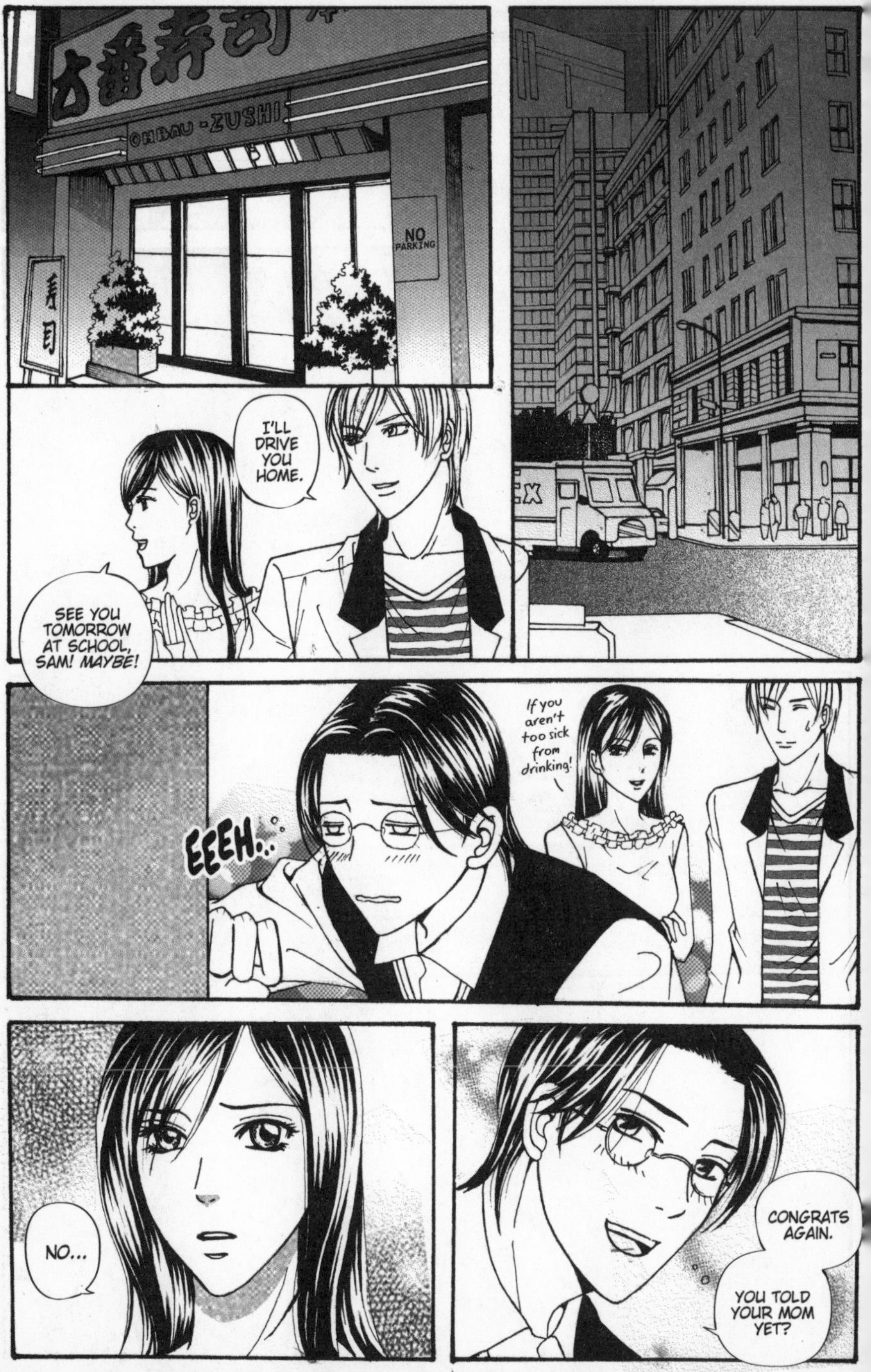
NO PARKING
I'LL DRIVE YOU HOME.
SEE YOU TOMORROW AT SCHOOL, SAM! *MAYBE!*
If you aren't too sick from drinking!
EEEH...
CONGRATS AGAIN.
YOU TOLD YOUR MOM YET?
NO...

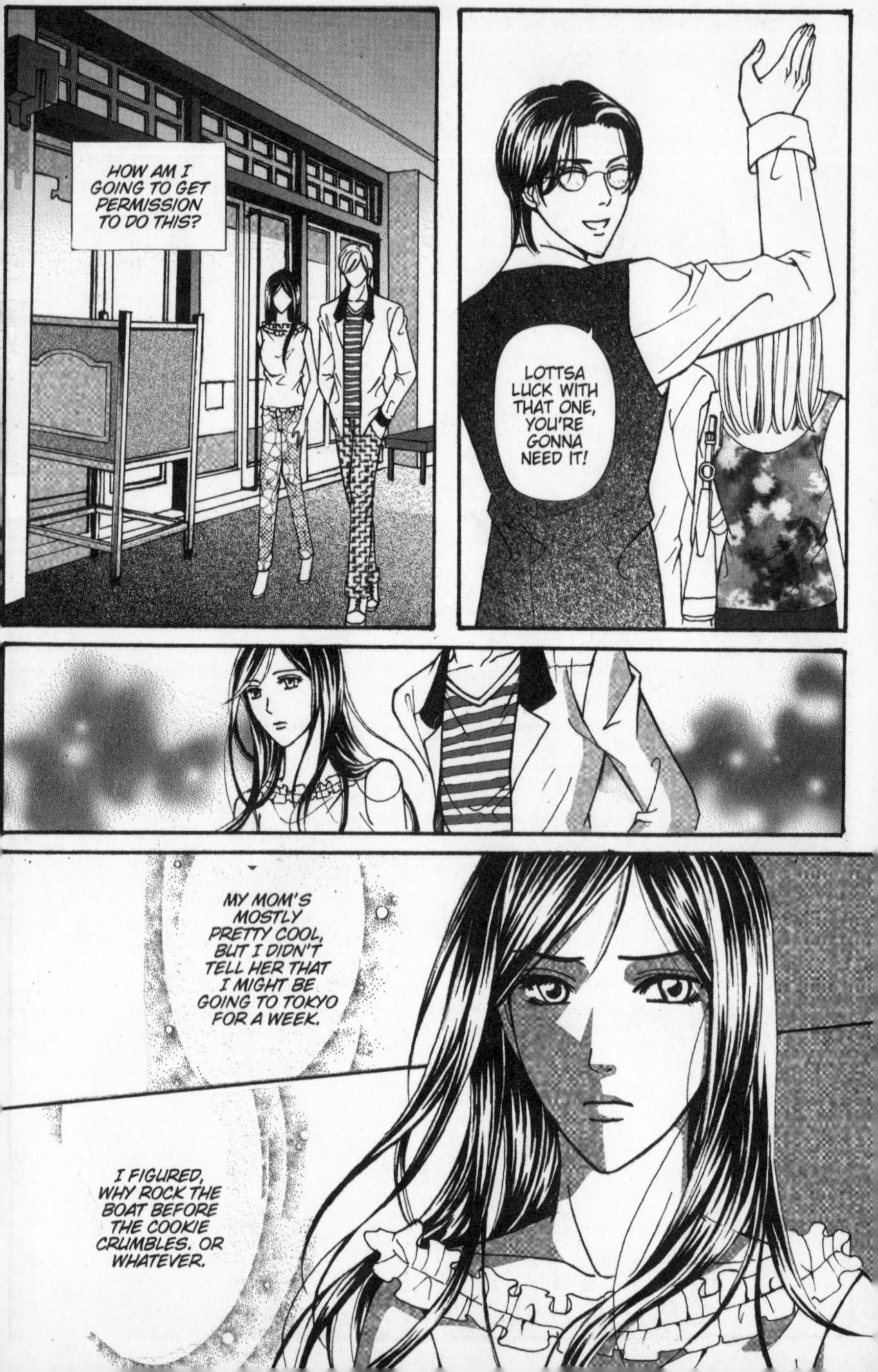
LOTTSA LUCK WITH THAT ONE, YOU'RE GONNA NEED IT!
HOW AM I GOING TO GET PERMISSION TO DO THIS?
MY MOM'S MOSTLY PRETTY COOL, BUT I DIDN'T TELL HER THAT I MIGHT BE GOING TO TOKYO FOR A WEEK.
I FIGURED, WHY ROCK THE BOAT BEFORE THE COOKIE CRUMBLES. OR WHATEVER.

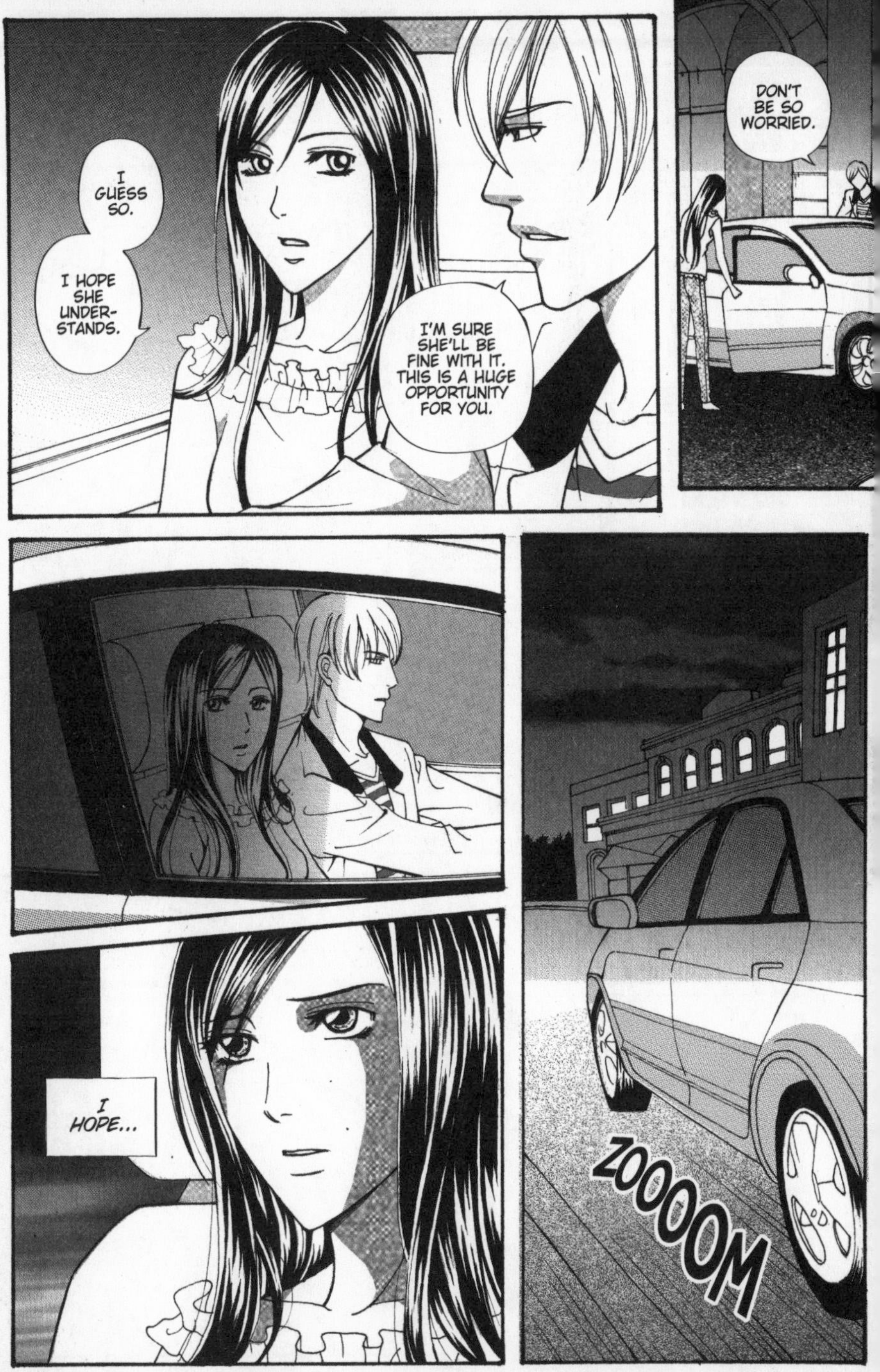
DON'T BE SO WORRIED.
I GUESS SO.
I HOPE SHE UNDER-STANDS.
I'M SURE SHE'LL BE FINE WITH IT. THIS IS A HUGE OPPORTUNITY FOR YOU.
ZOOOOM
I HOPE...

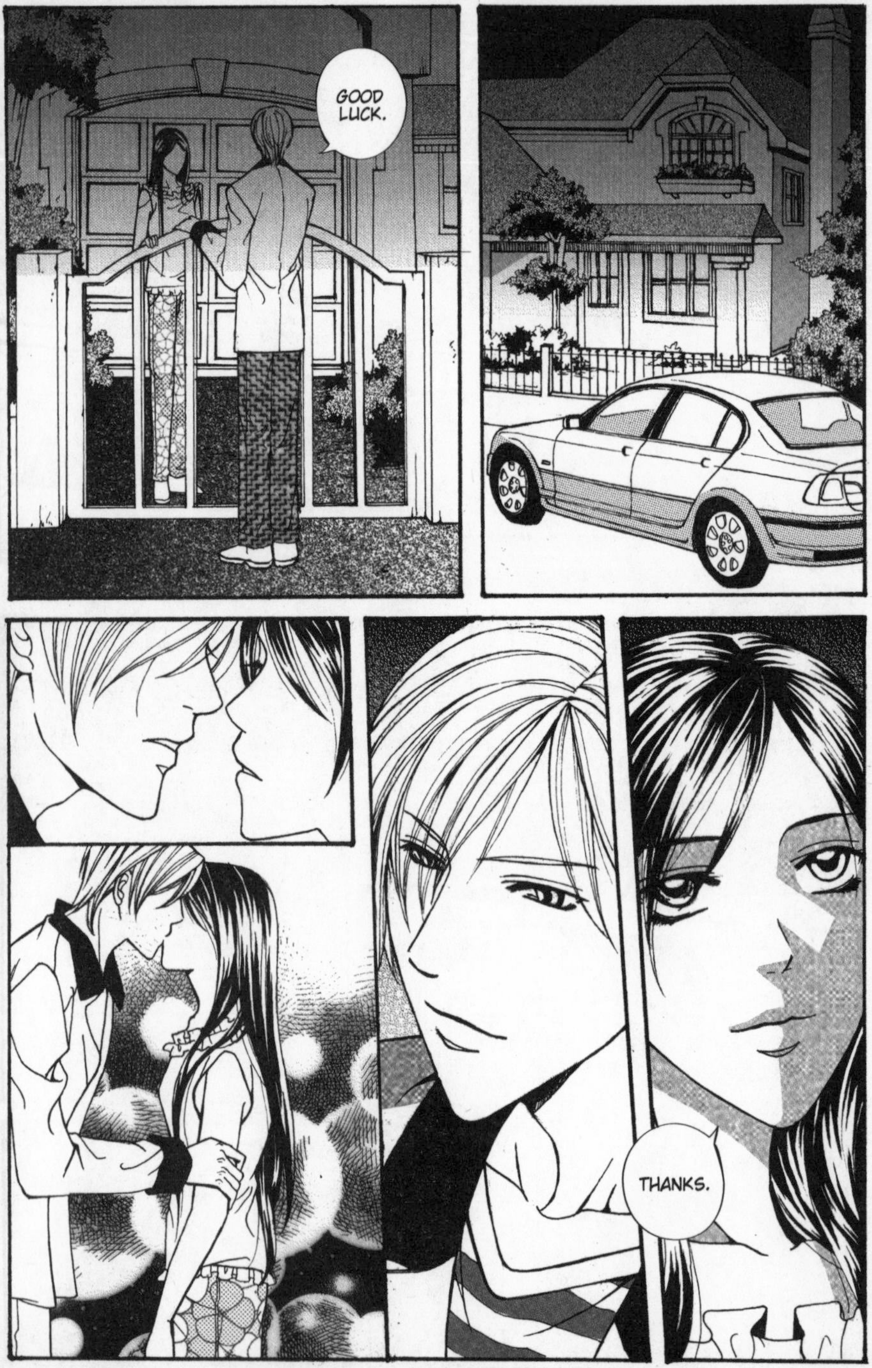
GOOD LUCK.
THANKS.

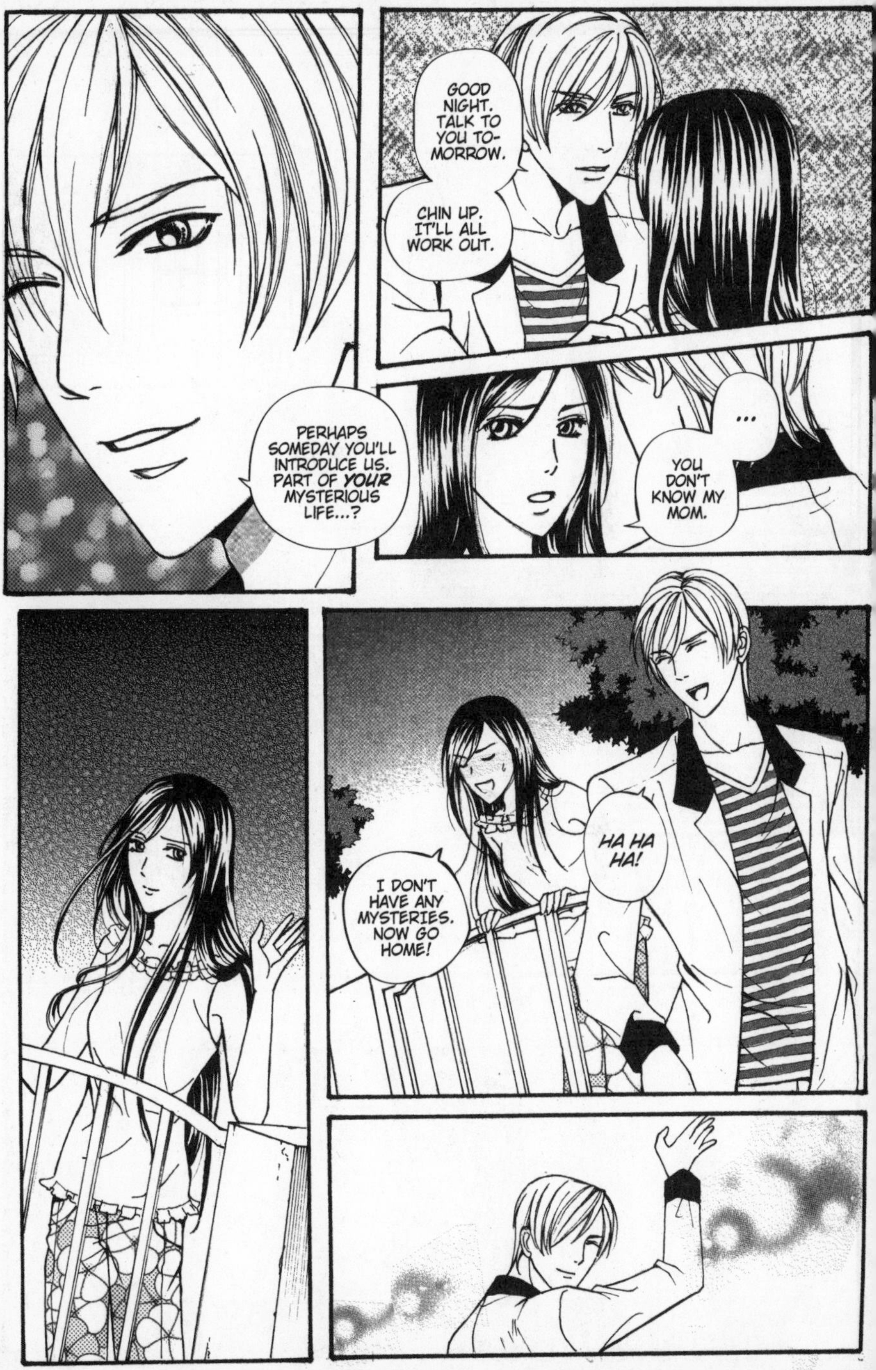
GOOD NIGHT. TALK TO YOU TO-MORROW.
CHIN UP. IT'LL ALL WORK OUT.
...
YOU DON'T KNOW MY MOM.
PERHAPS SOMEDAY YOU'LL INTRODUCE US. PART OF *YOUR* MYSTERIOUS LIFE...?
HA HA HA!
I DON'T HAVE ANY MYSTERIES. NOW GO HOME!

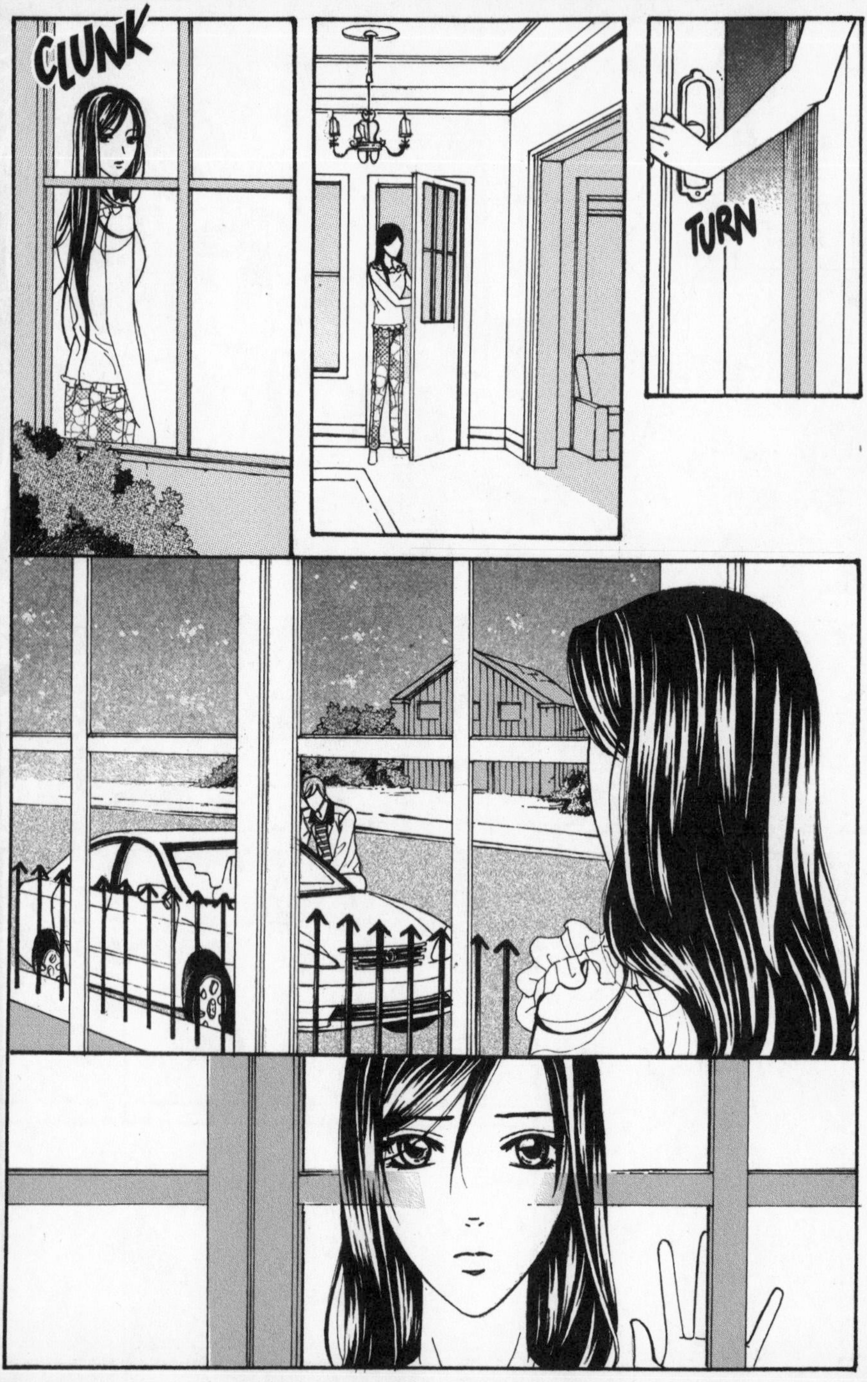
TURN
CLUNK

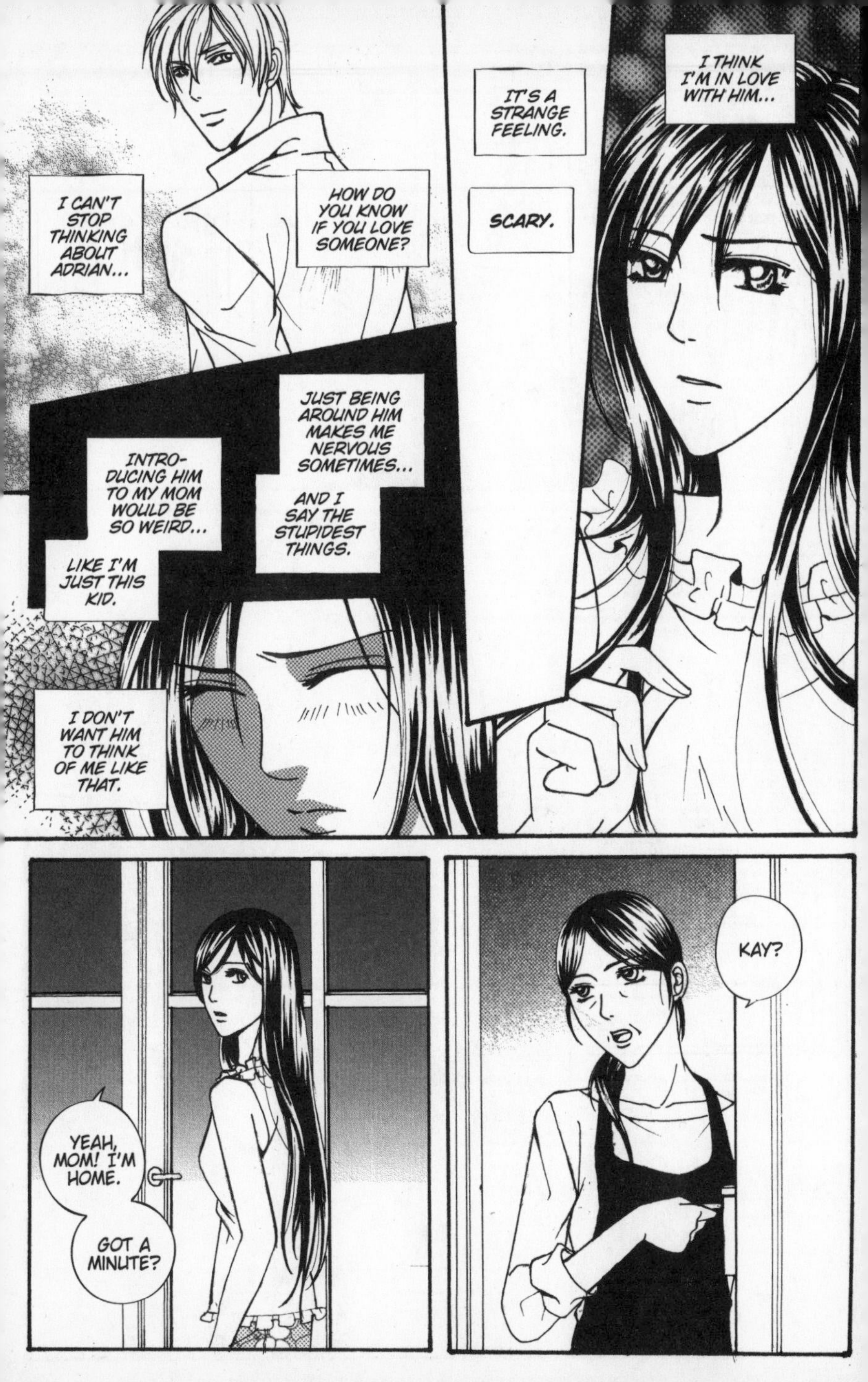
I THINK I'M IN LOVE WITH HIM...
IT'S A STRANGE FEELING.
SCARY.
HOW DO YOU KNOW IF YOU LOVE SOMEONE?
I CAN'T STOP THINKING ABOUT ADRIAN...
JUST BEING AROUND HIM MAKES ME NERVOUS SOMETIMES...
AND I SAY THE STUPIDEST THINGS.
INTRODUCING HIM TO MY MOM WOULD BE SO WEIRD...
LIKE I'M JUST THIS KID.
I DON'T WANT HIM TO THINK OF ME LIKE THAT.
KAY?
YEAH, MOM! I'M HOME.
GOT A MINUTE?

I DON'T KNOW...

THAT'S A LOT OF SCHOOL TO MISS.

I'LL TALK TO THE TEACHERS. MOM, PLEASE?

DON'T WHINE. LET ME THINK ABOUT IT.

ALL RIGHT.

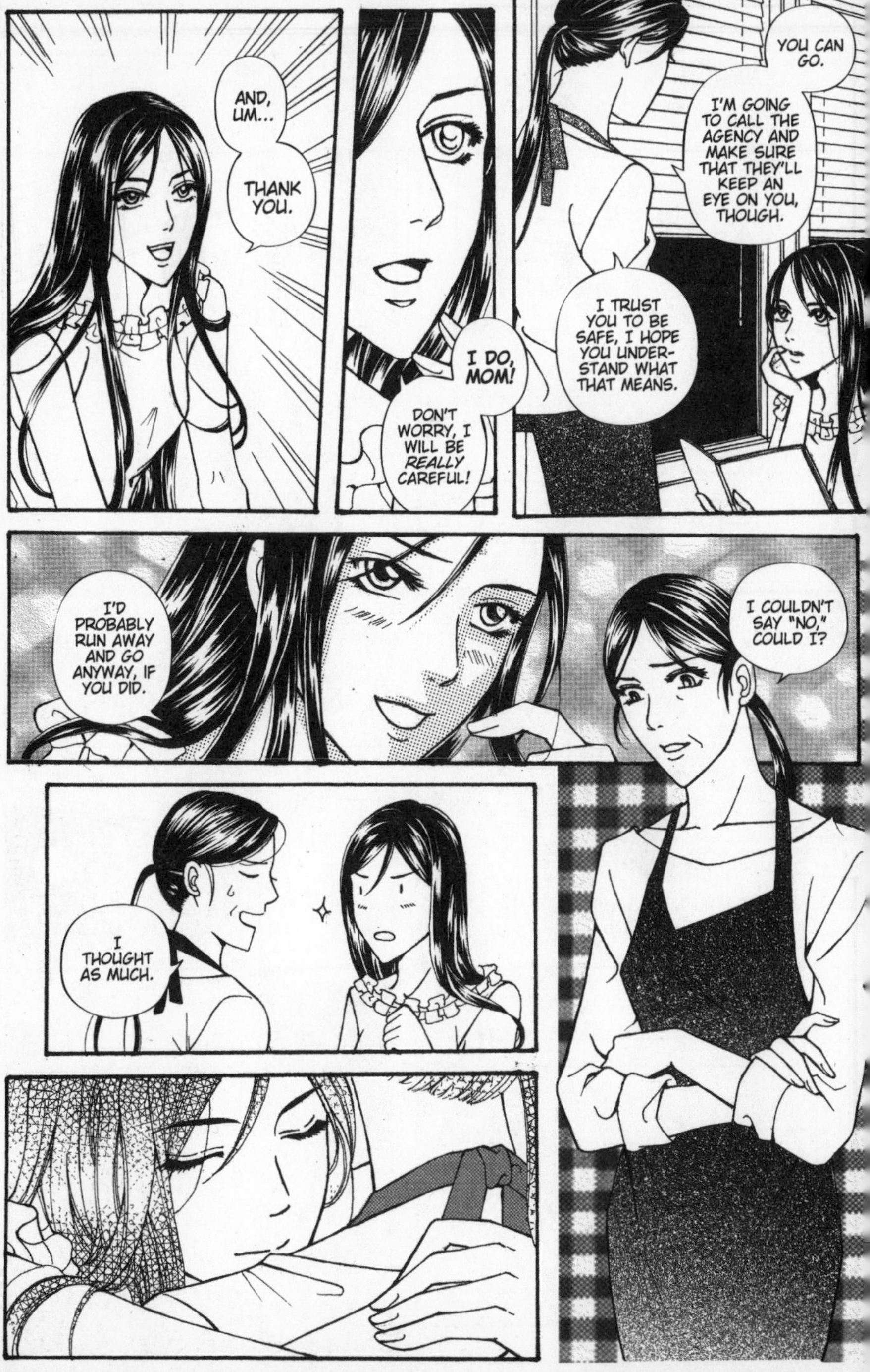
YOU CAN GO.
I'M GOING TO CALL THE AGENCY AND MAKE SURE THAT THEY'LL KEEP AN EYE ON YOU, THOUGH.
I TRUST YOU TO BE SAFE, I HOPE YOU UNDER-STAND WHAT THAT MEANS.
I DO, MOM!
DON'T WORRY, I WILL BE *REALLY* CAREFUL!
AND, UM...
THANK YOU.
I COULDN'T SAY "NO," COULD I?
I'D PROBABLY RUN AWAY AND GO ANYWAY, IF YOU DID.
I THOUGHT AS MUCH.

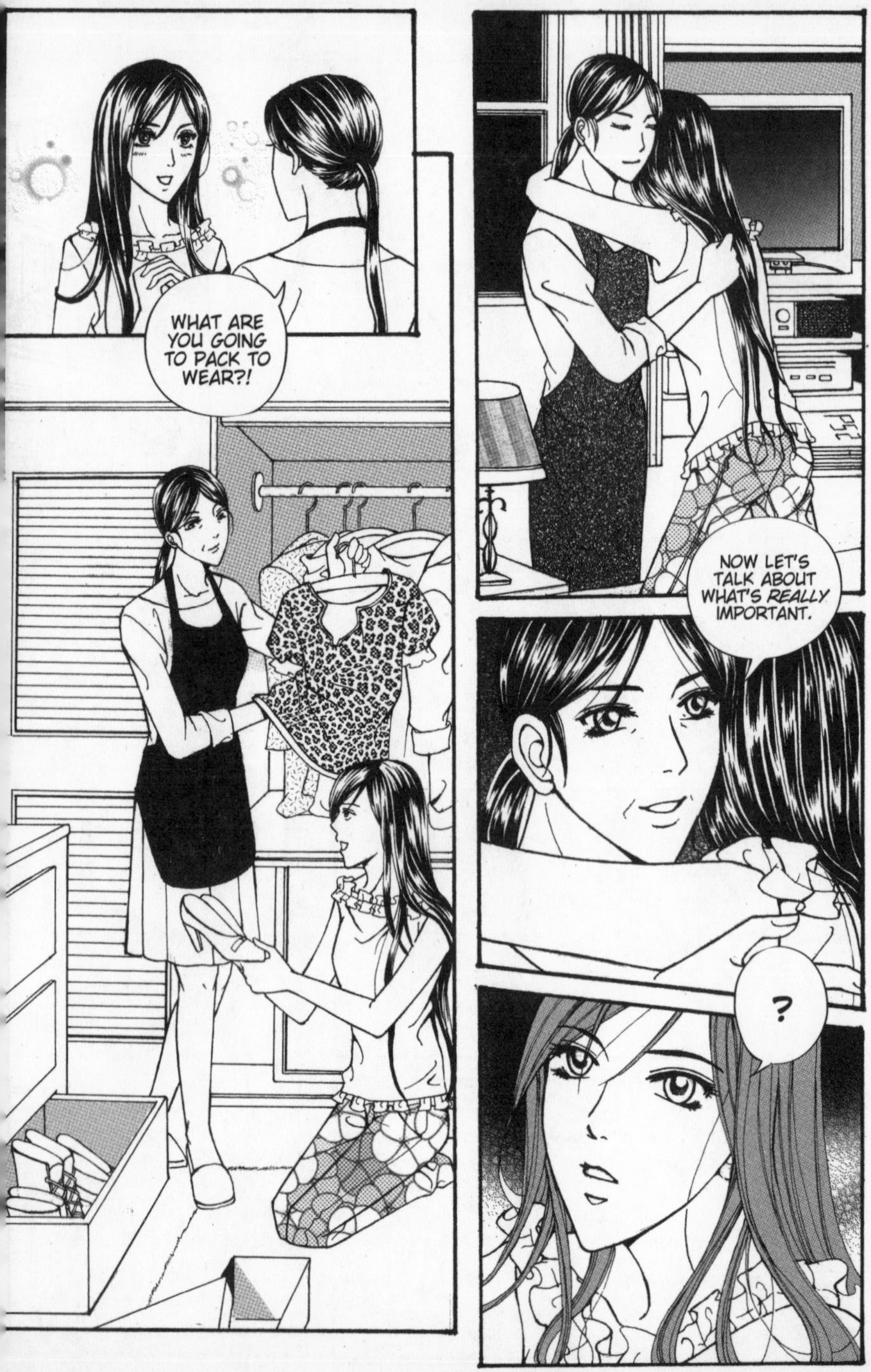
NOW LET'S TALK ABOUT WHAT'S *REALLY* IMPORTANT.
?
WHAT ARE YOU GOING TO PACK TO WEAR?!

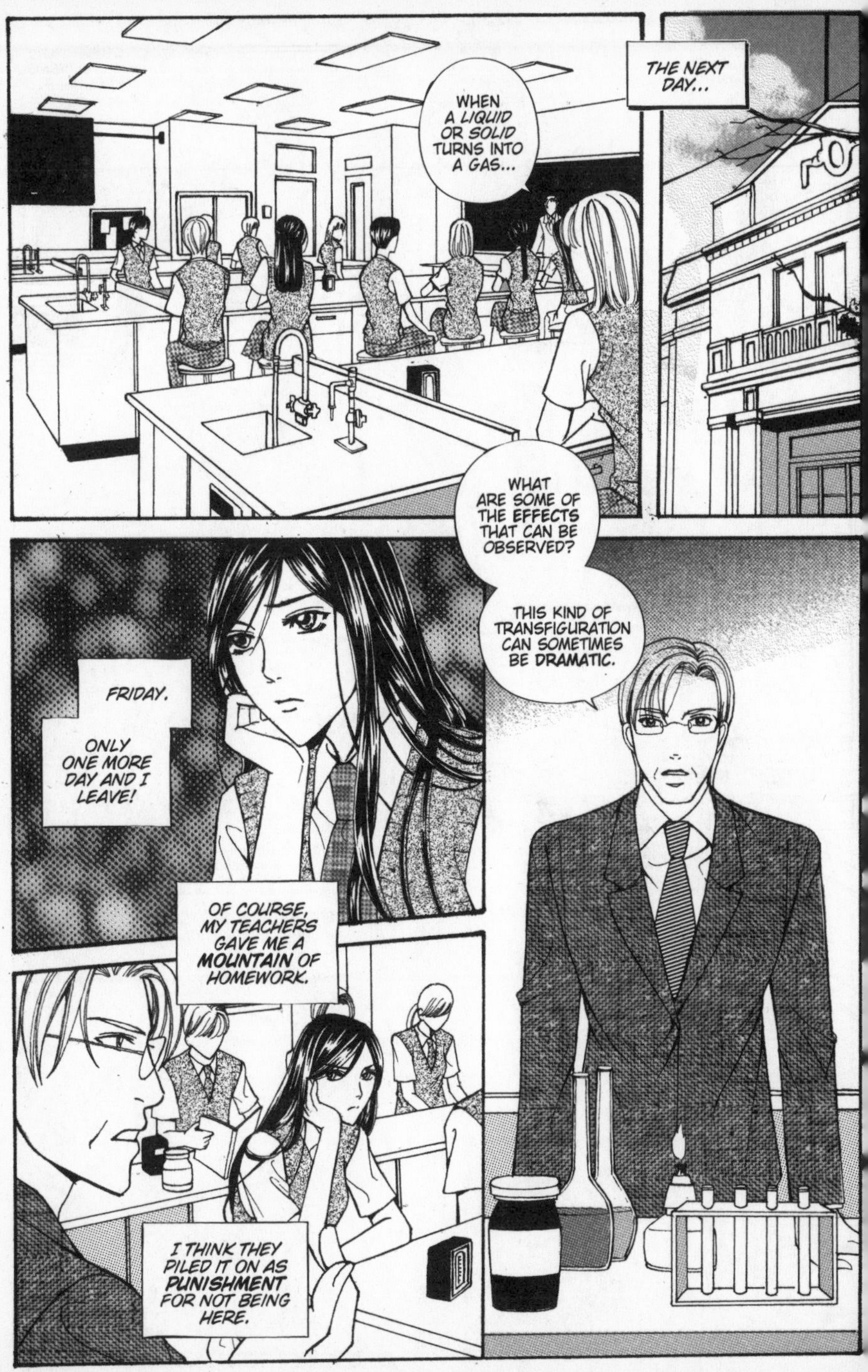
THE NEXT DAY...
WHEN A LIQUID OR SOLID TURNS INTO A GAS...
WHAT ARE SOME OF THE EFFECTS THAT CAN BE OBSERVED?
THIS KIND OF TRANSFIGURATION CAN SOMETIMES BE DRAMATIC.
FRIDAY.
ONLY ONE MORE DAY AND I LEAVE!
OF COURSE, MY TEACHERS GAVE ME A MOUNTAIN OF HOMEWORK.
I THINK THEY PILED IT ON AS PUNISHMENT FOR NOT BEING HERE.

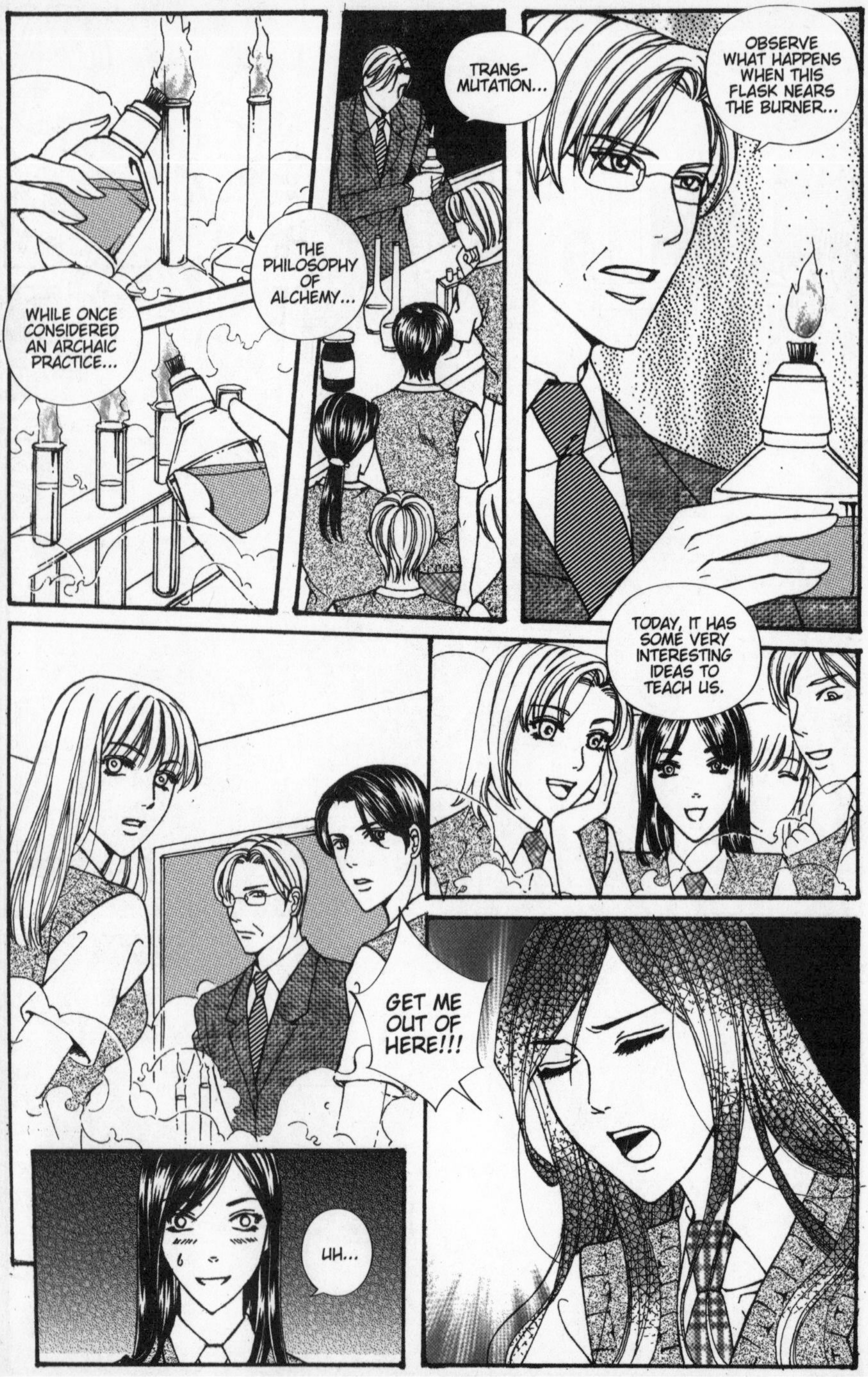
WHILE ONCE CONSIDERED AN ARCHAIC PRACTICE...
THE PHILOSOPHY OF ALCHEMY...
TRANS-MUTATION...
TODAY, IT HAS SOME VERY INTERESTING IDEAS TO TEACH US.
OBSERVE WHAT HAPPENS WHEN THIS FLASK NEARS THE BURNER...
GET ME OUT OF HERE!!!
UH...

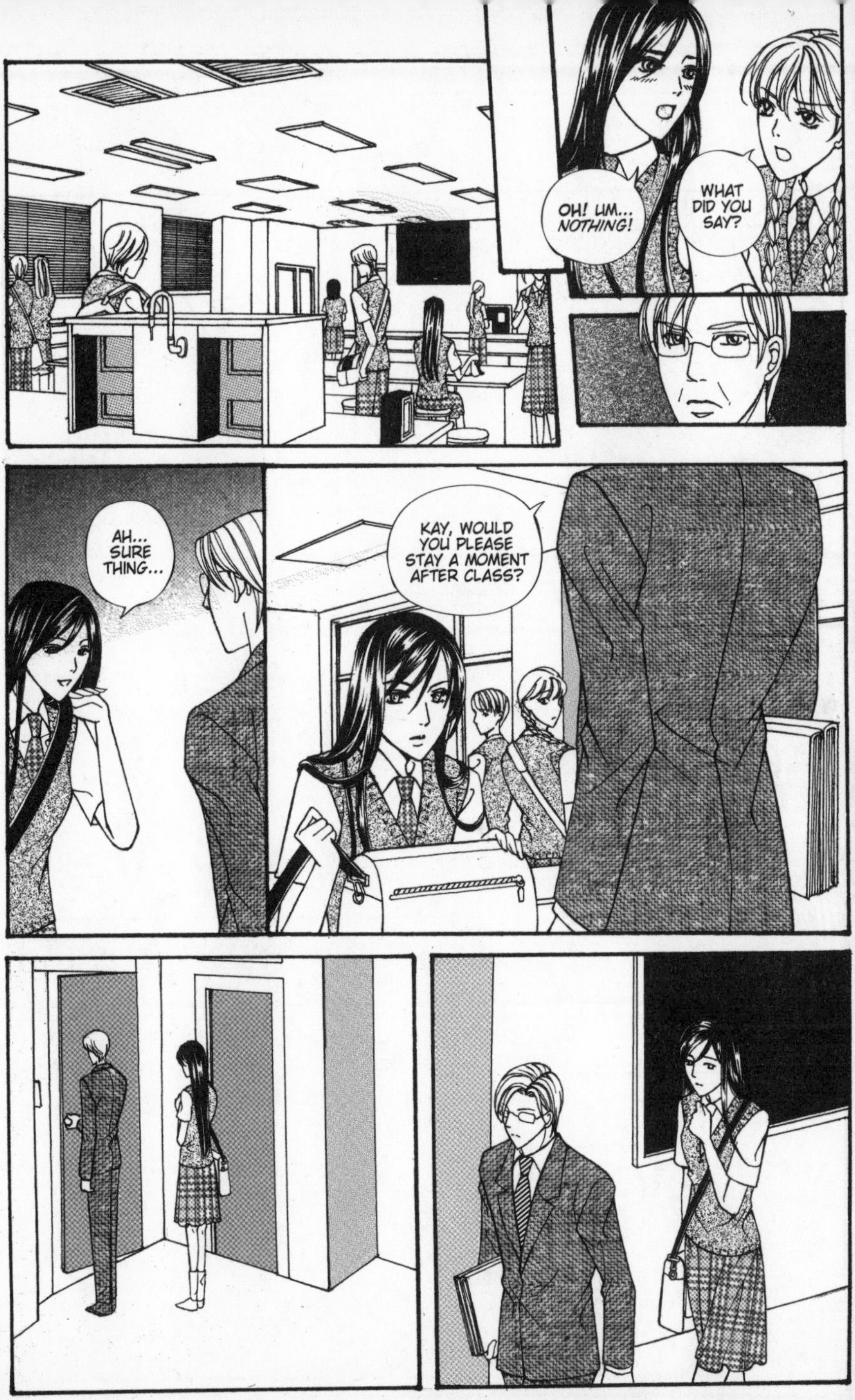
WHAT DID YOU SAY?
OH! UM... NOTHING!
KAY, WOULD YOU PLEASE STAY A MOMENT AFTER CLASS?
AH... SURE THING...

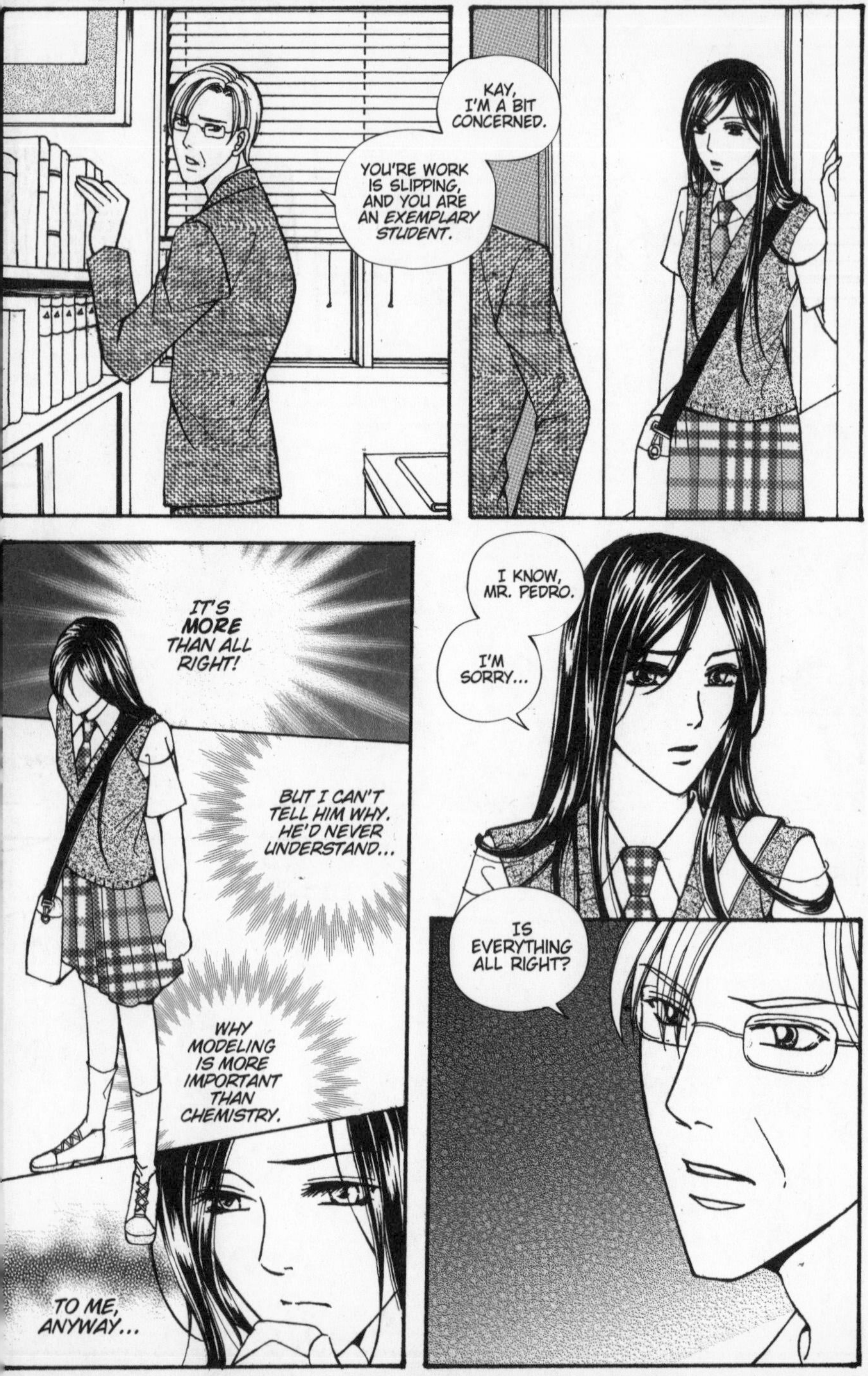
KAY, I'M A BIT CONCERNED.
YOU'RE WORK IS SLIPPING, AND YOU ARE AN *EXEMPLARY* STUDENT.
I KNOW, MR. PEDRO.
I'M SORRY...
IS EVERYTHING ALL RIGHT?
IT'S **MORE** THAN ALL RIGHT!
BUT I CAN'T TELL HIM WHY. HE'D NEVER UNDERSTAND...
WHY MODELING IS MORE IMPORTANT THAN CHEMISTRY.
TO ME, ANYWAY...

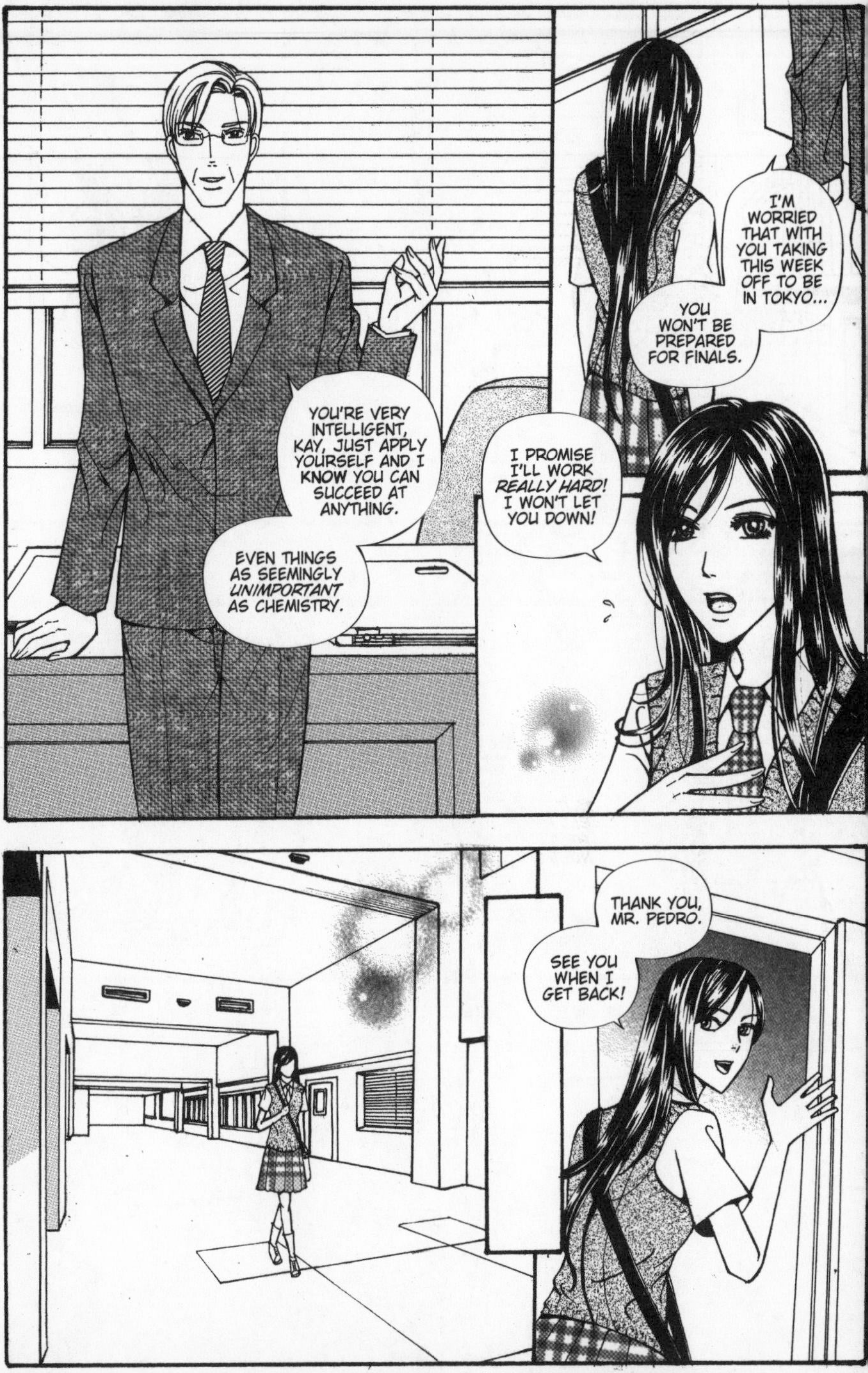
I'M WORRIED THAT WITH YOU TAKING THIS WEEK OFF TO BE IN TOKYO...
YOU WON'T BE PREPARED FOR FINALS.
I PROMISE I'LL WORK *REALLY HARD!* I WON'T LET YOU DOWN!
YOU'RE VERY INTELLIGENT, KAY, JUST APPLY YOURSELF AND I **KNOW** YOU CAN SUCCEED AT ANYTHING.
EVEN THINGS AS SEEMINGLY *UNIMPORTANT* AS CHEMISTRY.
THANK YOU, MR. PEDRO.
SEE YOU WHEN I GET BACK!

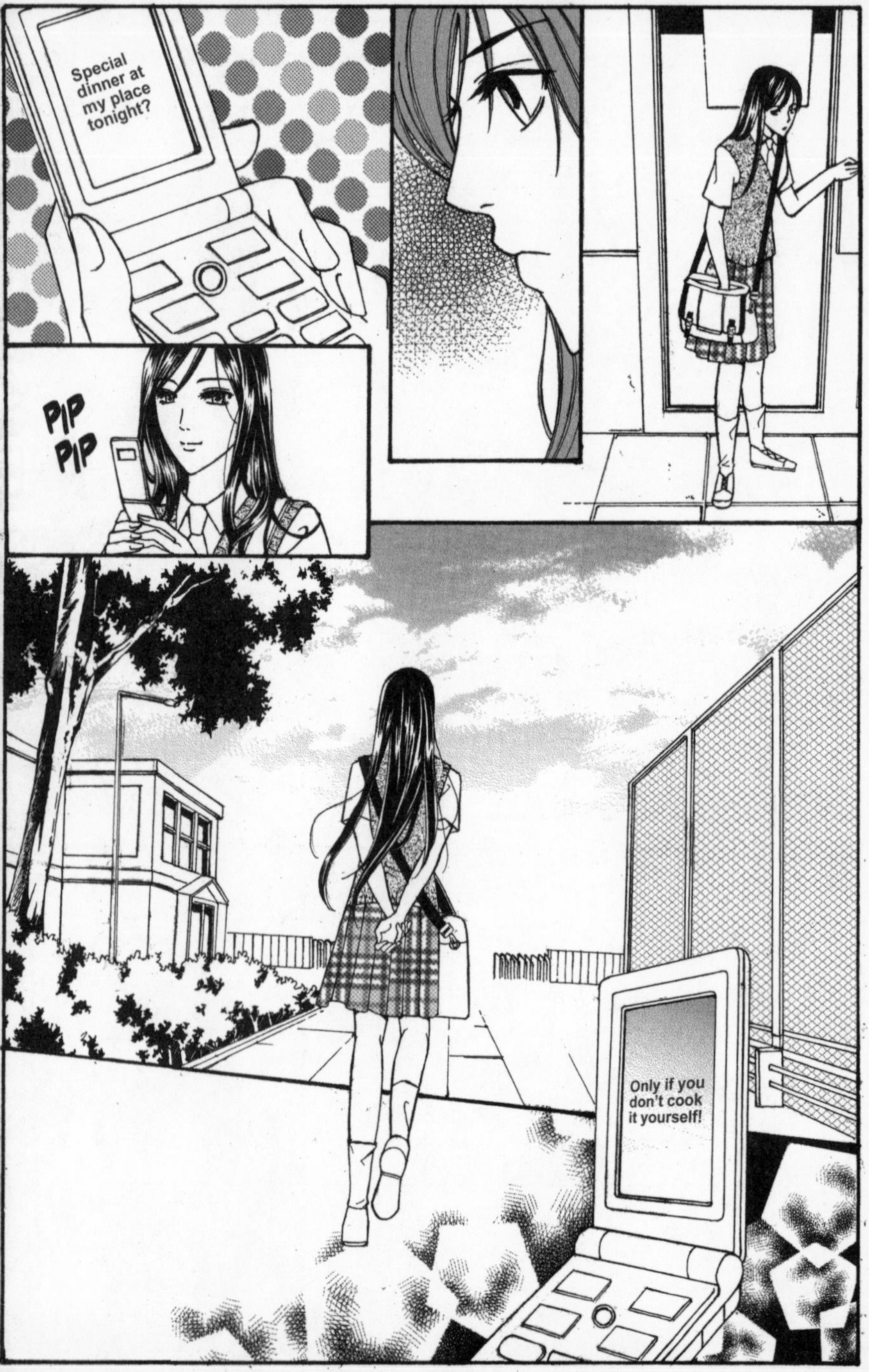
Special dinner at my place tonight?
PIP PIP
Only if you don't cook it yourself!

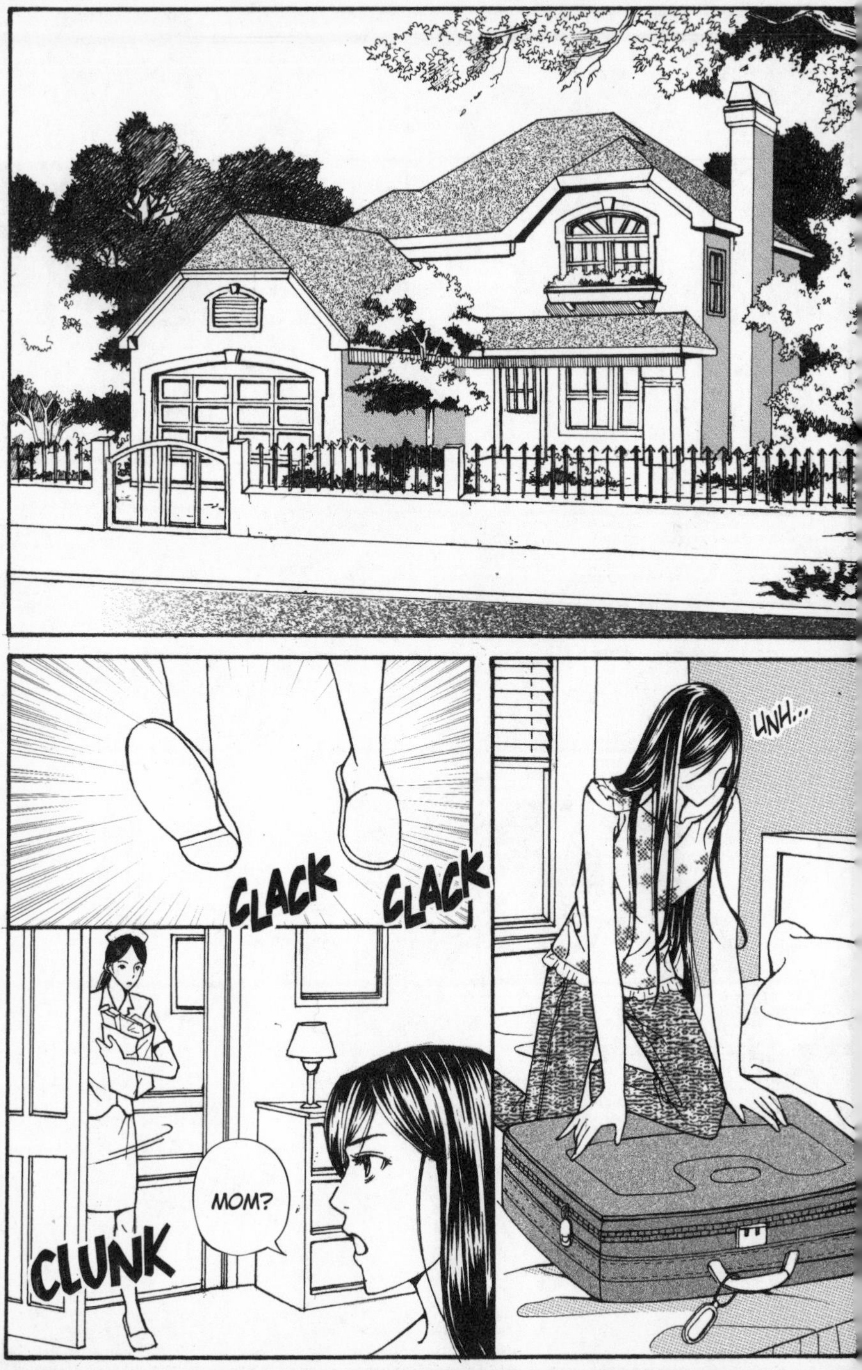
UNH...
CLACK
CLACK
MOM?
CLUNK

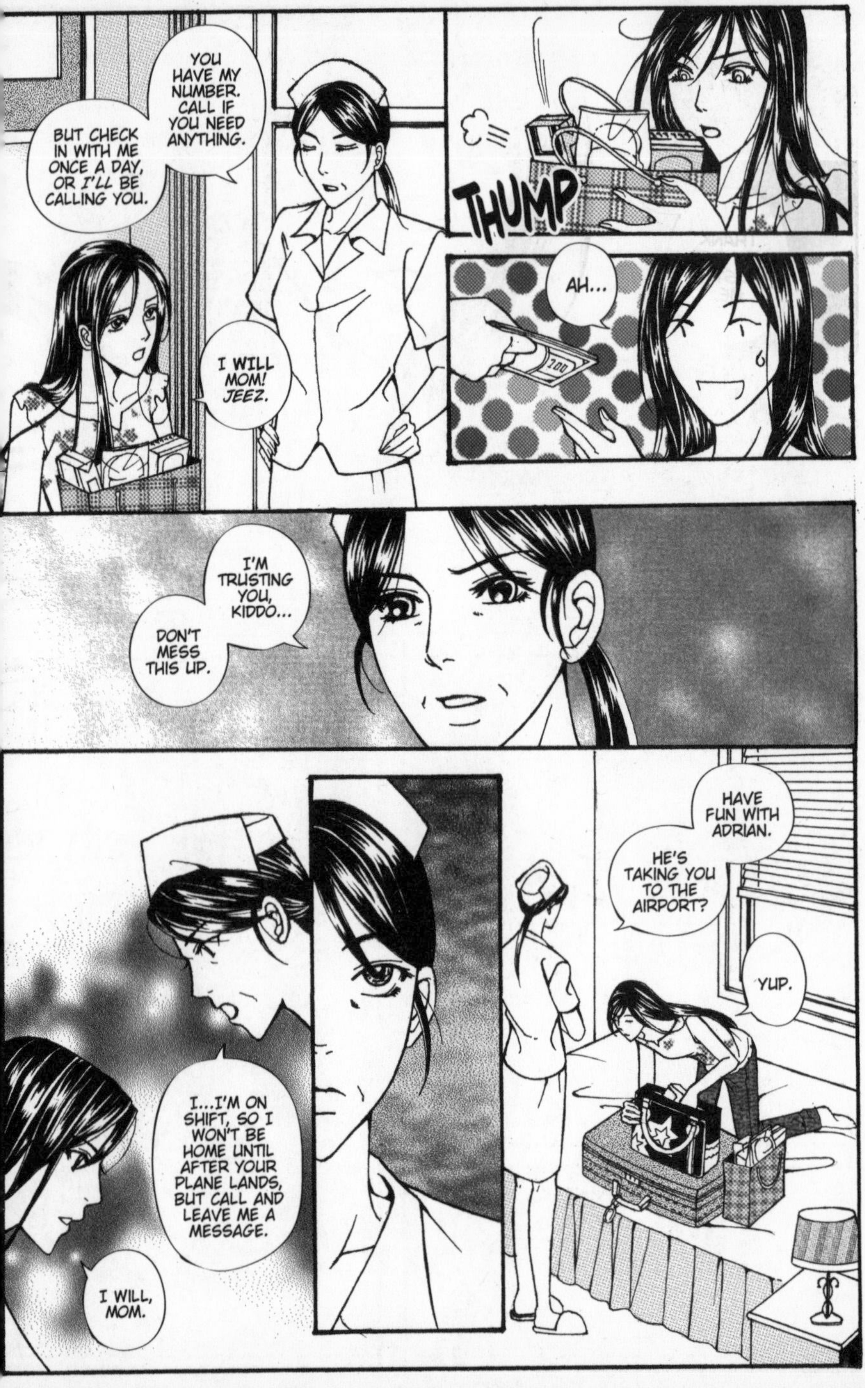
THUMP
AH...
YOU HAVE MY NUMBER. CALL IF YOU NEED ANYTHING.
BUT CHECK IN WITH ME ONCE A DAY, OR I'LL BE CALLING YOU.
I WILL MOM! JEEZ.
I'M TRUSTING YOU, KIDDO...
DON'T MESS THIS UP.
HAVE FUN WITH ADRIAN.
HE'S TAKING YOU TO THE AIRPORT?
YUP.
I...I'M ON SHIFT, SO I WON'T BE HOME UNTIL AFTER YOUR PLANE LANDS, BUT CALL AND LEAVE ME A MESSAGE.
I WILL, MOM.

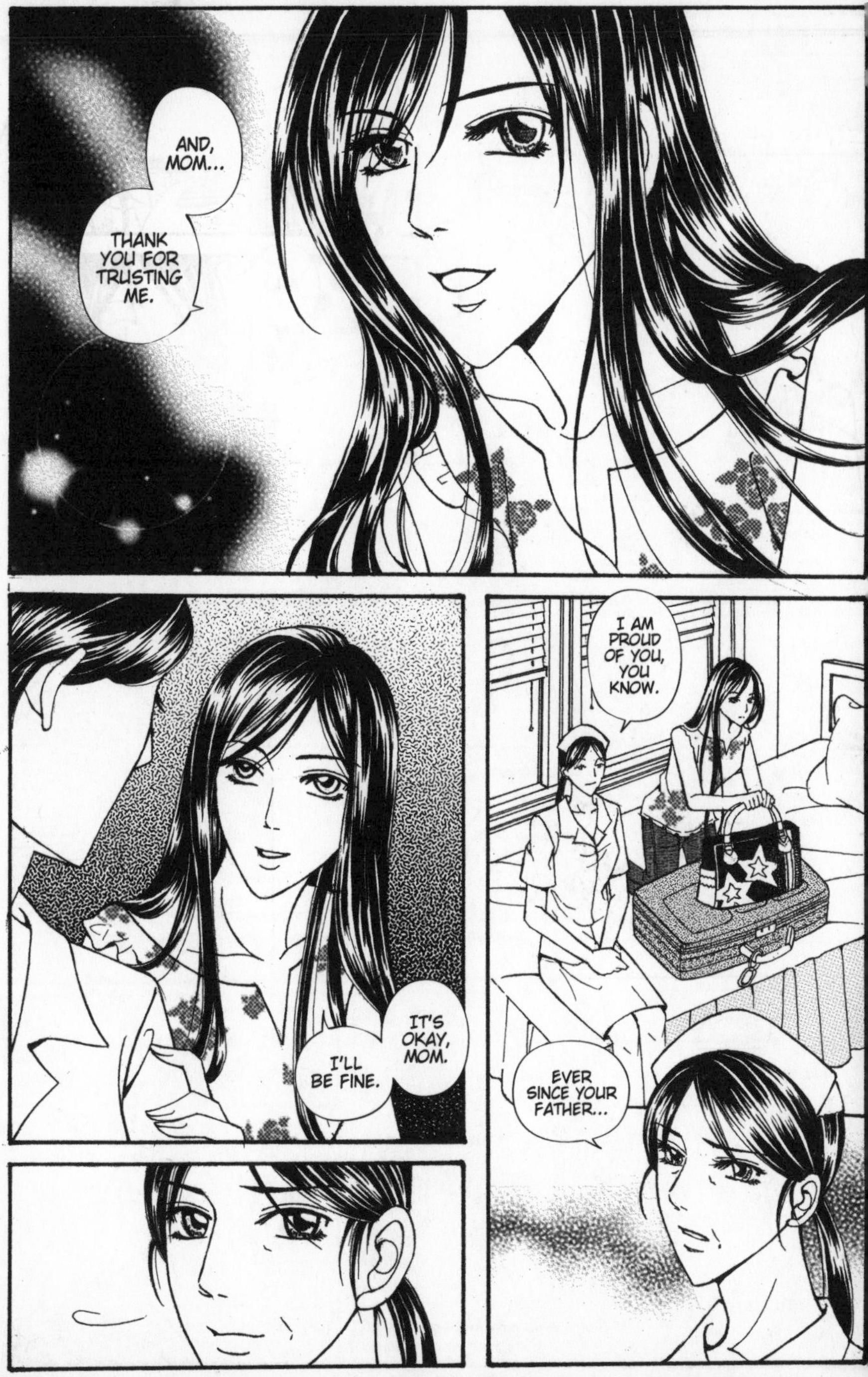
AND, MOM...
THANK YOU FOR TRUSTING ME.
I AM PROUD OF YOU, YOU KNOW.
EVER SINCE YOUR FATHER...
IT'S OKAY, MOM.
I'LL BE FINE.

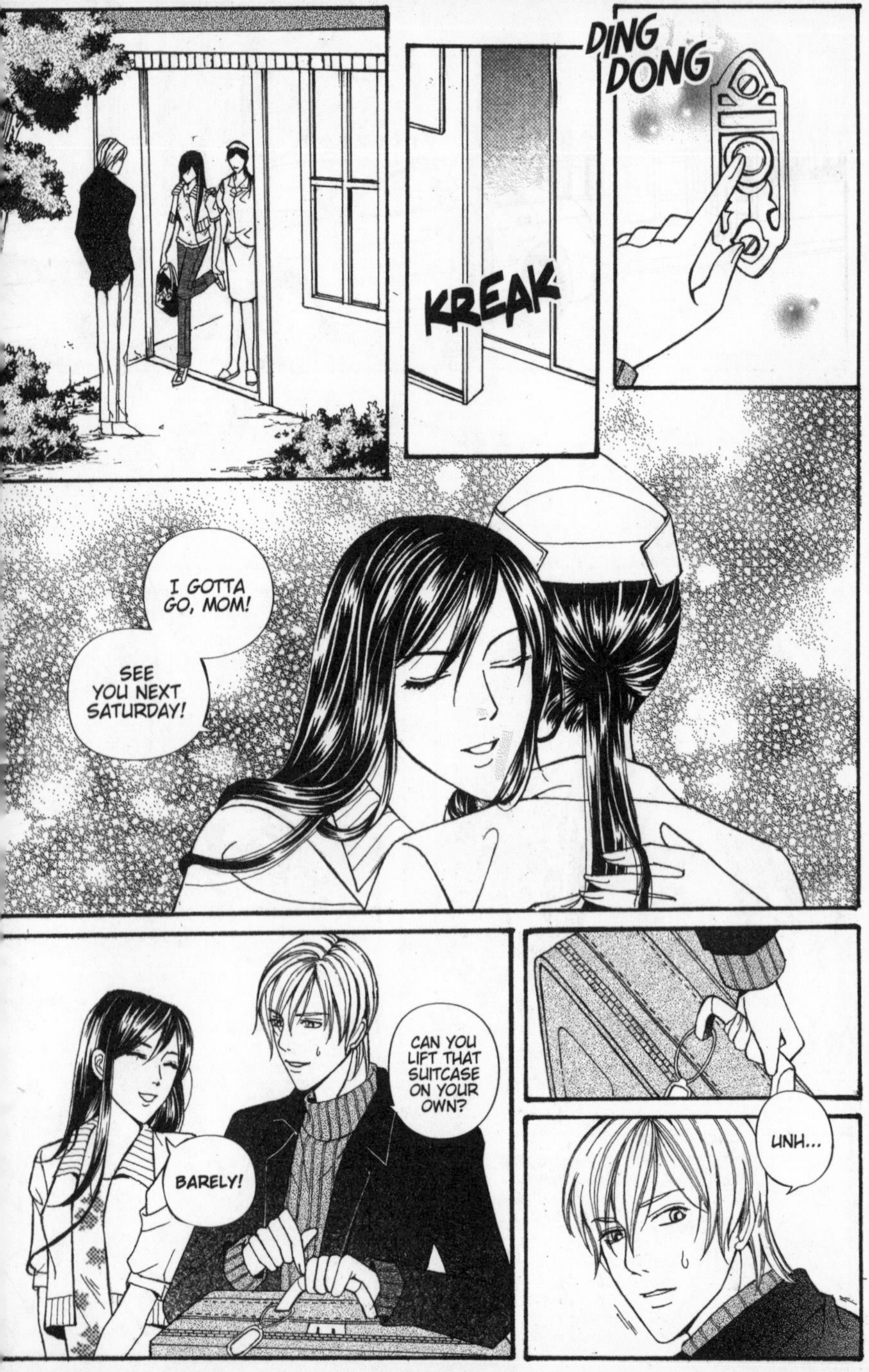
DING DONG
KREAK
I GOTTA GO, MOM!
SEE YOU NEXT SATURDAY!
UNH...
CAN YOU LIFT THAT SUITCASE ON YOUR OWN?
BARELY!

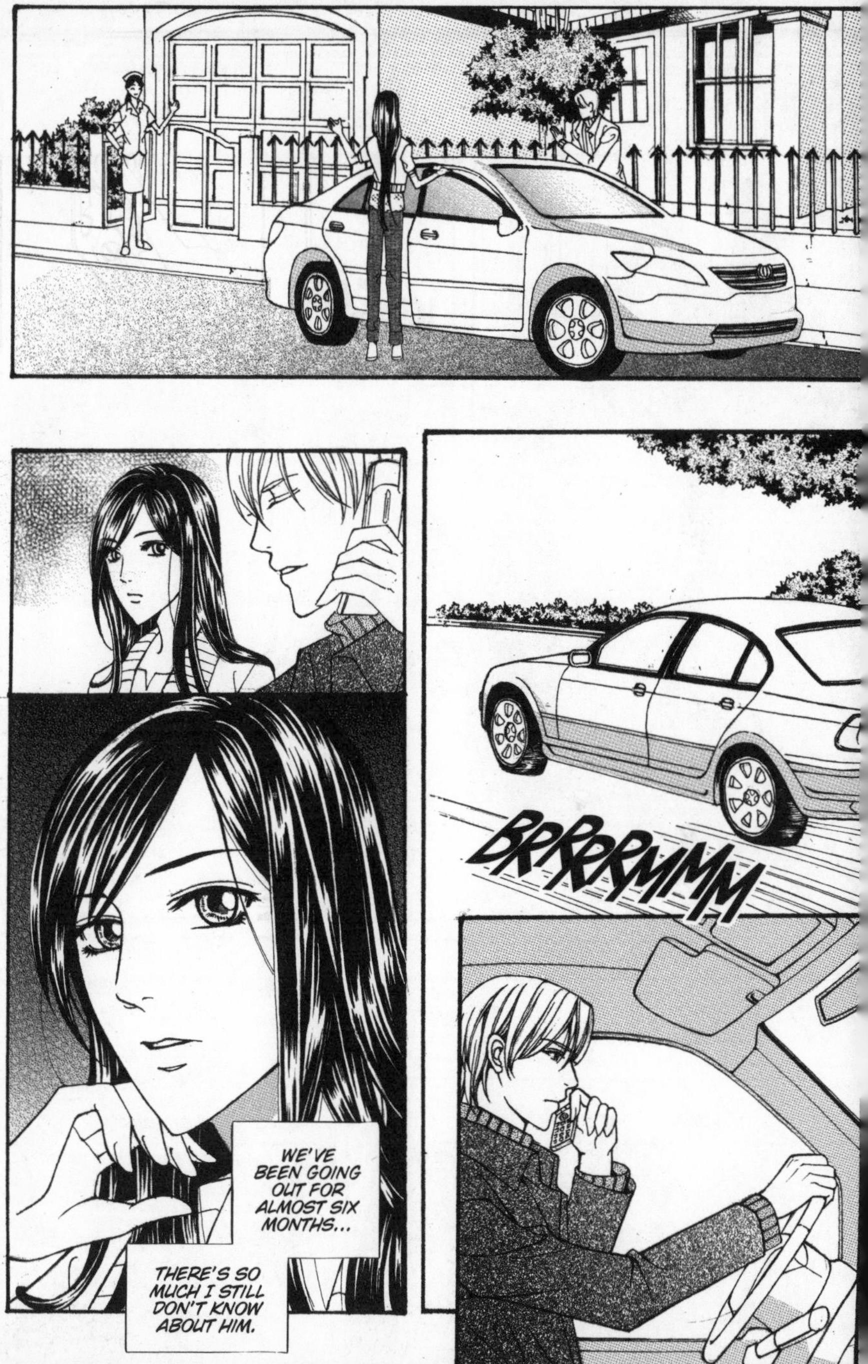
BRRRRMMMM
WE'VE BEEN GOING OUT FOR ALMOST SIX MONTHS...
THERE'S SO MUCH I STILL DON'T KNOW ABOUT HIM.

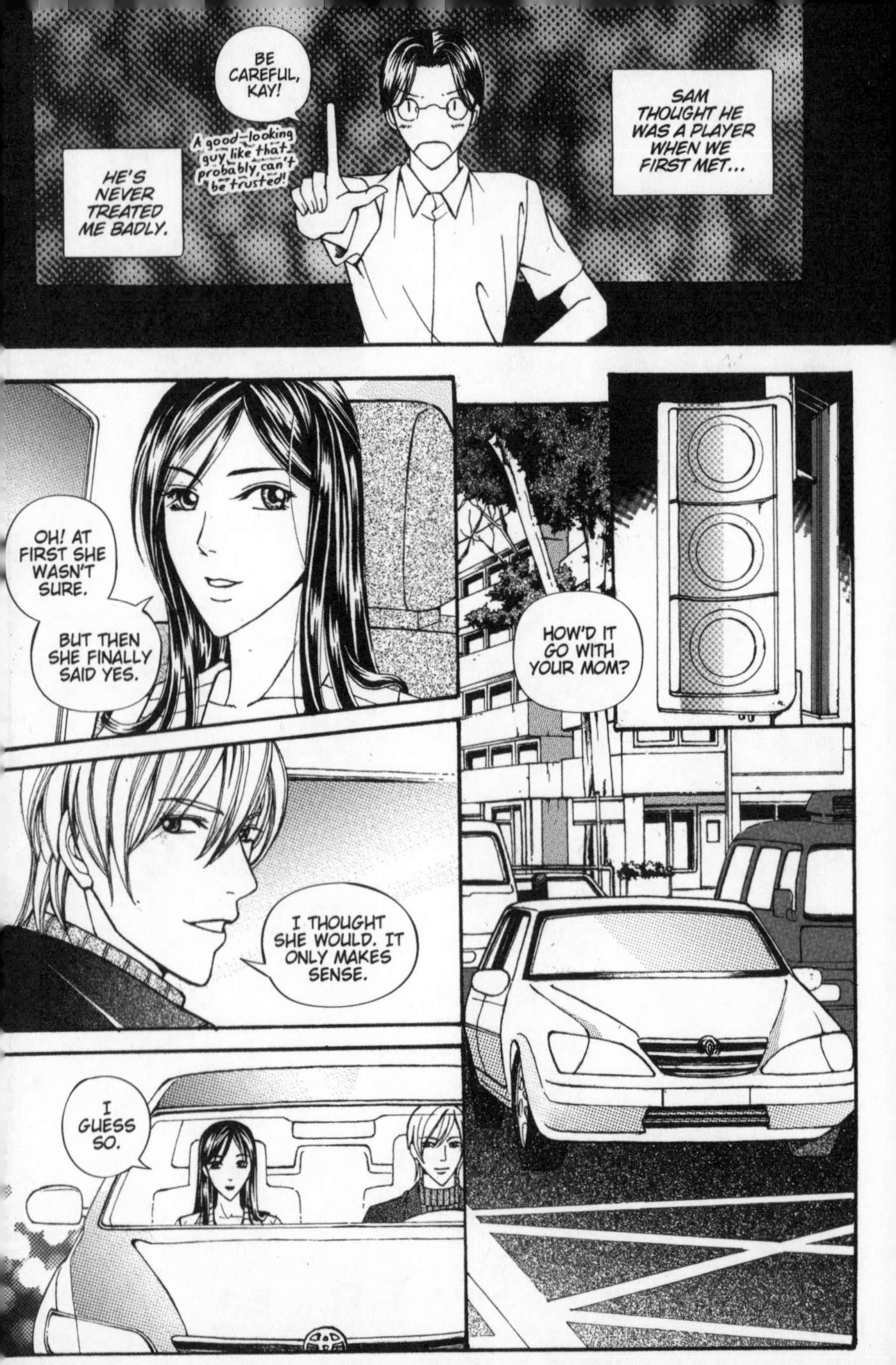
SAM THOUGHT HE WAS A PLAYER WHEN WE FIRST MET...
BE CAREFUL, KAY!
A good-looking guy like that probably can't be trusted!
HE'S NEVER TREATED ME BADLY.
HOW'D IT GO WITH YOUR MOM?
OH! AT FIRST SHE WASN'T SURE.
BUT THEN SHE FINALLY SAID YES.
I THOUGHT SHE WOULD. IT ONLY MAKES SENSE.
I GUESS SO.

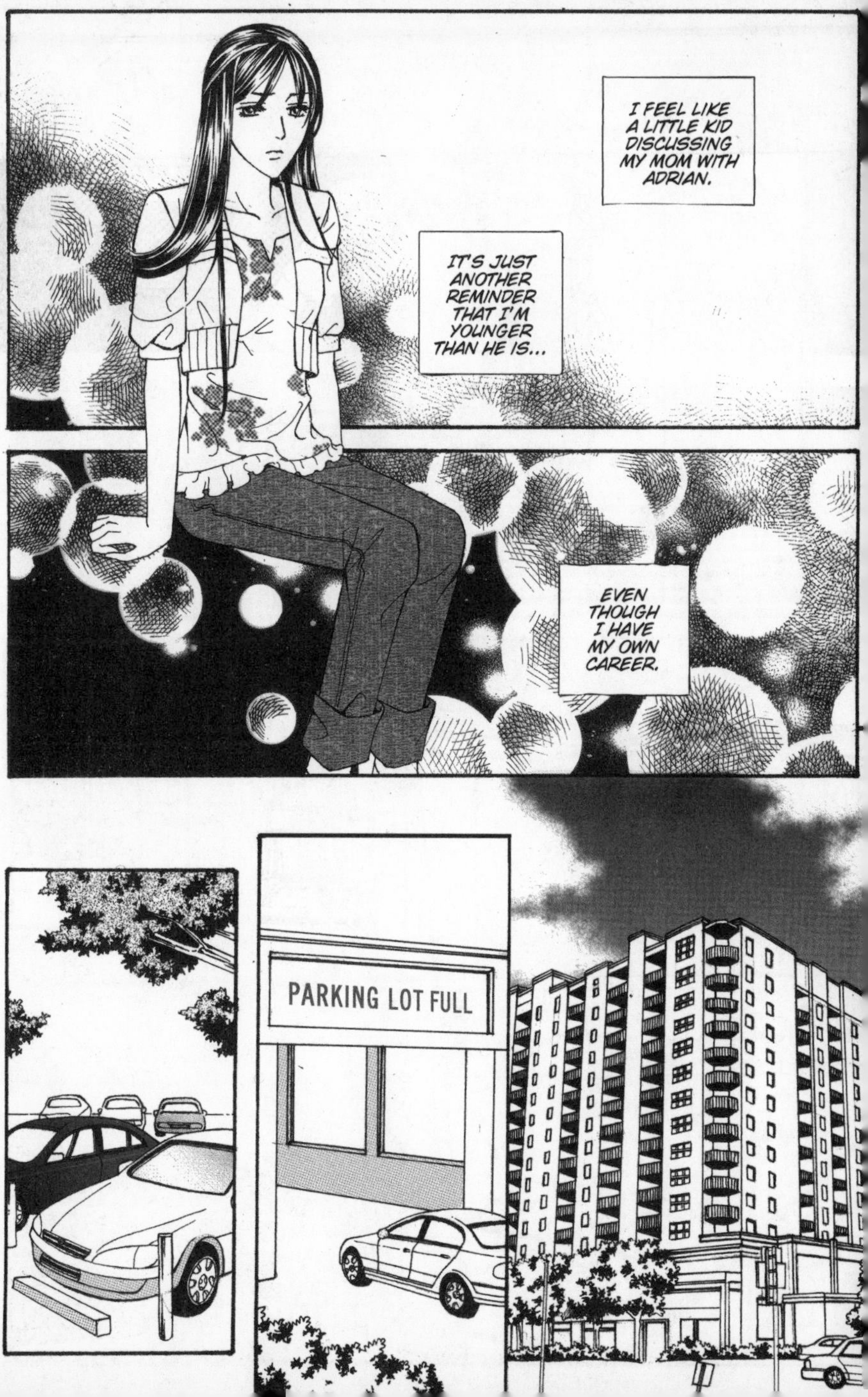
I FEEL LIKE A LITTLE KID DISCUSSING MY MOM WITH ADRIAN.
IT'S JUST ANOTHER REMINDER THAT I'M YOUNGER THAN HE IS...
EVEN THOUGH I HAVE MY OWN CAREER.
PARKING LOT FULL

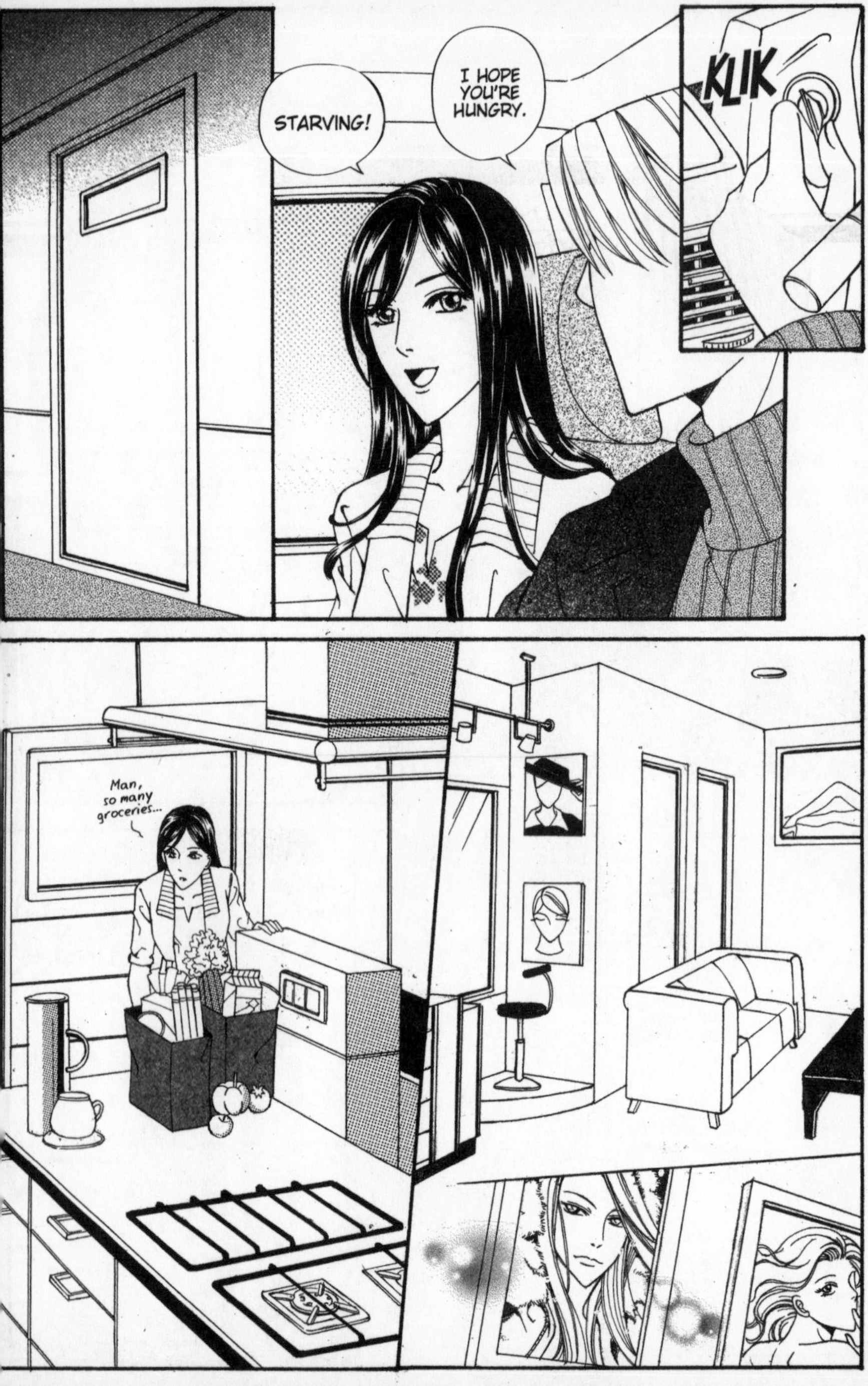
KLIK
I HOPE YOU'RE HUNGRY.
STARVING!
Man, so many groceries...

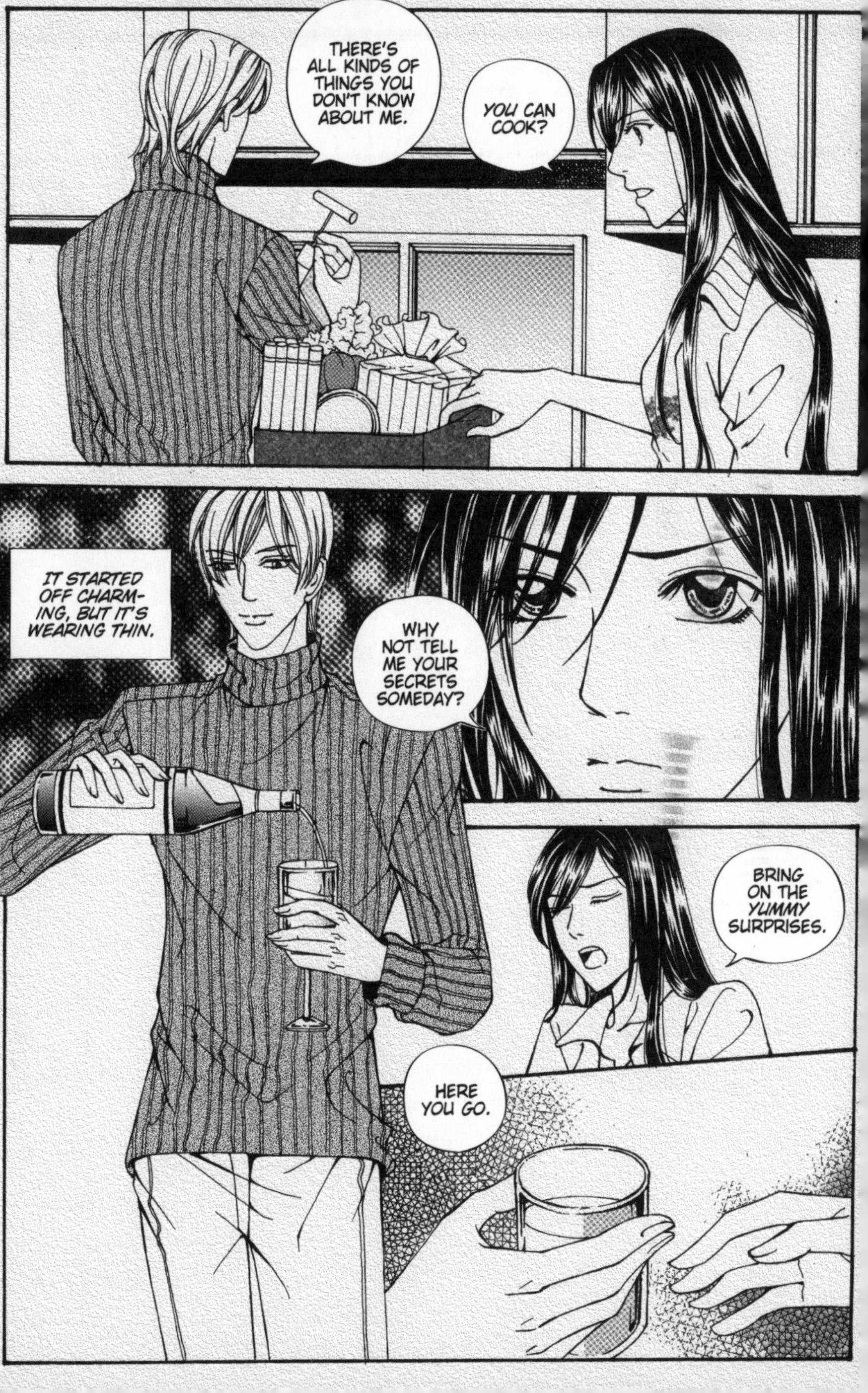
YOU CAN COOK?
THERE'S ALL KINDS OF THINGS YOU DON'T KNOW ABOUT ME.
WHY NOT TELL ME YOUR SECRETS SOMEDAY?
IT STARTED OFF CHARMING, BUT IT'S WEARING THIN.
BRING ON THE YUMMY SURPRISES.
HERE YOU GO.

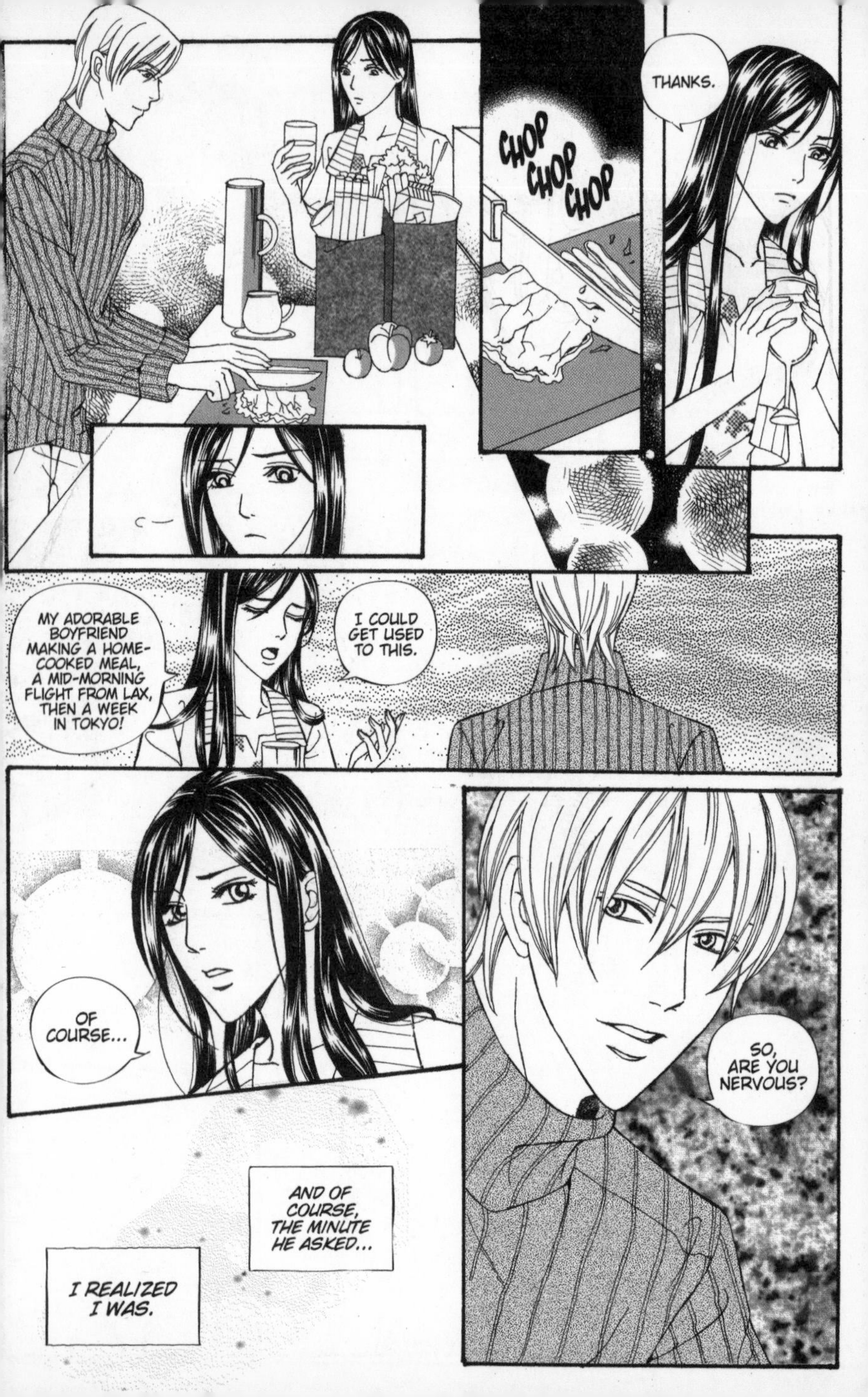
THANKS.
CHOP CHOP CHOP
I COULD GET USED TO THIS.
MY ADORABLE BOYFRIEND MAKING A HOME-COOKED MEAL, A MID-MORNING FLIGHT FROM LAX, THEN A WEEK IN TOKYO!
SO, ARE YOU NERVOUS?
OF COURSE...
AND OF COURSE, THE MINUTE HE ASKED...
I REALIZED I WAS.

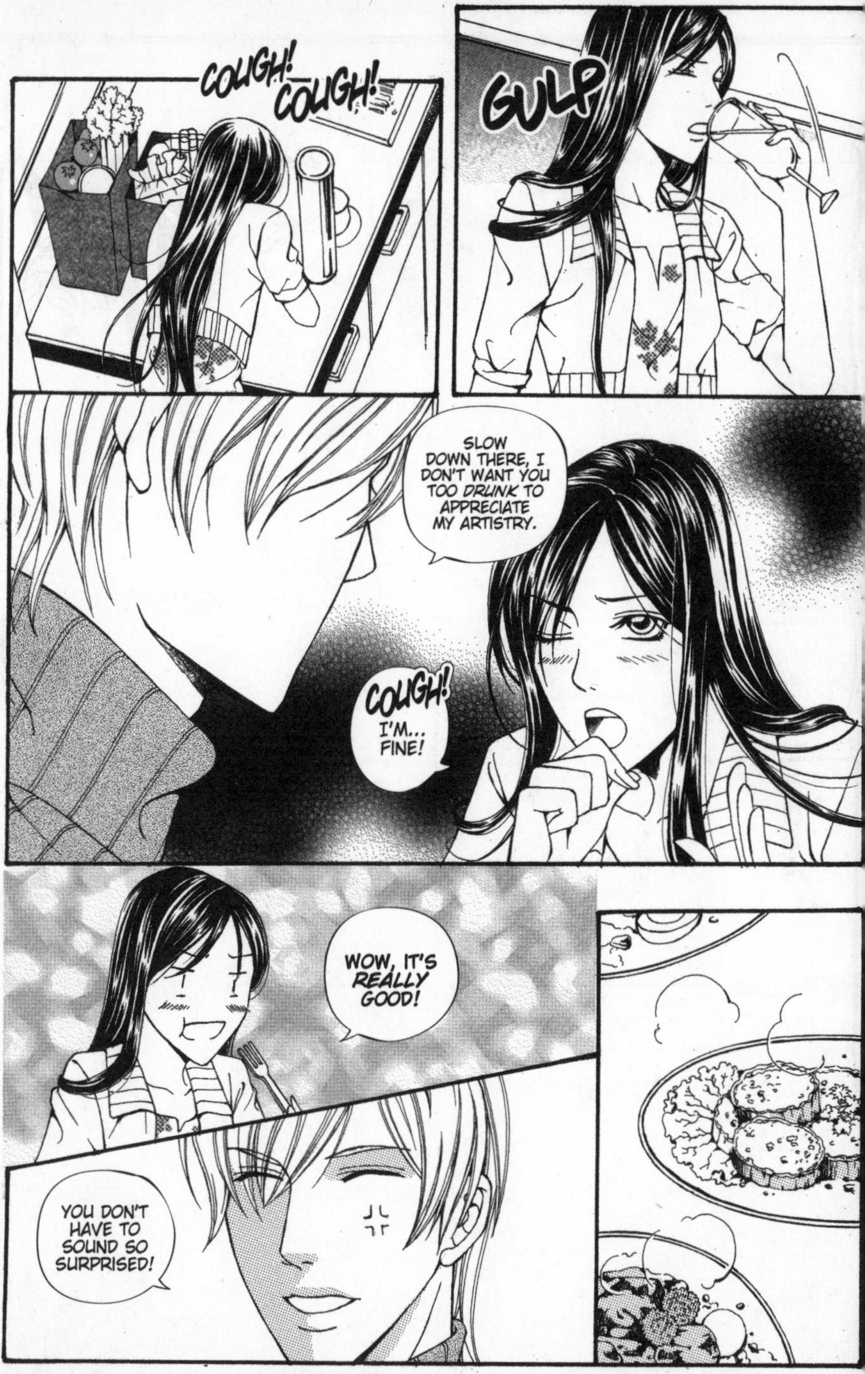
GULP
COUGH! COUGH!
SLOW DOWN THERE, I DON'T WANT YOU TOO *DRUNK* TO APPRECIATE MY ARTISTRY.
COUGH! I'M... FINE!
WOW, IT'S *REALLY* GOOD!
YOU DON'T HAVE TO SOUND SO SURPRISED!

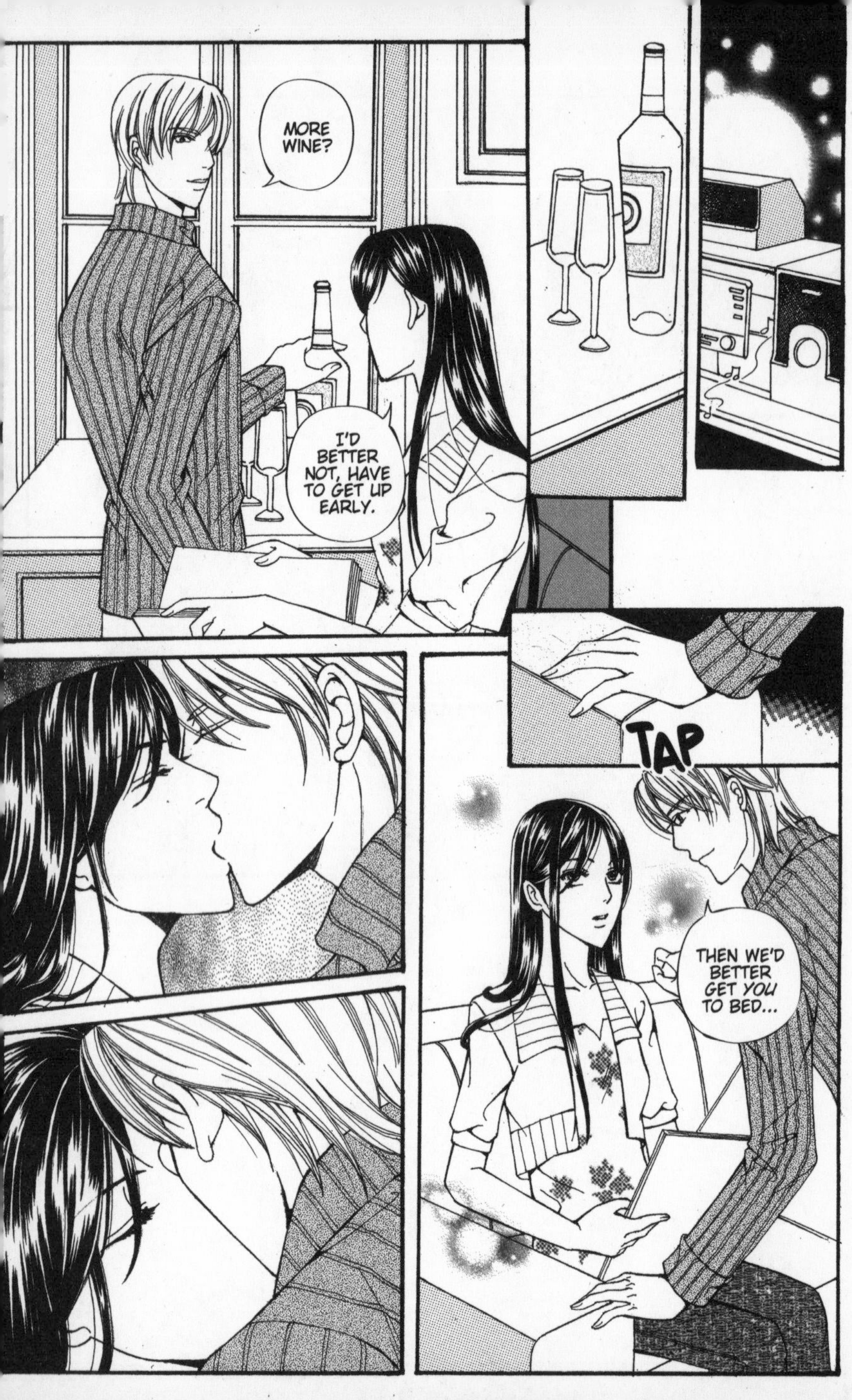
MORE WINE?
I'D BETTER NOT, HAVE TO GET UP EARLY.
TAP
THEN WE'D BETTER GET *YOU* TO BED...

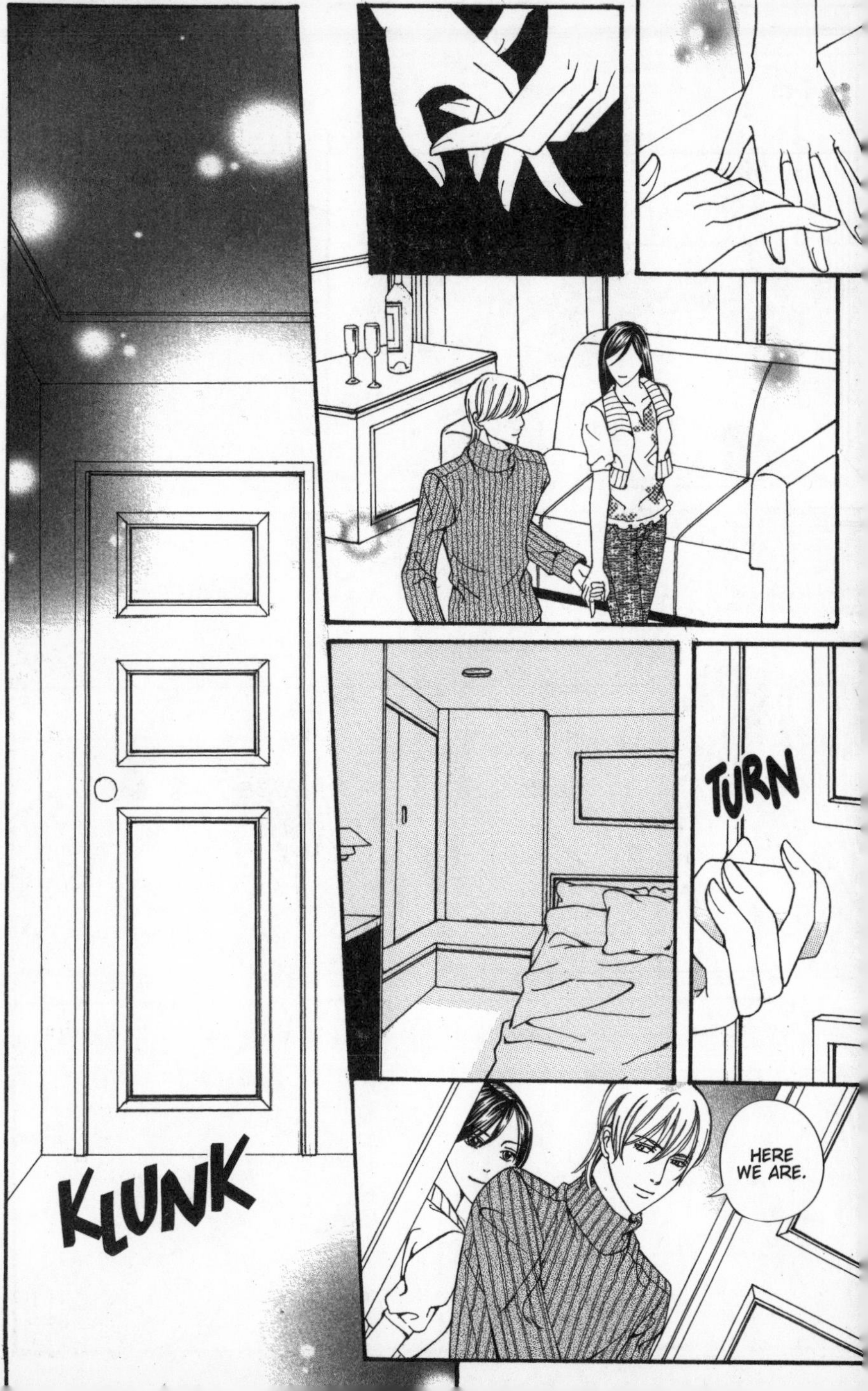
TURN
HERE WE ARE.
KLUNK

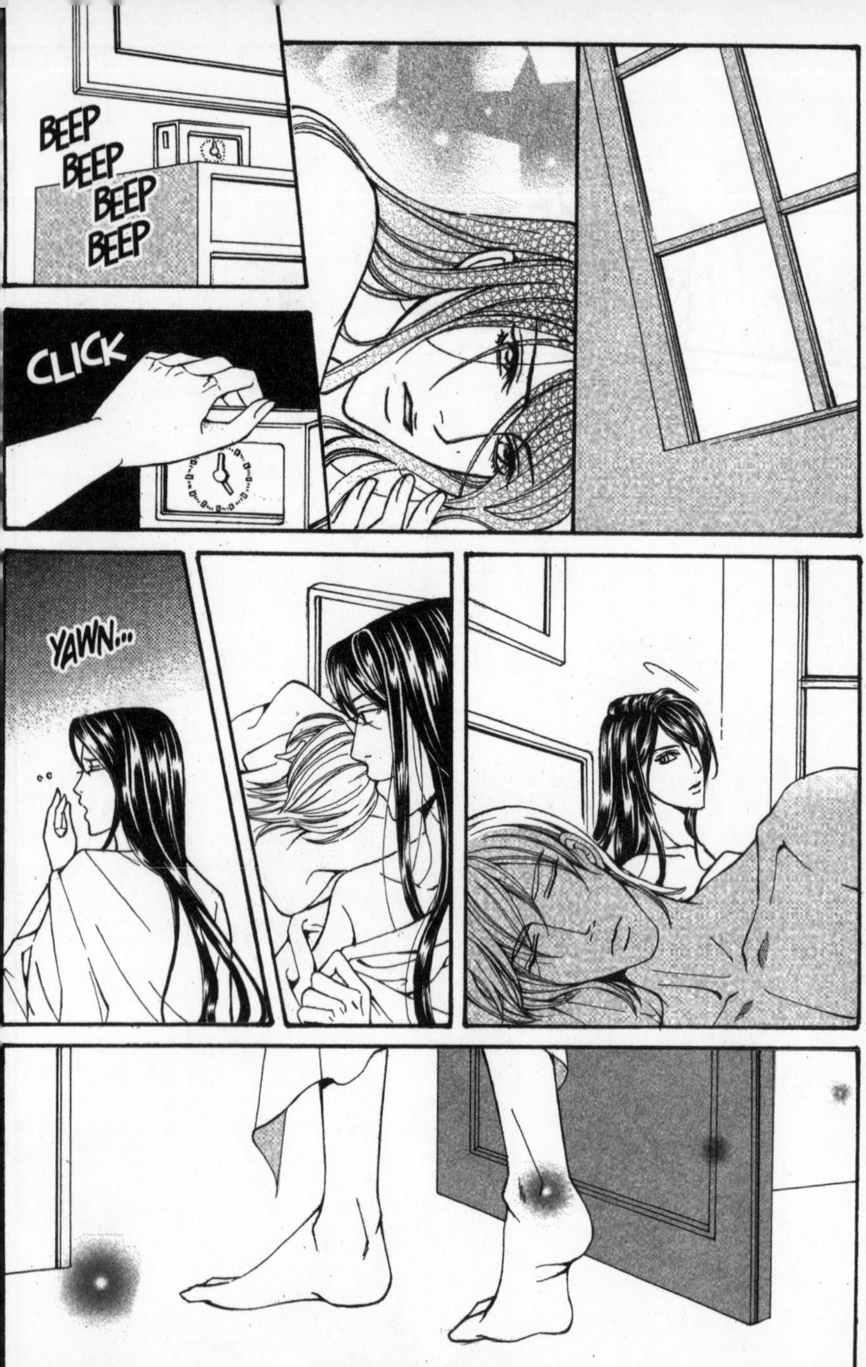
BEEP
BEEP
BEEP
BEEP
CLICK
YAWN...

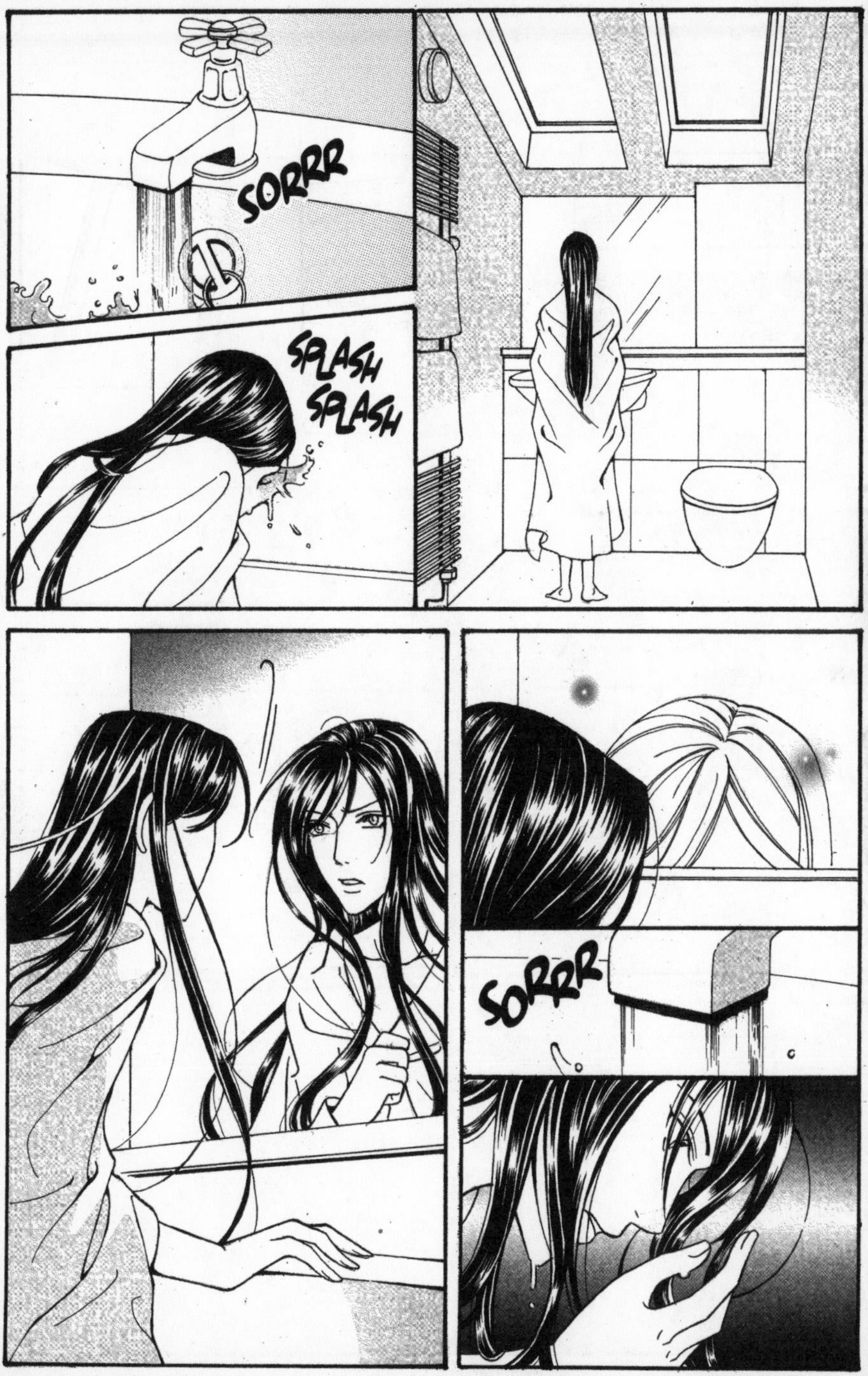
SORRR
SPLASH
SPLASH
SORRR

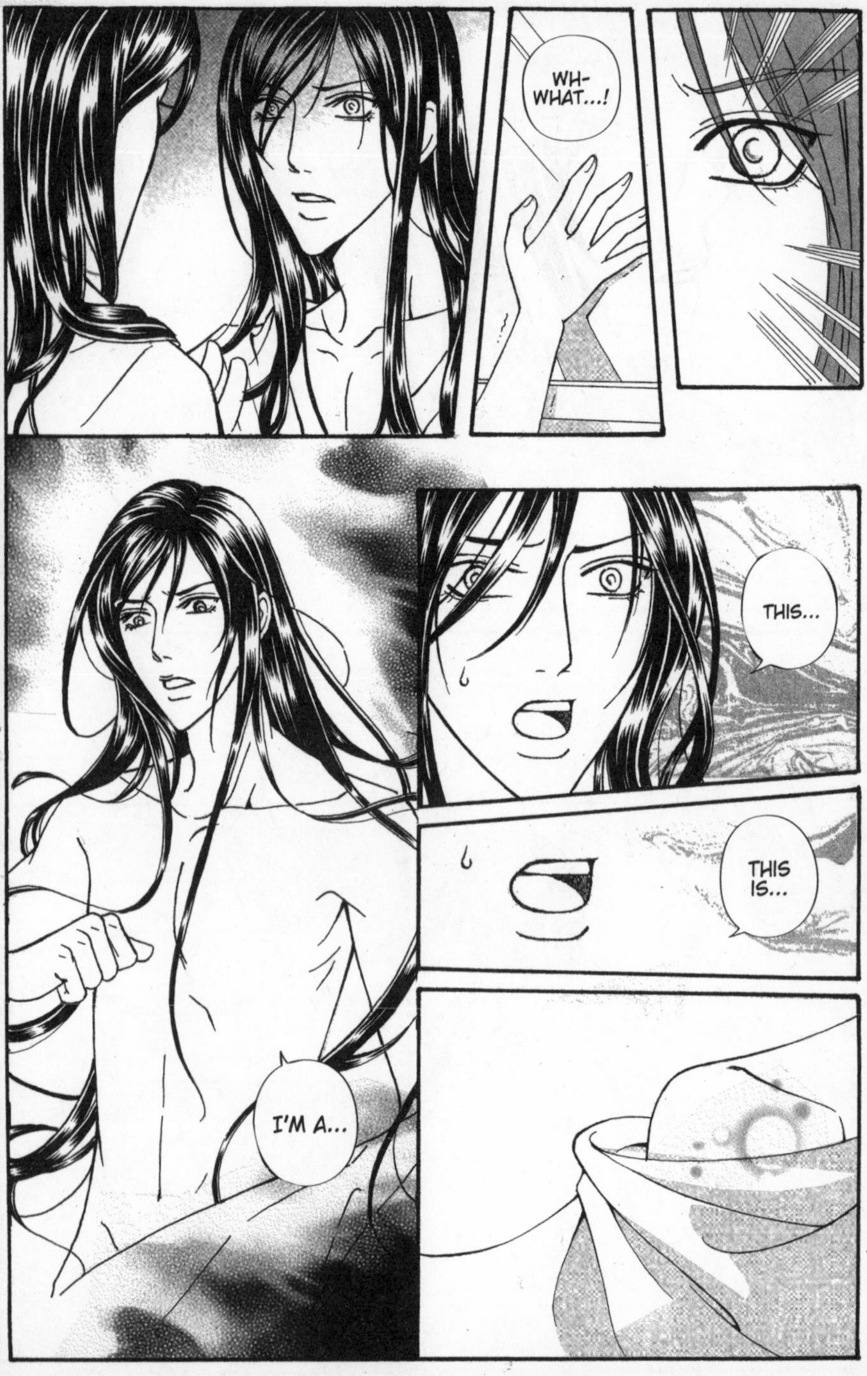
WH-
WHAT...!
THIS...
THIS
IS...
I'M A...

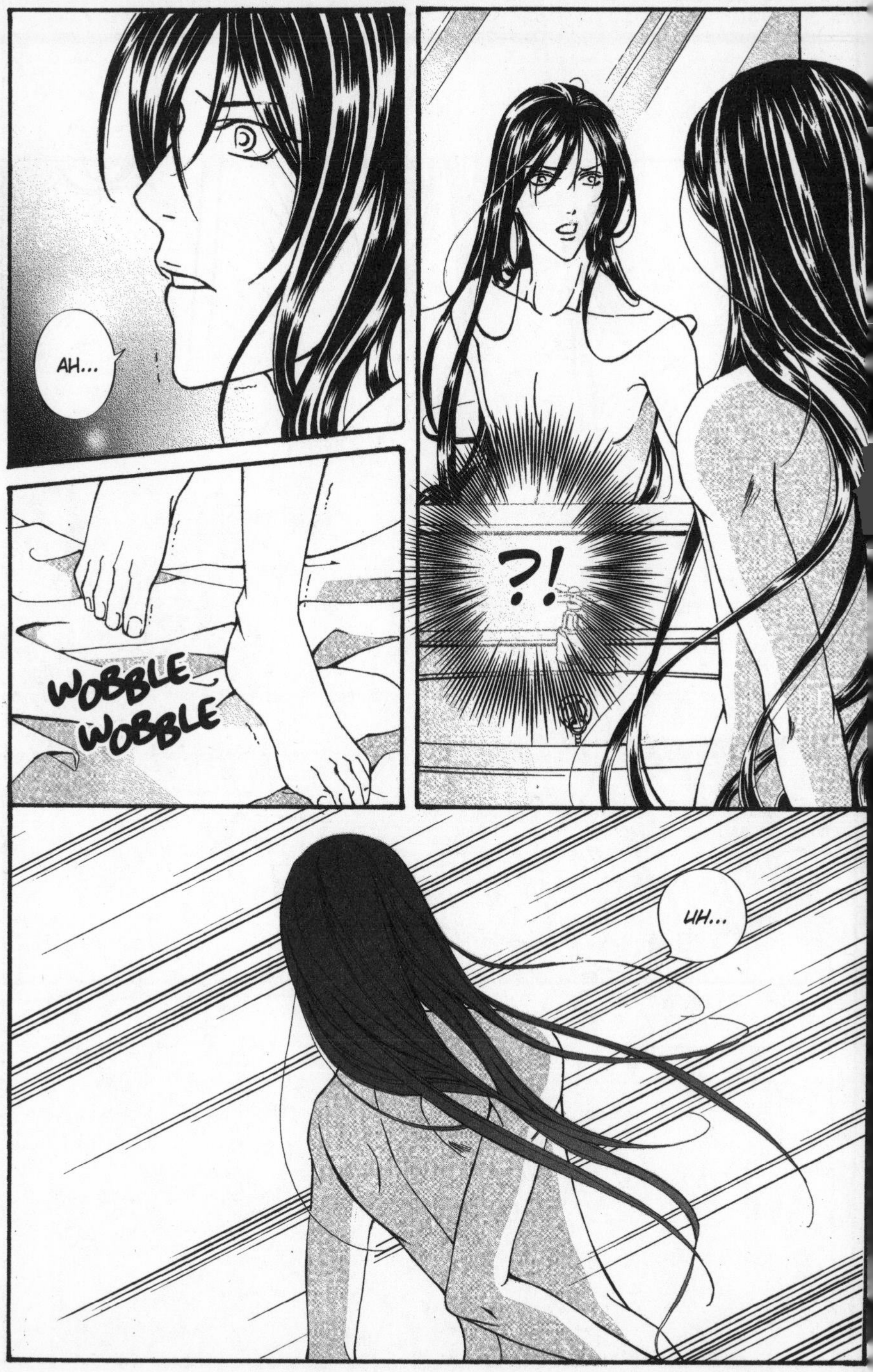
?!
AH...
WOBBLE WOBBLE
UH...

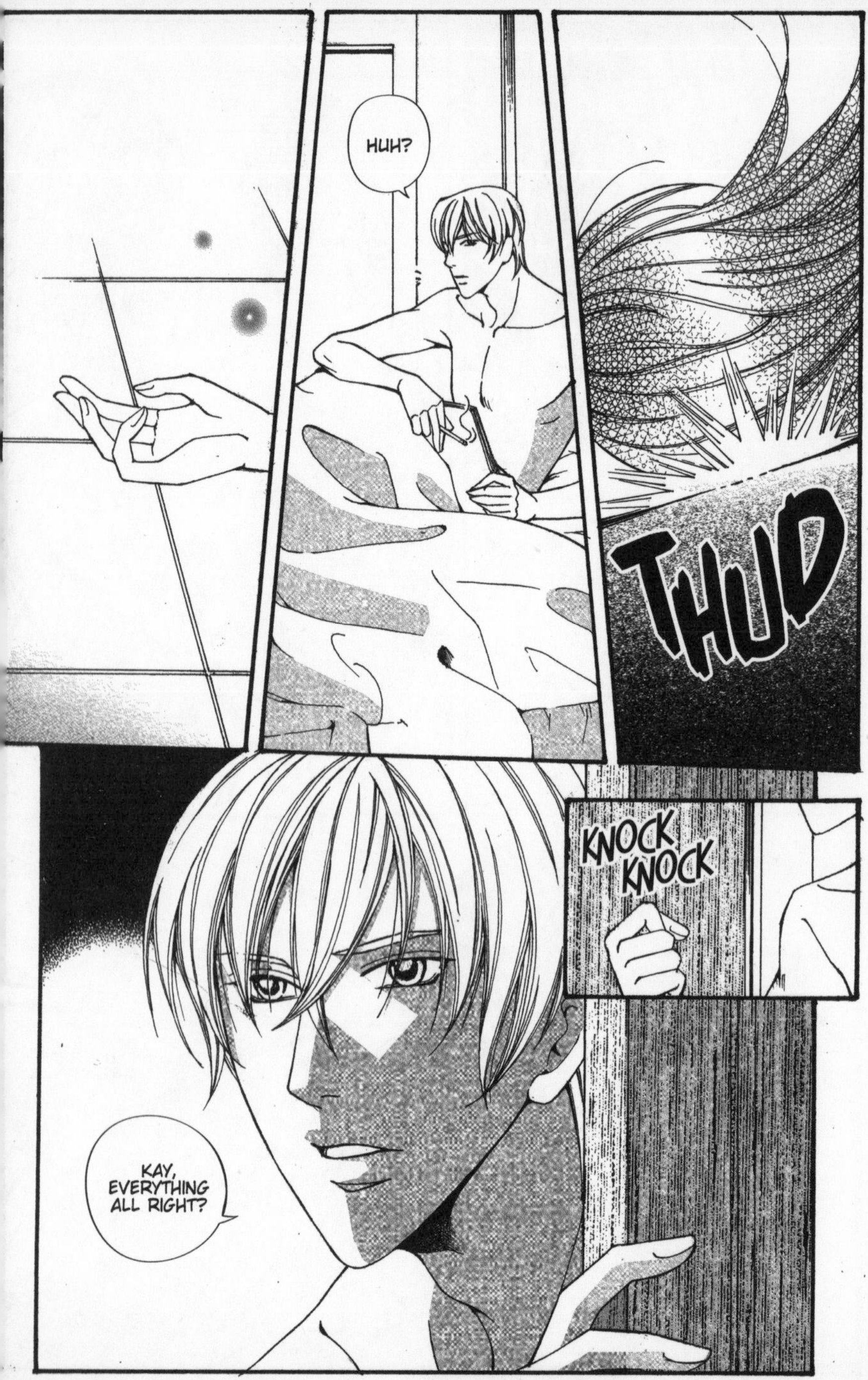
THUD
HUH?
KNOCK KNOCK
KAY, EVERYTHING ALL RIGHT?

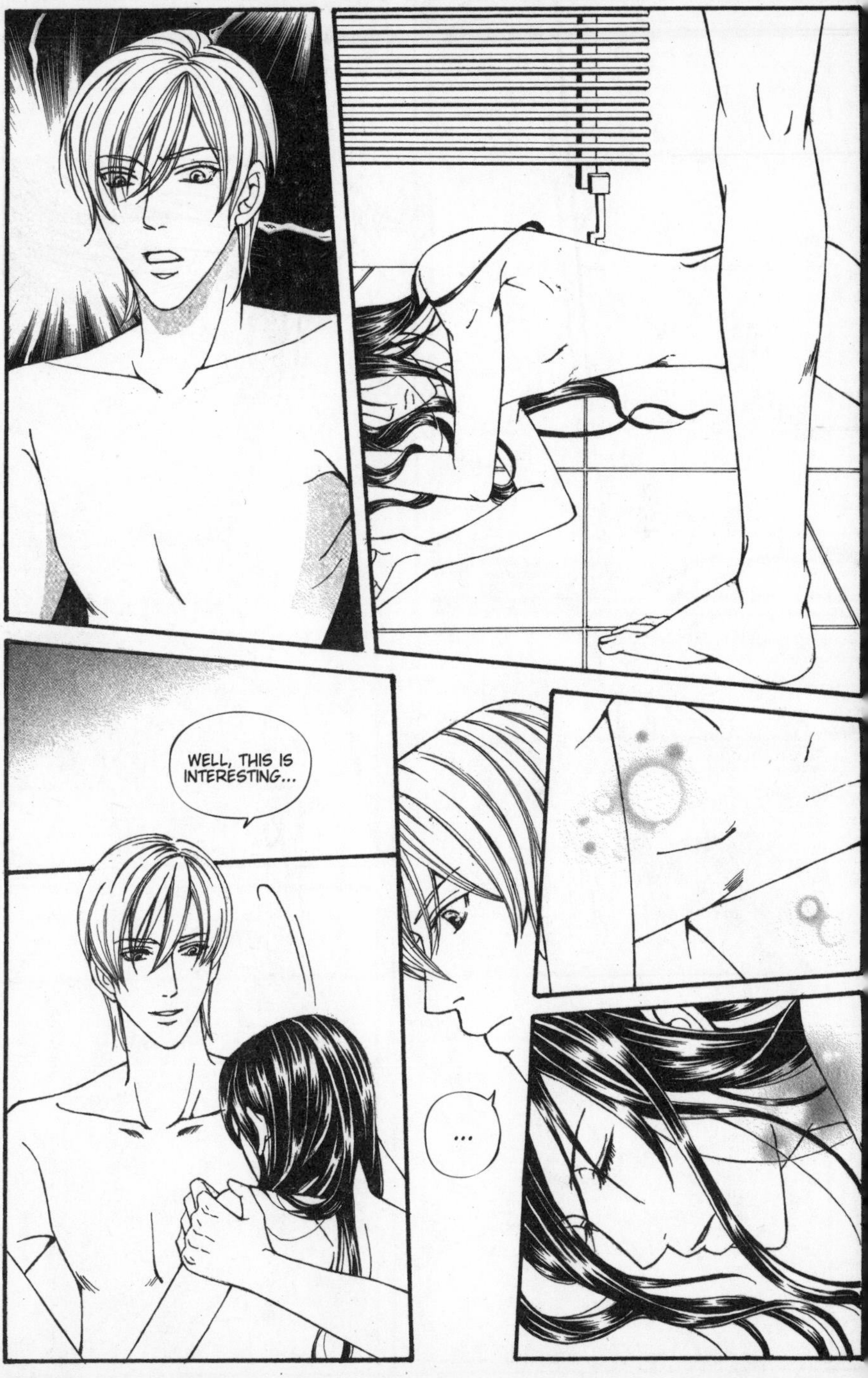
...
WELL, THIS IS INTERESTING...

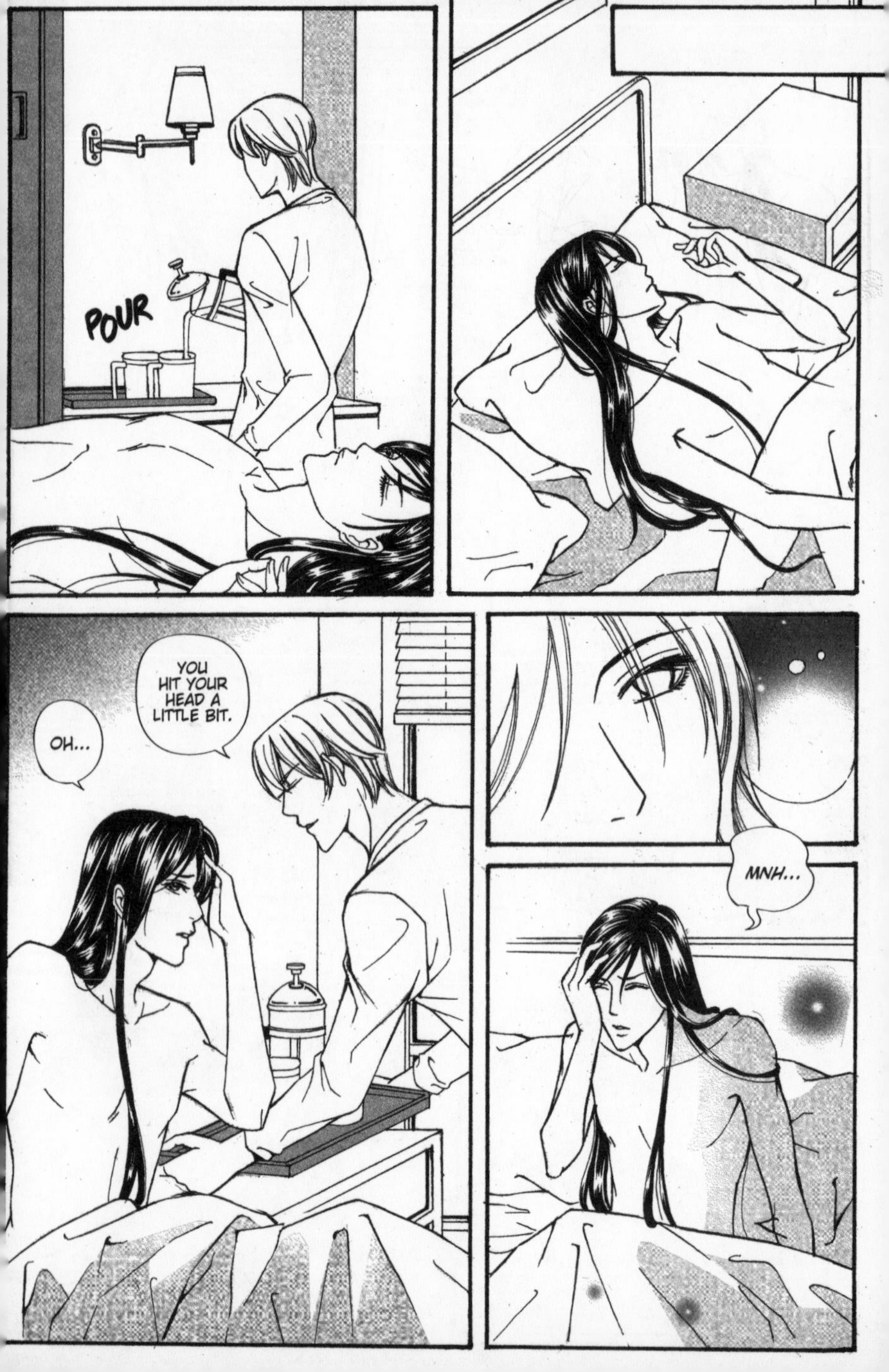
POUR
MNH...
YOU HIT YOUR HEAD A LITTLE BIT.
OH...

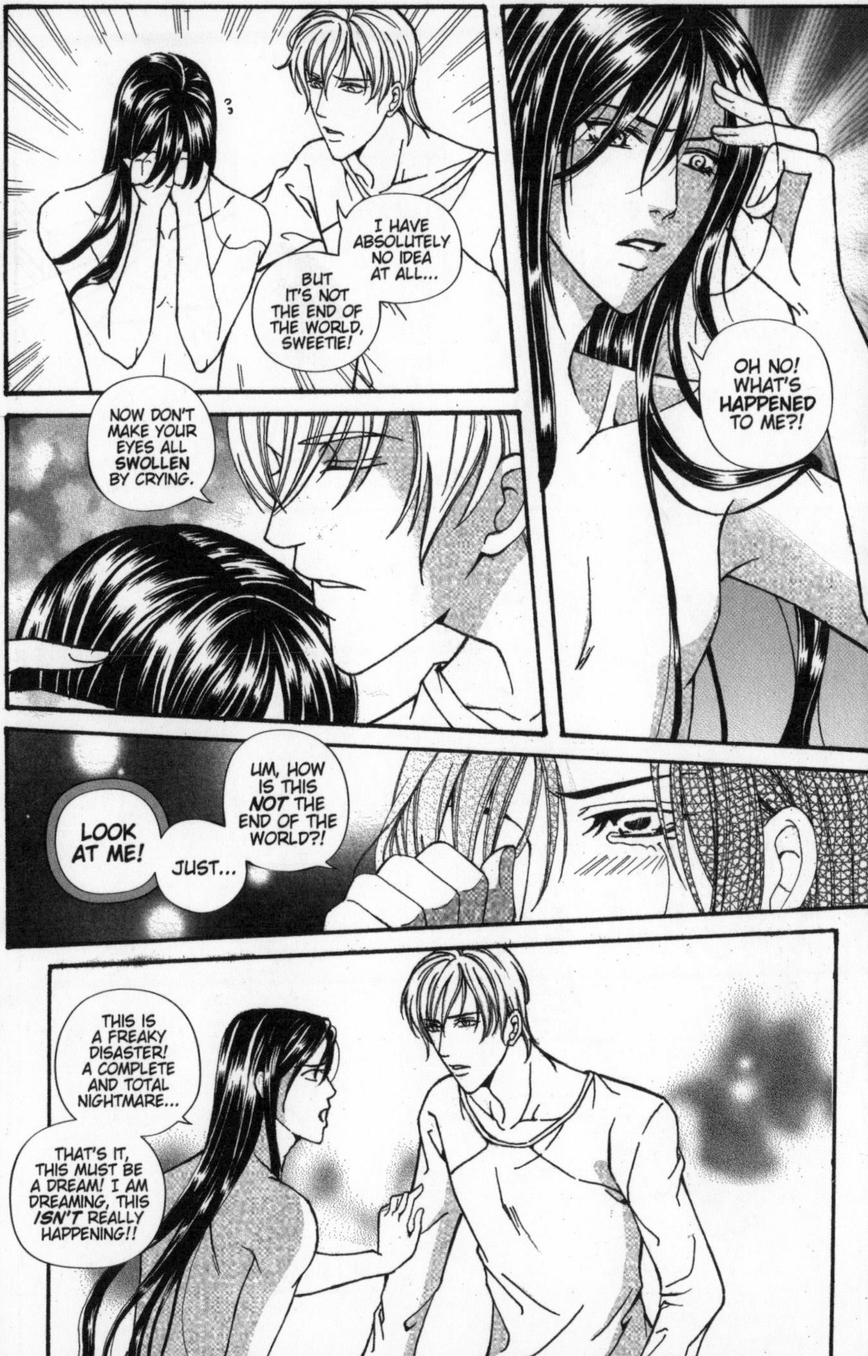
OH NO! WHAT'S **HAPPENED** TO ME?!
?
I HAVE ABSOLUTELY NO IDEA AT ALL...
BUT IT'S NOT THE END OF THE WORLD, SWEETIE!
NOW DON'T MAKE YOUR EYES ALL **SWOLLEN** BY CRYING.
UM, HOW IS THIS ***NOT*** THE END OF THE WORLD?!
JUST...
LOOK AT ME!
THIS IS A FREAKY DISASTER! A COMPLETE AND TOTAL NIGHTMARE...
THAT'S IT, THIS MUST BE A DREAM! I AM DREAMING, THIS ***ISN'T*** REALLY HAPPENING!!

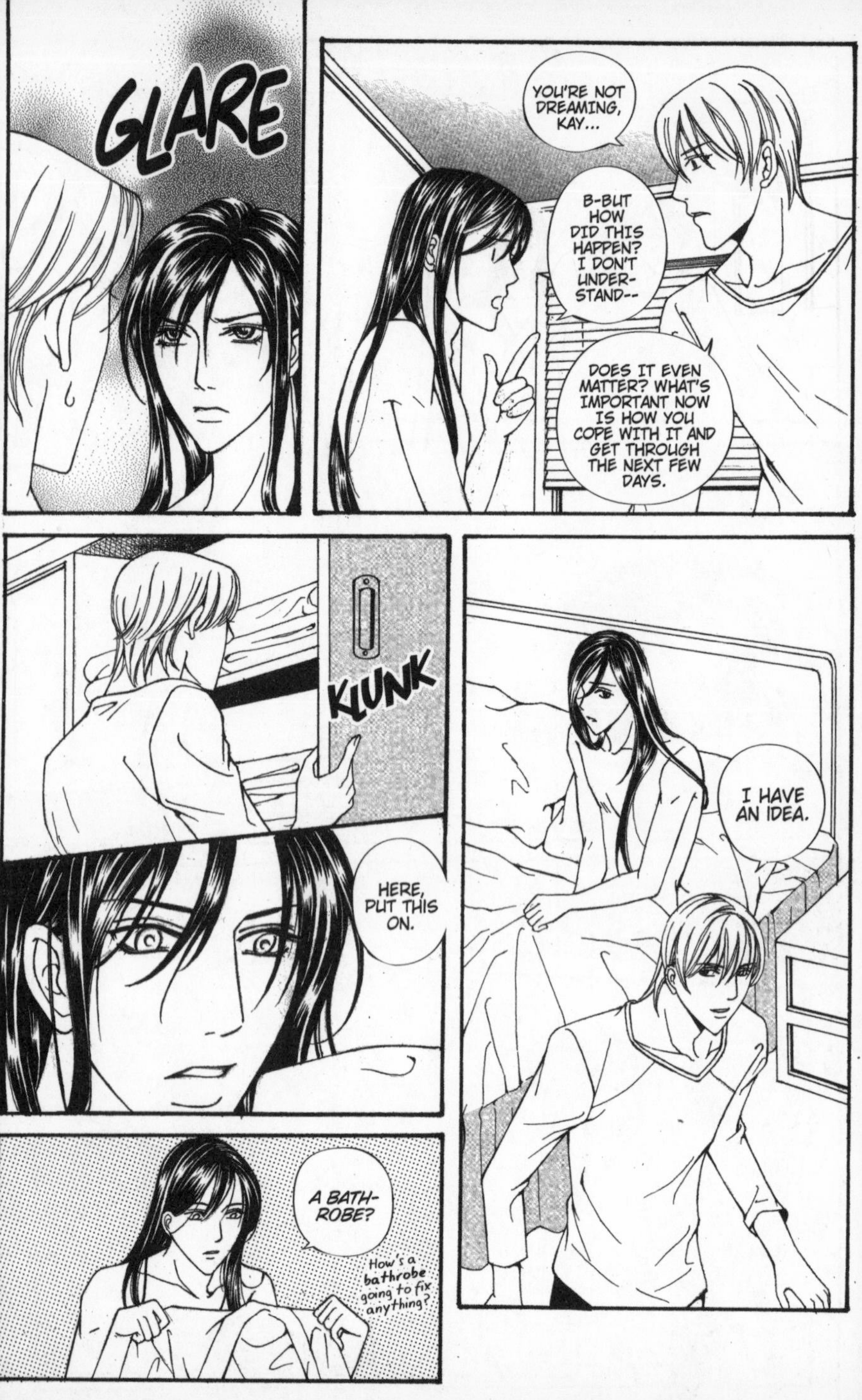
YOU'RE NOT DREAMING, KAY...
B-BUT HOW DID THIS HAPPEN? I DON'T UNDER-STAND--
DOES IT EVEN MATTER? WHAT'S IMPORTANT NOW IS HOW YOU COPE WITH IT AND GET THROUGH THE NEXT FEW DAYS.
GLARE
I HAVE AN IDEA.
KLUNK
HERE, PUT THIS ON.
A BATH-ROBE?
How's a bathrobe going to fix anything?

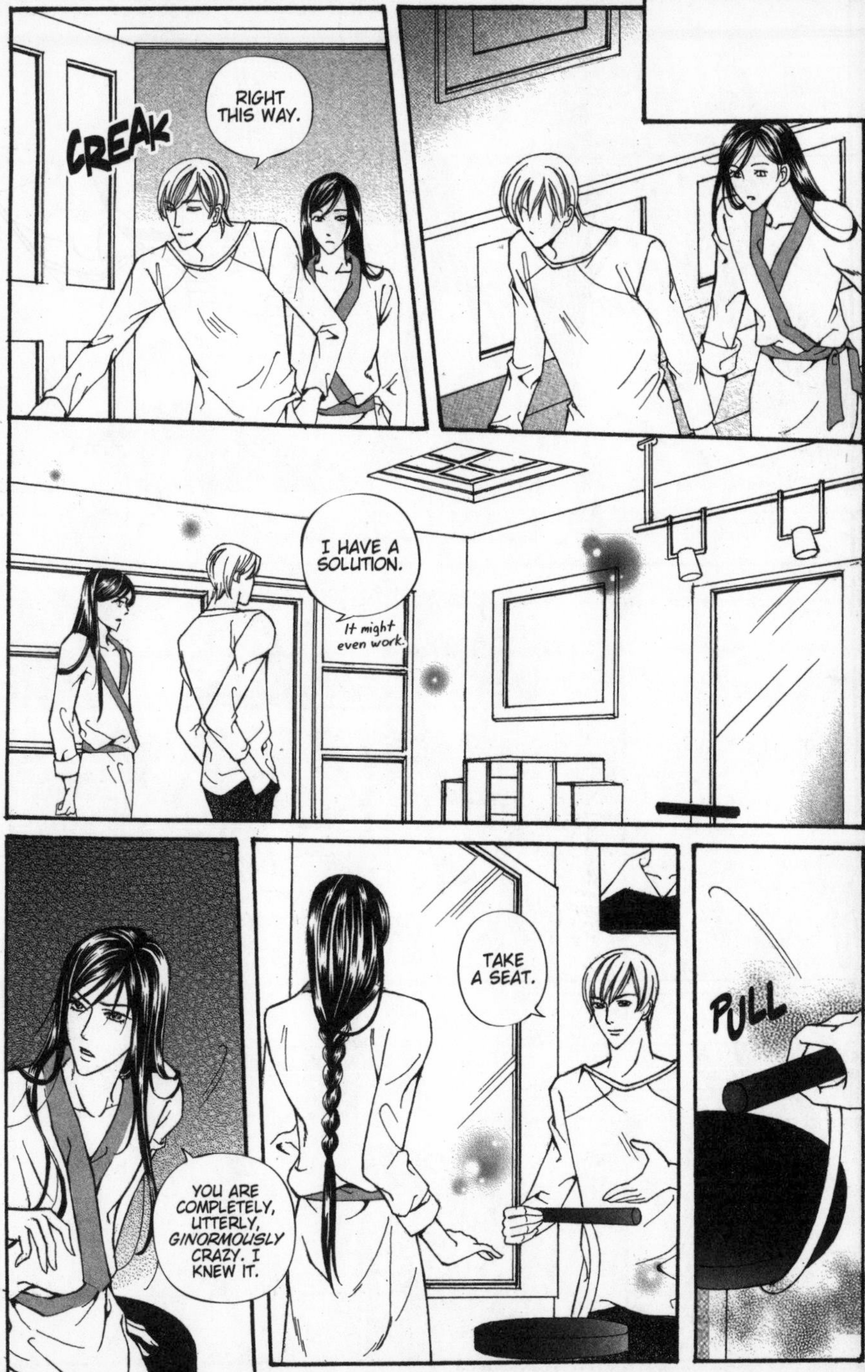
RIGHT THIS WAY.
CREAK
I HAVE A SOLUTION.
It might even work.
PULL
TAKE A SEAT.
YOU ARE COMPLETELY, UTTERLY, GINORMOUSLY CRAZY. I KNEW IT.

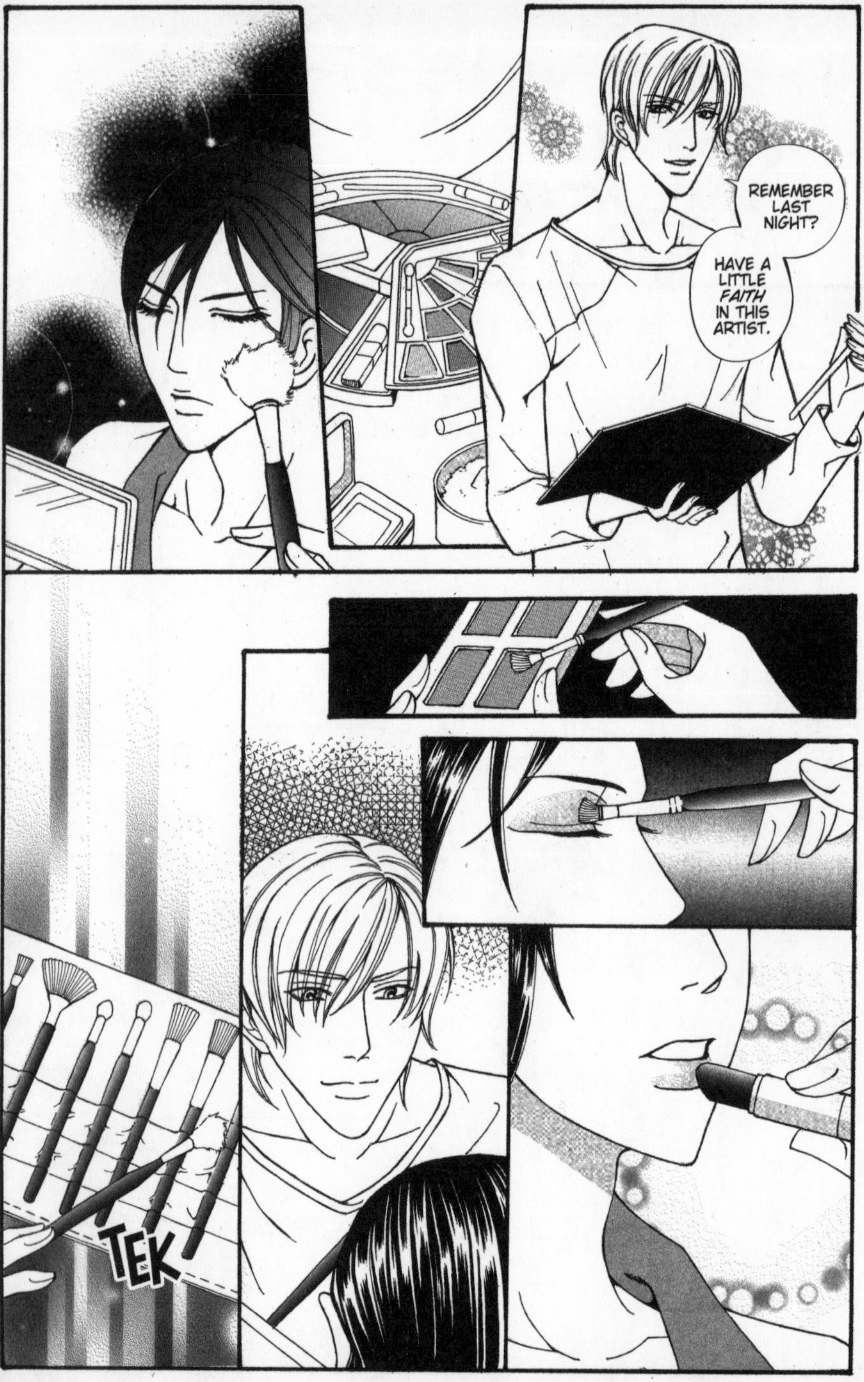
REMEMBER LAST NIGHT?
HAVE A LITTLE *FAITH* IN THIS ARTIST.
TEK

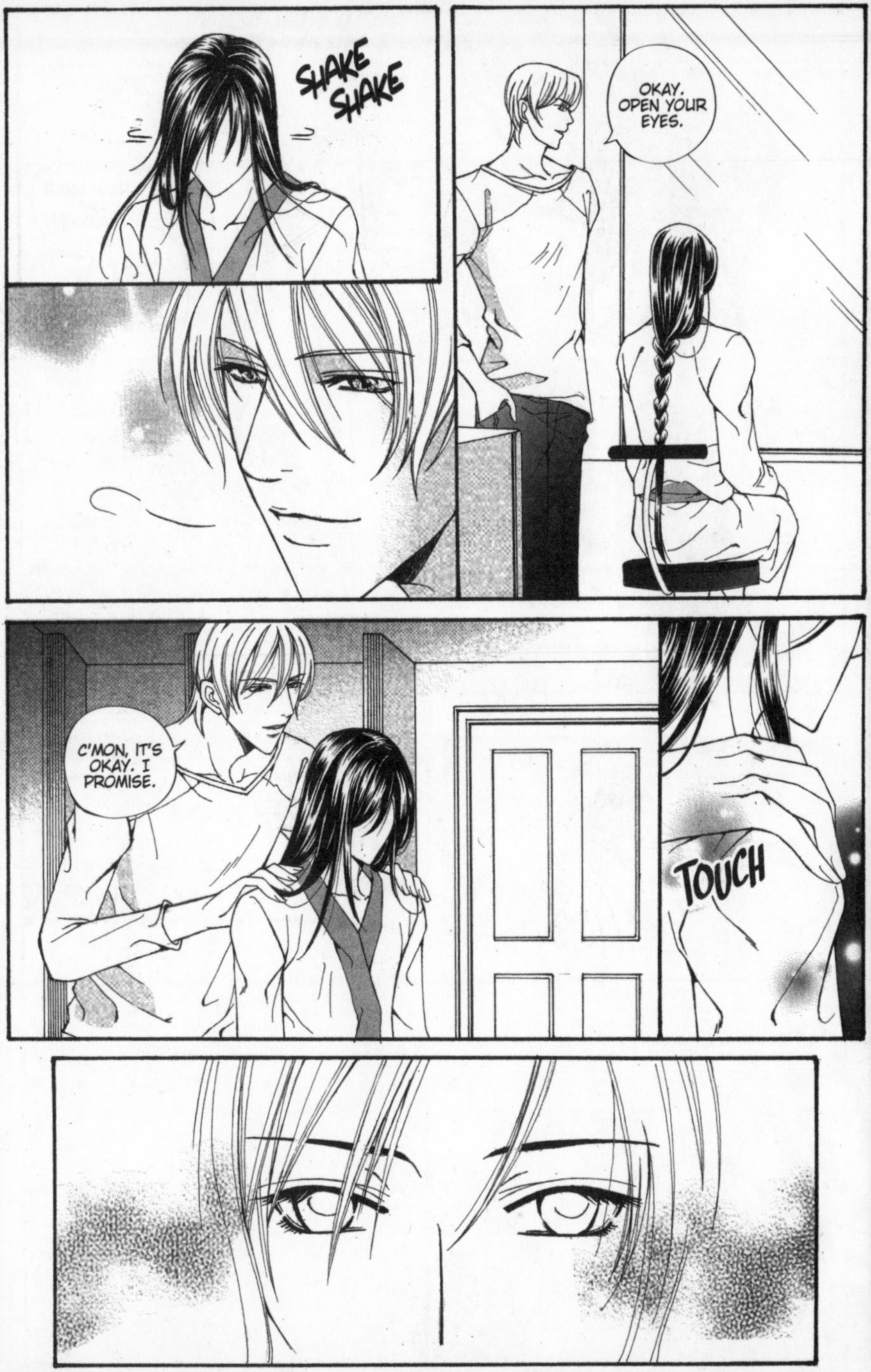
OKAY. OPEN YOUR EYES.
SHAKE SHAKE
TOUCH
C'MON, IT'S OKAY. I PROMISE.

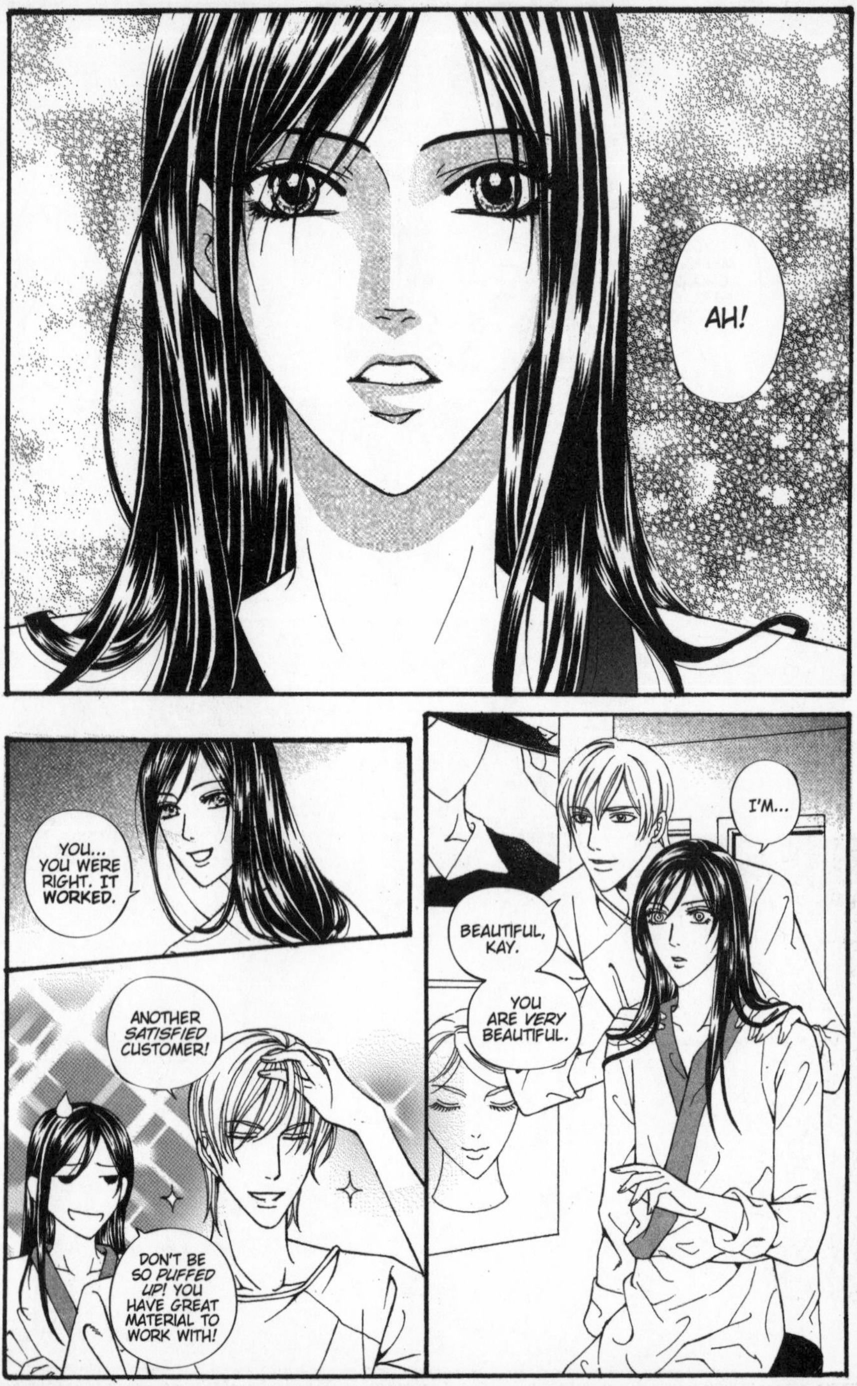
AH!
I'M...
BEAUTIFUL, KAY.
YOU ARE *VERY* BEAUTIFUL.
YOU... YOU WERE RIGHT. IT WORKED.
ANOTHER *SATISFIED* CUSTOMER!
DON'T BE SO *PUFFED UP*! YOU HAVE GREAT MATERIAL TO WORK WITH!

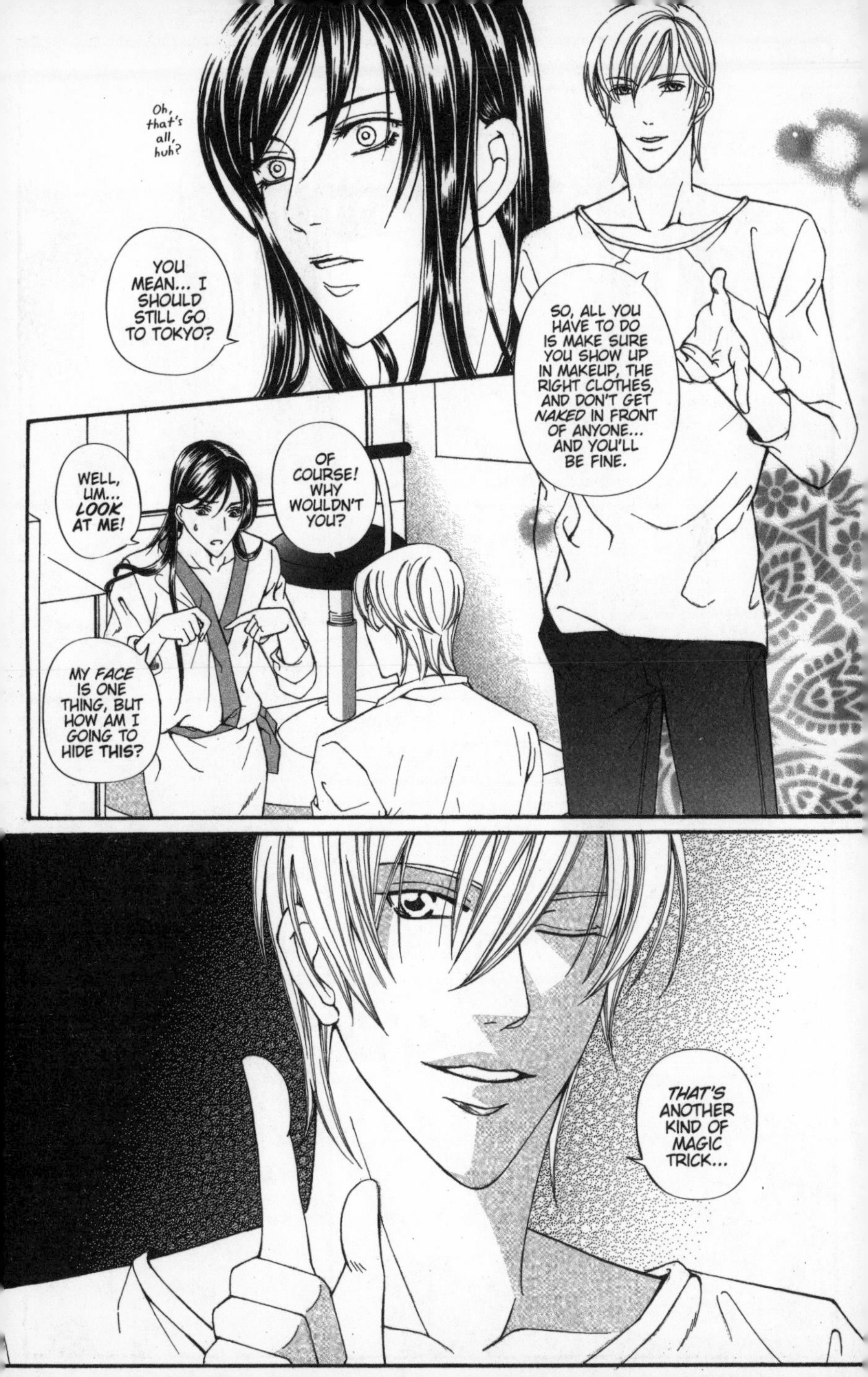
SO, ALL YOU HAVE TO DO IS MAKE SURE YOU SHOW UP IN MAKEUP, THE RIGHT CLOTHES, AND DON'T GET *NAKED* IN FRONT OF ANYONE... AND YOU'LL BE FINE.
Oh, that's all, huh?
YOU MEAN... I SHOULD STILL GO TO TOKYO?
OF COURSE! WHY WOULDN'T YOU?
WELL, UM... ***LOOK*** AT ME!
MY *FACE* IS ONE THING, BUT HOW AM I GOING TO HIDE THIS?
THAT'S ANOTHER KIND OF MAGIC TRICK...

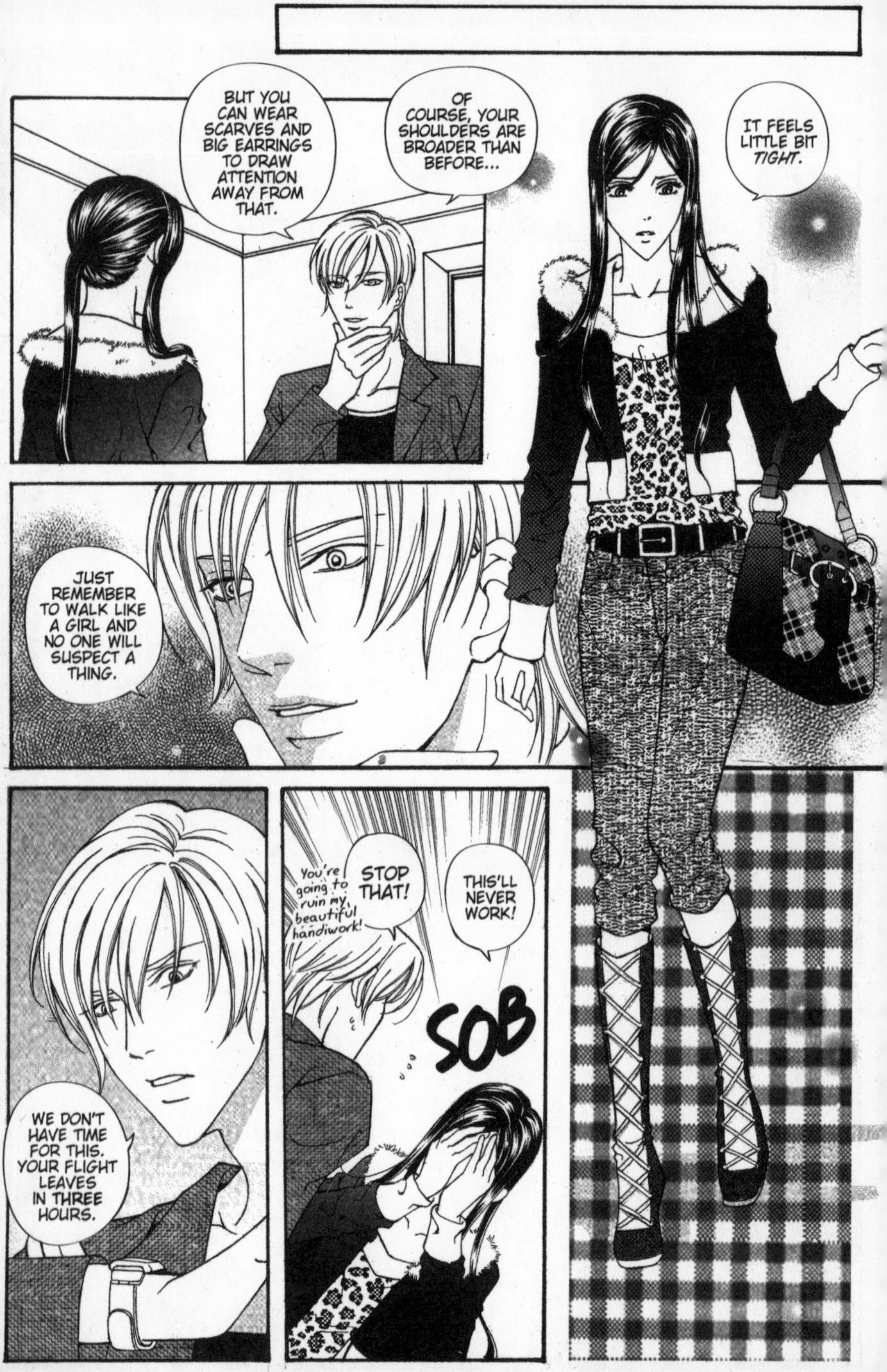
IT FEELS LITTLE BIT *TIGHT*.
OF COURSE, YOUR SHOULDERS ARE BROADER THAN BEFORE...
BUT YOU CAN WEAR SCARVES AND BIG EARRINGS TO DRAW ATTENTION AWAY FROM THAT.
JUST REMEMBER TO WALK LIKE A GIRL AND NO ONE WILL SUSPECT A THING.
THIS'LL NEVER WORK!
STOP THAT!
You're going to ruin my beautiful handiwork!
SOB
WE DON'T HAVE TIME FOR THIS. YOUR FLIGHT LEAVES IN THREE HOURS.

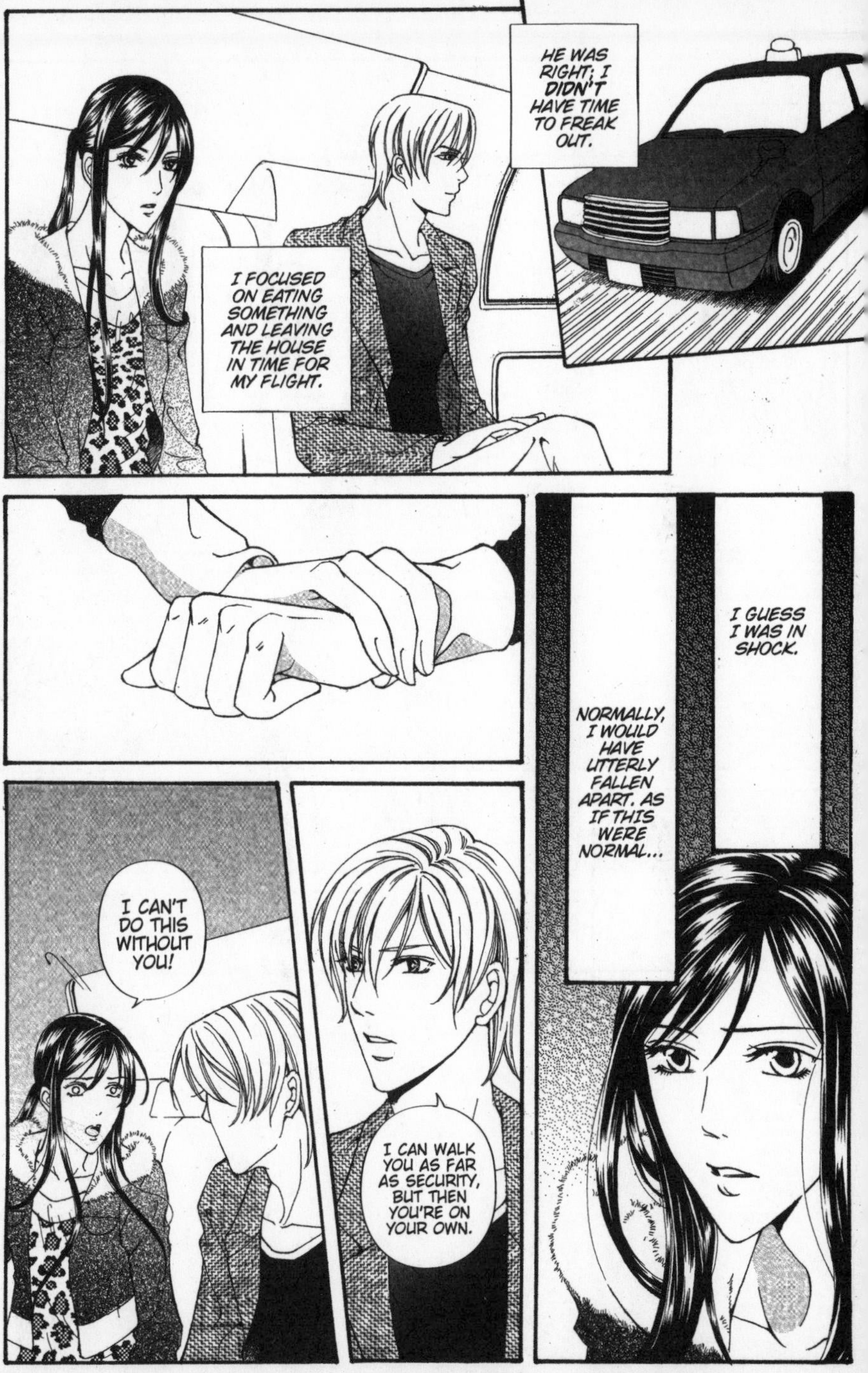
HE WAS RIGHT; I DIDN'T HAVE TIME TO FREAK OUT.
I FOCUSED ON EATING SOMETHING AND LEAVING THE HOUSE IN TIME FOR MY FLIGHT.
I GUESS I WAS IN SHOCK.
NORMALLY, I WOULD HAVE UTTERLY FALLEN APART. AS IF THIS WERE NORMAL...
I CAN WALK YOU AS FAR AS SECURITY, BUT THEN YOU'RE ON YOUR OWN.
I CAN'T DO THIS WITHOUT YOU!

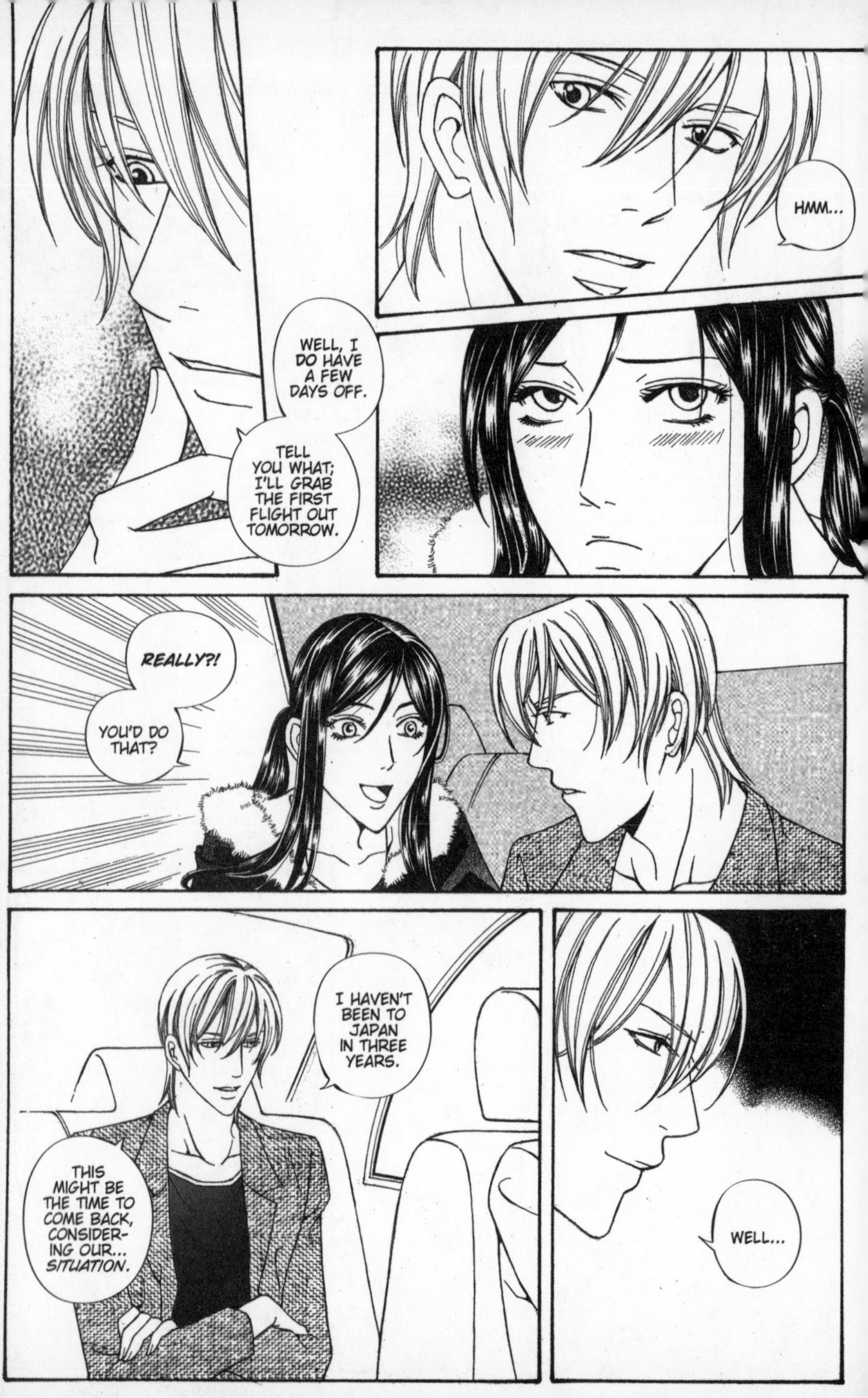
HMM...
WELL, I DO HAVE A FEW DAYS OFF.
TELL YOU WHAT; I'LL GRAB THE FIRST FLIGHT OUT TOMORROW.
REALLY?!
YOU'D DO THAT?
WELL...
I HAVEN'T BEEN TO JAPAN IN THREE YEARS.
THIS MIGHT BE THE TIME TO COME BACK, CONSIDERING OUR... *SITUATION*.

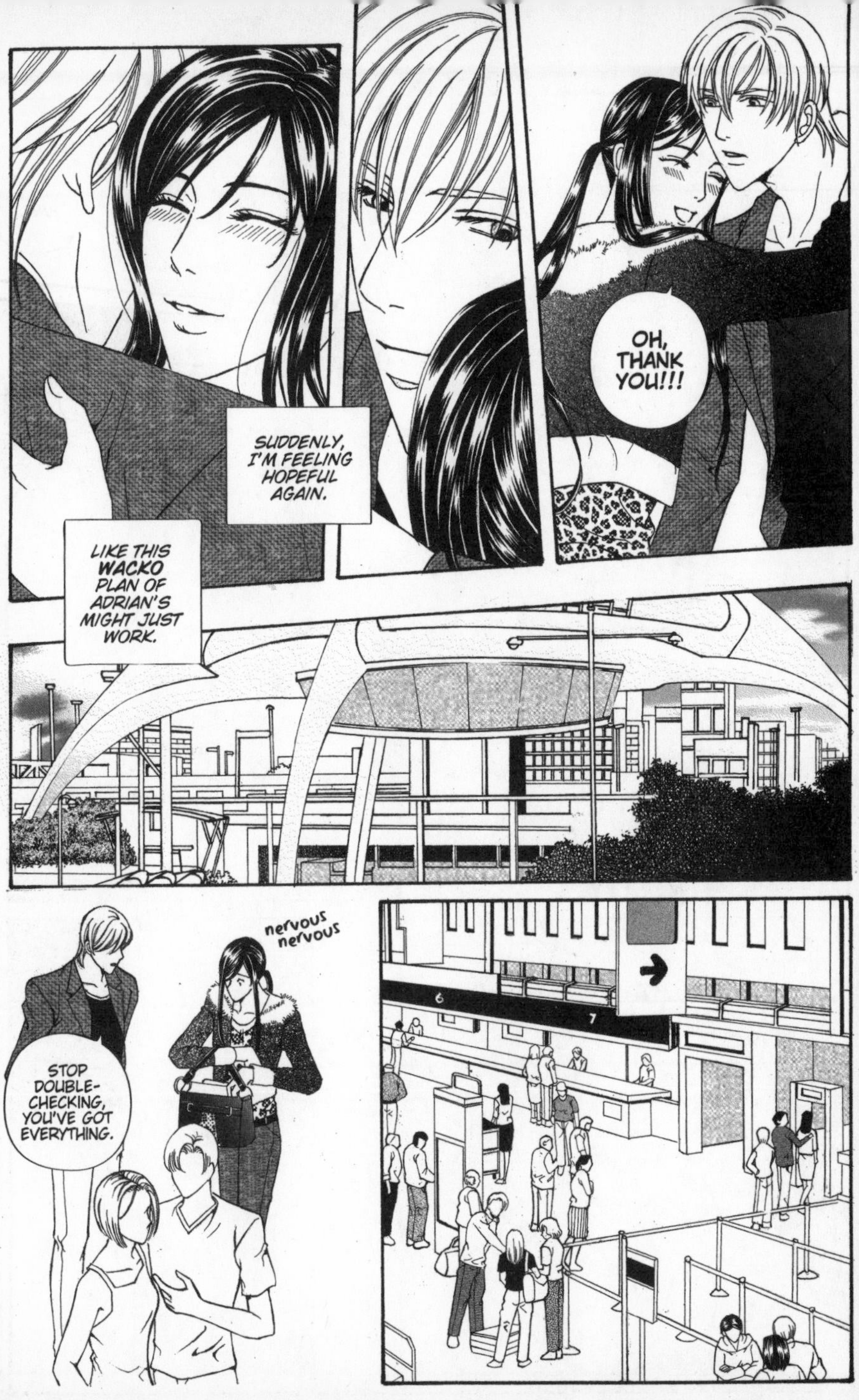
OH, THANK YOU!!!
SUDDENLY, I'M FEELING HOPEFUL AGAIN.
LIKE THIS **WACKO** PLAN OF ADRIAN'S MIGHT JUST WORK.
nervous nervous
STOP DOUBLE-CHECKING, YOU'VE GOT EVERYTHING.

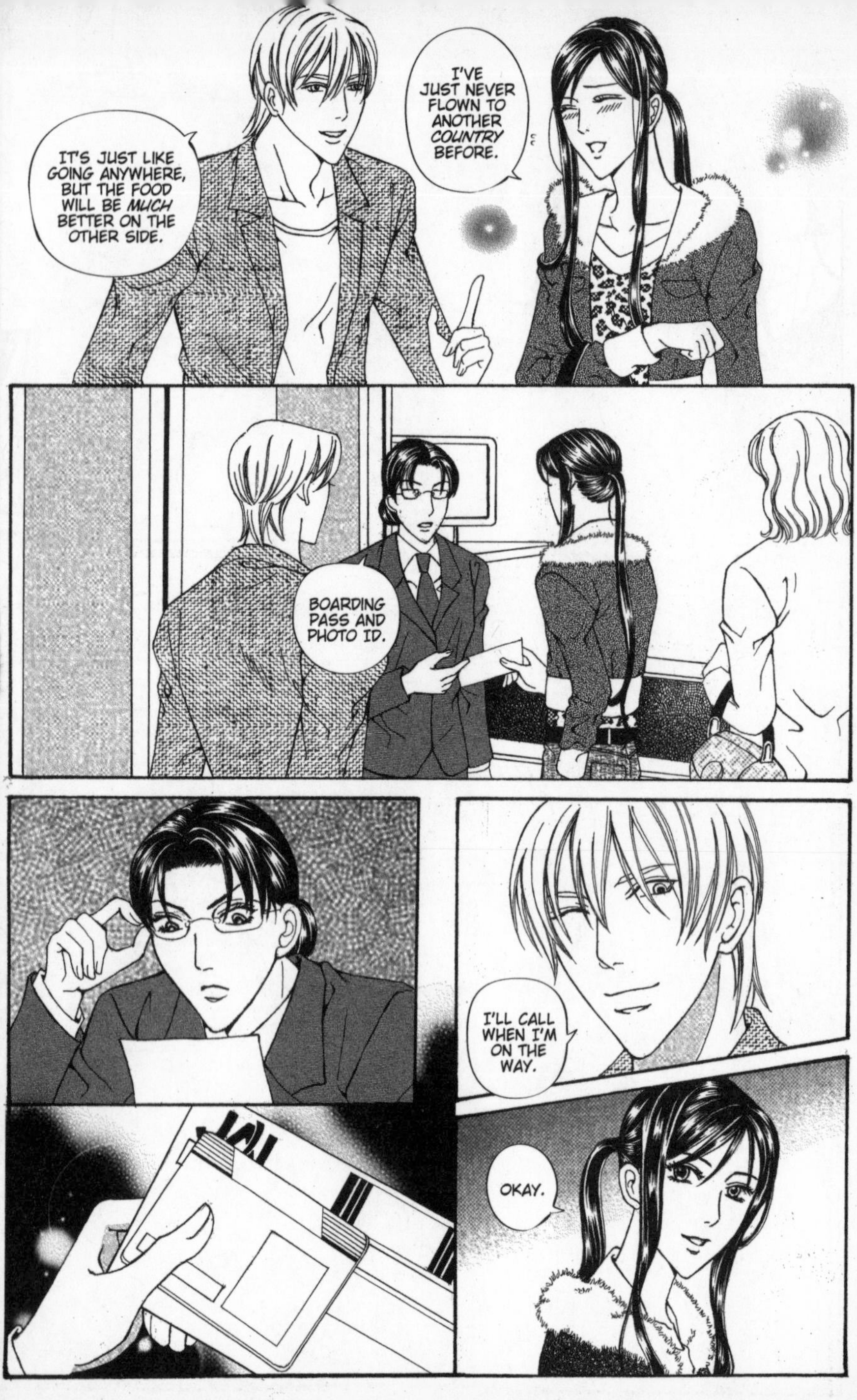
I'VE JUST NEVER FLOWN TO ANOTHER *COUNTRY* BEFORE.
IT'S JUST LIKE GOING ANYWHERE, BUT THE FOOD WILL BE *MUCH* BETTER ON THE OTHER SIDE.
BOARDING PASS AND PHOTO ID.
I'LL CALL WHEN I'M ON THE WAY.
OKAY.

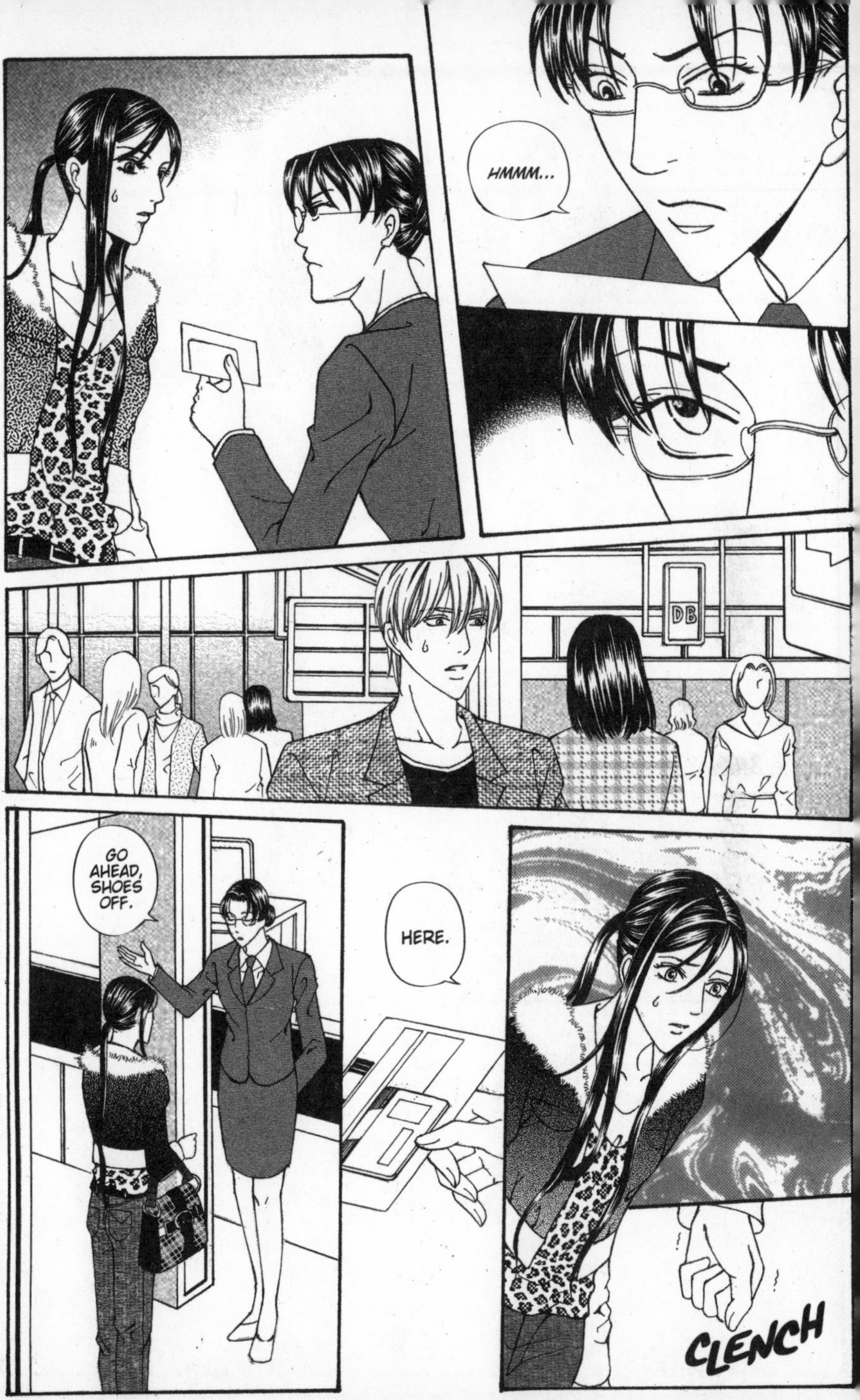
HMMM...
CLENCH
HERE.
GO AHEAD, SHOES OFF.

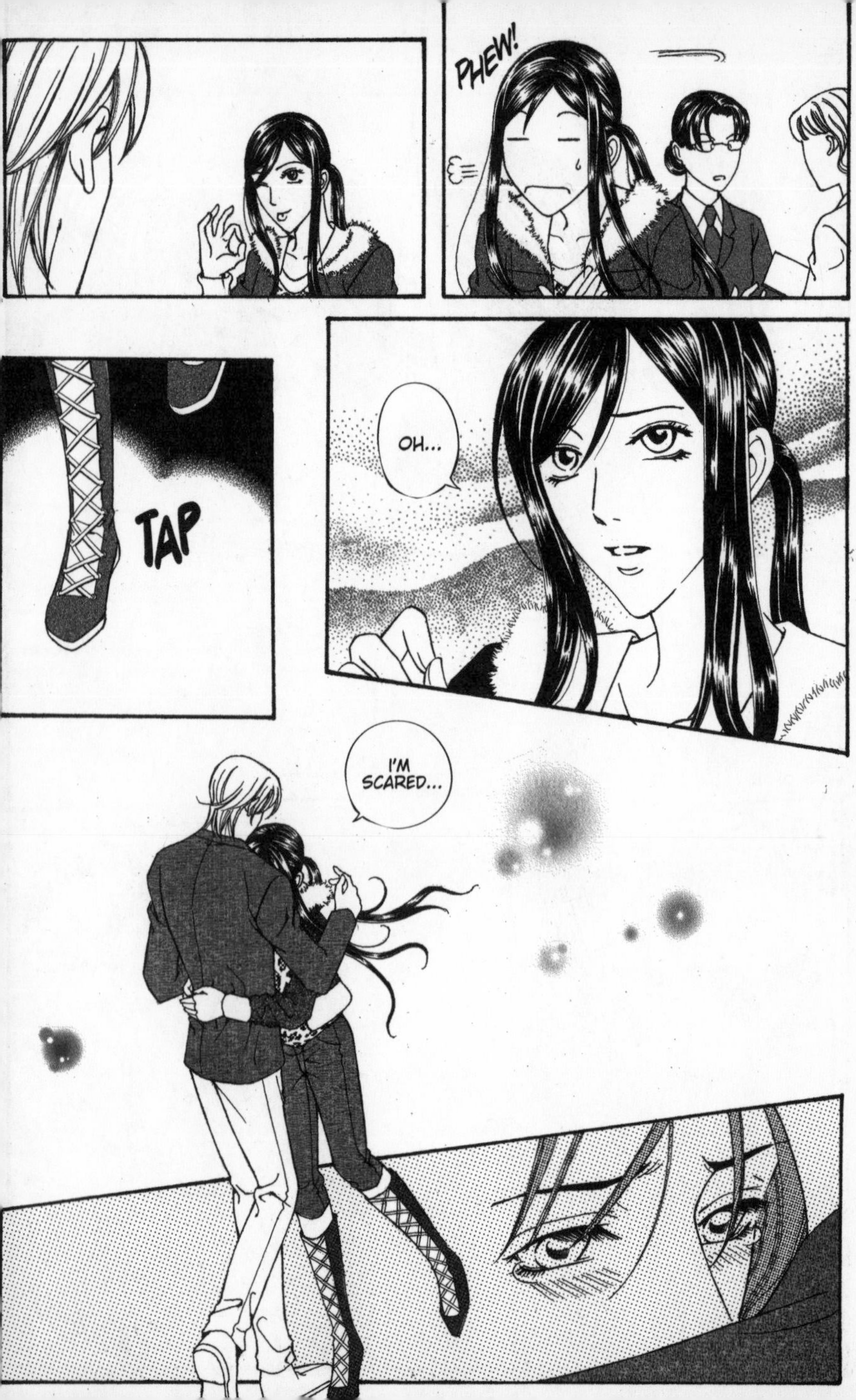
PHEW!
OH...
TAP
I'M SCARED...

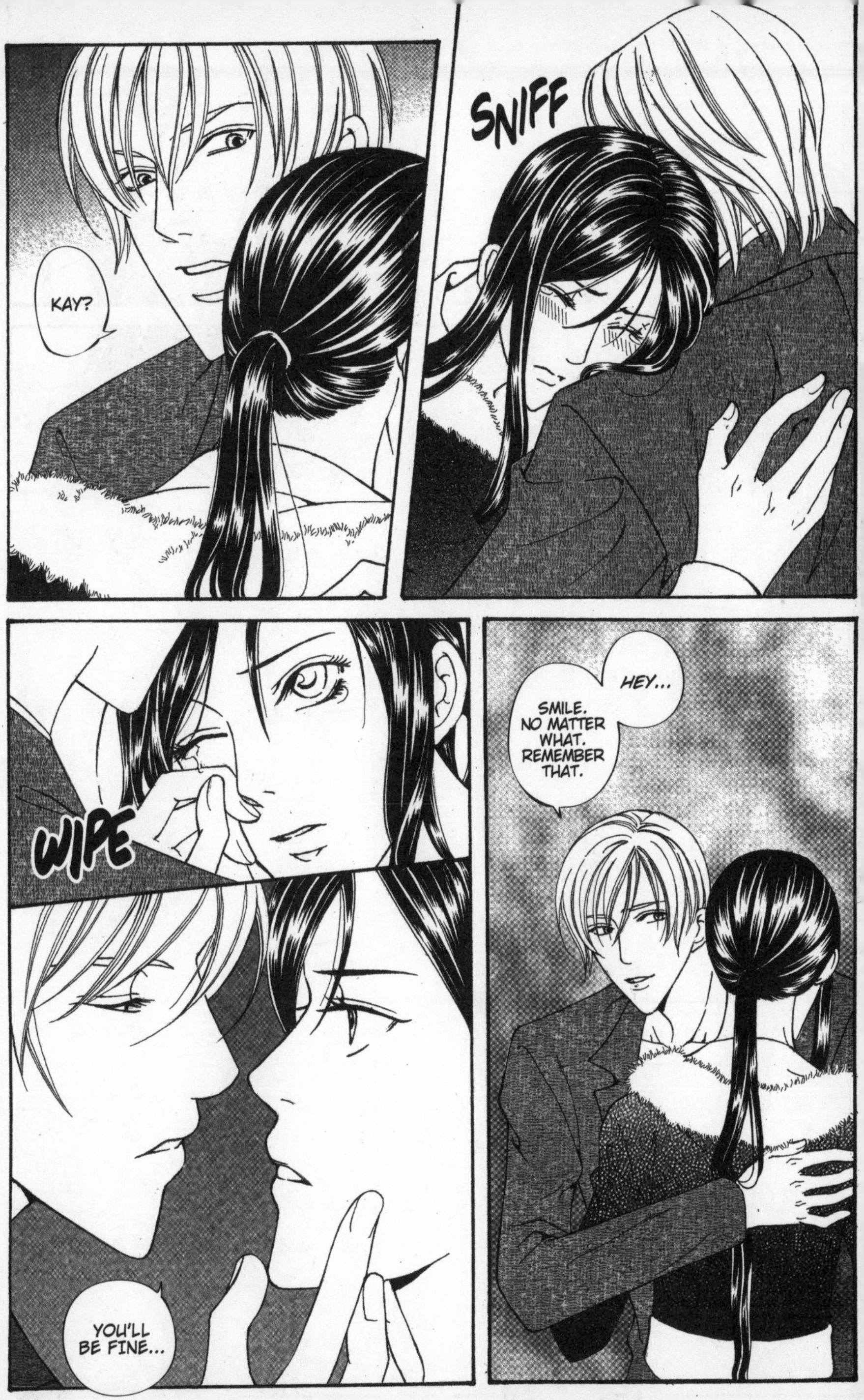
SNIFF
KAY?
HEY...
SMILE. NO MATTER WHAT. REMEMBER THAT.
WIPE
YOU'LL BE FINE...

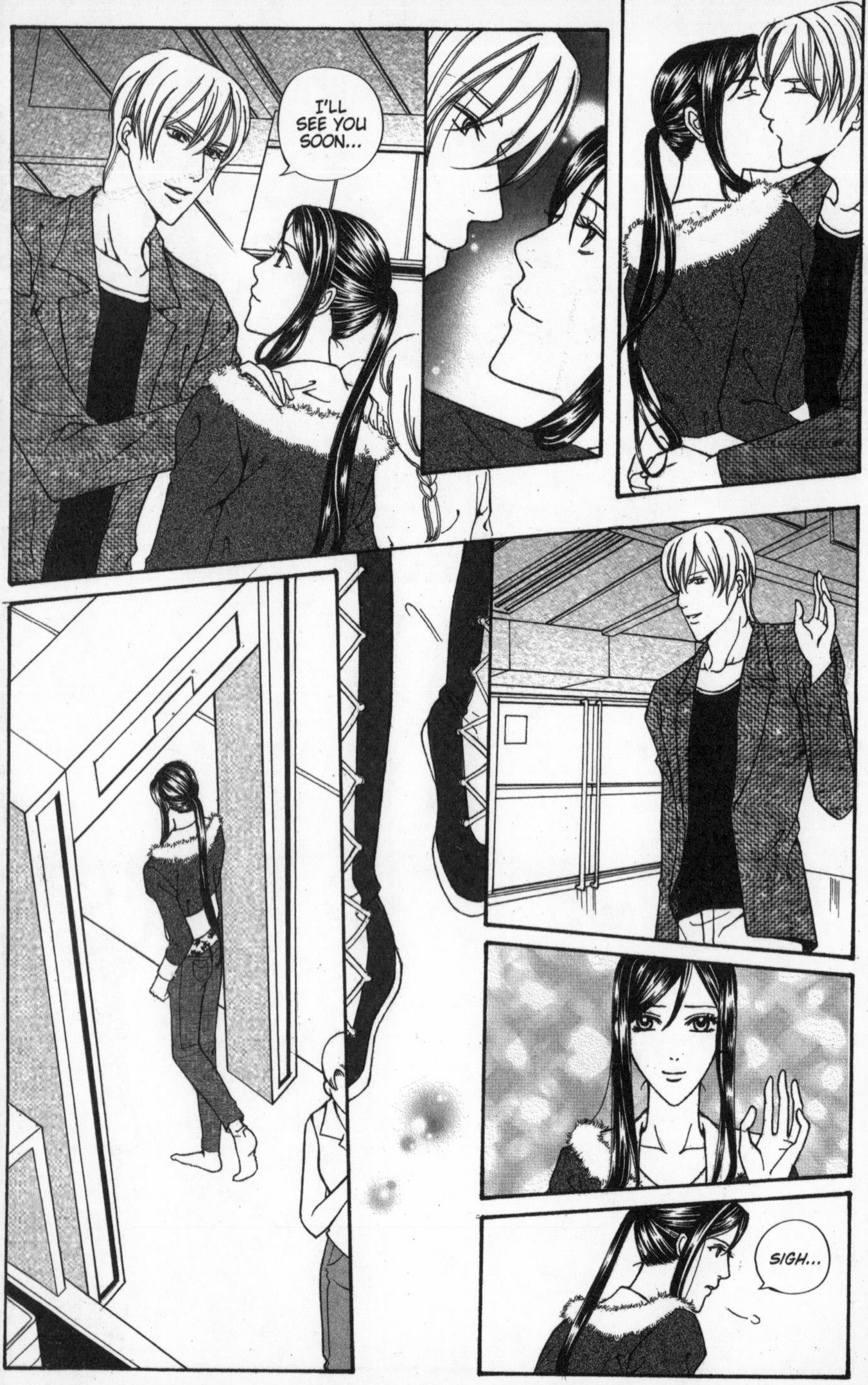
I'LL SEE YOU SOON...
SIGH...

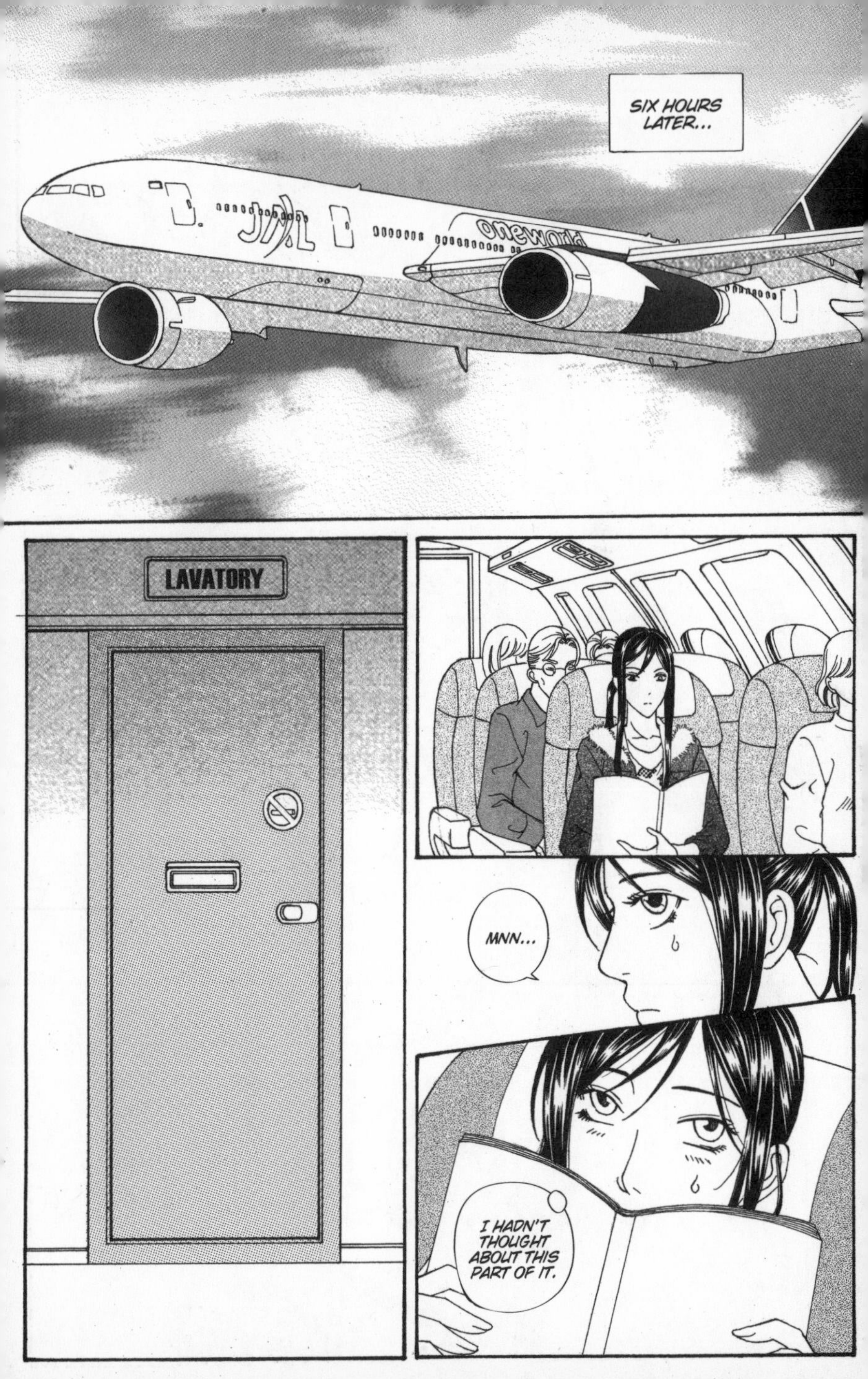
SIX HOURS LATER...
oneworld
MNN...
I HADN'T THOUGHT ABOUT THIS PART OF IT.
LAVATORY

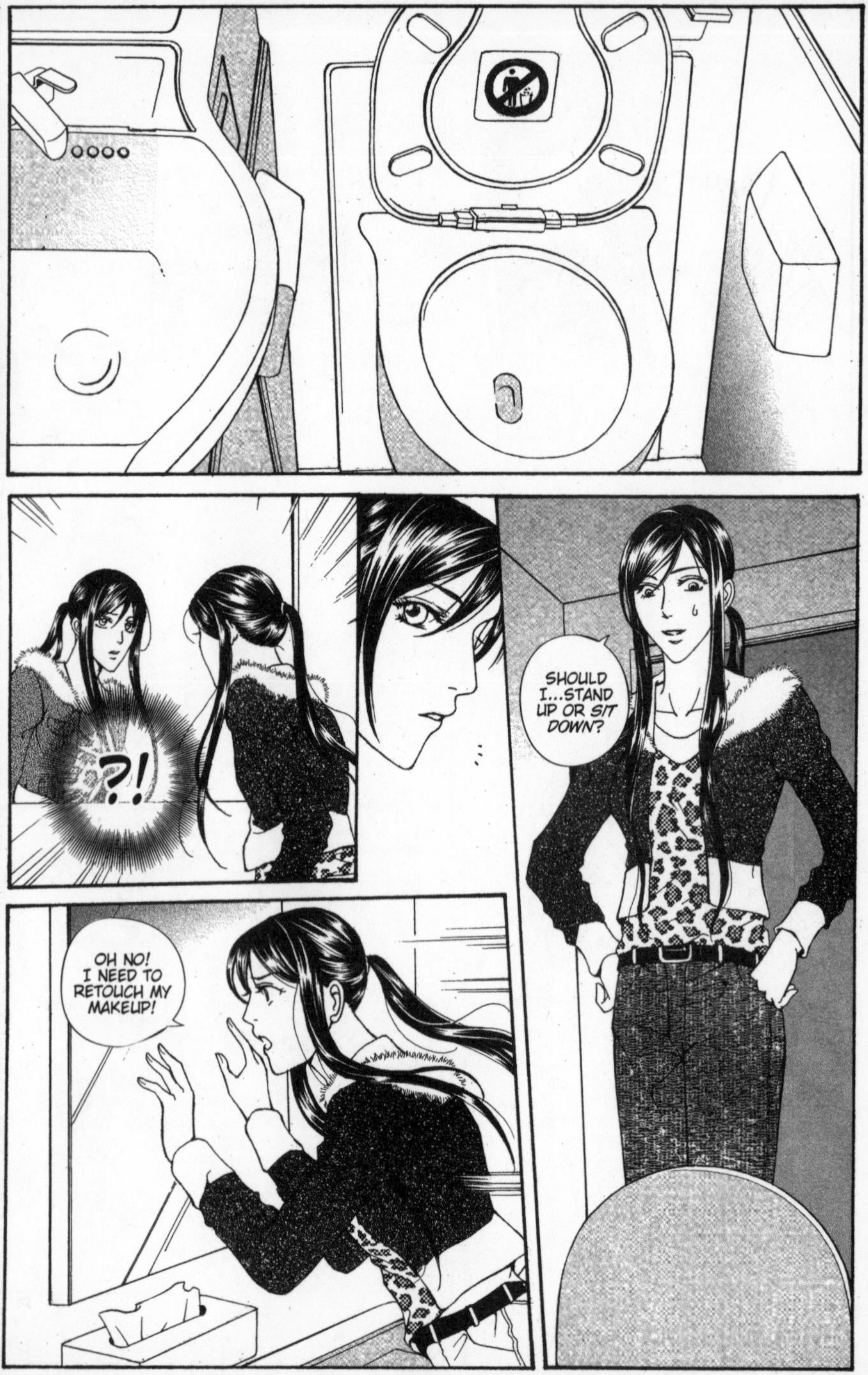
SHOULD I...STAND UP OR SIT DOWN?
...
?!
OH NO! I NEED TO RETOUCH MY MAKEUP!

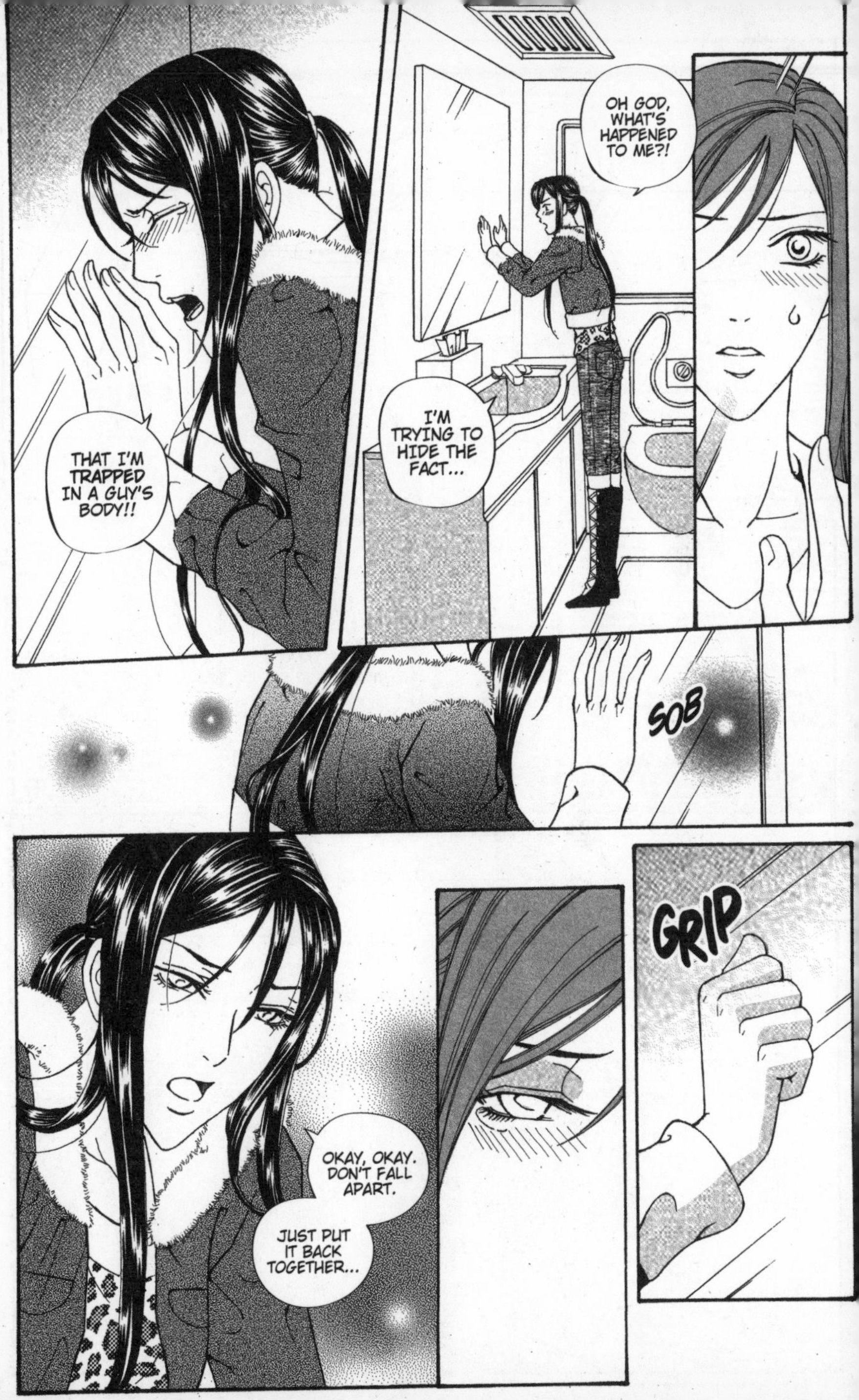
OH GOD, WHAT'S HAPPENED TO ME?!
I'M TRYING TO HIDE THE FACT...
THAT I'M TRAPPED IN A GUY'S BODY!!
SOB
GRIP
OKAY, OKAY. DON'T FALL APART.
JUST PUT IT BACK TOGETHER...

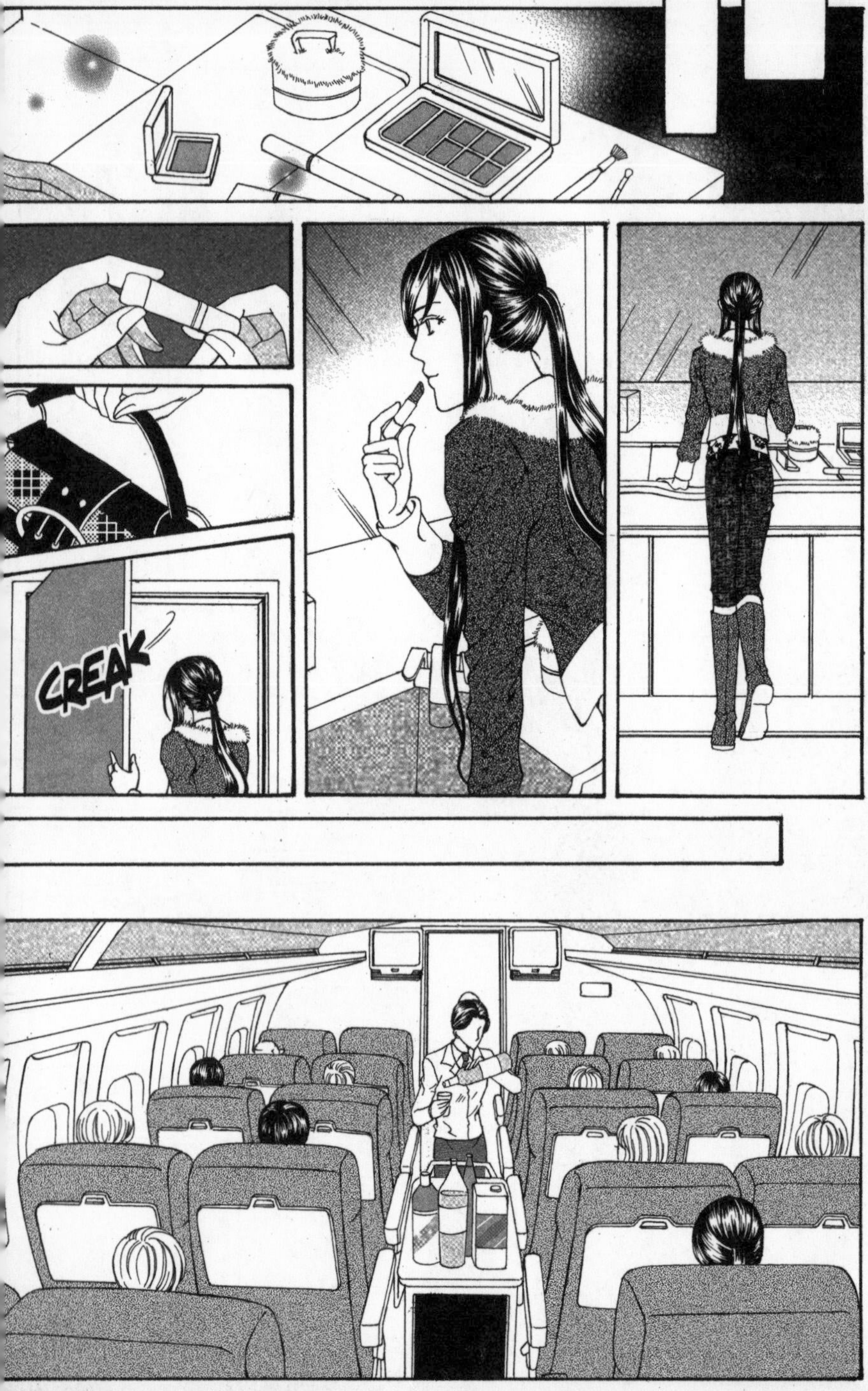
CREAK

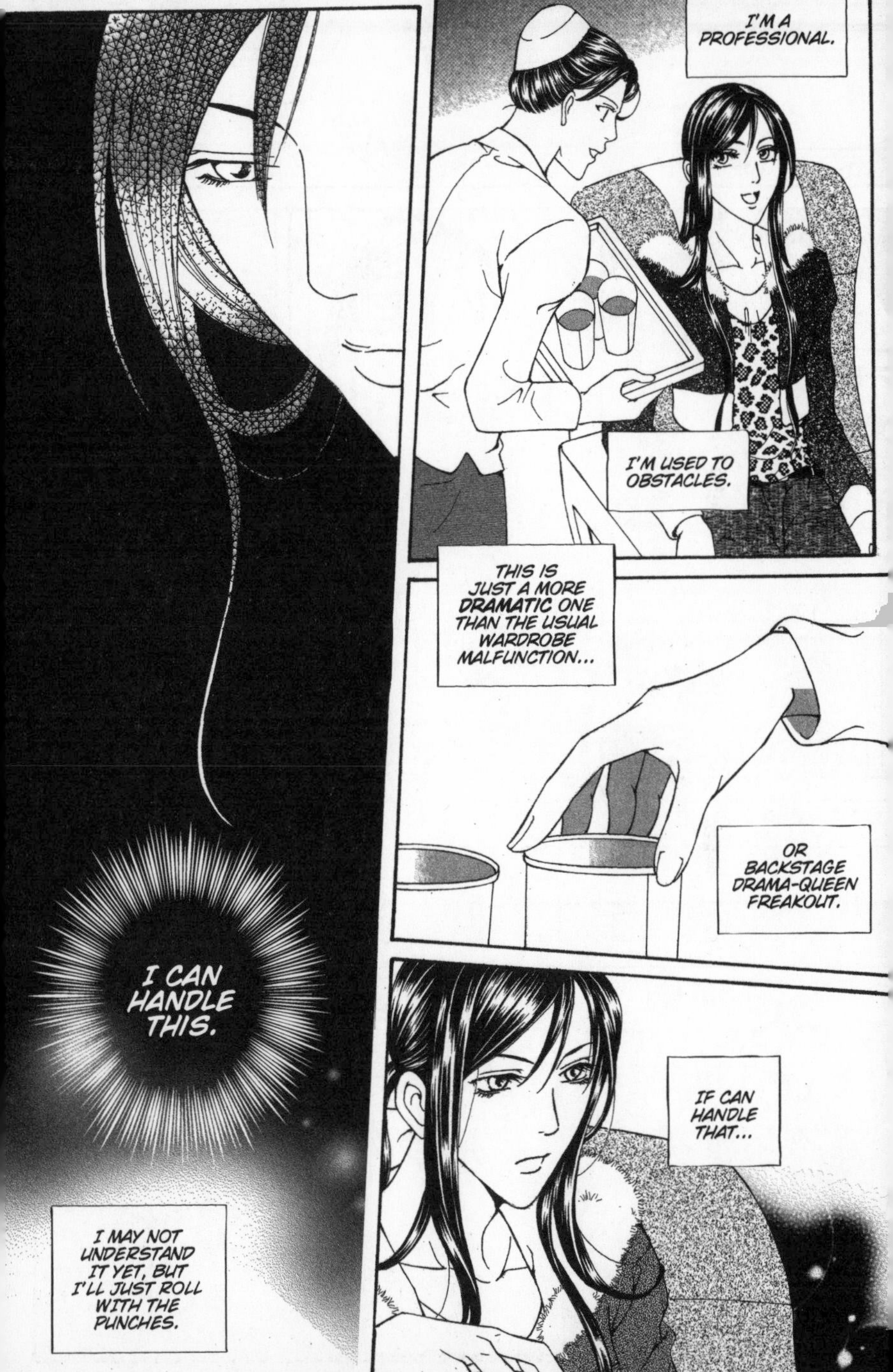
I'M A PROFESSIONAL.
I'M USED TO OBSTACLES.
THIS IS JUST A MORE **DRAMATIC** ONE THAN THE USUAL WARDROBE MALFUNCTION...
OR BACKSTAGE DRAMA-QUEEN FREAKOUT.
IF CAN HANDLE THAT...
I CAN HANDLE THIS.
I MAY NOT UNDERSTAND IT YET, BUT I'LL JUST ROLL WITH THE PUNCHES.

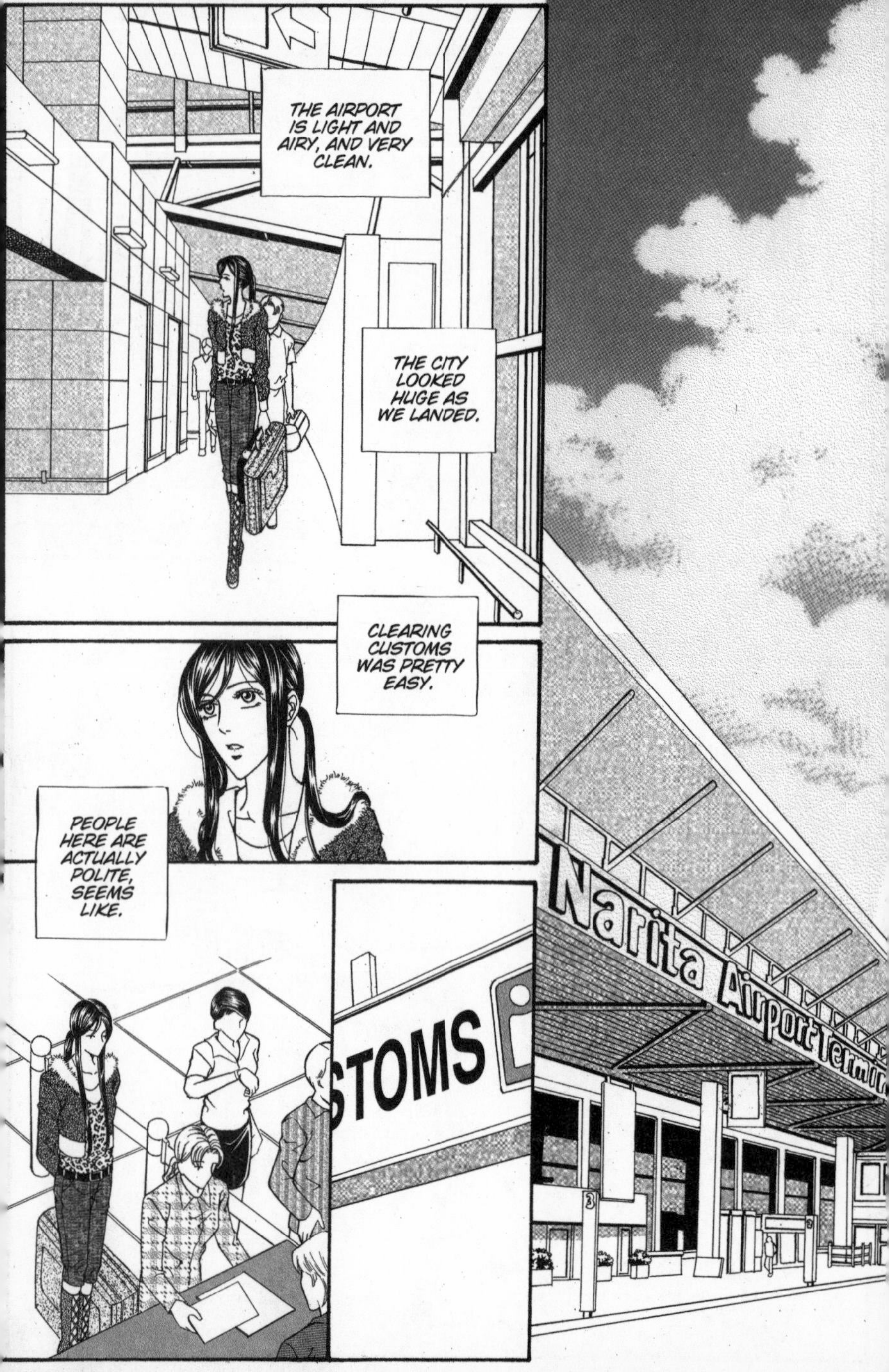
Narita Airport Termin
THE AIRPORT IS LIGHT AND AIRY, AND VERY CLEAN.
THE CITY LOOKED HUGE AS WE LANDED.
CLEARING CUSTOMS WAS PRETTY EASY.
PEOPLE HERE ARE ACTUALLY POLITE, SEEMS LIKE.
STOMS

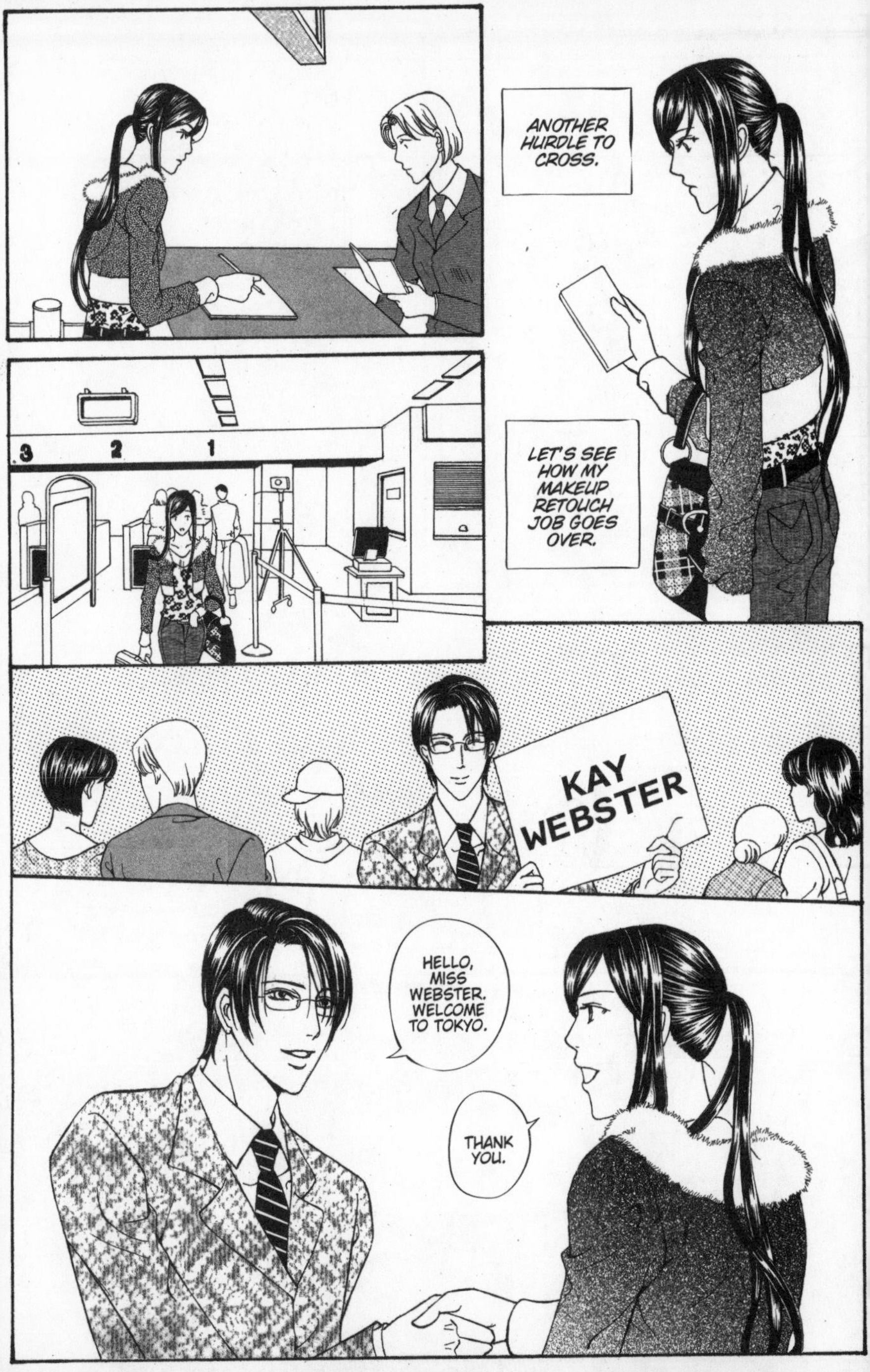
ANOTHER HURDLE TO CROSS.
LET'S SEE HOW MY MAKEUP RETOUCH JOB GOES OVER.
3
2
1
KAY WEBSTER
HELLO, MISS WEBSTER. WELCOME TO TOKYO.
THANK YOU.

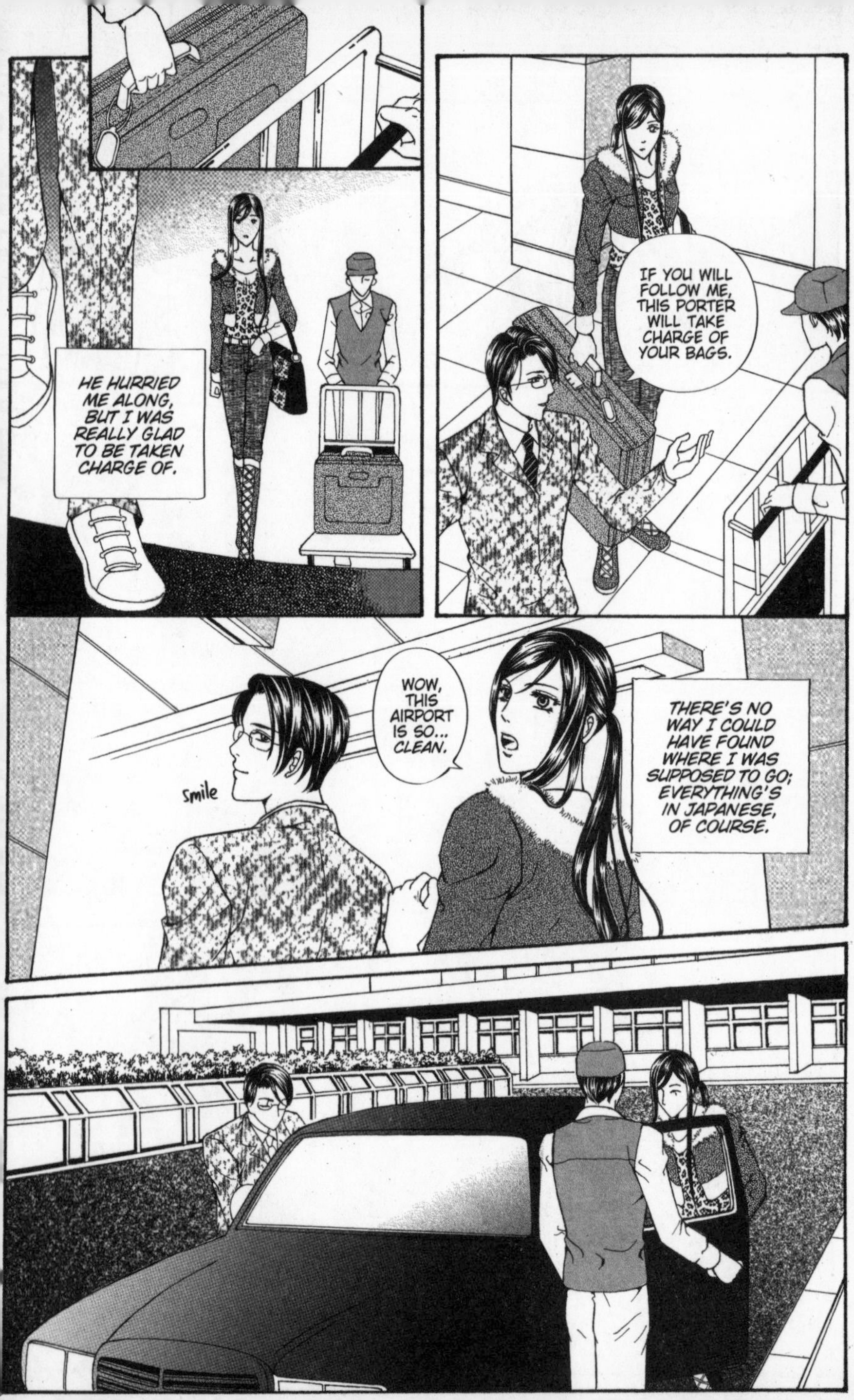
IF YOU WILL FOLLOW ME, THIS PORTER WILL TAKE CHARGE OF YOUR BAGS.
HE HURRIED ME ALONG, BUT I WAS REALLY GLAD TO BE TAKEN CHARGE OF.
THERE'S NO WAY I COULD HAVE FOUND WHERE I WAS SUPPOSED TO GO; EVERYTHING'S IN JAPANESE, OF COURSE.
WOW, THIS AIRPORT IS SO... CLEAN.
Smile

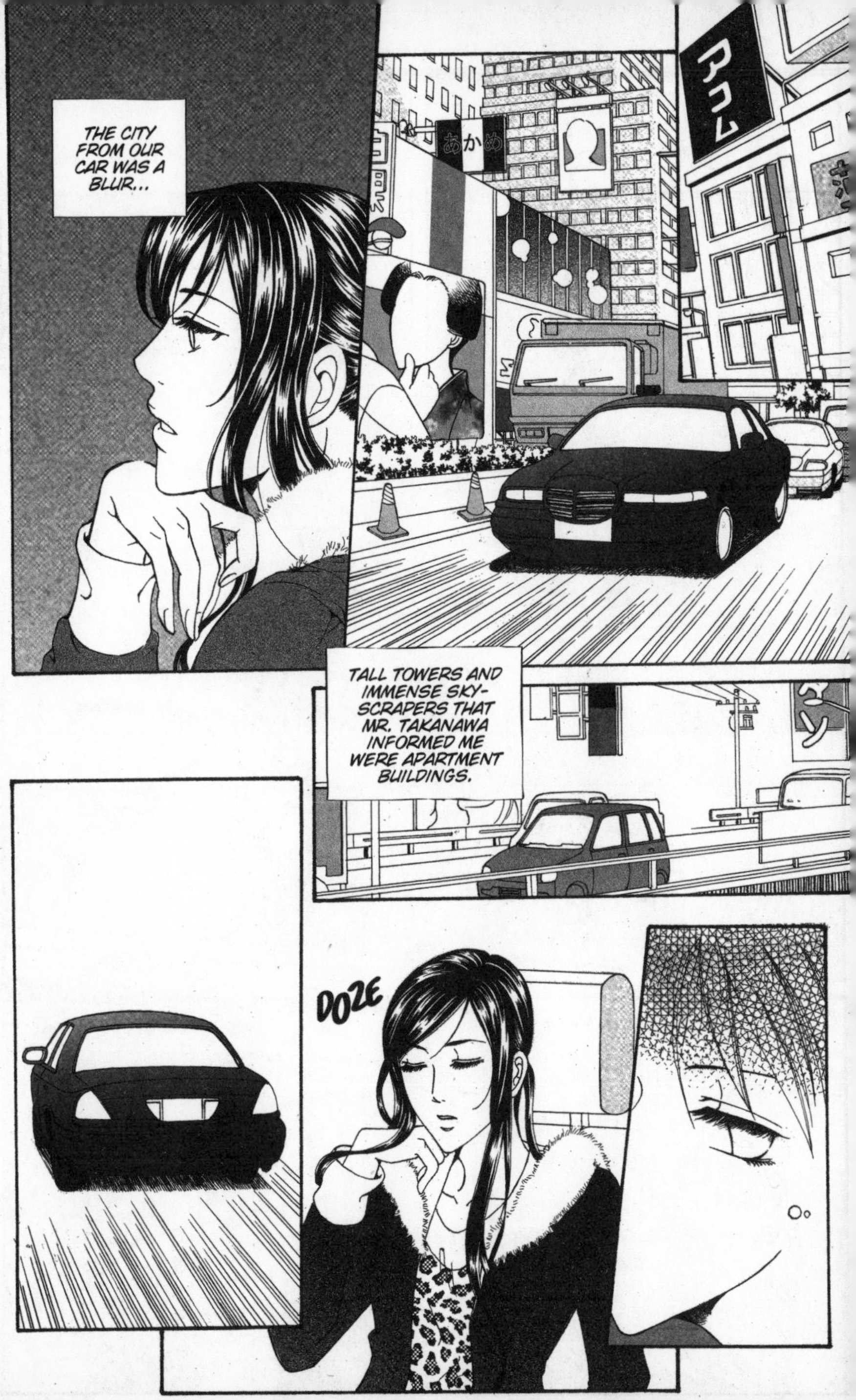
THE CITY FROM OUR CAR WAS A BLUR...
TALL TOWERS AND IMMENSE SKY-SCRAPERS THAT MR. TAKANAWA INFORMED ME WERE APARTMENT BUILDINGS.
Oo
DOZE

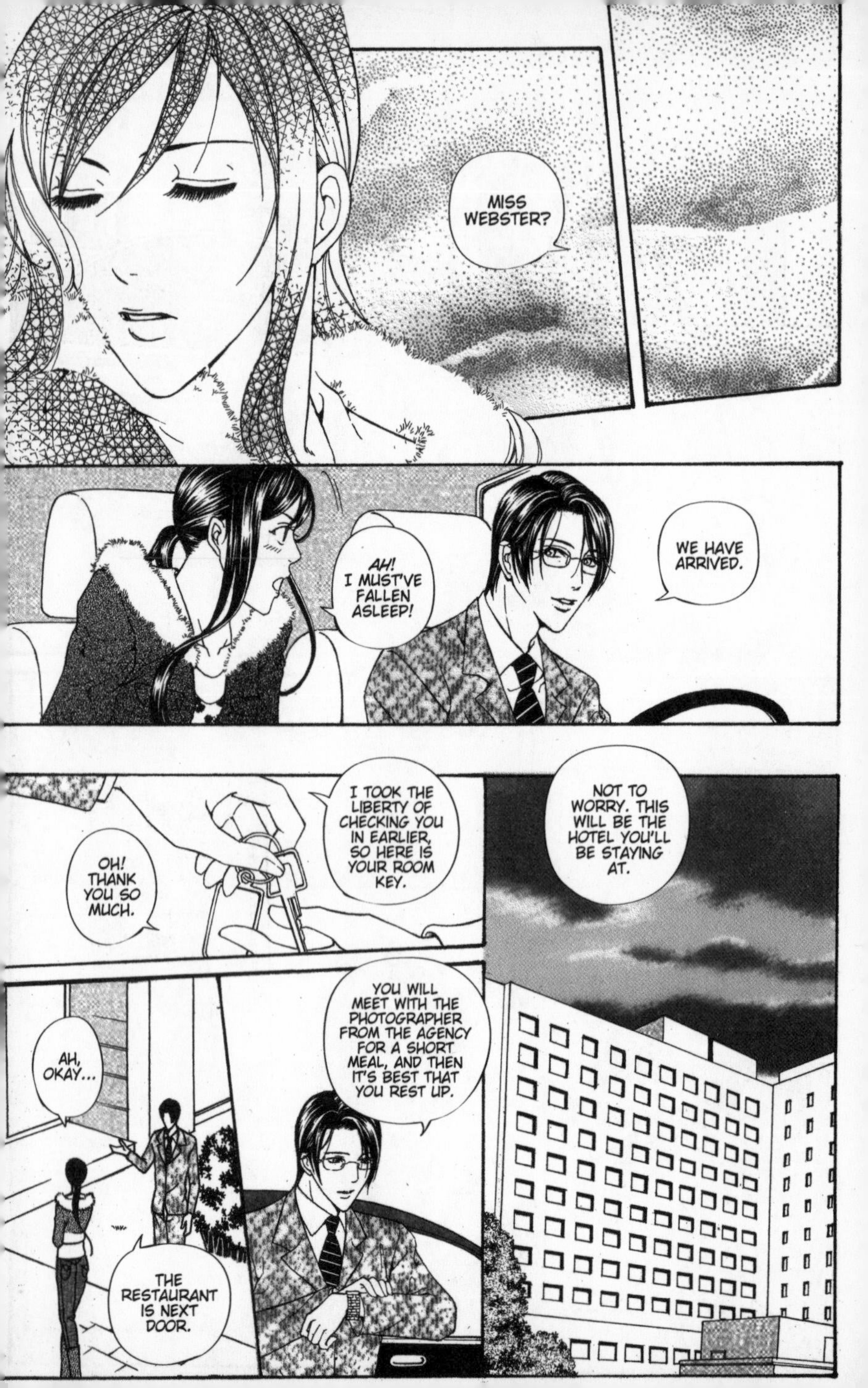
MISS WEBSTER?
WE HAVE ARRIVED.
AH! I MUST'VE FALLEN ASLEEP!
NOT TO WORRY. THIS WILL BE THE HOTEL YOU'LL BE STAYING AT.
I TOOK THE LIBERTY OF CHECKING YOU IN EARLIER, SO HERE IS YOUR ROOM KEY.
OH! THANK YOU SO MUCH.
YOU WILL MEET WITH THE PHOTOGRAPHER FROM THE AGENCY FOR A SHORT MEAL, AND THEN IT'S BEST THAT YOU REST UP.
AH, OKAY...
THE RESTAURANT IS NEXT DOOR.

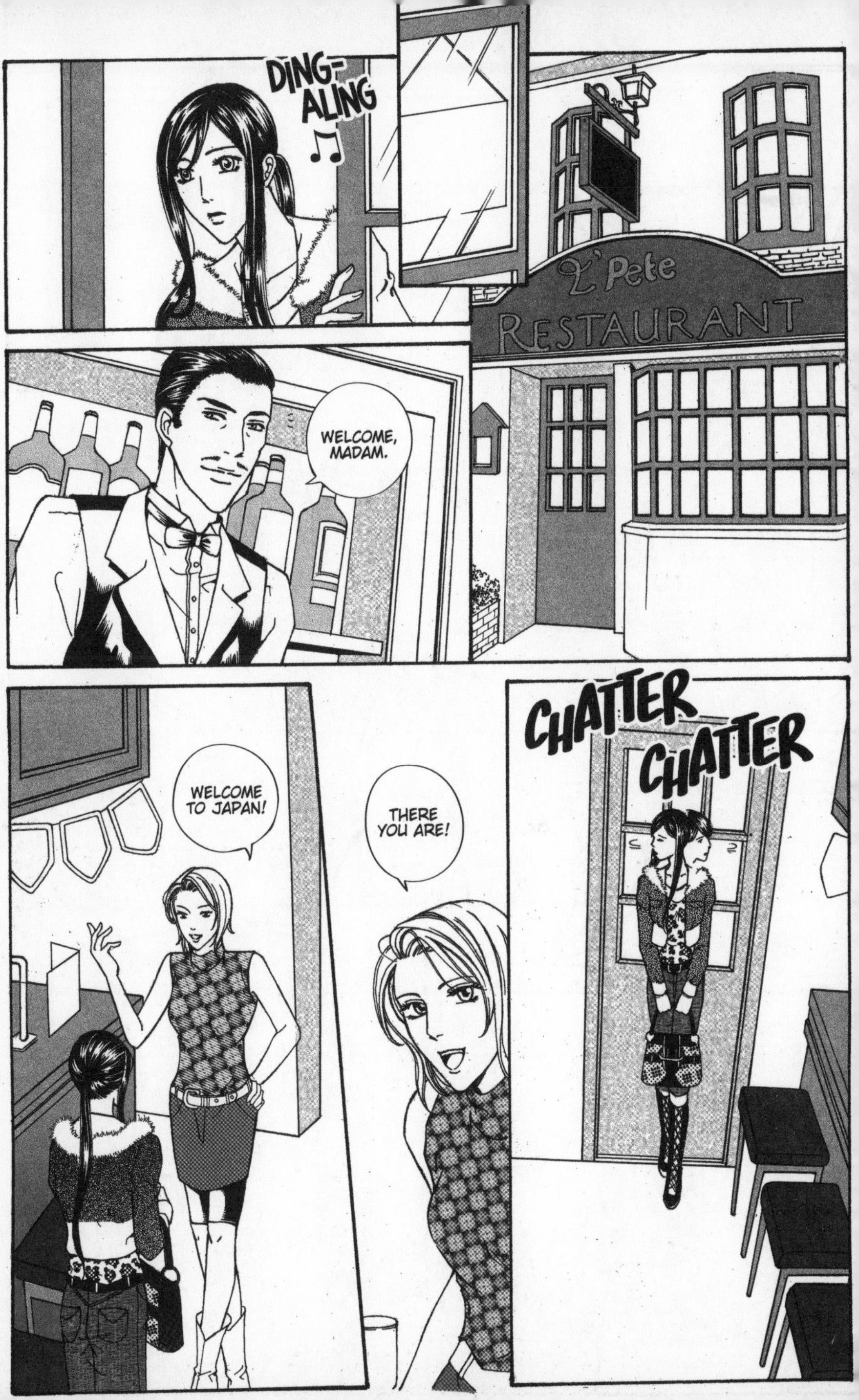
L'Pete
RESTAURANT
DING-ALING
WELCOME, MADAM.
CHATTER CHATTER
THERE YOU ARE!
WELCOME TO JAPAN!

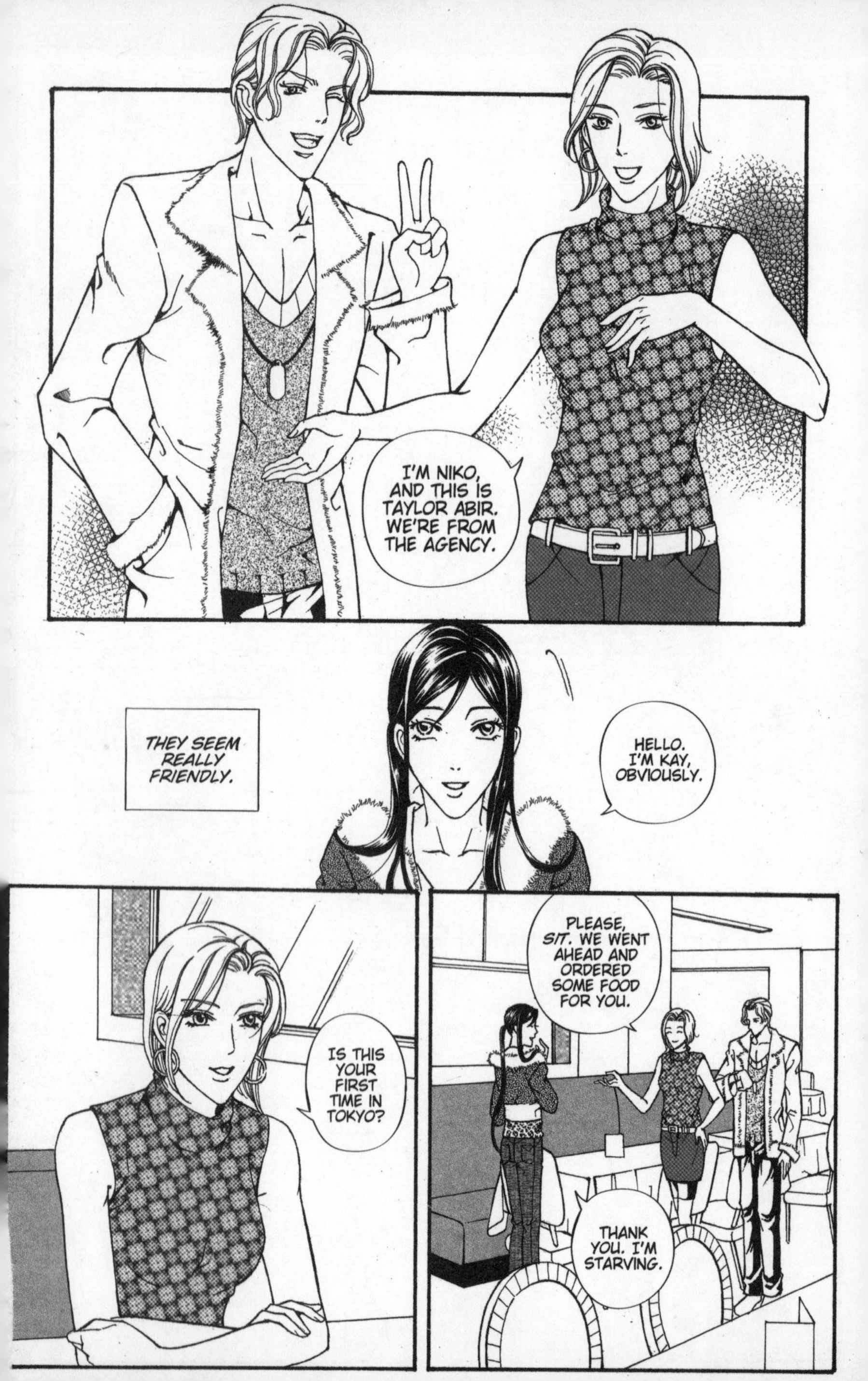
I'M NIKO, AND THIS IS TAYLOR ABIR. WE'RE FROM THE AGENCY.
HELLO. I'M KAY, OBVIOUSLY.
THEY SEEM REALLY FRIENDLY.
PLEASE, SIT. WE WENT AHEAD AND ORDERED SOME FOOD FOR YOU.
THANK YOU. I'M STARVING.
IS THIS YOUR FIRST TIME IN TOKYO?

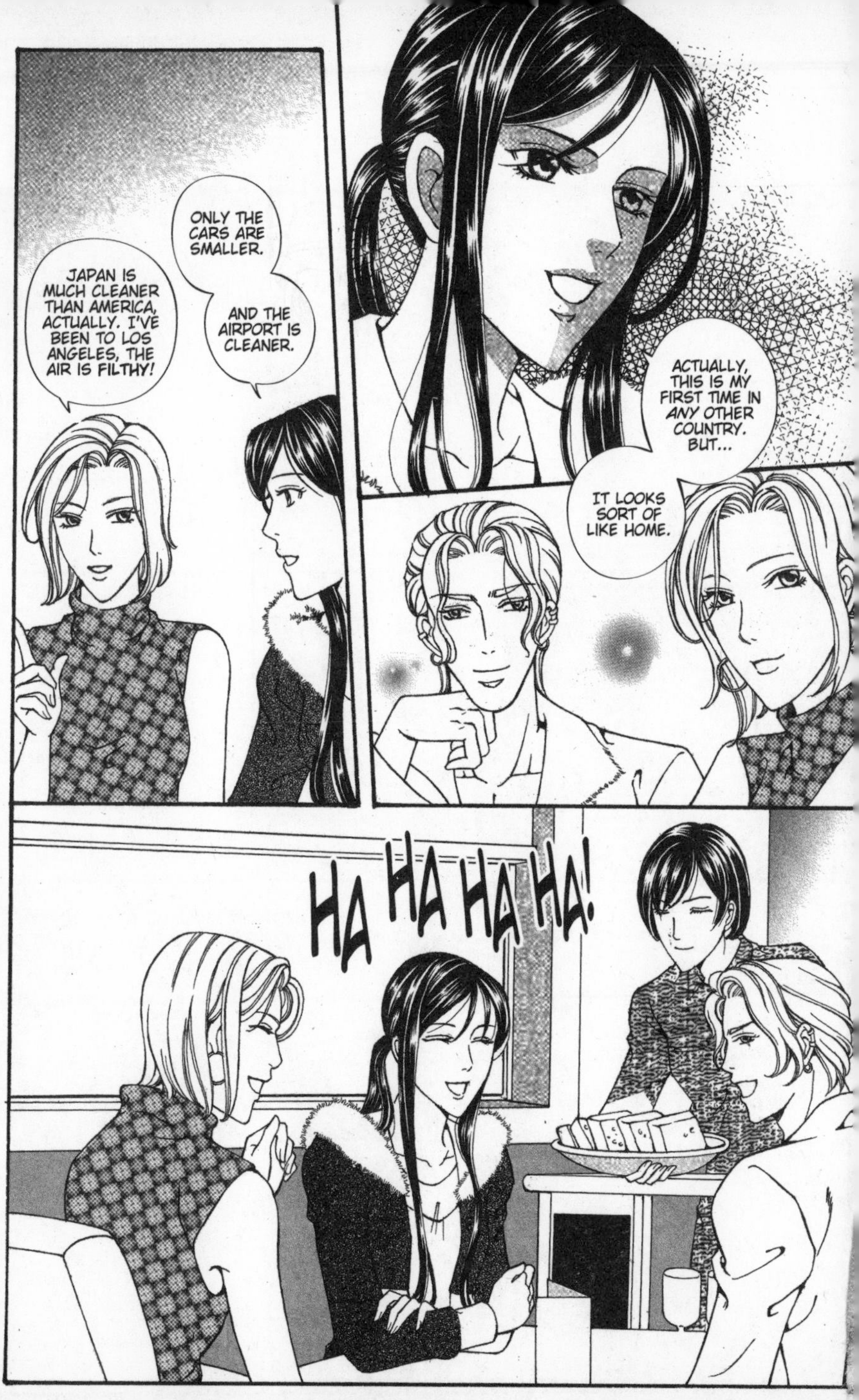

ACTUALLY, THIS IS MY FIRST TIME IN ANY OTHER COUNTRY. BUT...
IT LOOKS SORT OF LIKE HOME.
ONLY THE CARS ARE SMALLER.
AND THE AIRPORT IS CLEANER.
JAPAN IS MUCH CLEANER THAN AMERICA, ACTUALLY. I'VE BEEN TO LOS ANGELES, THE AIR IS FILTHY!
HA HA HA HA HA!

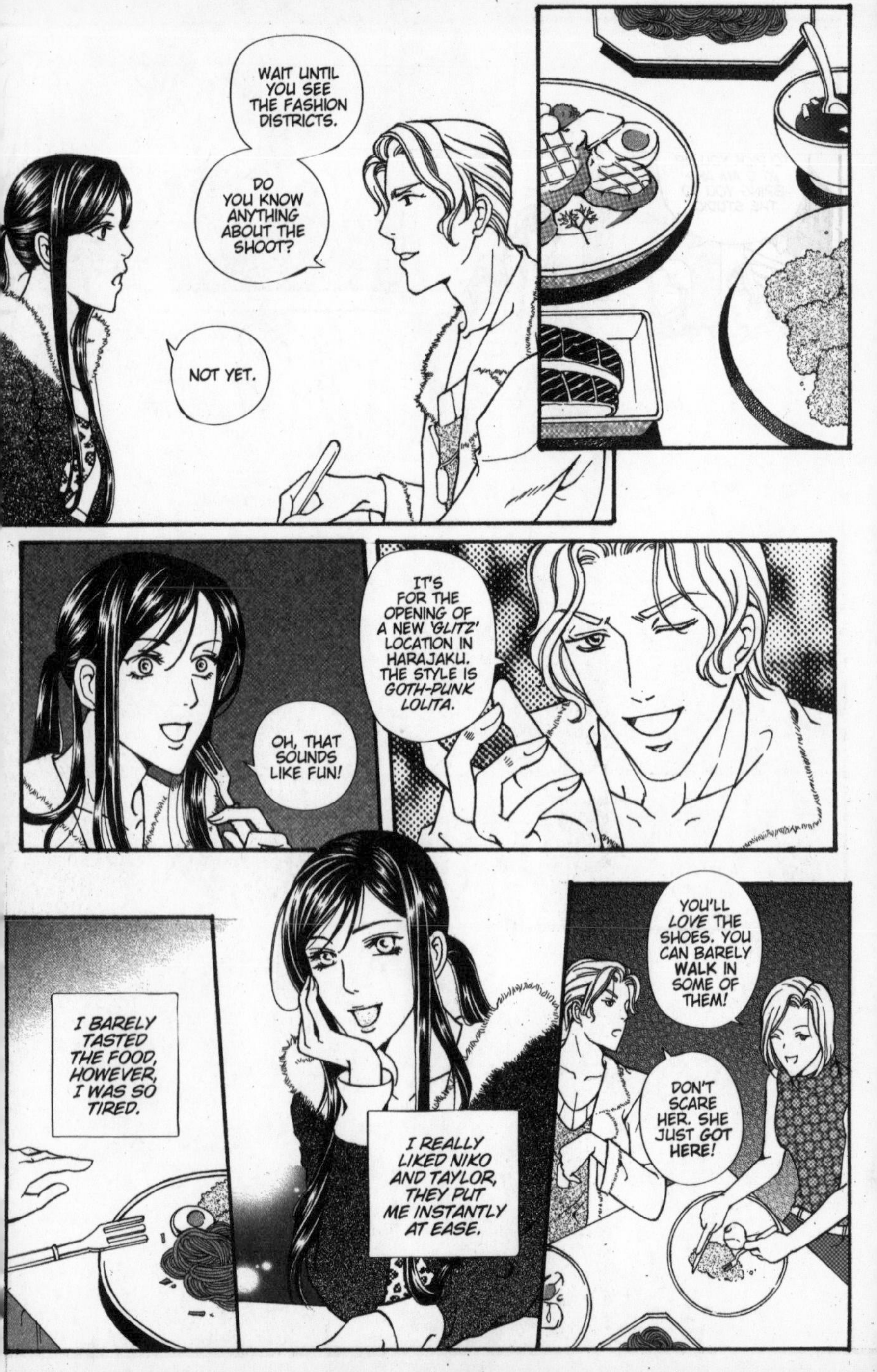
WAIT UNTIL YOU SEE THE FASHION DISTRICTS.
DO YOU KNOW ANYTHING ABOUT THE SHOOT?
NOT YET.
IT'S FOR THE OPENING OF A NEW 'GLITZ' LOCATION IN HARAJAKU. THE STYLE IS GOTH-PUNK LOLITA.
OH, THAT SOUNDS LIKE FUN!
YOU'LL LOVE THE SHOES. YOU CAN BARELY WALK IN SOME OF THEM!
DON'T SCARE HER. SHE JUST GOT HERE!
I REALLY LIKED NIKO AND TAYLOR, THEY PUT ME INSTANTLY AT EASE.
I BARELY TASTED THE FOOD, HOWEVER, I WAS SO TIRED.

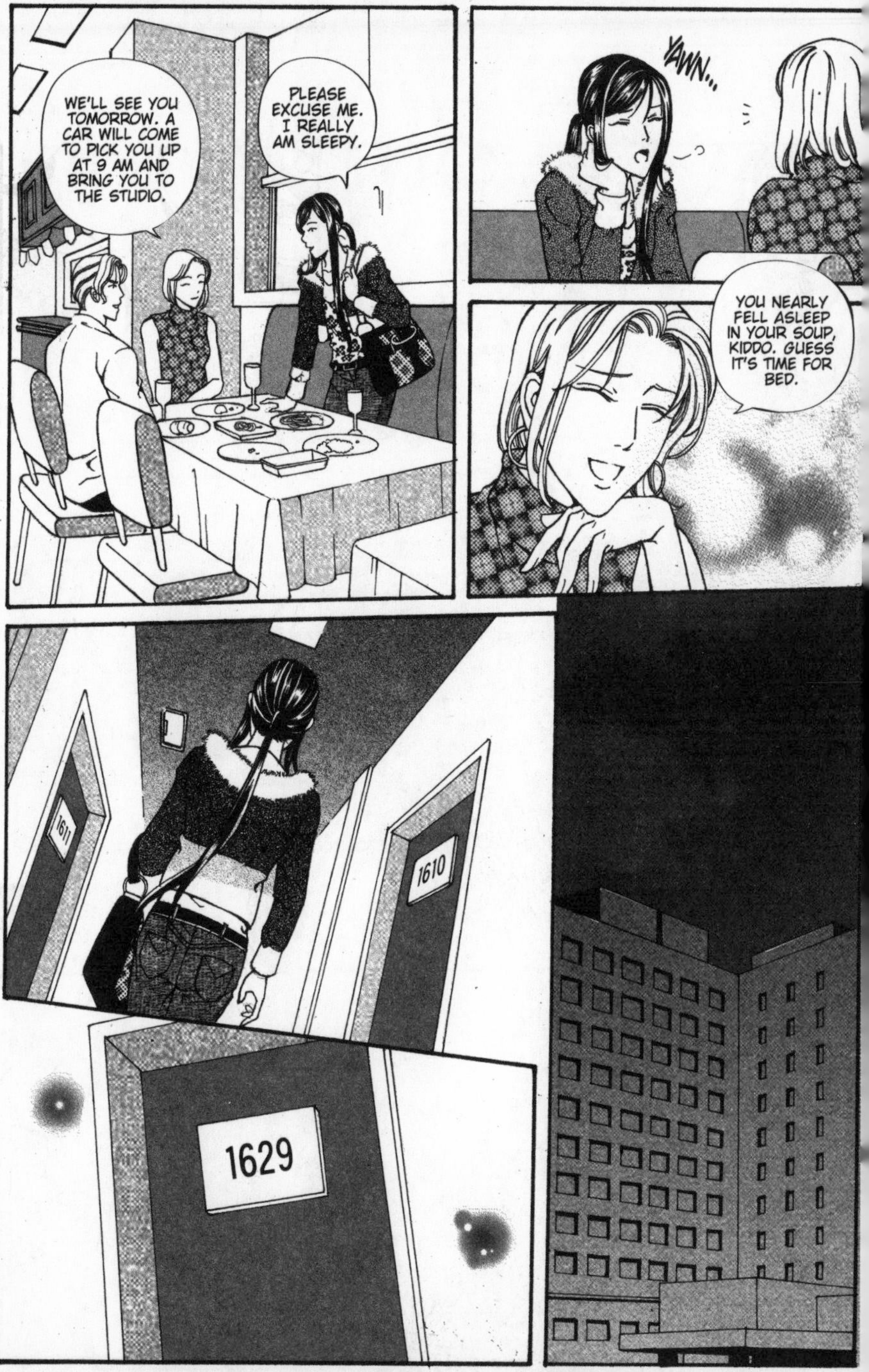
YAWN...
YOU NEARLY FELL ASLEEP IN YOUR SOUP, KIDDO. GUESS IT'S TIME FOR BED.
PLEASE EXCUSE ME. I REALLY AM SLEEPY.
WE'LL SEE YOU TOMORROW. A CAR WILL COME TO PICK YOU UP AT 9 AM AND BRING YOU TO THE STUDIO.
1611
1610
1629

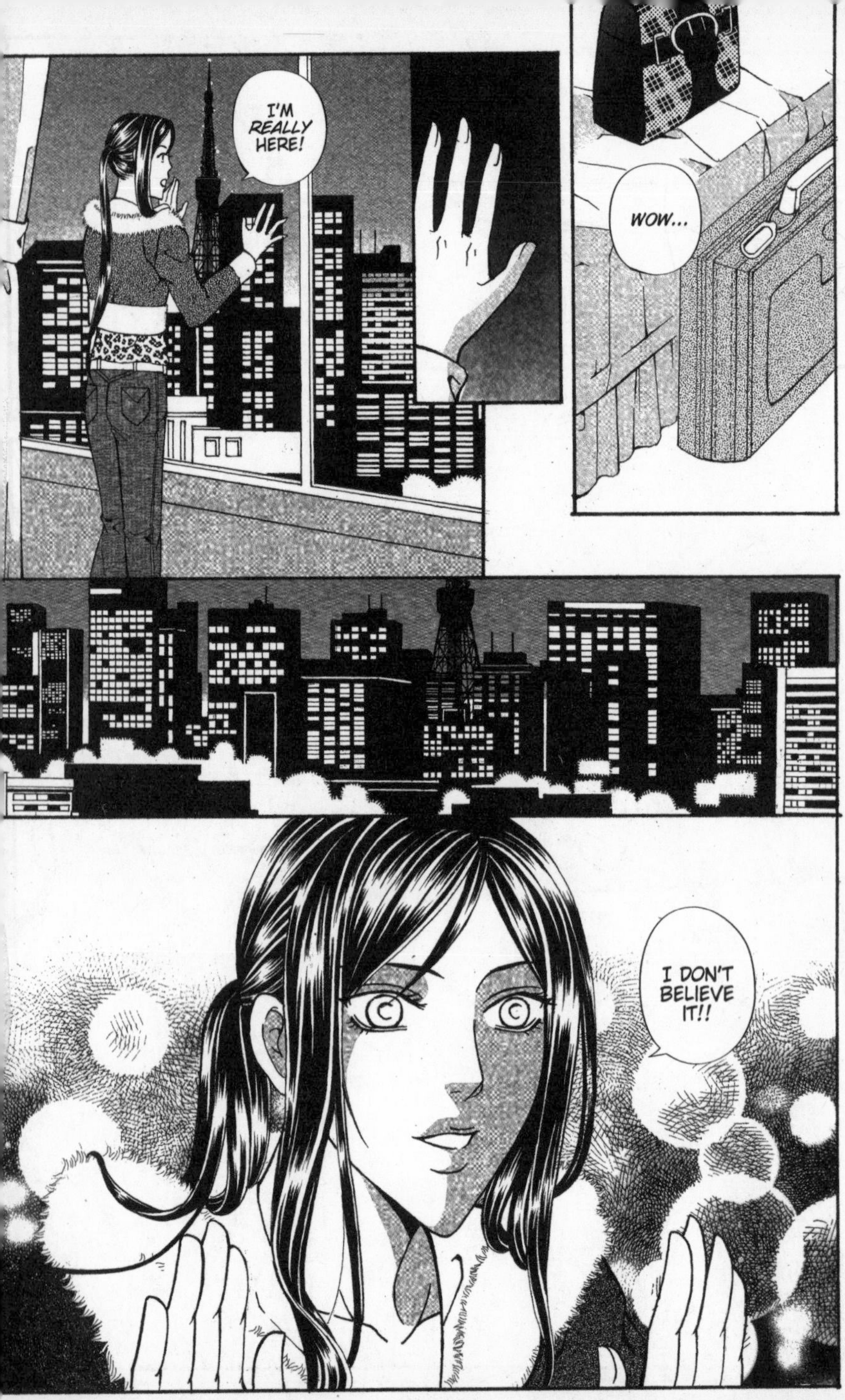
WOW...
I'M REALLY HERE!
I DON'T BELIEVE IT!!

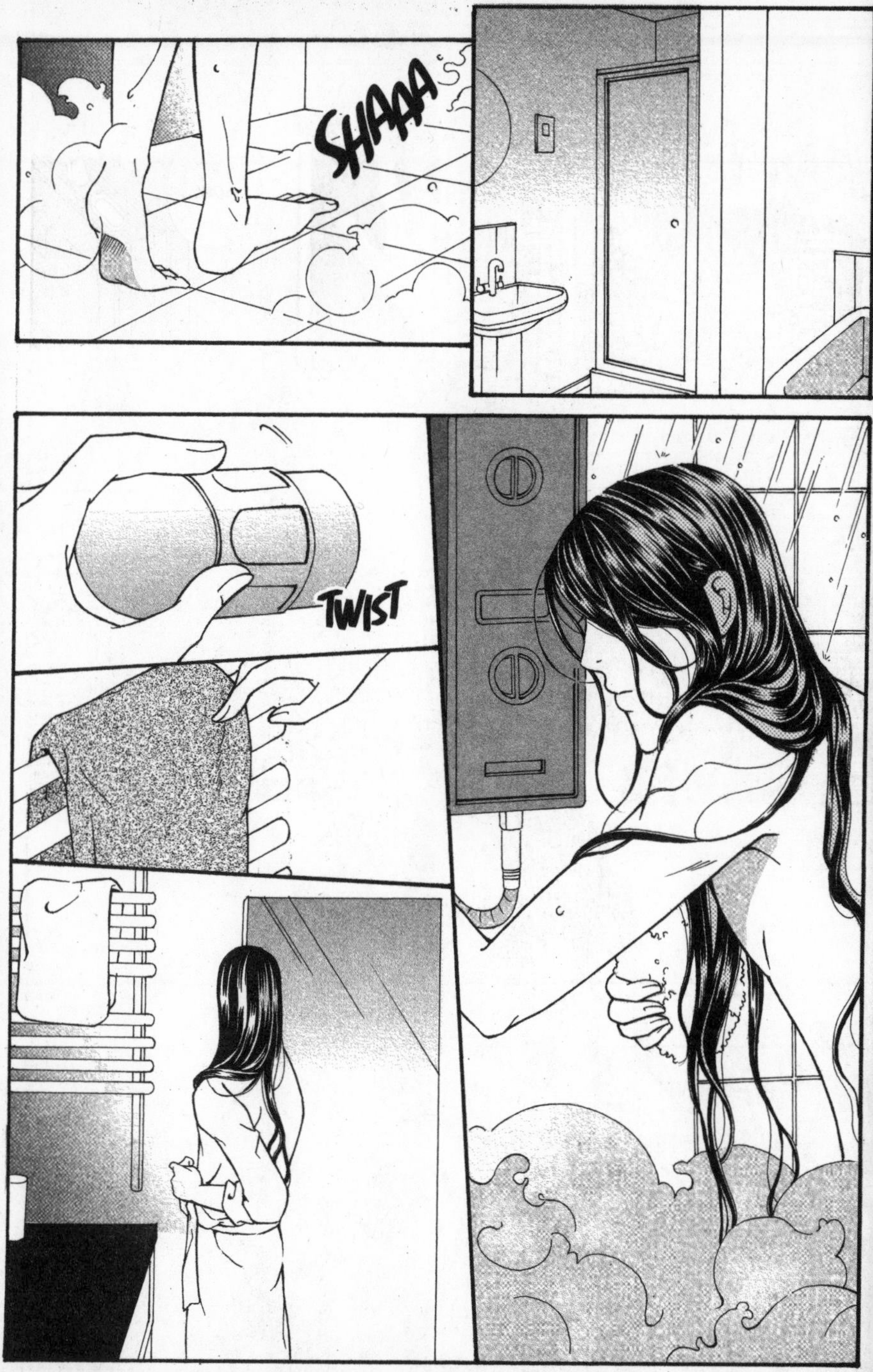
SHAAA
TWIST

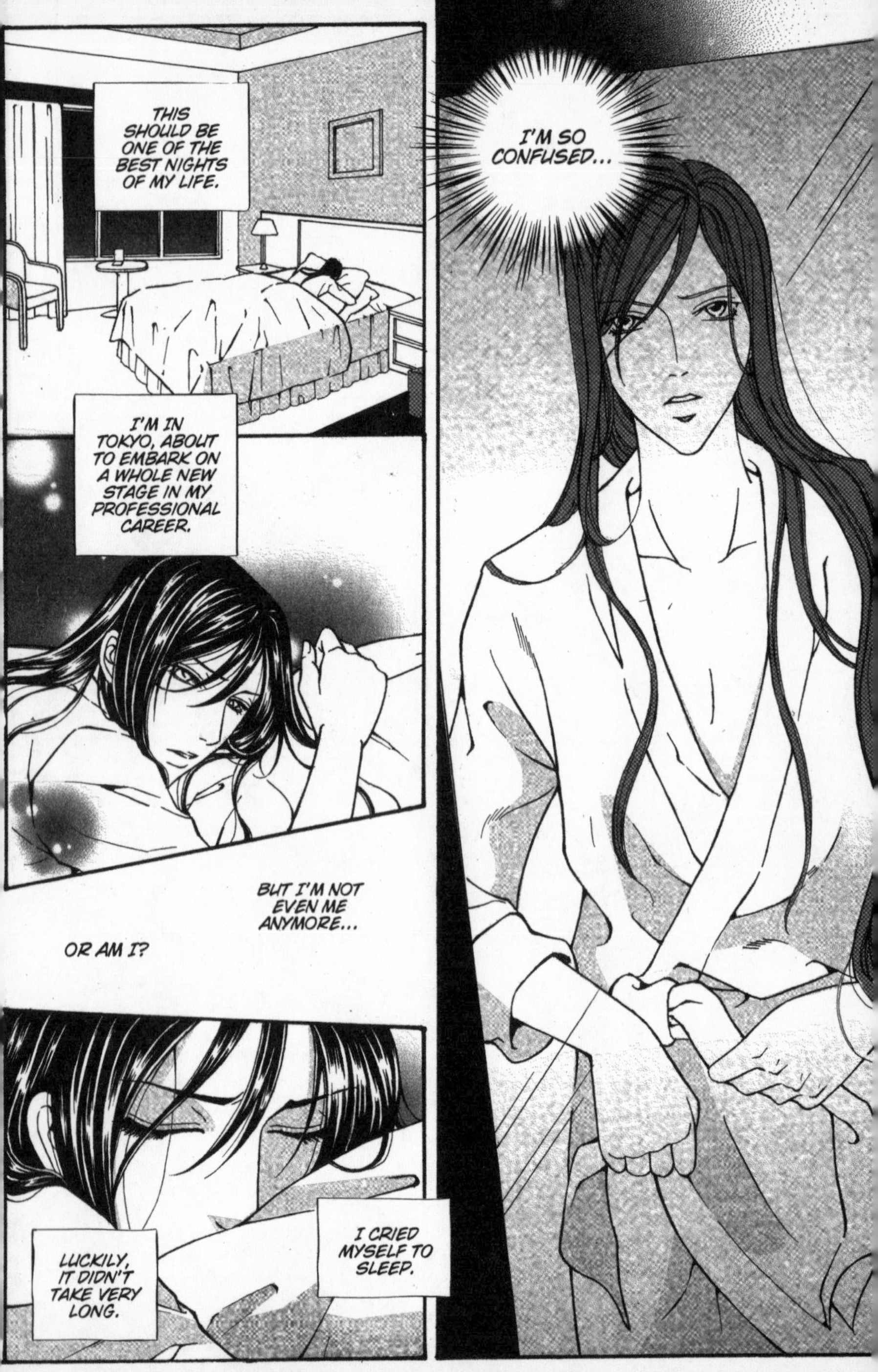
I'M SO CONFUSED...
THIS SHOULD BE ONE OF THE BEST NIGHTS OF MY LIFE.
I'M IN TOKYO, ABOUT TO EMBARK ON A WHOLE NEW STAGE IN MY PROFESSIONAL CAREER.
BUT I'M NOT EVEN ME ANYMORE...
OR AM I?
I CRIED MYSELF TO SLEEP.
LUCKILY, IT DIDN'T TAKE VERY LONG.

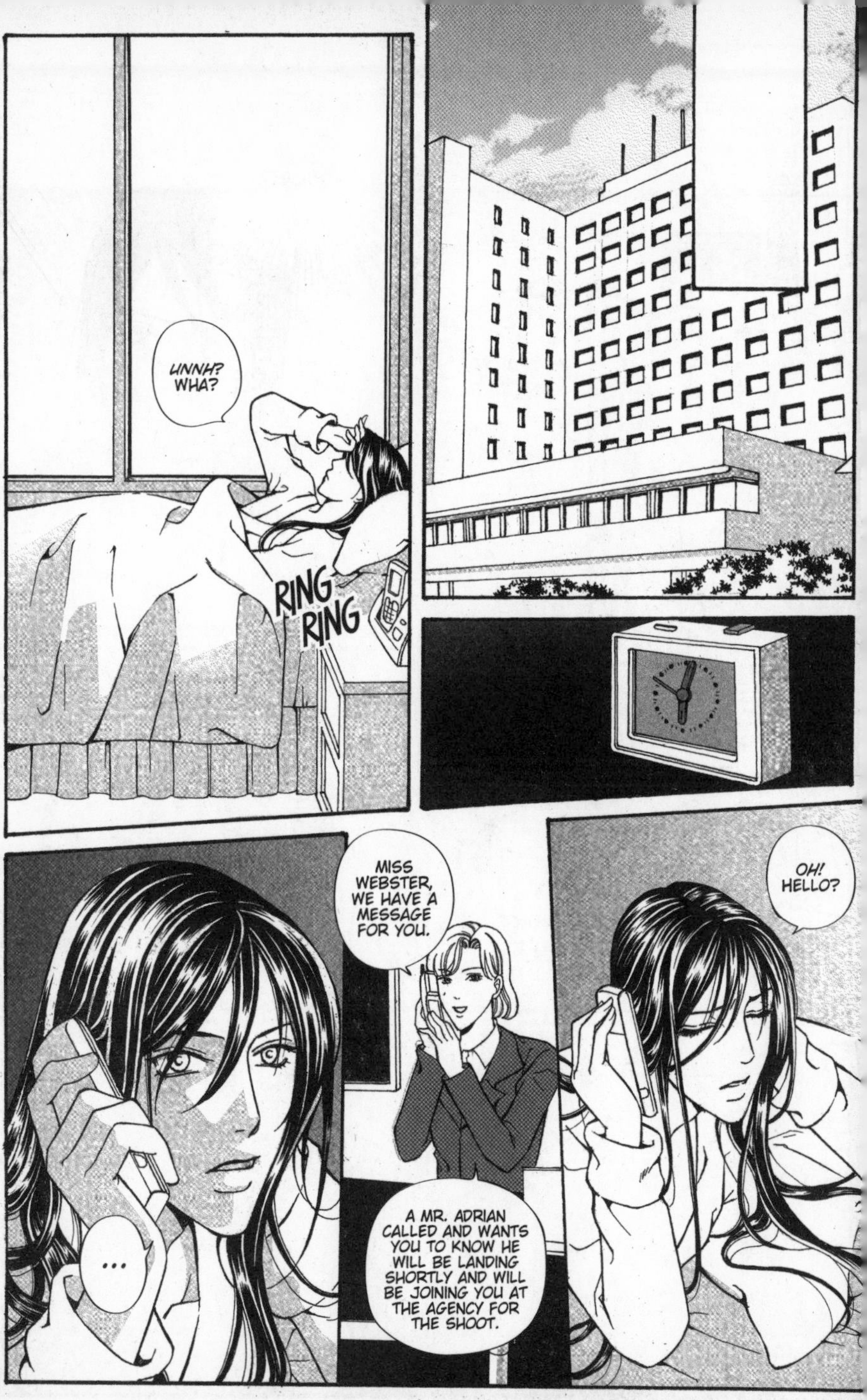
UNNH? WHA?
RING RING
OH! HELLO?
MISS WEBSTER, WE HAVE A MESSAGE FOR YOU.
A MR. ADRIAN CALLED AND WANTS YOU TO KNOW HE WILL BE LANDING SHORTLY AND WILL BE JOINING YOU AT THE AGENCY FOR THE SHOOT.
...

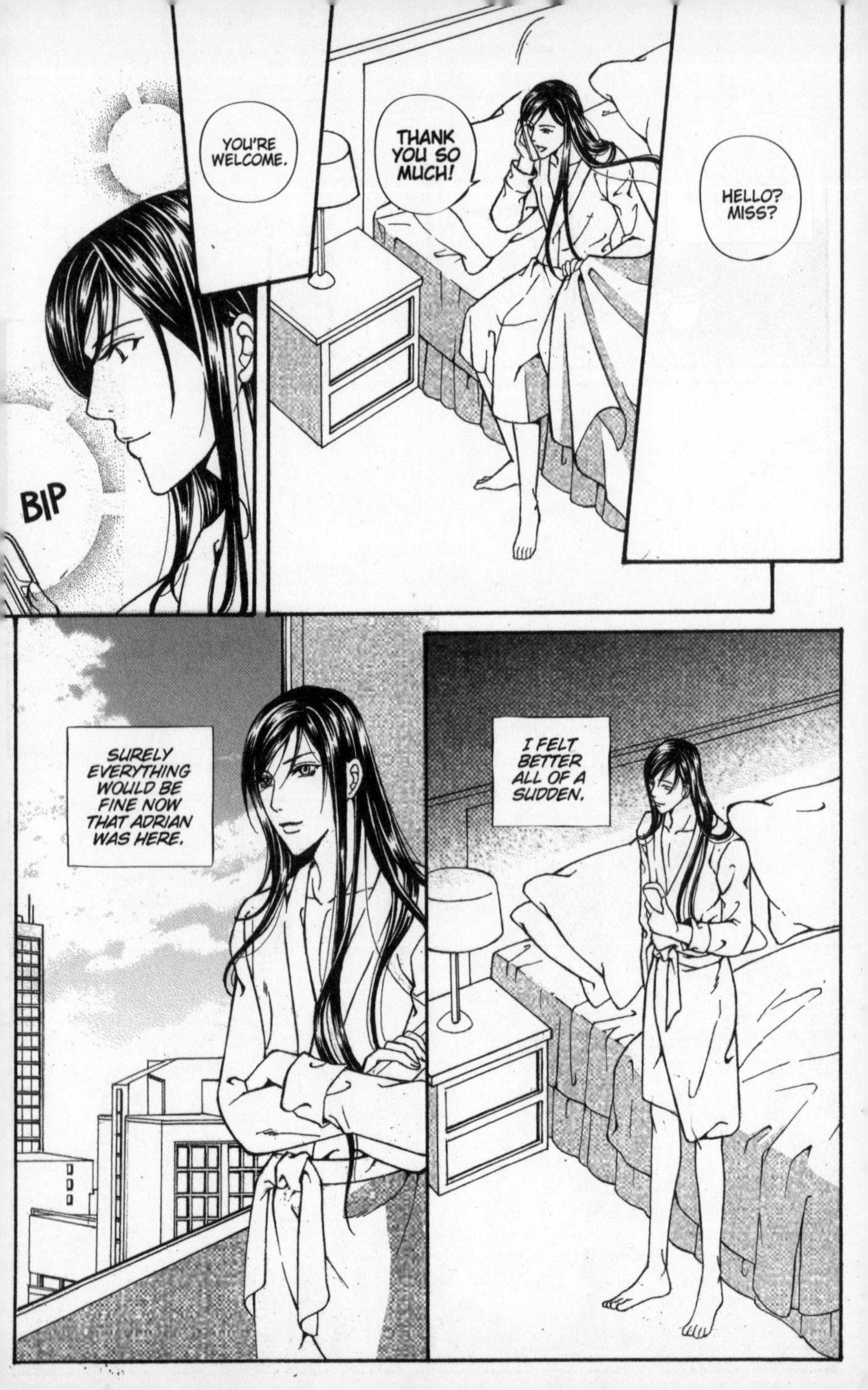
HELLO? MISS?
THANK YOU SO MUCH!
YOU'RE WELCOME.
BIP
I FELT BETTER ALL OF A SUDDEN.
SURELY EVERYTHING WOULD BE FINE NOW THAT ADRIAN WAS HERE.

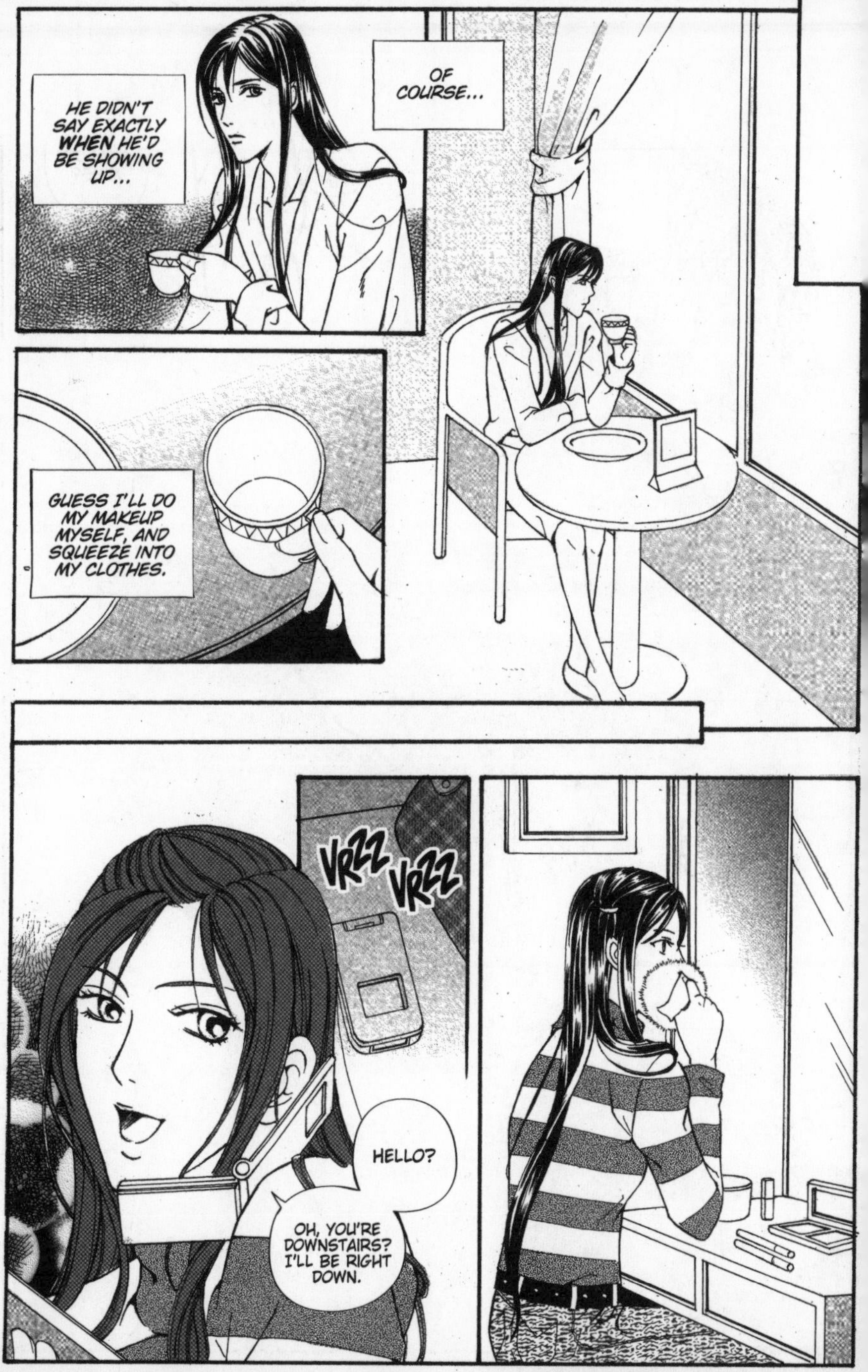
OF COURSE...
HE DIDN'T SAY EXACTLY WHEN HE'D BE SHOWING UP...
GUESS I'LL DO MY MAKEUP MYSELF, AND SQUEEZE INTO MY CLOTHES.
VRZZ VRZZ
HELLO?
OH, YOU'RE DOWNSTAIRS? I'LL BE RIGHT DOWN.

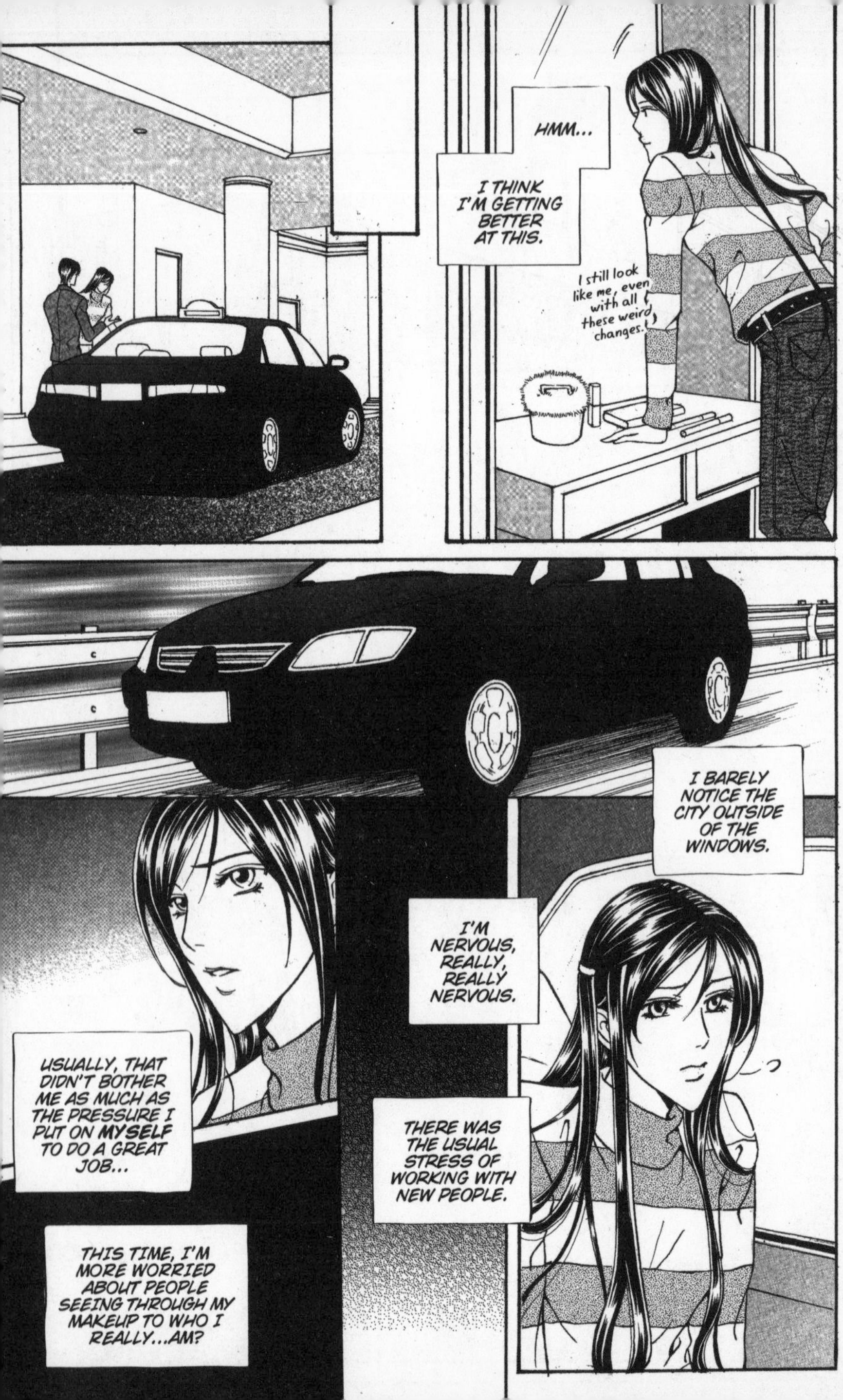
HMM...
I THINK I'M GETTING BETTER AT THIS.
I still look like me, even with all these weird changes.
I BARELY NOTICE THE CITY OUTSIDE OF THE WINDOWS.
I'M NERVOUS, REALLY, REALLY NERVOUS.
THERE WAS THE USUAL STRESS OF WORKING WITH NEW PEOPLE.
USUALLY, THAT DIDN'T BOTHER ME AS MUCH AS THE PRESSURE I PUT ON MYSELF TO DO A GREAT JOB...
THIS TIME, I'M MORE WORRIED ABOUT PEOPLE SEEING THROUGH MY MAKEUP TO WHO I REALLY...AM?

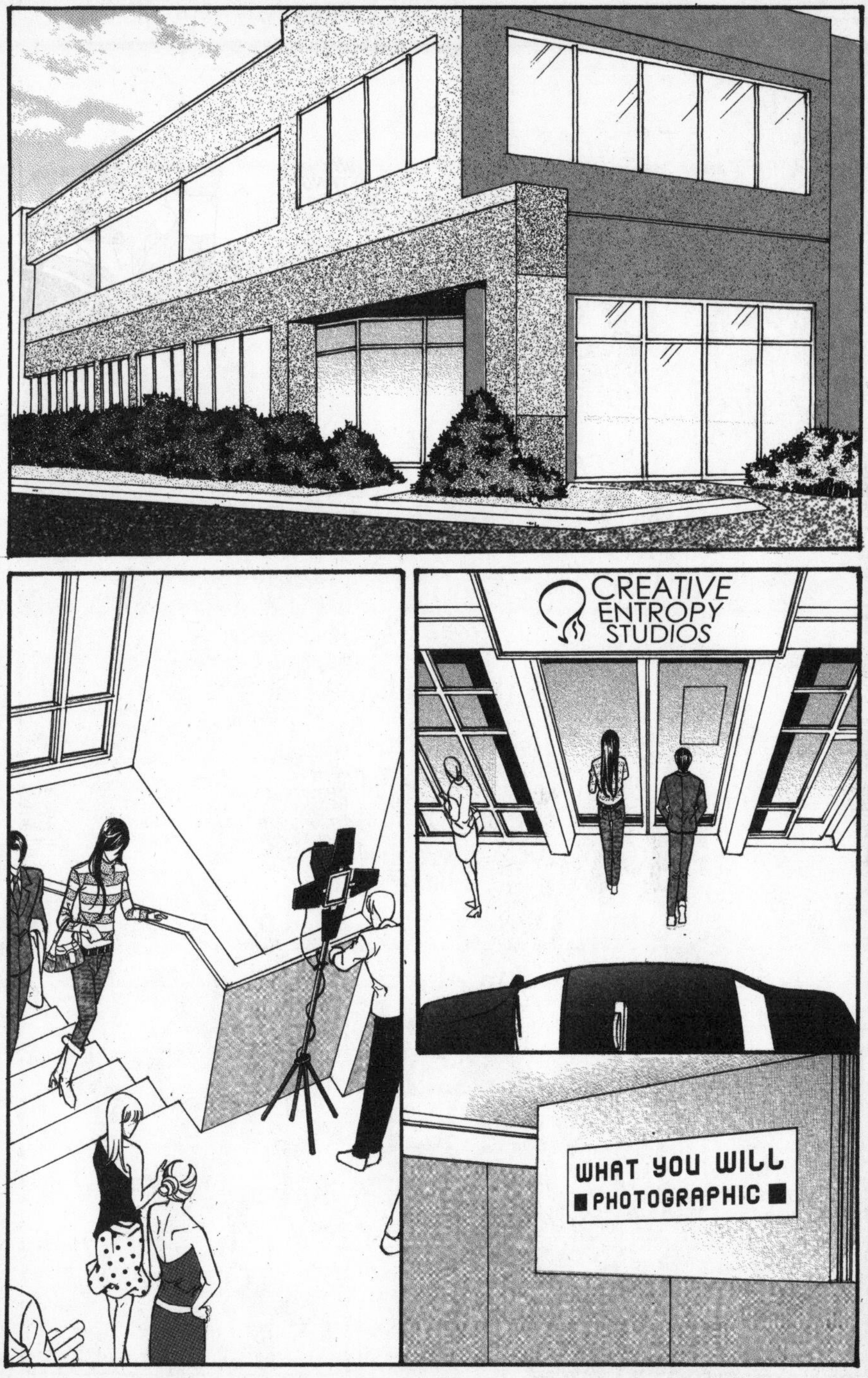
CREATIVE
ENTROPY
STUDIOS
WHAT YOU WILL
PHOTOGRAPHIC

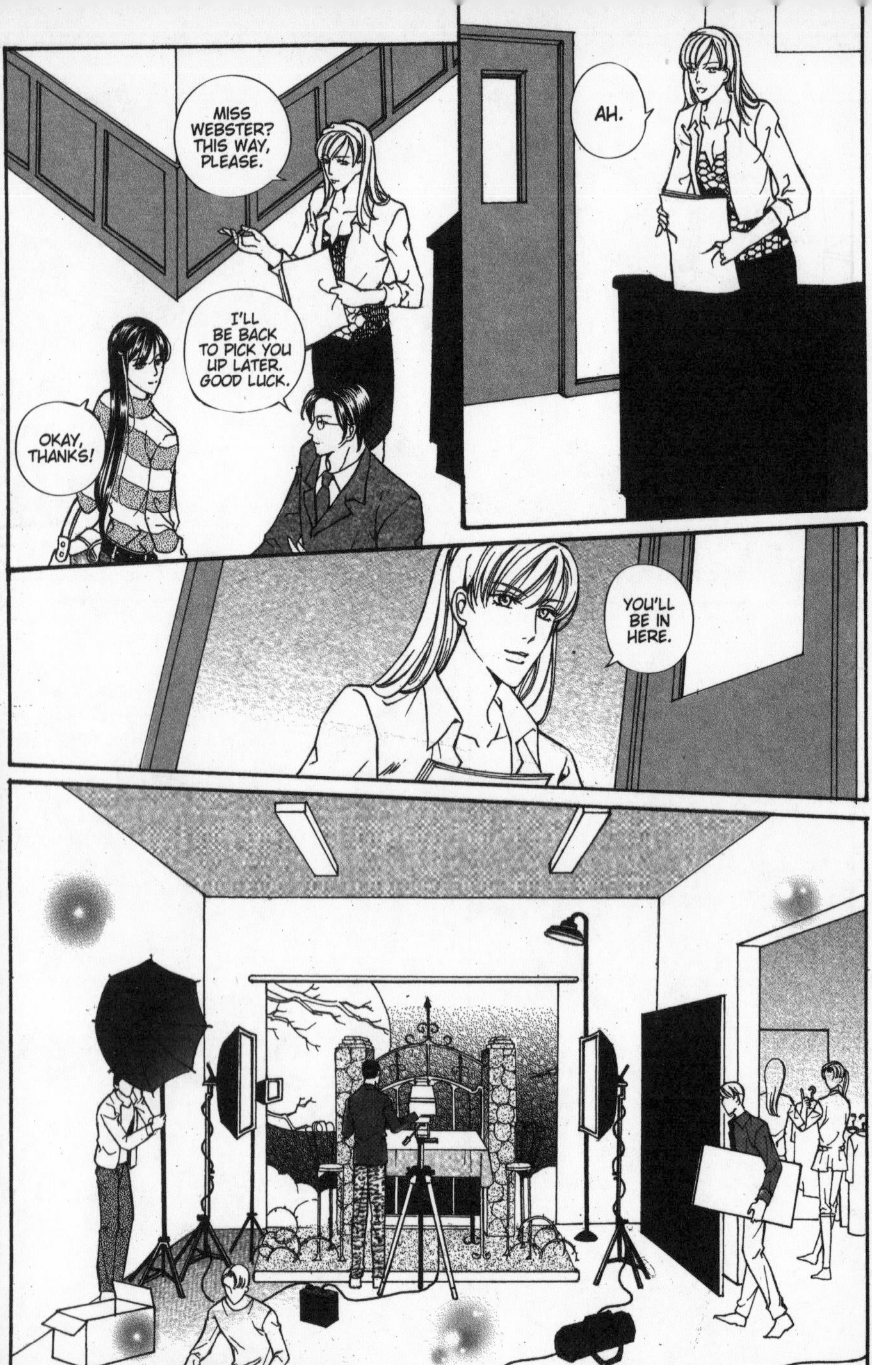
AH.
MISS WEBSTER? THIS WAY, PLEASE.
I'LL BE BACK TO PICK YOU UP LATER. GOOD LUCK.
OKAY, THANKS!
YOU'LL BE IN HERE.

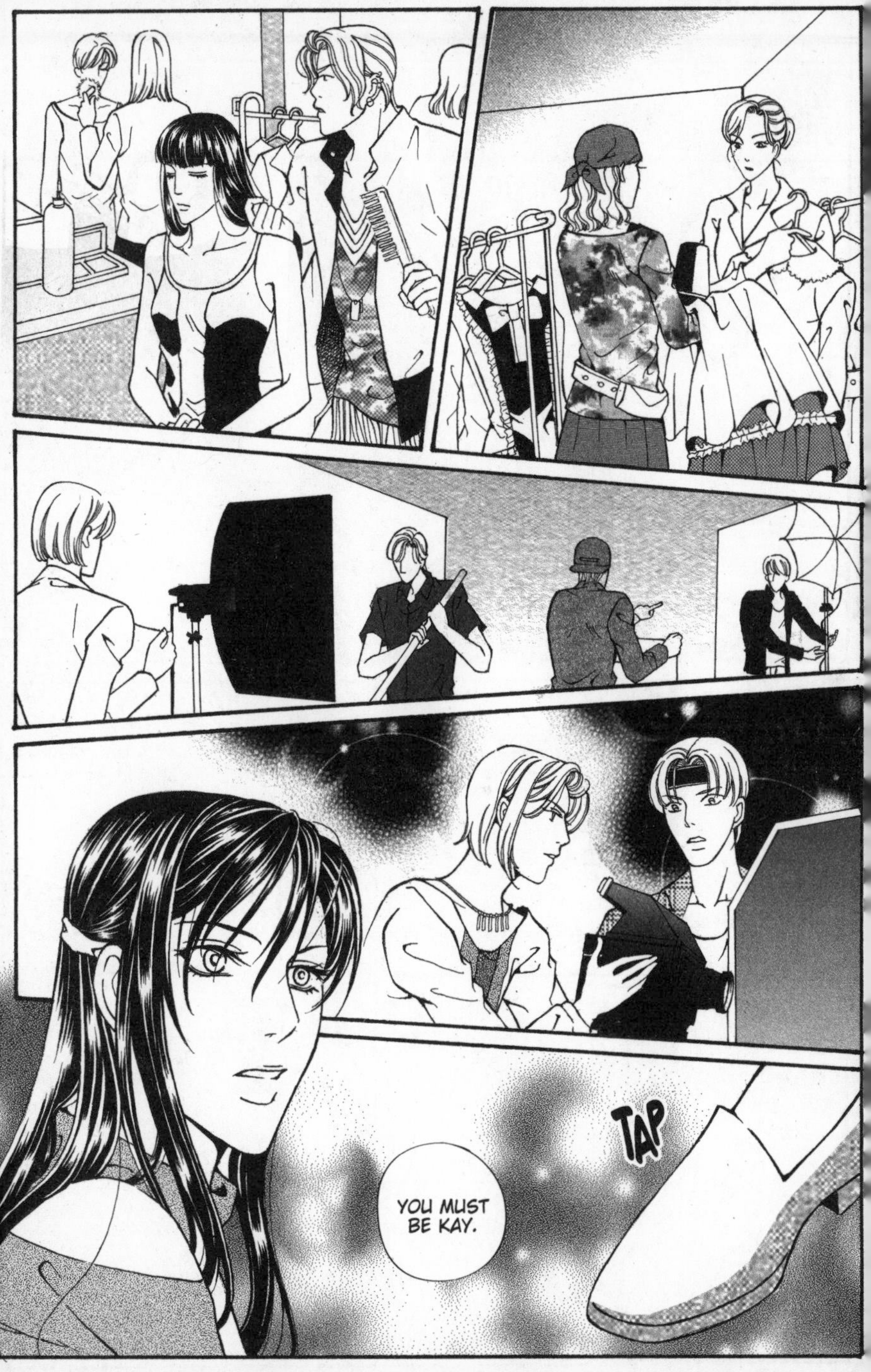
TAP
YOU MUST BE KAY.

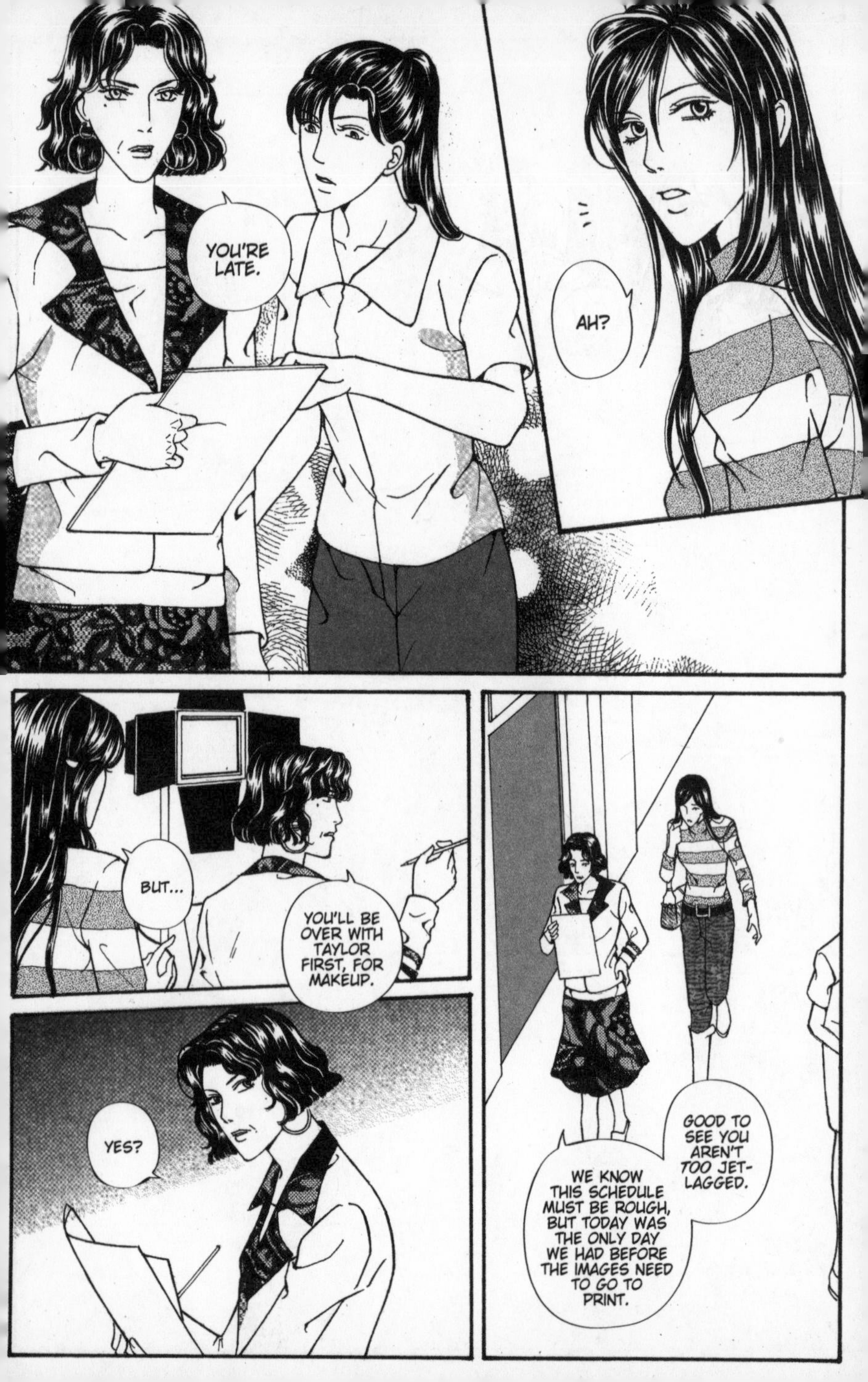
AH?
YOU'RE LATE.
GOOD TO SEE YOU AREN'T *TOO* JET-LAGGED.
WE KNOW THIS SCHEDULE MUST BE ROUGH, BUT TODAY WAS THE ONLY DAY WE HAD BEFORE THE IMAGES NEED TO GO TO PRINT.
YOU'LL BE OVER WITH TAYLOR FIRST, FOR MAKEUP.
BUT...
YES?

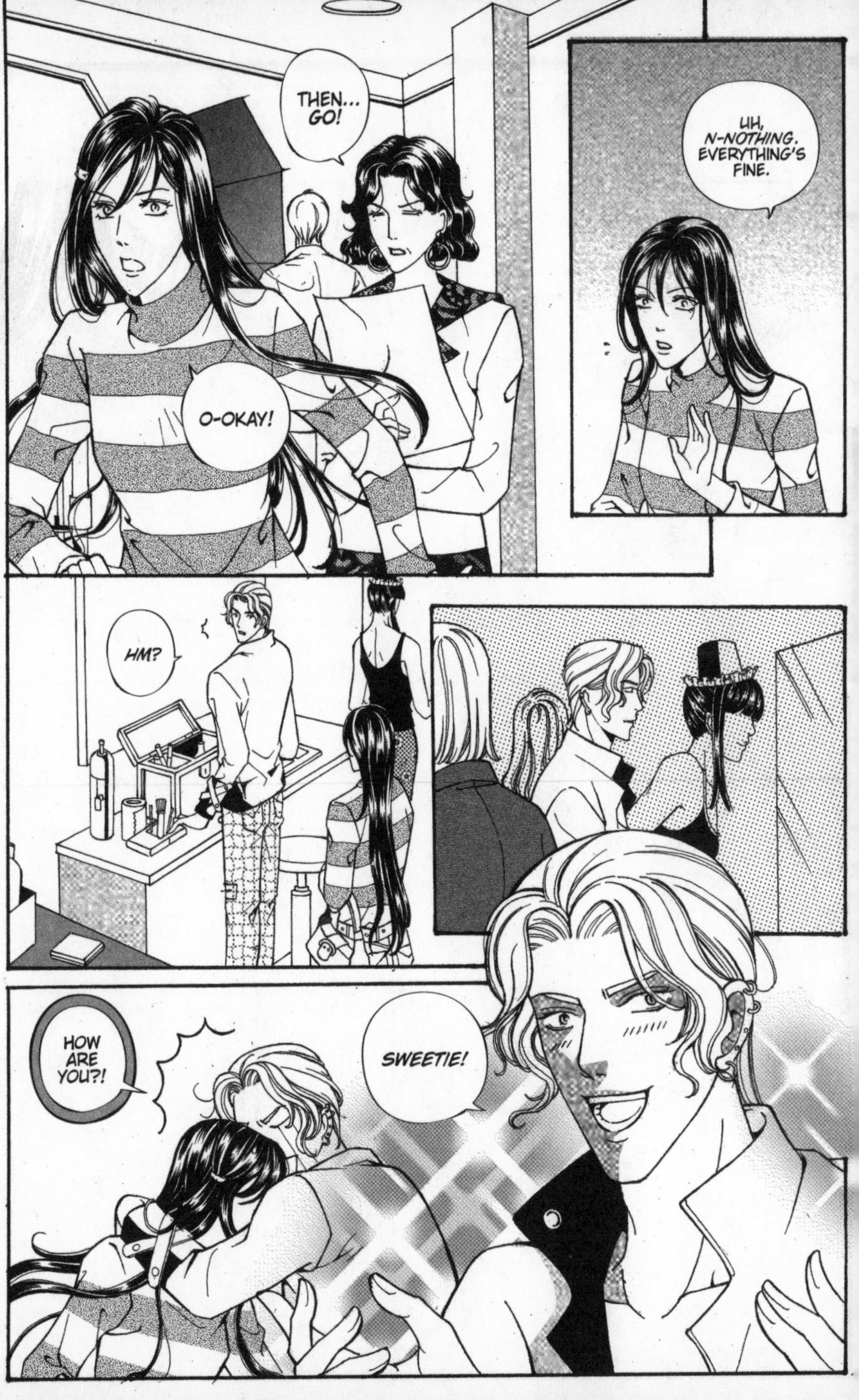
UH, N-NOTHING. EVERYTHING'S FINE.
THEN... GO!
O-OKAY!
HM?
SWEETIE!
HOW ARE YOU?!

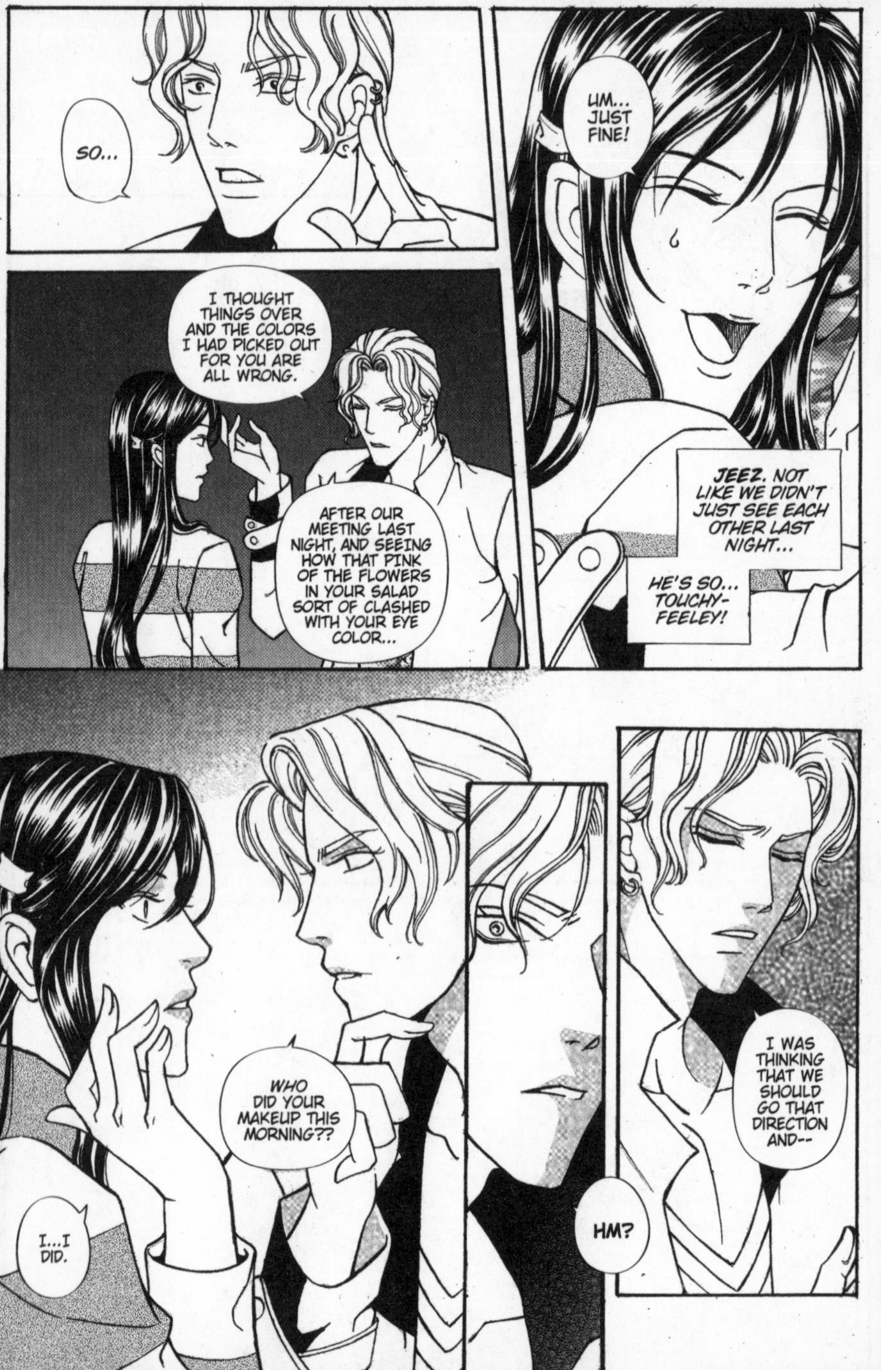
UM... JUST FINE!
JEEZ. NOT LIKE WE DIDN'T JUST SEE EACH OTHER LAST NIGHT...
HE'S SO... TOUCHY-FEELEY!
SO...
I THOUGHT THINGS OVER AND THE COLORS I HAD PICKED OUT FOR YOU ARE ALL WRONG.
AFTER OUR MEETING LAST NIGHT, AND SEEING HOW THAT PINK OF THE FLOWERS IN YOUR SALAD SORT OF CLASHED WITH YOUR EYE COLOR...
I WAS THINKING THAT WE SHOULD GO THAT DIRECTION AND--
HM?
WHO DID YOUR MAKEUP THIS MORNING??
I...I DID.

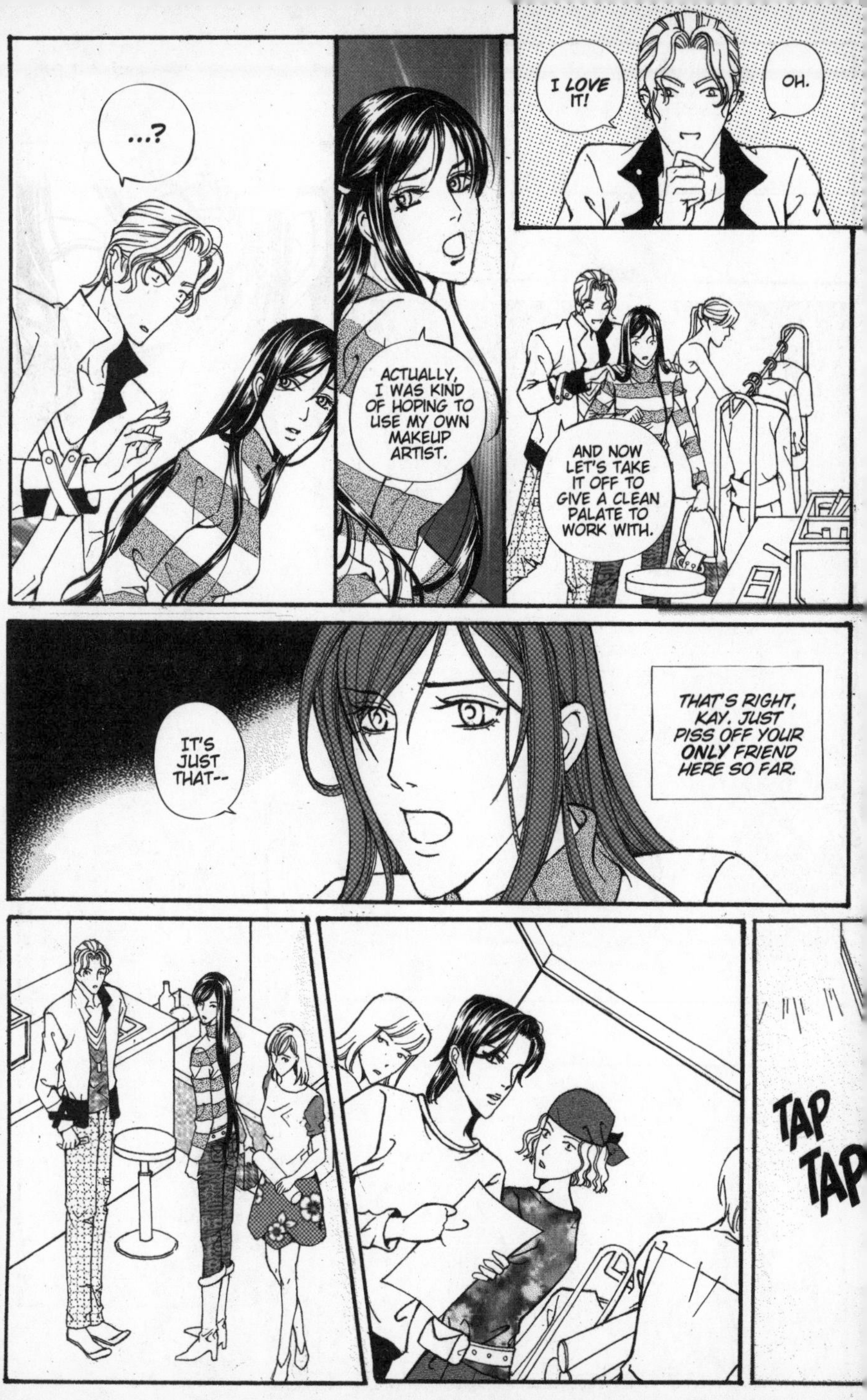
OH.
I LOVE IT!
AND NOW LET'S TAKE IT OFF TO GIVE A CLEAN PALATE TO WORK WITH.
ACTUALLY, I WAS KIND OF HOPING TO USE MY OWN MAKEUP ARTIST.
...?
THAT'S RIGHT, KAY. JUST PISS OFF YOUR ONLY FRIEND HERE SO FAR.
IT'S JUST THAT--
TAP TAP

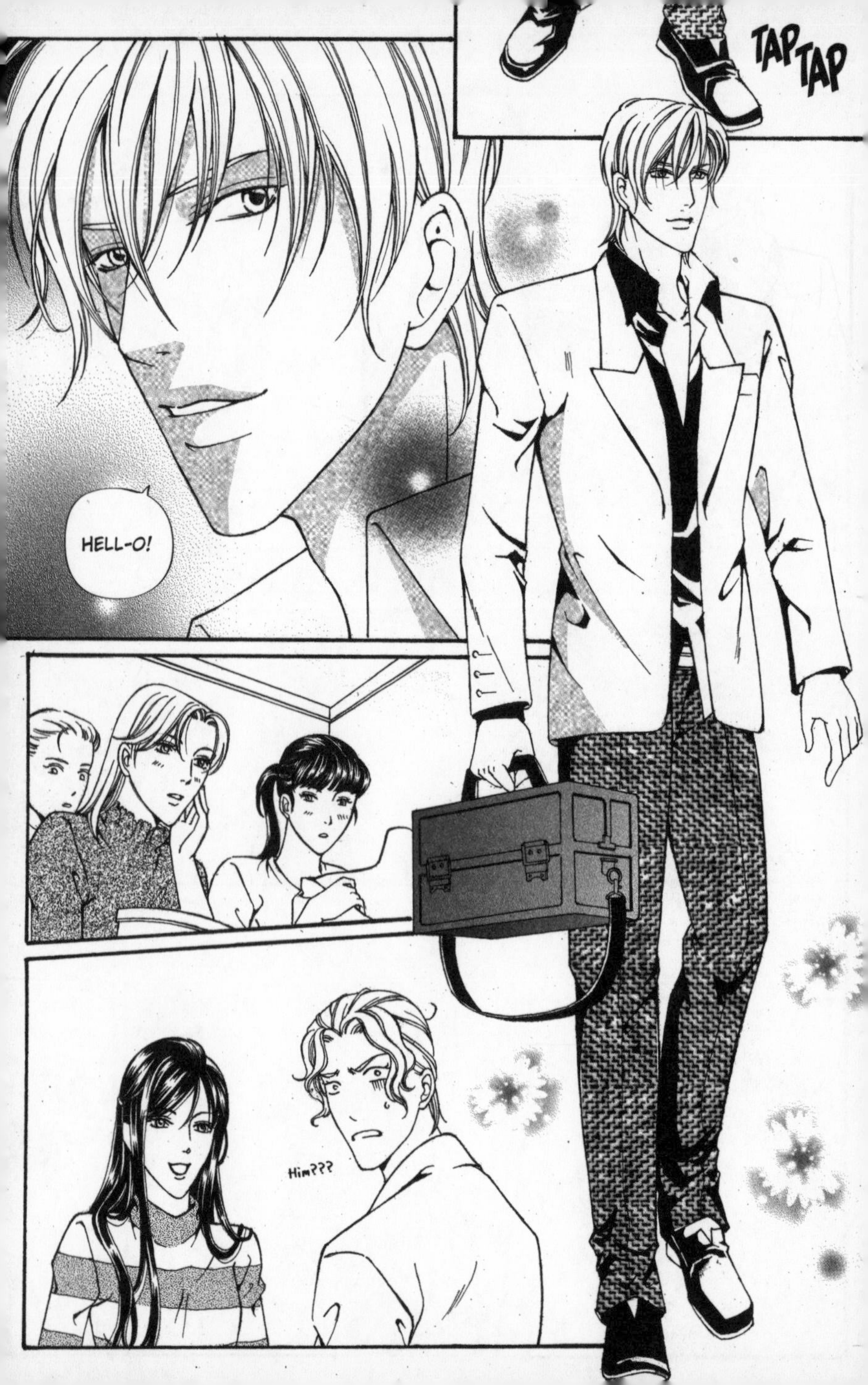
TAP TAP
HELL-O!
Him???

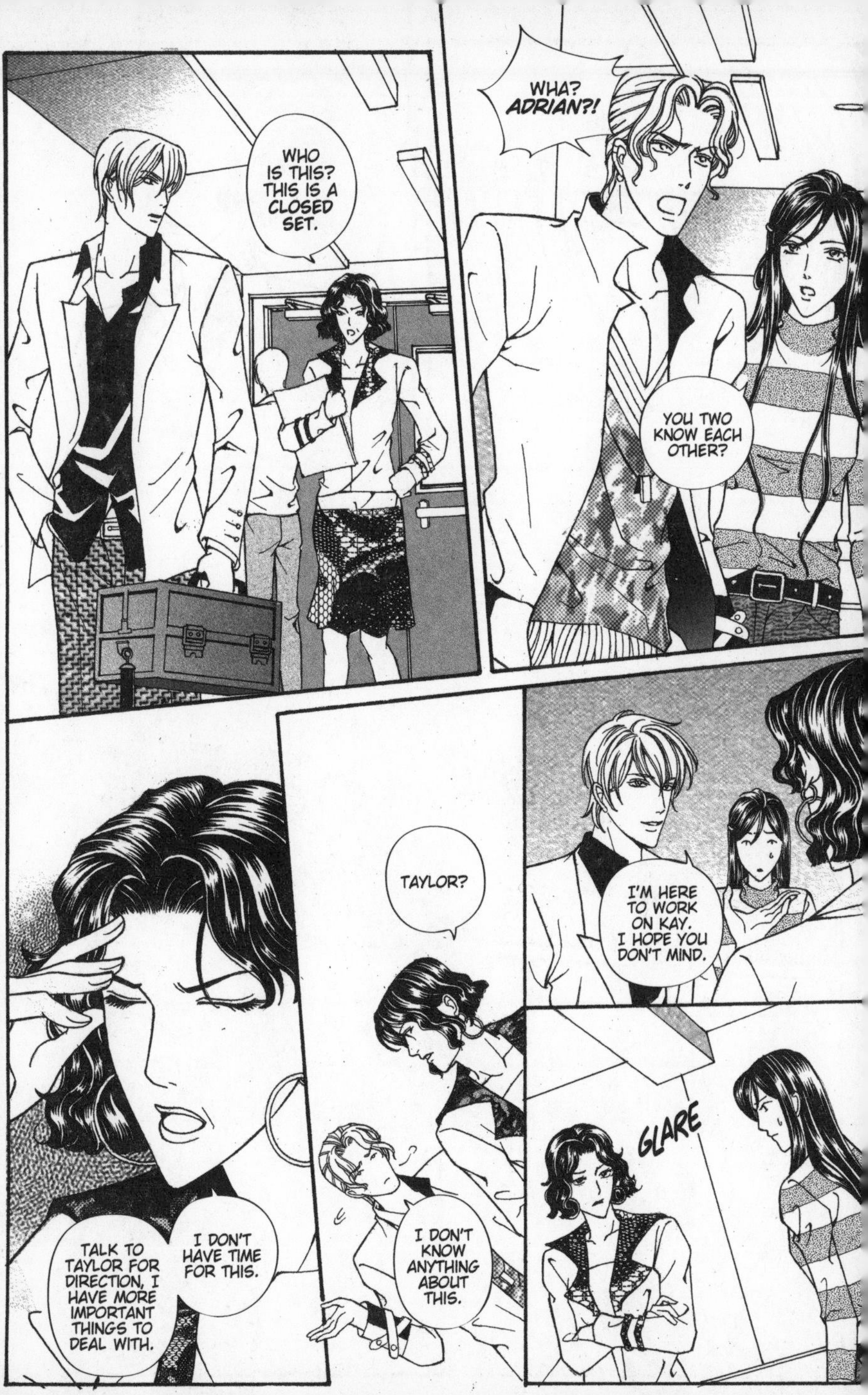
WHA? ADRIAN?!
YOU TWO KNOW EACH OTHER?
WHO IS THIS? THIS IS A CLOSED SET.
I'M HERE TO WORK ON KAY. I HOPE YOU DON'T MIND.
GLARE
TAYLOR?
I DON'T KNOW ANYTHING ABOUT THIS.
I DON'T HAVE TIME FOR THIS.
TALK TO TAYLOR FOR DIRECTION, I HAVE MORE IMPORTANT THINGS TO DEAL WITH.

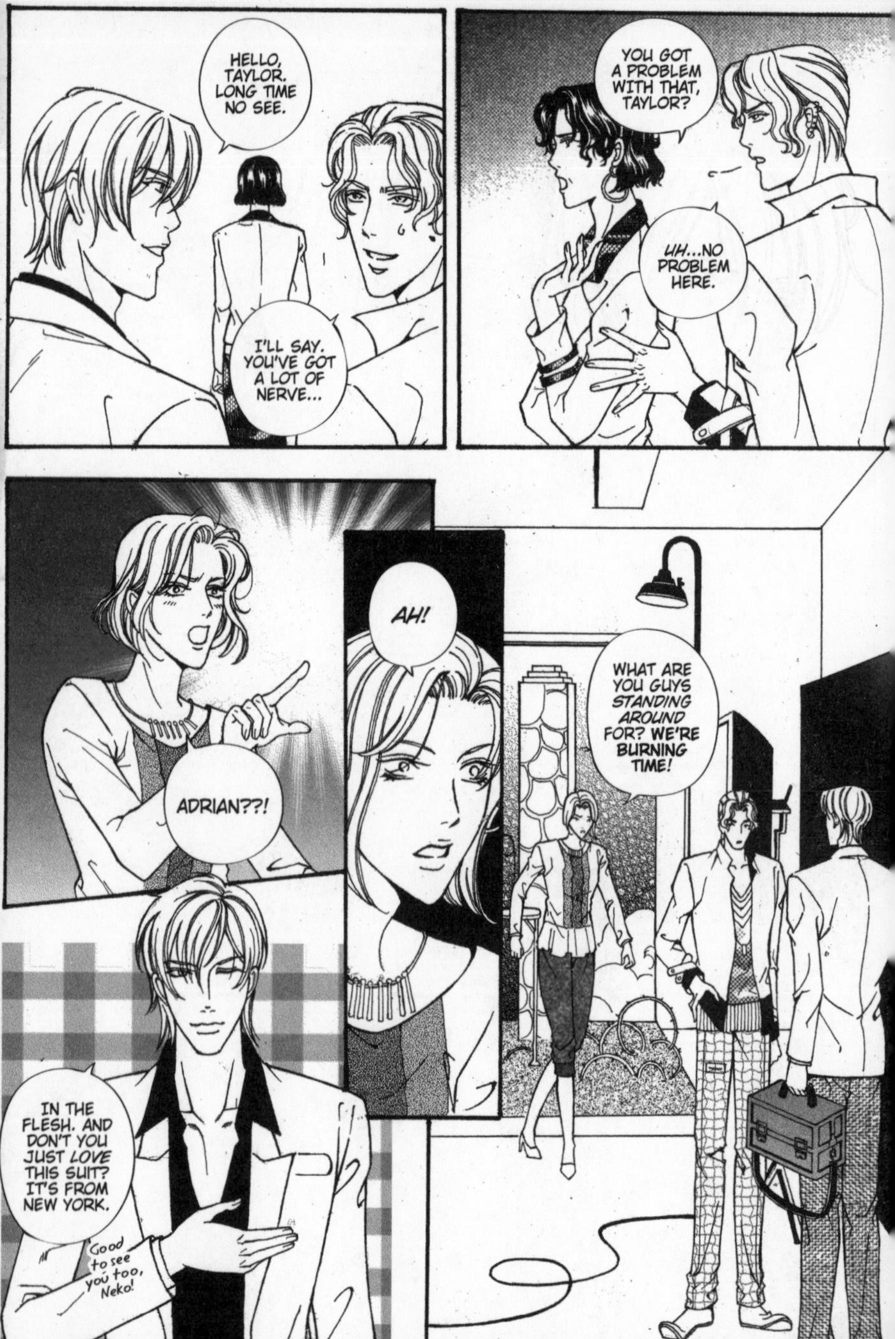
YOU GOT A PROBLEM WITH THAT, TAYLOR?
UH...NO PROBLEM HERE.
HELLO, TAYLOR. LONG TIME NO SEE.
I'LL SAY. YOU'VE GOT A LOT OF NERVE...
WHAT ARE YOU GUYS *STANDING AROUND* FOR? WE'RE BURNING TIME!
AH!
ADRIAN??!
IN THE FLESH. AND DON'T YOU JUST *LOVE* THIS SUIT? IT'S FROM NEW YORK.
Good to see you too, Neko!

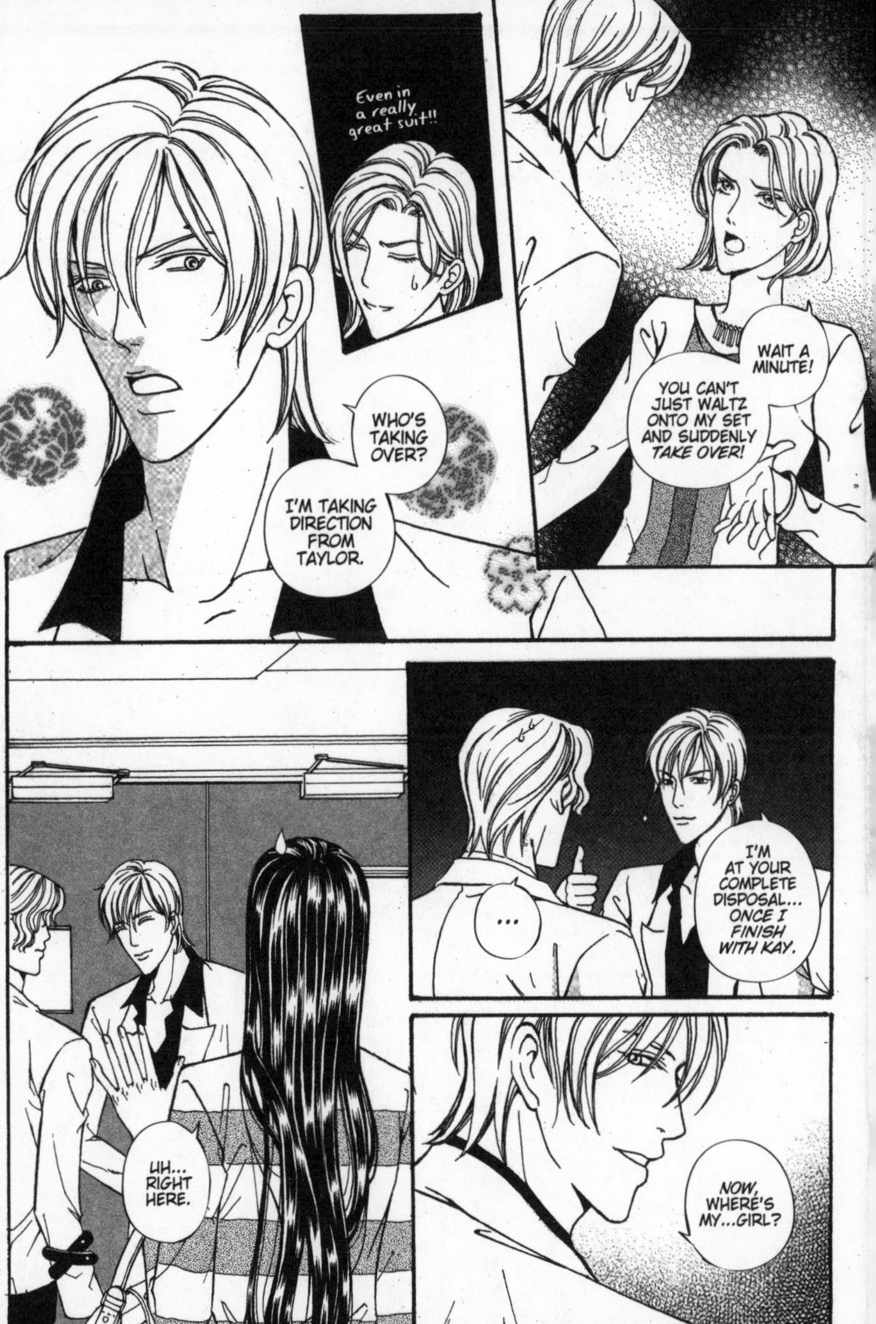
WAIT A MINUTE!
YOU CAN'T JUST WALTZ ONTO MY SET AND SUDDENLY *TAKE OVER!*
Even in a really great suit!!
WHO'S TAKING OVER?
I'M TAKING DIRECTION FROM TAYLOR.
I'M AT YOUR COMPLETE DISPOSAL... ONCE I FINISH WITH KAY.
...
NOW, WHERE'S MY...GIRL?
UH... RIGHT HERE.

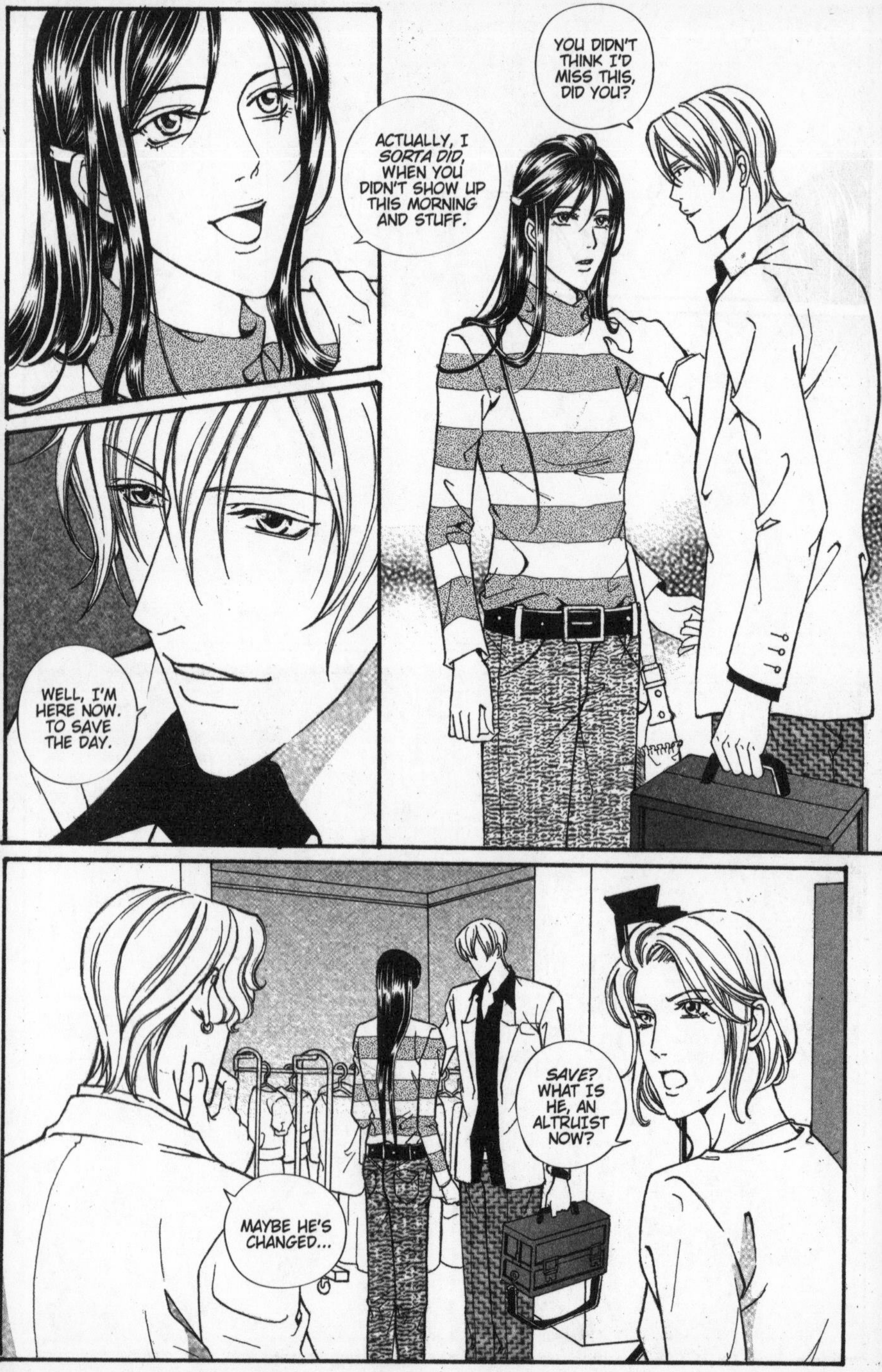
YOU DIDN'T THINK I'D MISS THIS, DID YOU?
ACTUALLY, I *SORTA DID*, WHEN YOU DIDN'T SHOW UP THIS MORNING AND STUFF.
WELL, I'M HERE NOW. TO SAVE THE DAY.
SAVE? WHAT IS HE, AN ALTRUIST NOW?
MAYBE HE'S CHANGED...

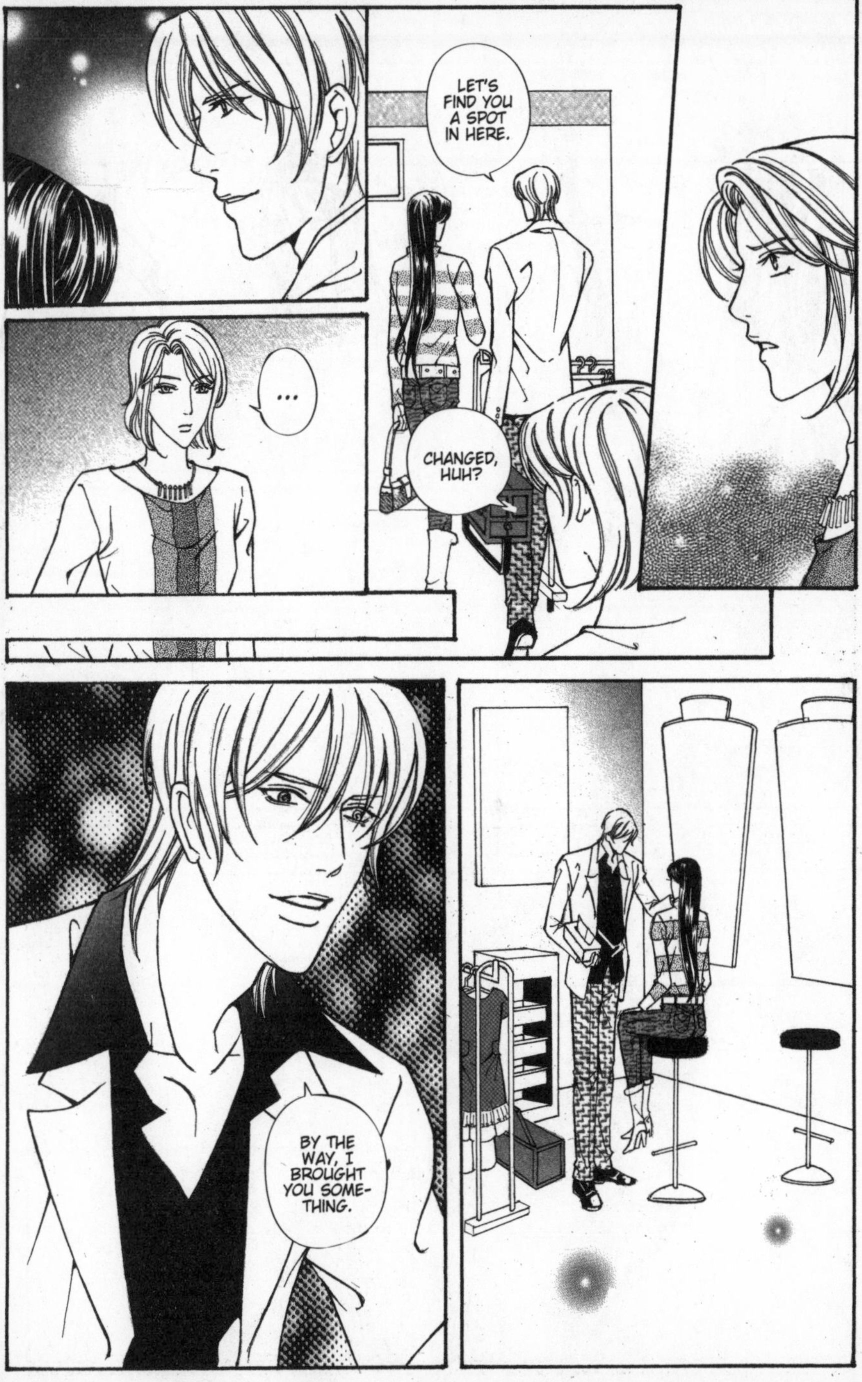
LET'S FIND YOU A SPOT IN HERE.
CHANGED, HUH?
...
BY THE WAY, I BROUGHT YOU SOME-THING.

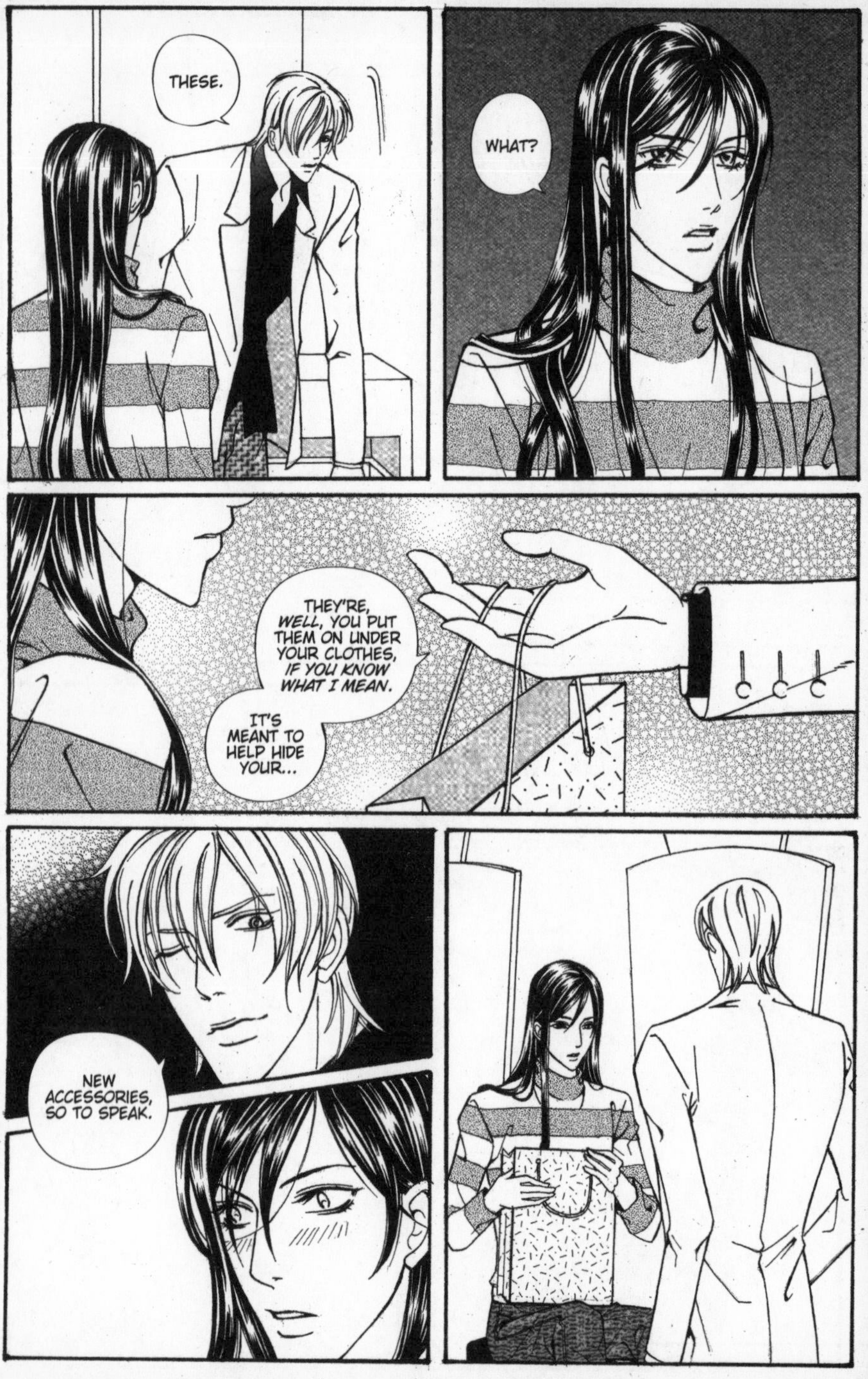
THESE.
WHAT?
THEY'RE, *WELL,* YOU PUT THEM ON UNDER YOUR CLOTHES, *IF YOU KNOW WHAT I MEAN.*
IT'S MEANT TO HELP HIDE YOUR...
NEW ACCESSORIES, SO TO SPEAK.

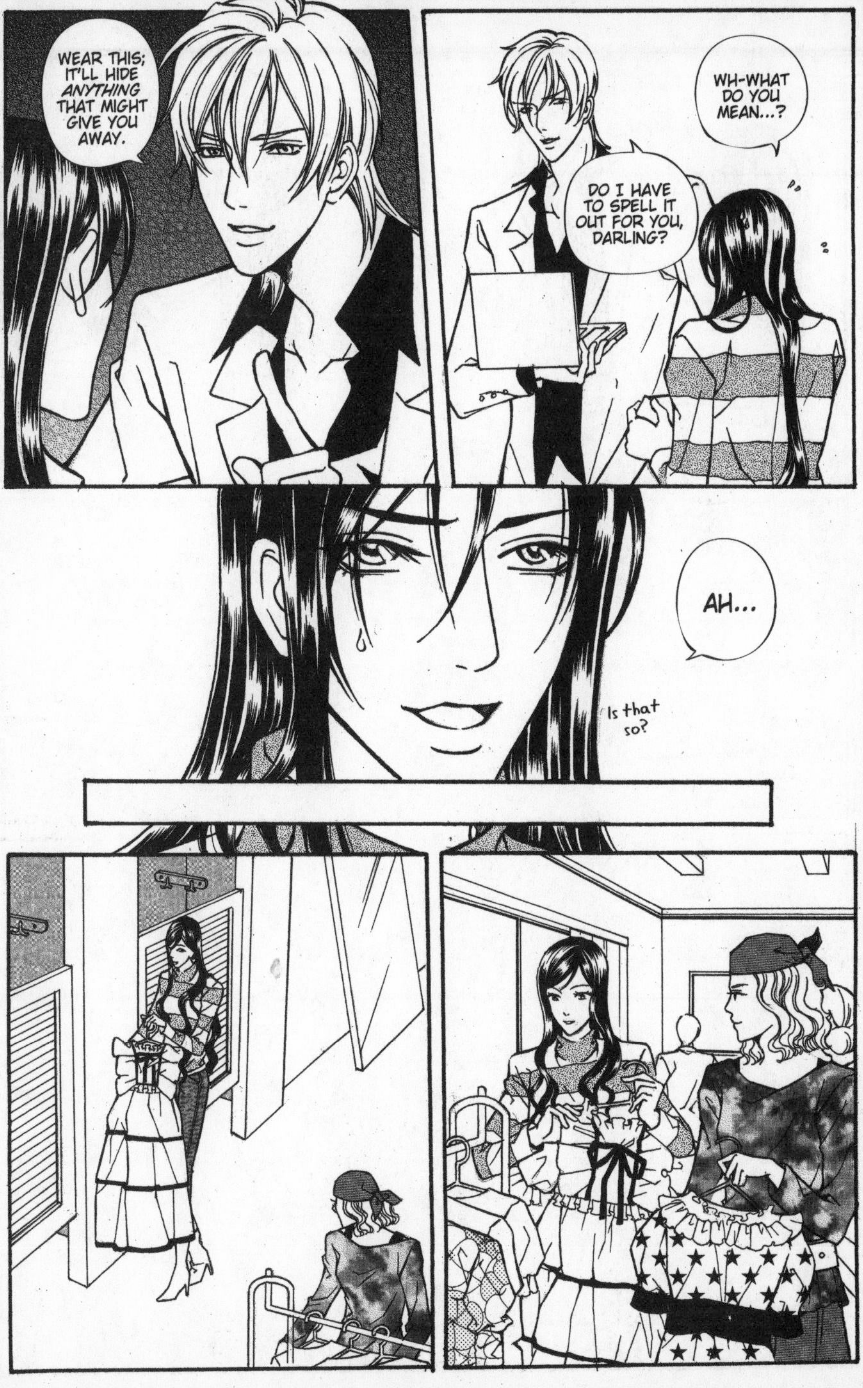
WH-WHAT DO YOU MEAN...?
DO I HAVE TO SPELL IT OUT FOR YOU, DARLING?
WEAR THIS; IT'LL HIDE *ANYTHING* THAT MIGHT GIVE YOU AWAY.
AH...
Is that so?

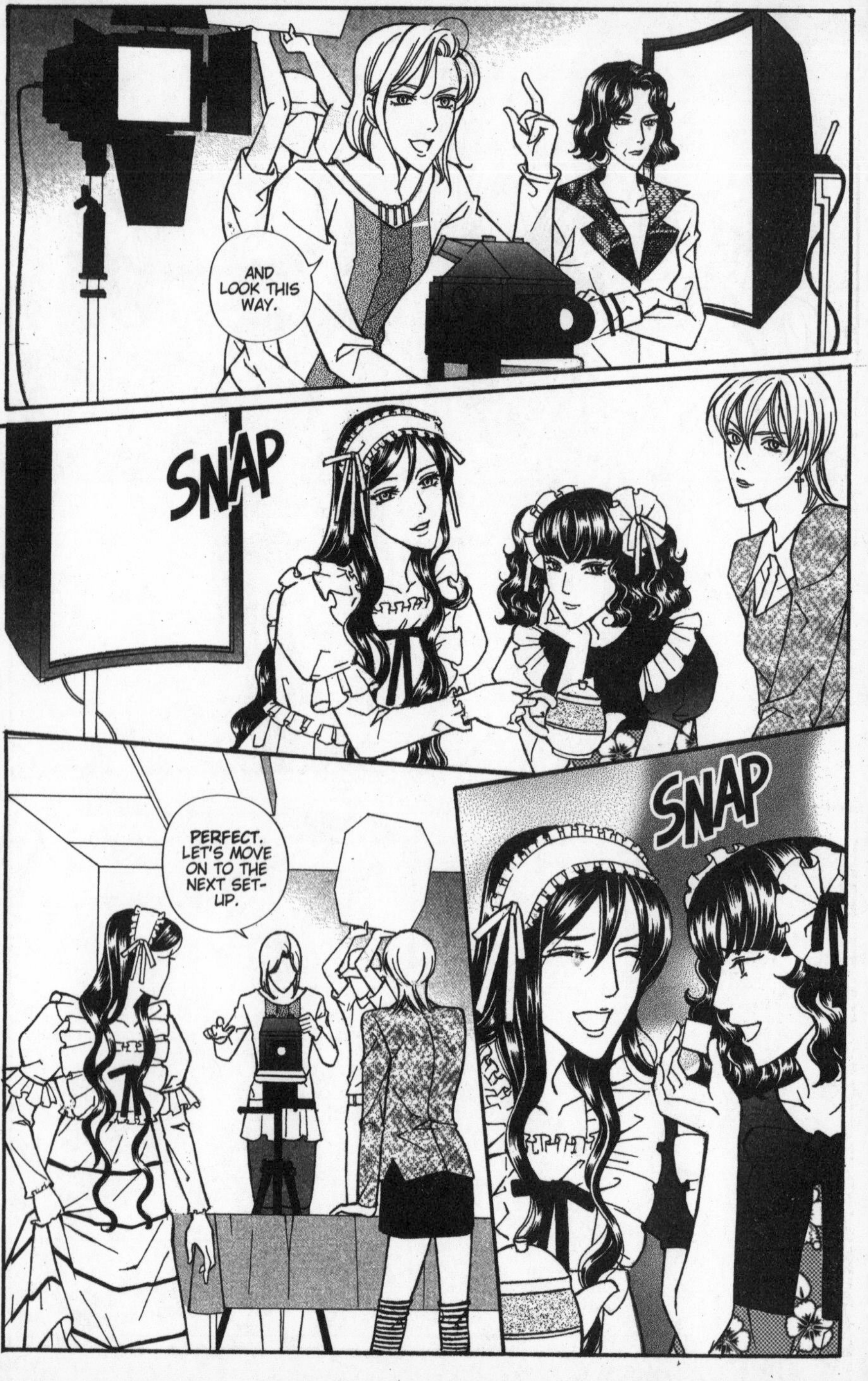
AND LOOK THIS WAY.
SNAP
SNAP
PERFECT. LET'S MOVE ON TO THE NEXT SET-UP.

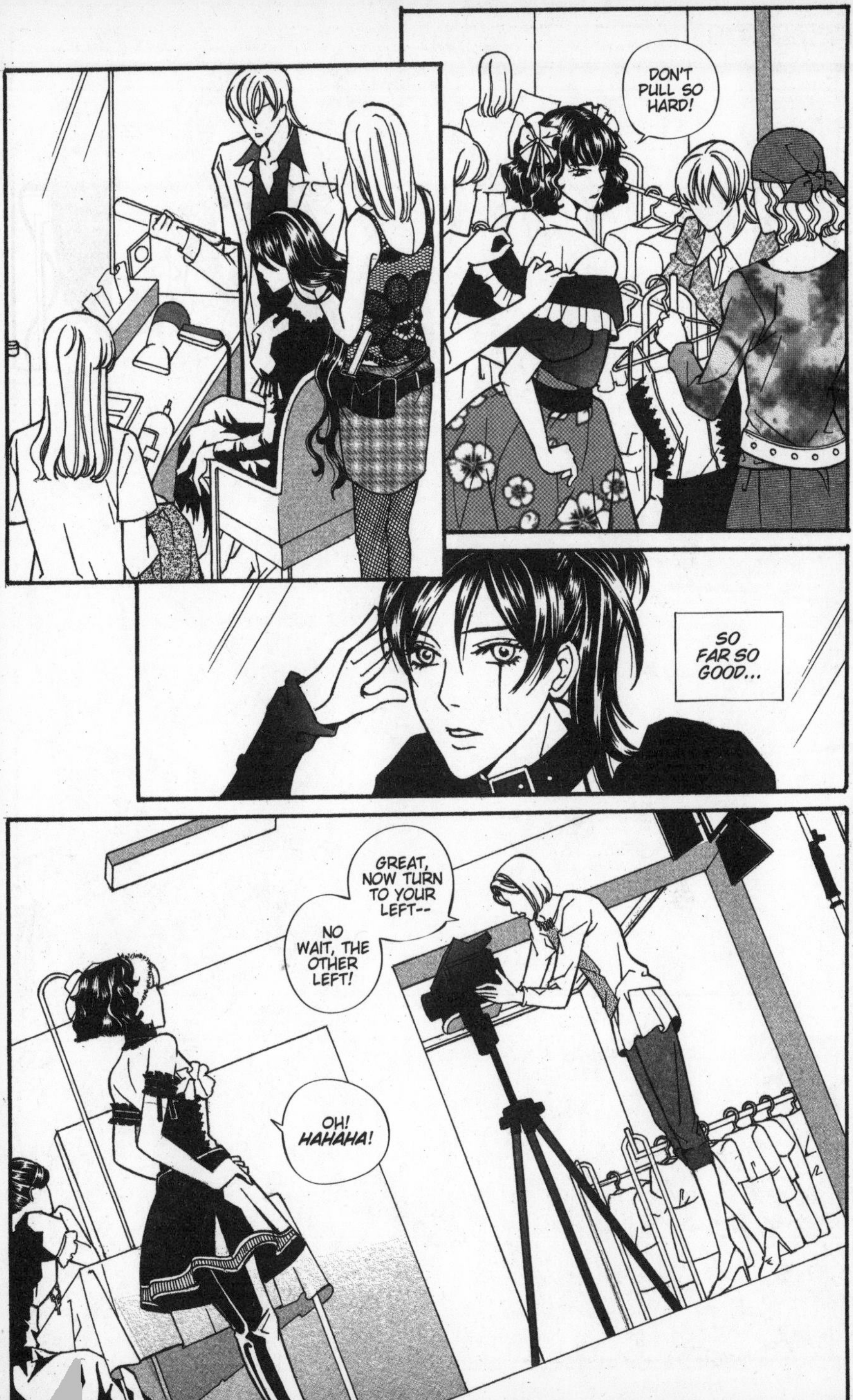
DON'T PULL SO HARD!
SO FAR SO GOOD...
GREAT, NOW TURN TO YOUR LEFT--
NO WAIT, THE OTHER LEFT!
OH! HAHAHA!

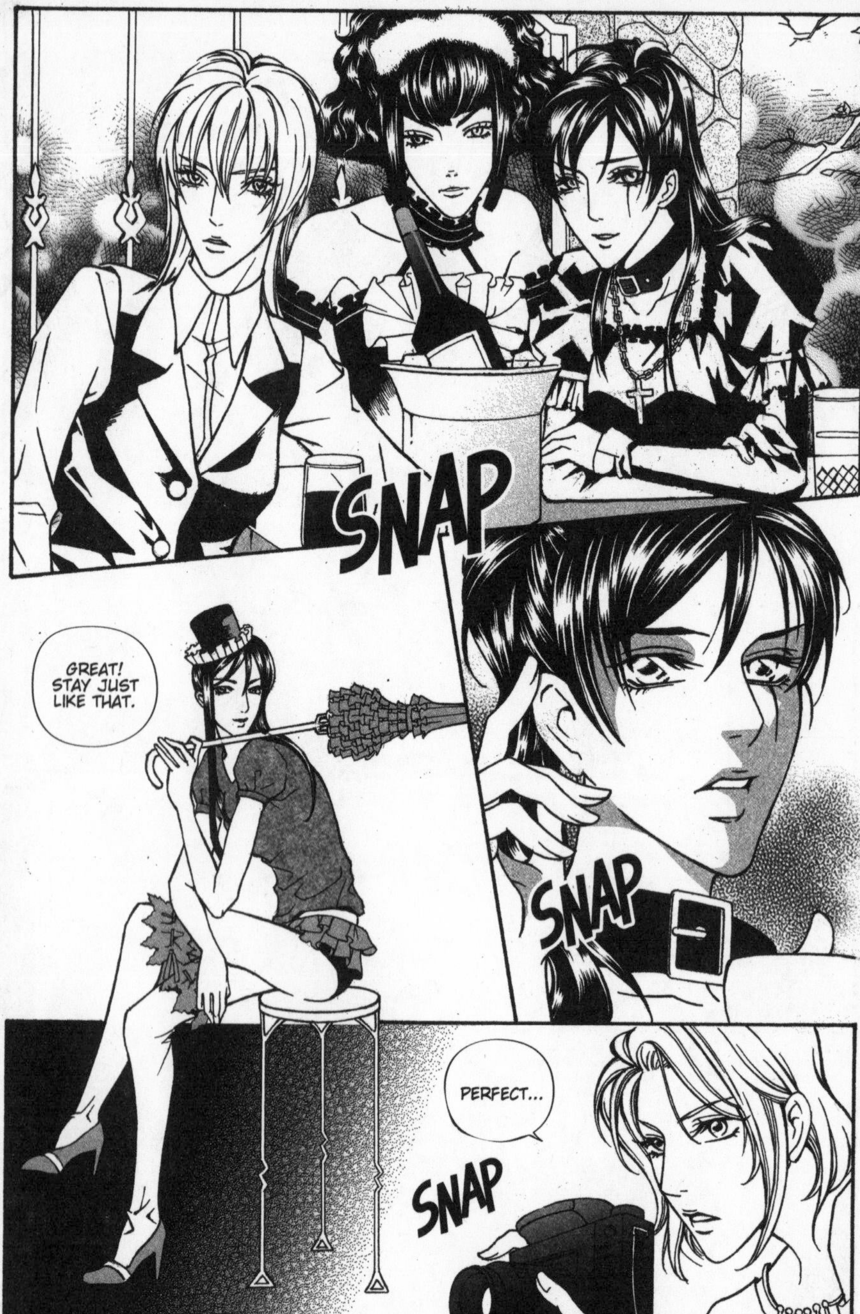
SNAP
SNAP
GREAT! STAY JUST LIKE THAT.
PERFECT...
SNAP

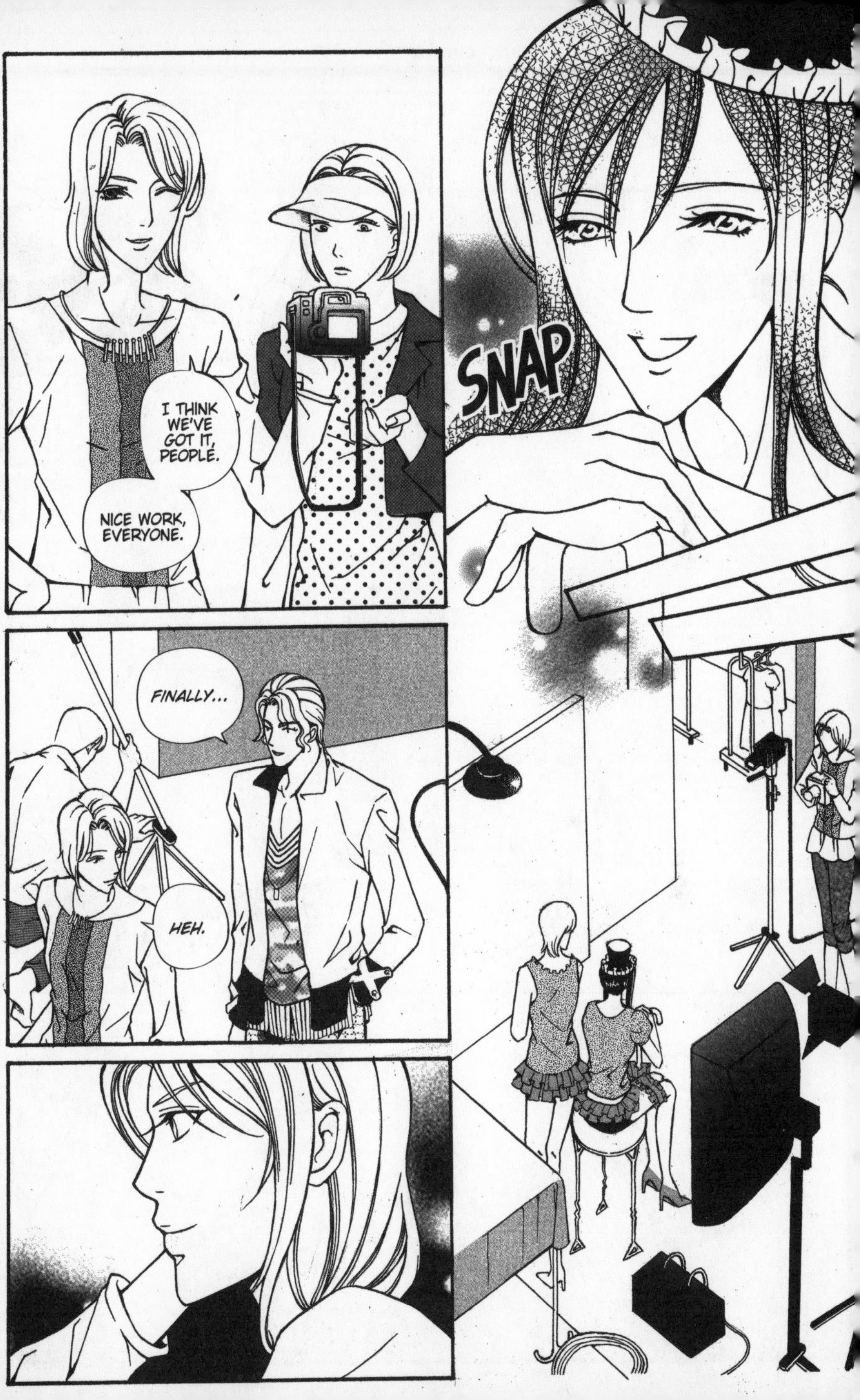
SNAP
I THINK WE'VE GOT IT, PEOPLE.
NICE WORK, EVERYONE.
FINALLY...
HEH.

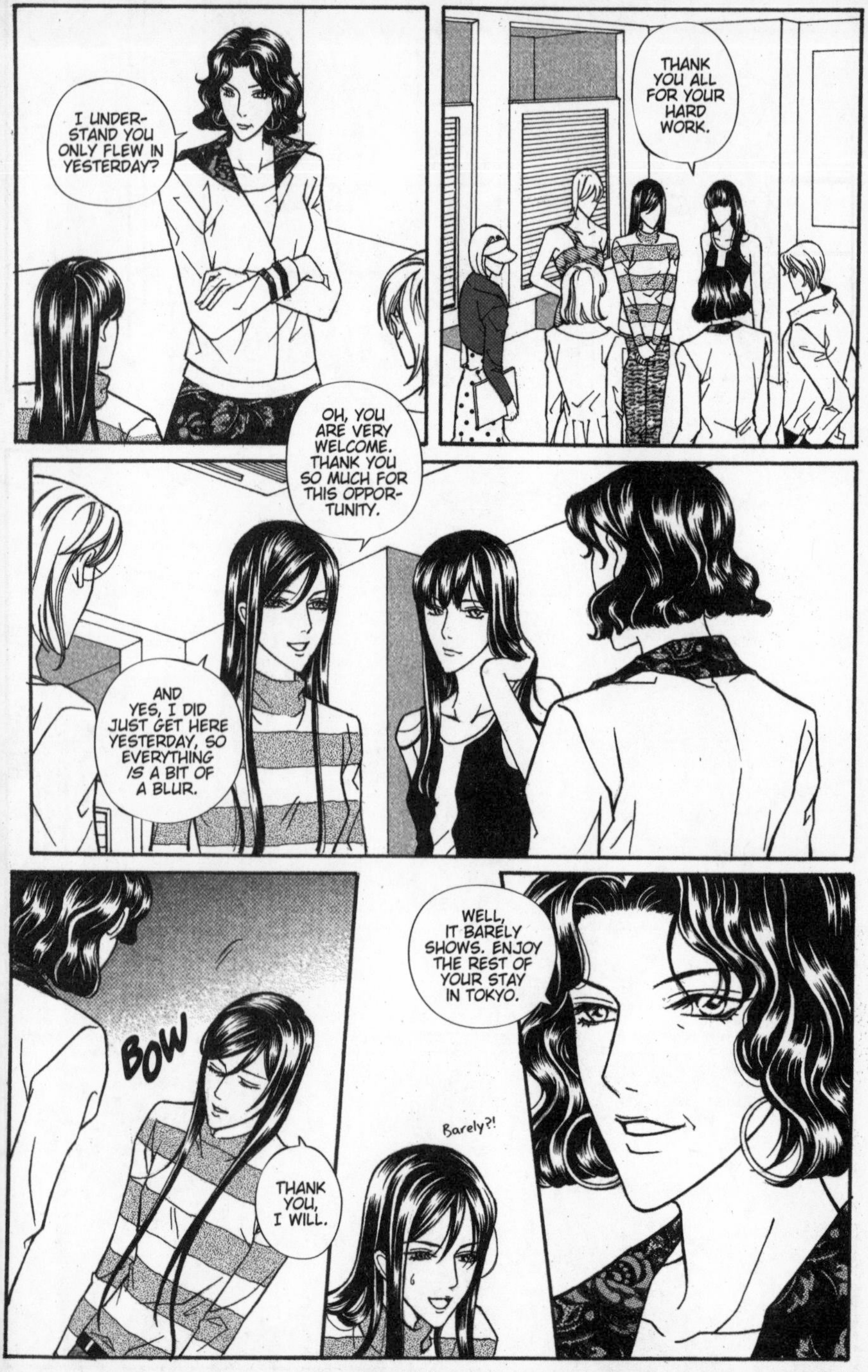
THANK YOU ALL FOR YOUR HARD WORK.
I UNDER-STAND YOU ONLY FLEW IN YESTERDAY?
OH, YOU ARE VERY WELCOME. THANK YOU SO MUCH FOR THIS OPPOR-TUNITY.
AND YES, I DID JUST GET HERE YESTERDAY, SO EVERYTHING *IS* A BIT OF A BLUR.
WELL, IT BARELY SHOWS. ENJOY THE REST OF YOUR STAY IN TOKYO.
BOW
THANK YOU, I WILL.
Barely?!

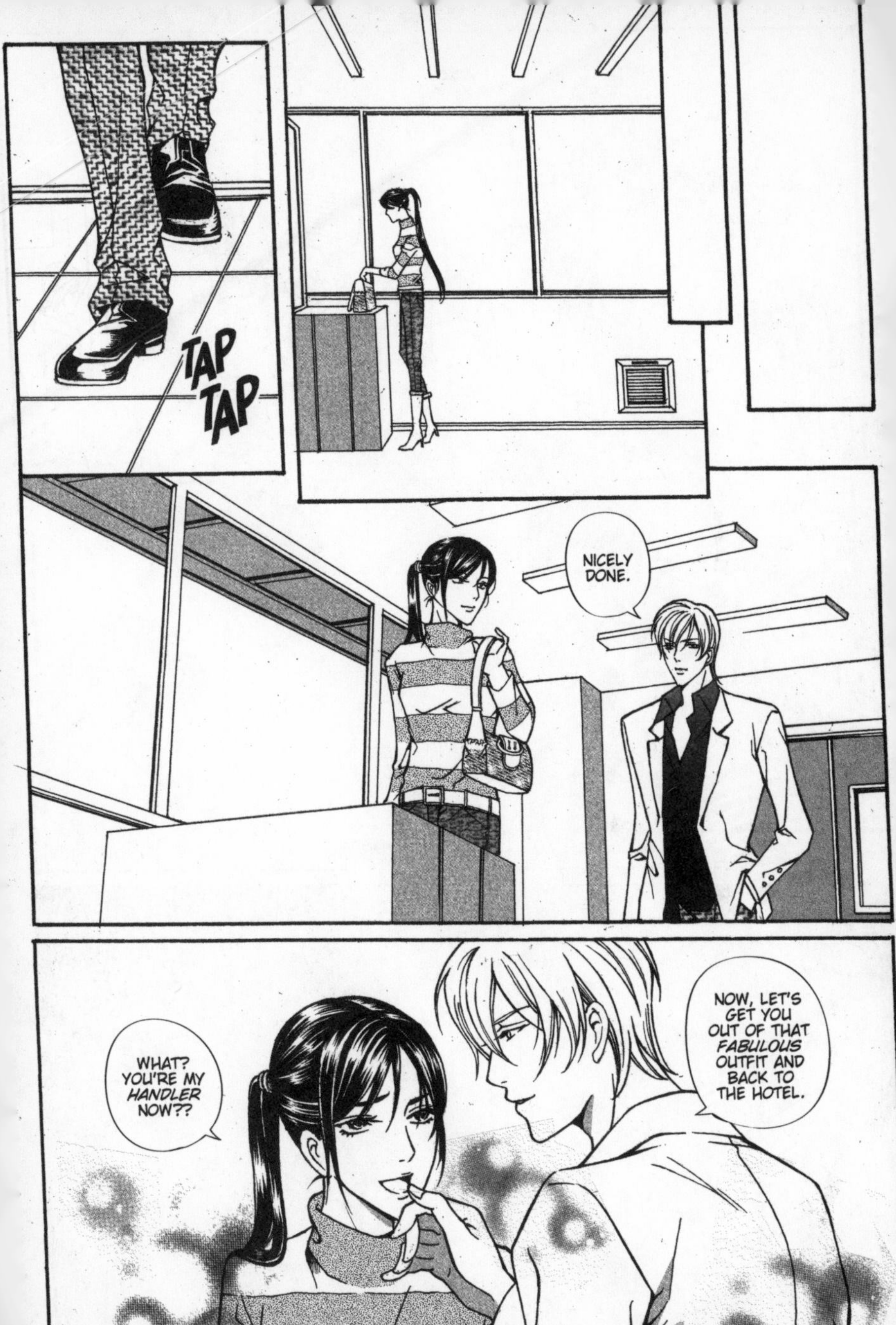
TAP TAP
NICELY DONE.
NOW, LET'S GET YOU OUT OF THAT *FABULOUS* OUTFIT AND BACK TO THE HOTEL.
WHAT? YOU'RE MY *HANDLER* NOW??

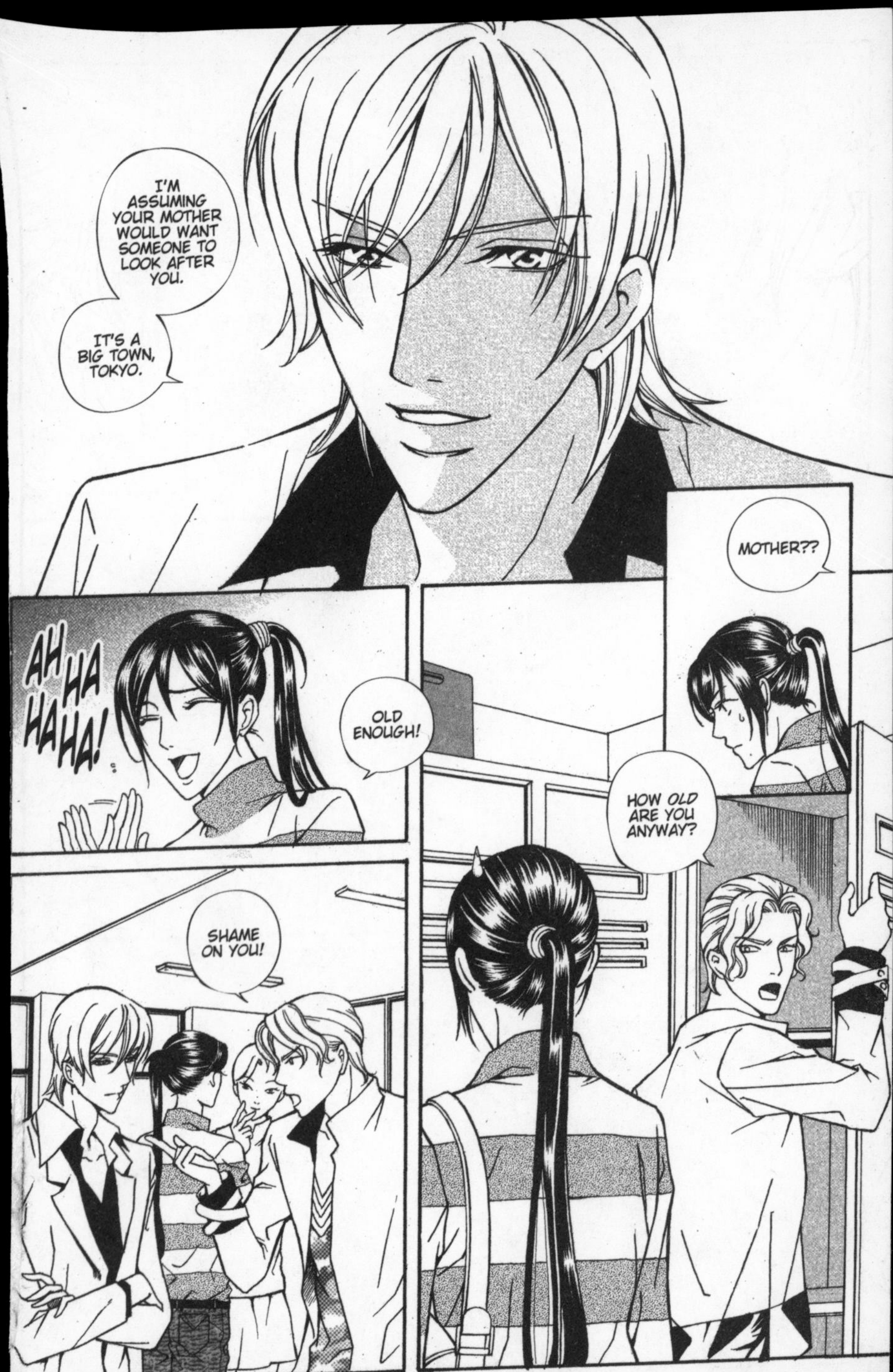
I'M ASSUMING YOUR MOTHER WOULD WANT SOMEONE TO LOOK AFTER YOU.
IT'S A BIG TOWN, TOKYO.
MOTHER??
HOW OLD ARE YOU ANYWAY?
AH HA HA HA!
OLD ENOUGH!
SHAME ON YOU!

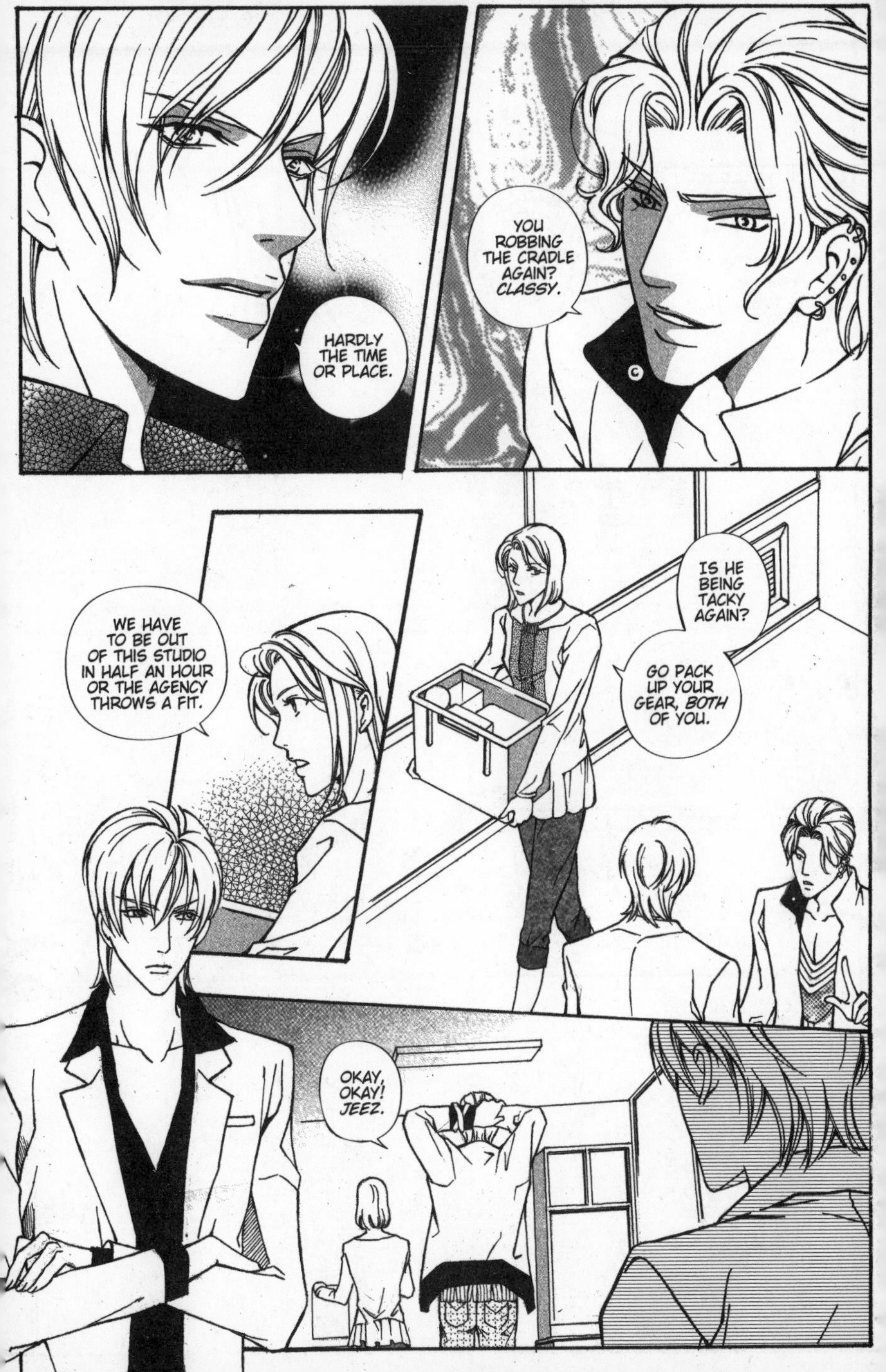

YOU ROBBING THE CRADLE AGAIN? *CLASSY*.
HARDLY THE TIME OR PLACE.
IS HE BEING TACKY AGAIN?
GO PACK UP YOUR GEAR, *BOTH* OF YOU.
WE HAVE TO BE OUT OF THIS STUDIO IN HALF AN HOUR OR THE AGENCY THROWS A FIT.
OKAY, OKAY! JEEZ.

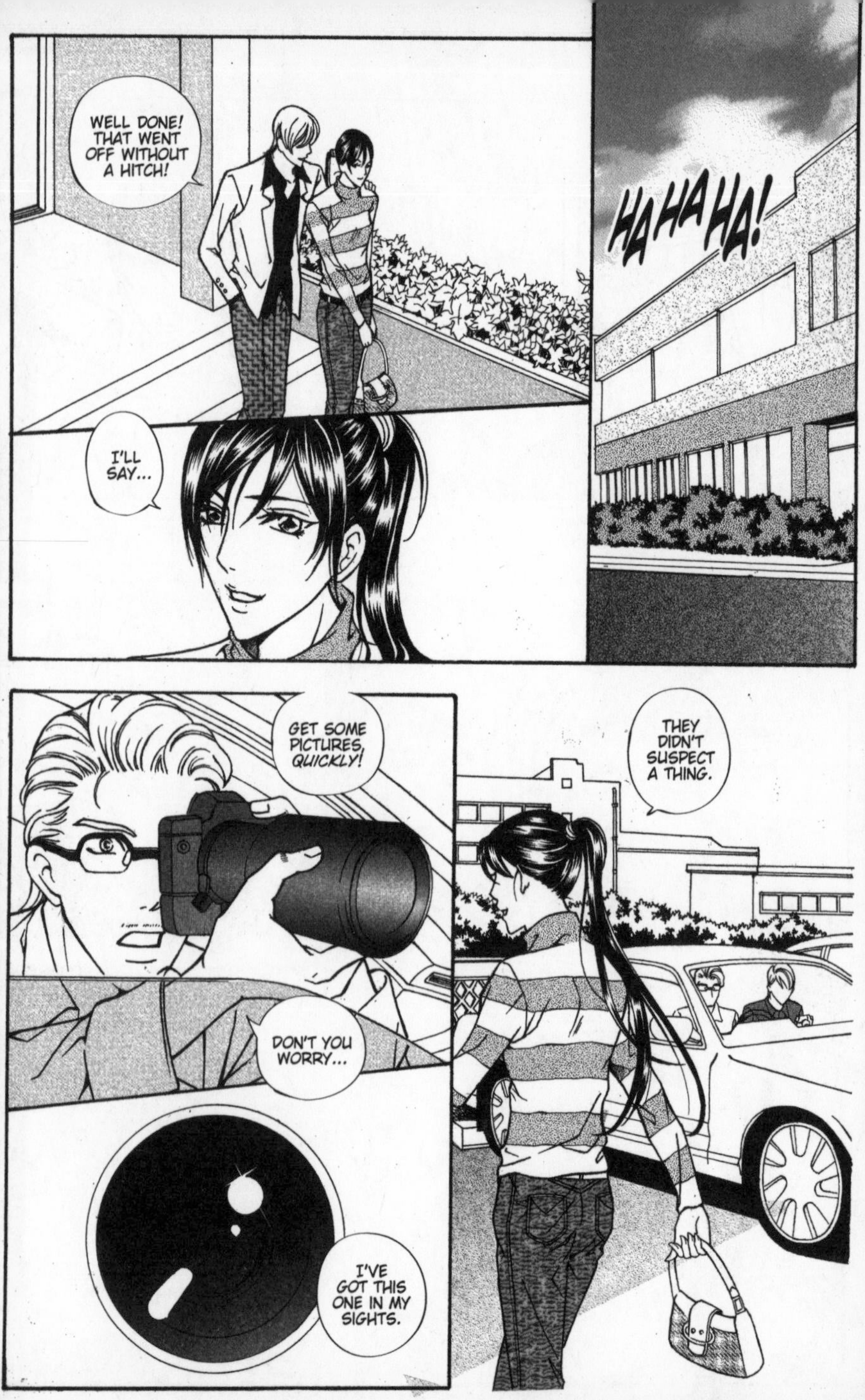
HA HA HA!
WELL DONE! THAT WENT OFF WITHOUT A HITCH!
I'LL SAY...
THEY DIDN'T SUSPECT A THING.
GET SOME PICTURES, QUICKLY!
DON'T YOU WORRY...
I'VE GOT THIS ONE IN MY SIGHTS.

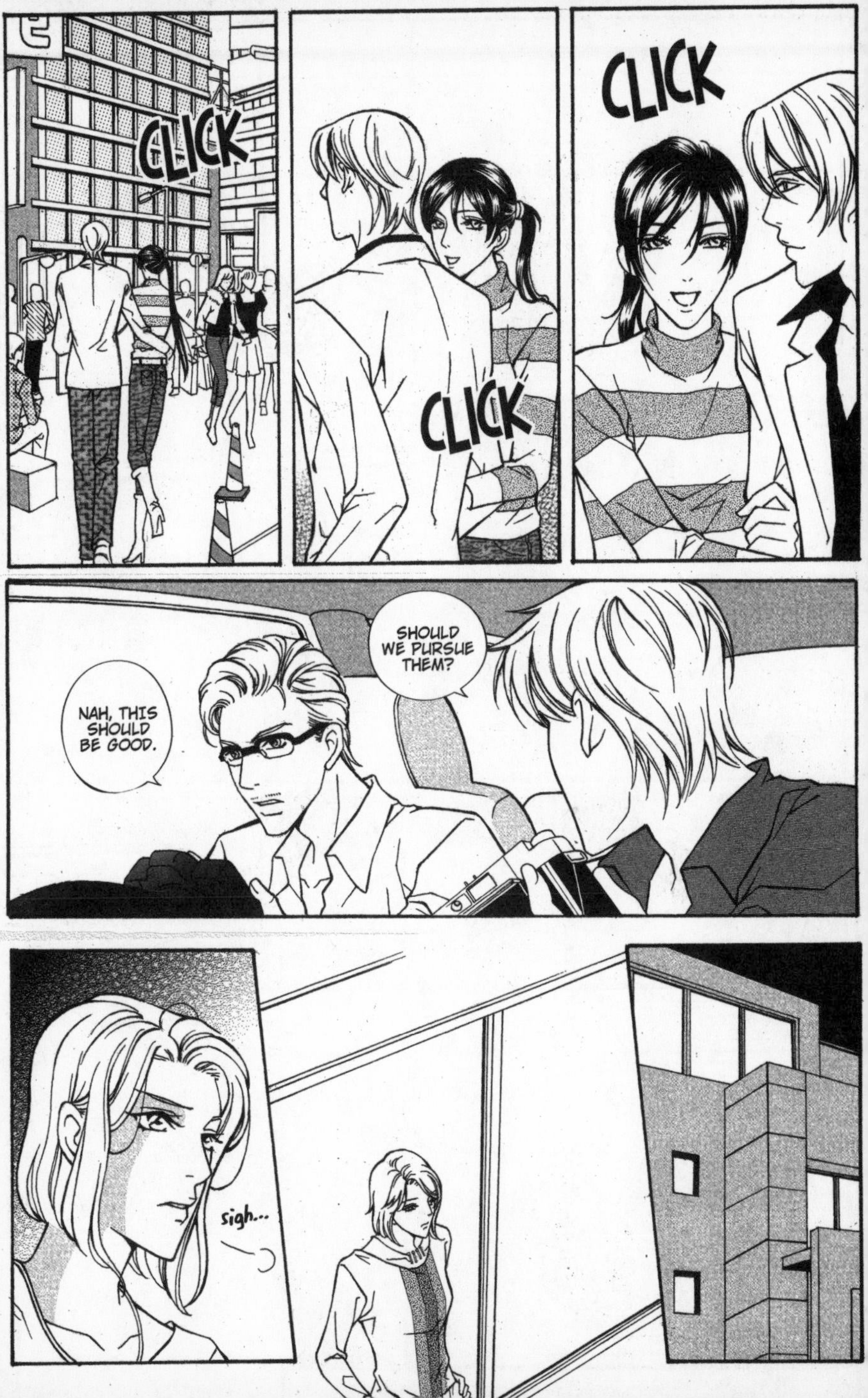
CLICK
CLICK
CLICK
SHOULD WE PURSUE THEM?
NAH, THIS SHOULD BE GOOD.
sigh...

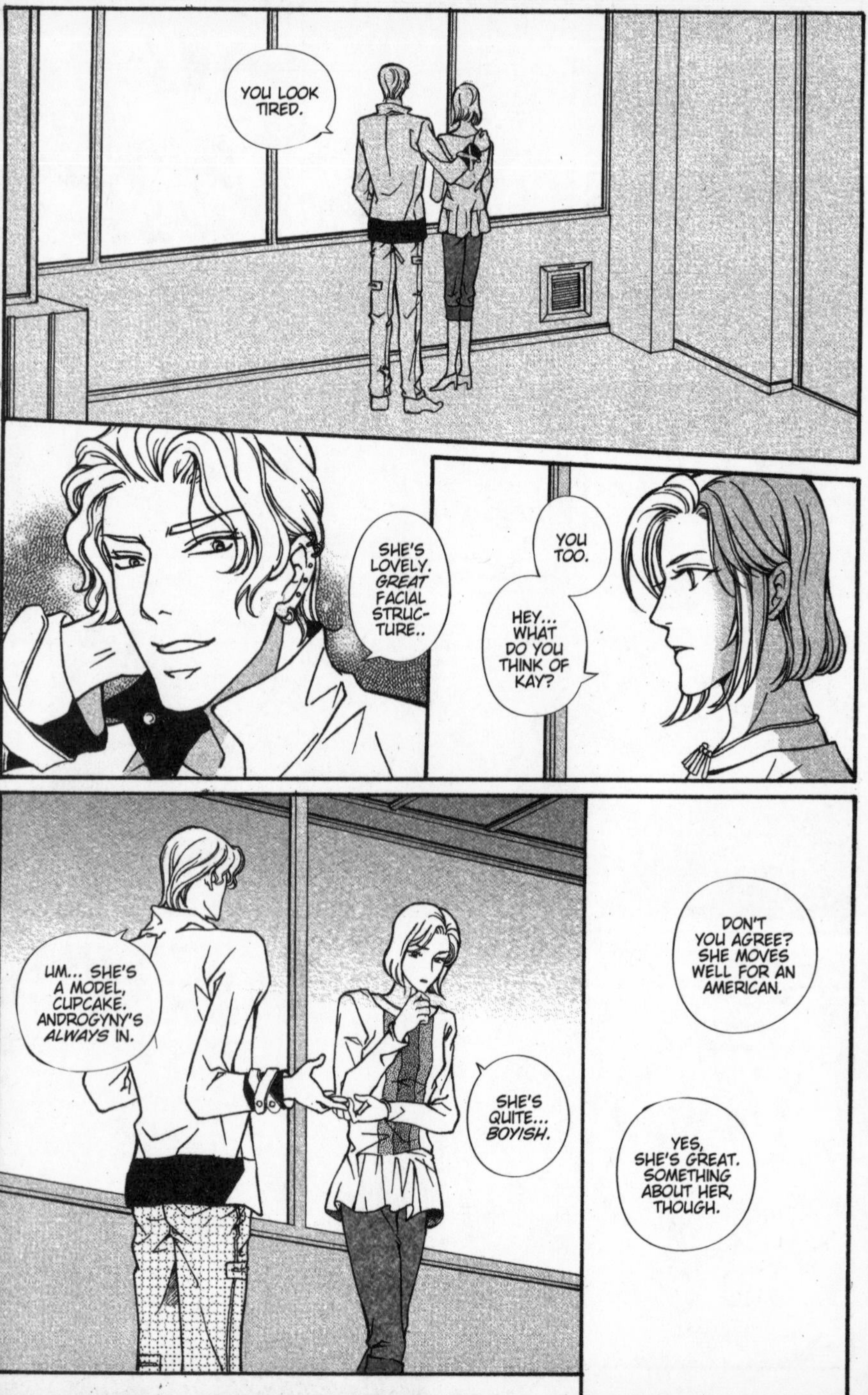
YOU LOOK TIRED.
YOU TOO.
HEY... WHAT DO YOU THINK OF KAY?
SHE'S LOVELY. *GREAT* FACIAL STRUCTURE..
DON'T YOU AGREE? SHE MOVES WELL FOR AN AMERICAN.
YES, SHE'S GREAT. SOMETHING ABOUT HER, THOUGH.
SHE'S QUITE... *BOYISH*.
UM... SHE'S A MODEL, CUPCAKE. ANDROGYNY'S *ALWAYS* IN.

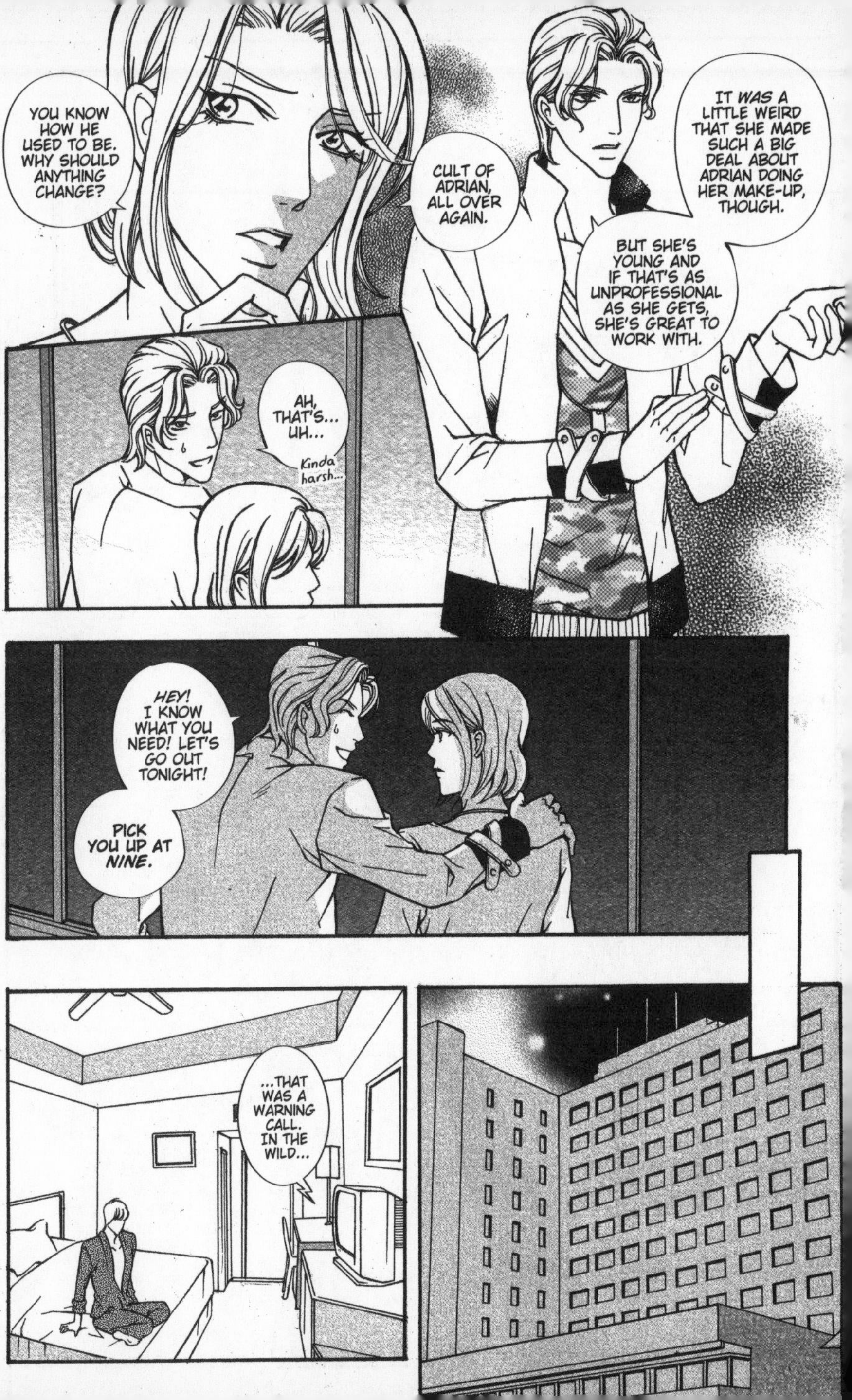
IT WAS A LITTLE WEIRD THAT SHE MADE SUCH A BIG DEAL ABOUT ADRIAN DOING HER MAKE-UP, THOUGH.
CULT OF ADRIAN, ALL OVER AGAIN.
BUT SHE'S YOUNG AND IF THAT'S AS UNPROFESSIONAL AS SHE GETS, SHE'S GREAT TO WORK WITH.
YOU KNOW HOW HE USED TO BE. WHY SHOULD ANYTHING CHANGE?
AH, THAT'S... UH...
Kinda harsh...
HEY! I KNOW WHAT YOU NEED! LET'S GO OUT TONIGHT!
PICK YOU UP AT NINE.
...THAT WAS A WARNING CALL. IN THE WILD...

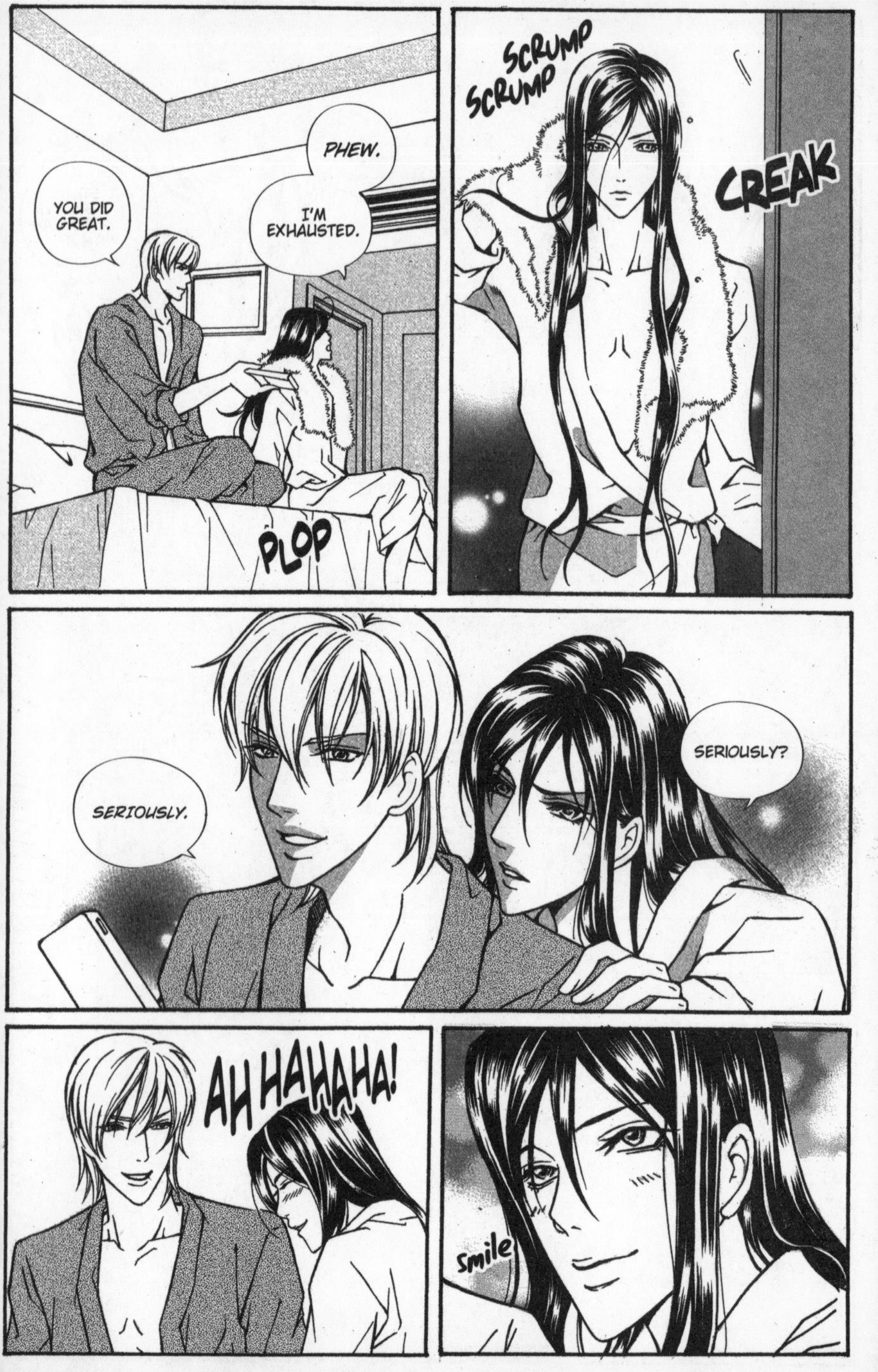
SCRUMP
SCRUMP
CREAK
PHEW.
I'M EXHAUSTED.
YOU DID GREAT.
PLOP
SERIOUSLY?
SERIOUSLY.
Smile
AH HAHAHA!

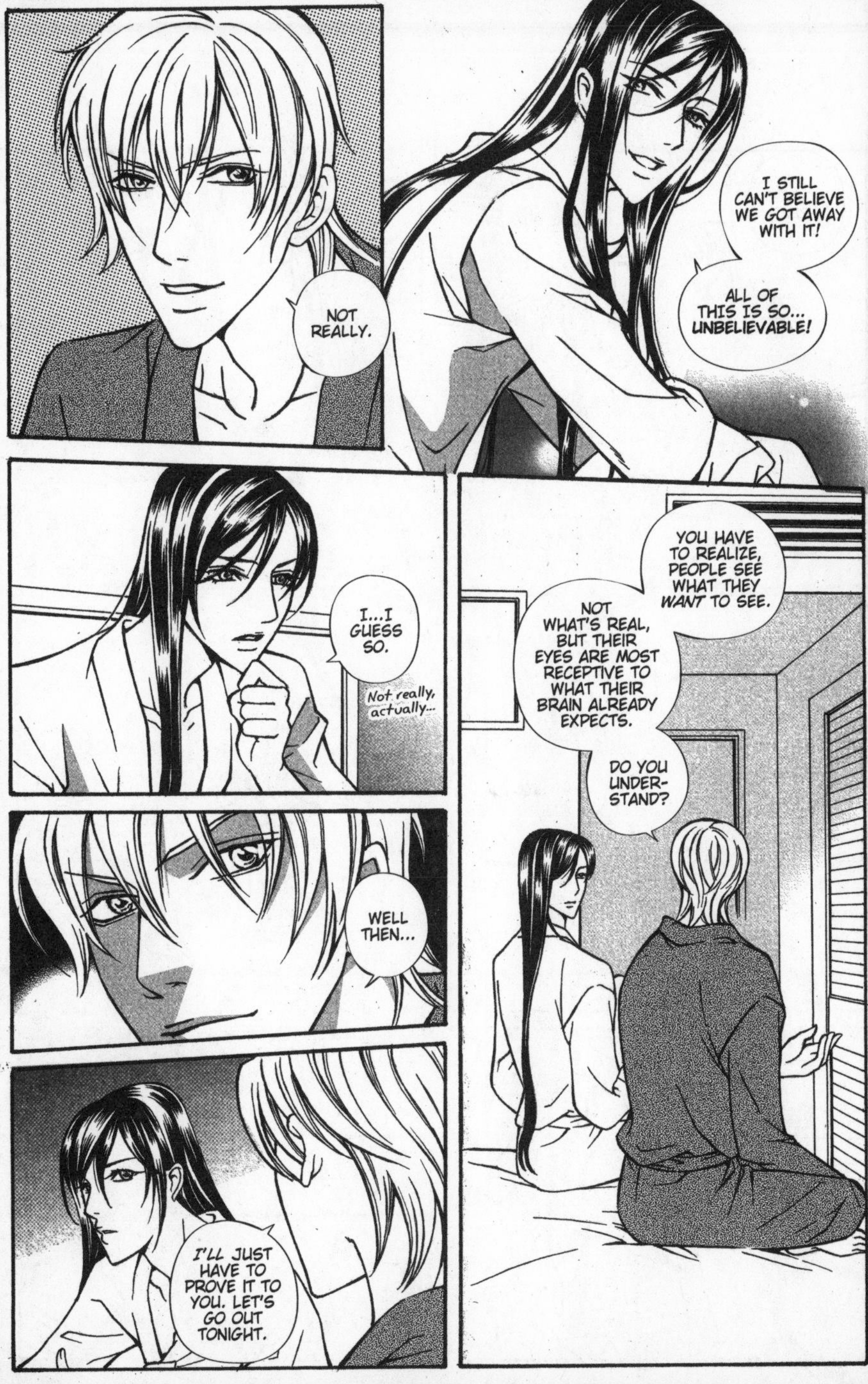
I STILL CAN'T BELIEVE WE GOT AWAY WITH IT!
ALL OF THIS IS SO... UNBELIEVABLE!
NOT REALLY.
YOU HAVE TO REALIZE, PEOPLE SEE WHAT THEY *WANT* TO SEE.
NOT WHAT'S REAL, BUT THEIR EYES ARE MOST RECEPTIVE TO WHAT THEIR BRAIN ALREADY EXPECTS.
DO YOU UNDER-STAND?
I...I GUESS SO.
Not really, actually...
WELL THEN...
I'LL JUST HAVE TO PROVE IT TO YOU. LET'S GO OUT TONIGHT.

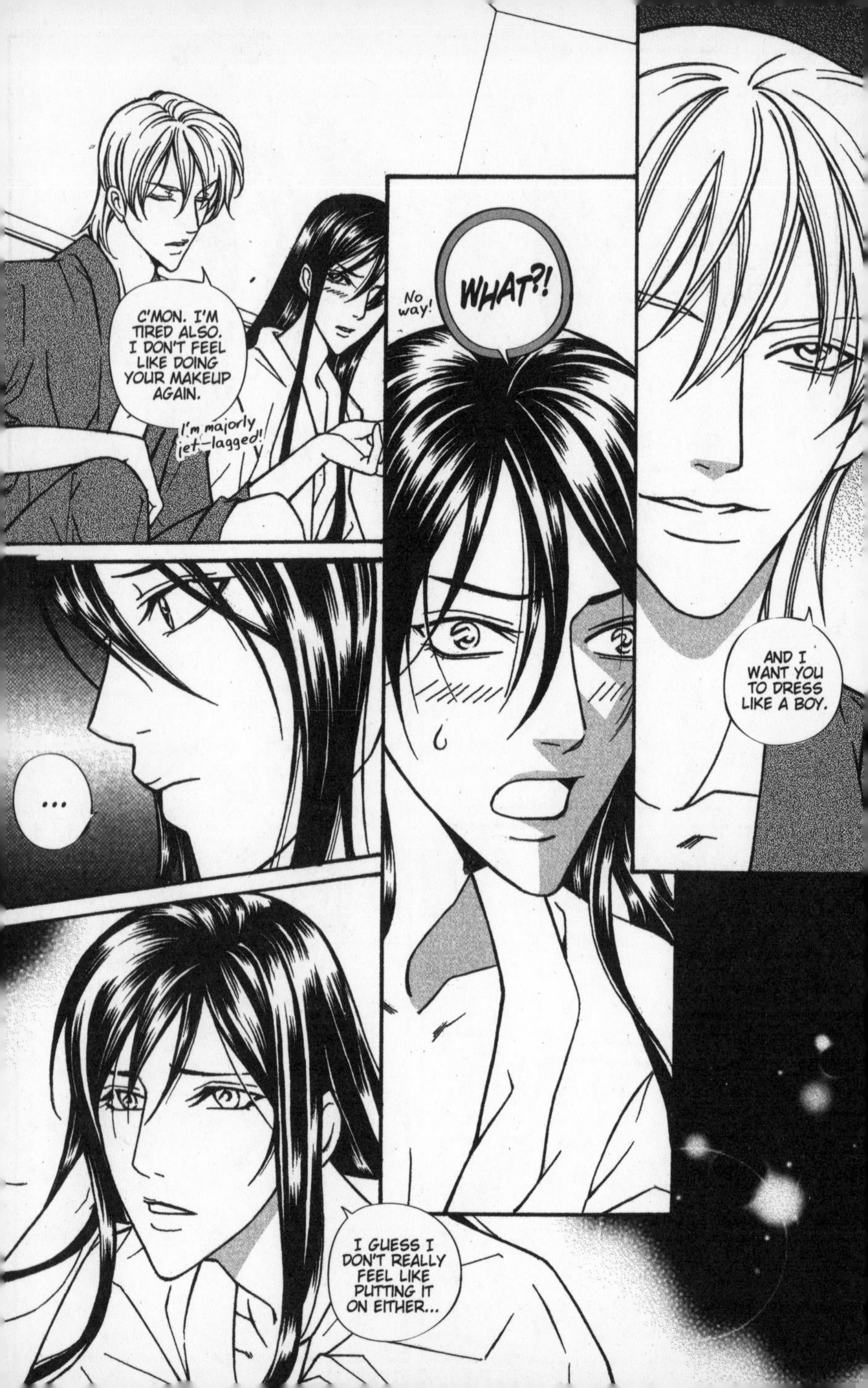
C'MON. I'M TIRED ALSO. I DON'T FEEL LIKE DOING YOUR MAKEUP AGAIN.
I'm majorly jet-lagged!
...
I GUESS I DON'T REALLY FEEL LIKE PUTTING IT ON EITHER...
AND I WANT YOU TO DRESS LIKE A BOY.
WHAT?!
No way!

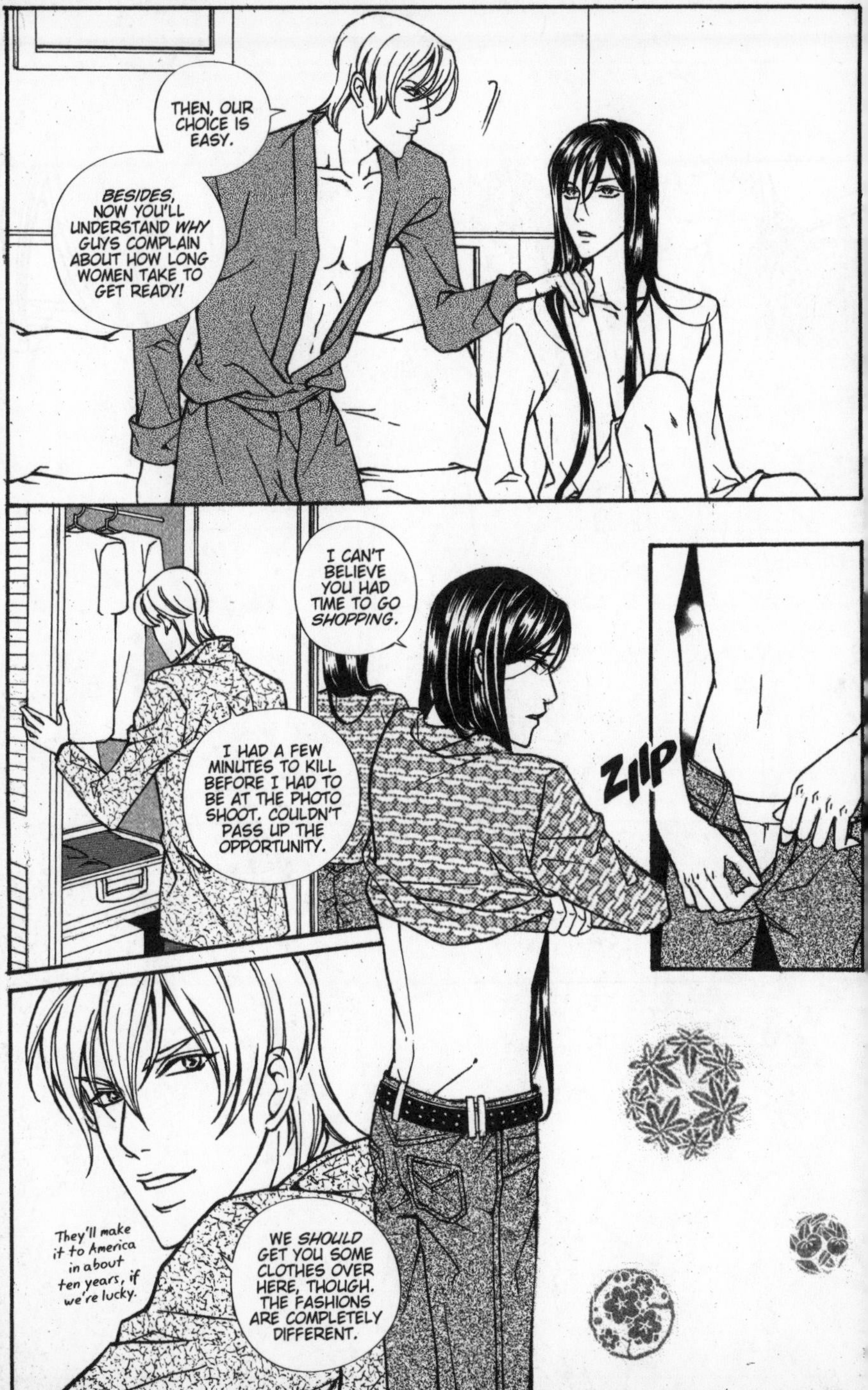
THEN, OUR CHOICE IS EASY.
BESIDES, NOW YOU'LL UNDERSTAND *WHY* GUYS COMPLAIN ABOUT HOW LONG WOMEN TAKE TO GET READY!
ZIIP
I CAN'T BELIEVE YOU HAD TIME TO GO *SHOPPING.*
I HAD A FEW MINUTES TO KILL BEFORE I HAD TO BE AT THE PHOTO SHOOT. COULDN'T PASS UP THE OPPORTUNITY.
WE *SHOULD* GET YOU SOME CLOTHES OVER HERE, THOUGH. THE FASHIONS ARE COMPLETELY DIFFERENT.
They'll make it to America in about ten years, if we're lucky.

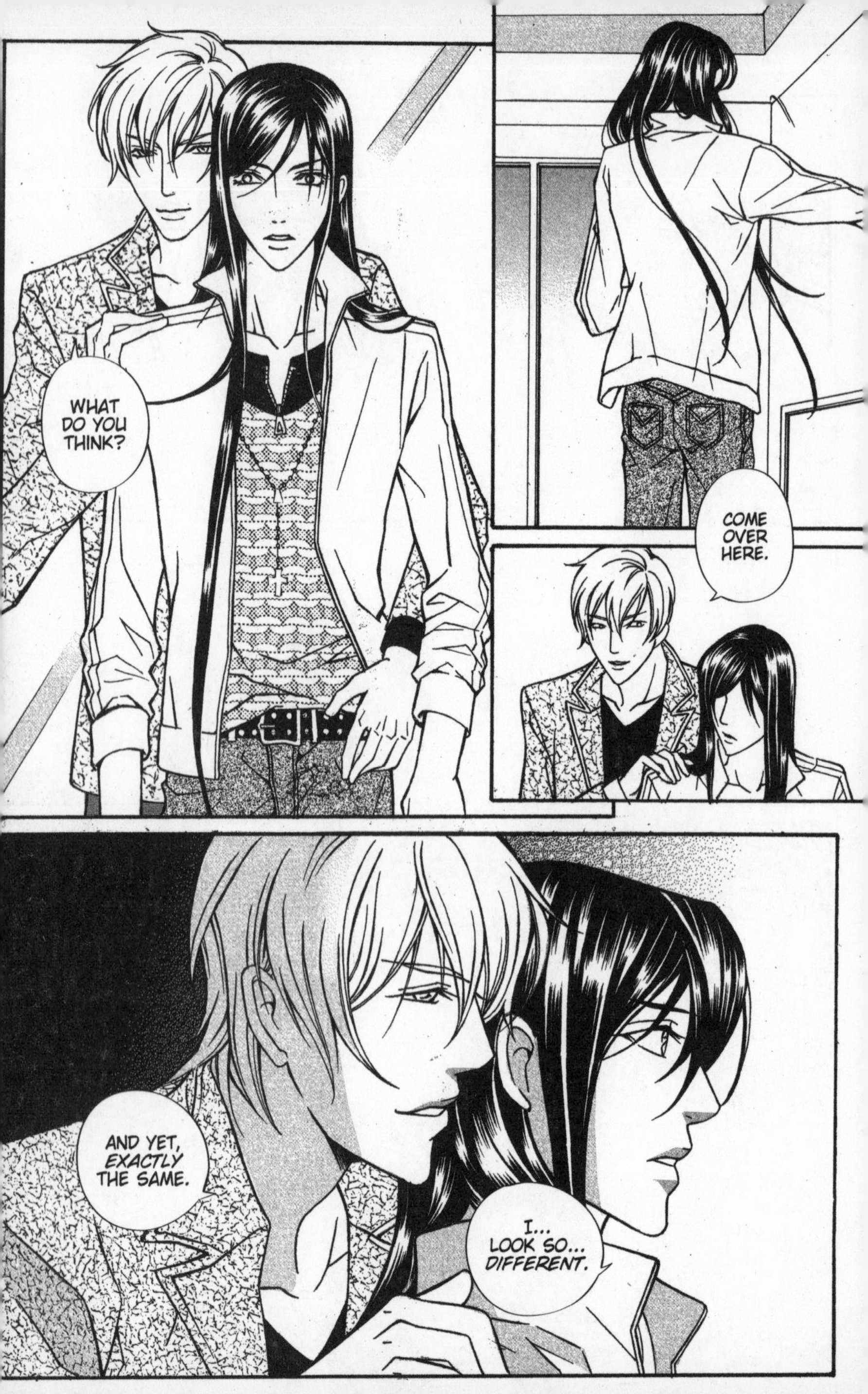
COME OVER HERE.
WHAT DO YOU THINK?
I... LOOK SO... *DIFFERENT*.
AND YET, *EXACTLY* THE SAME.

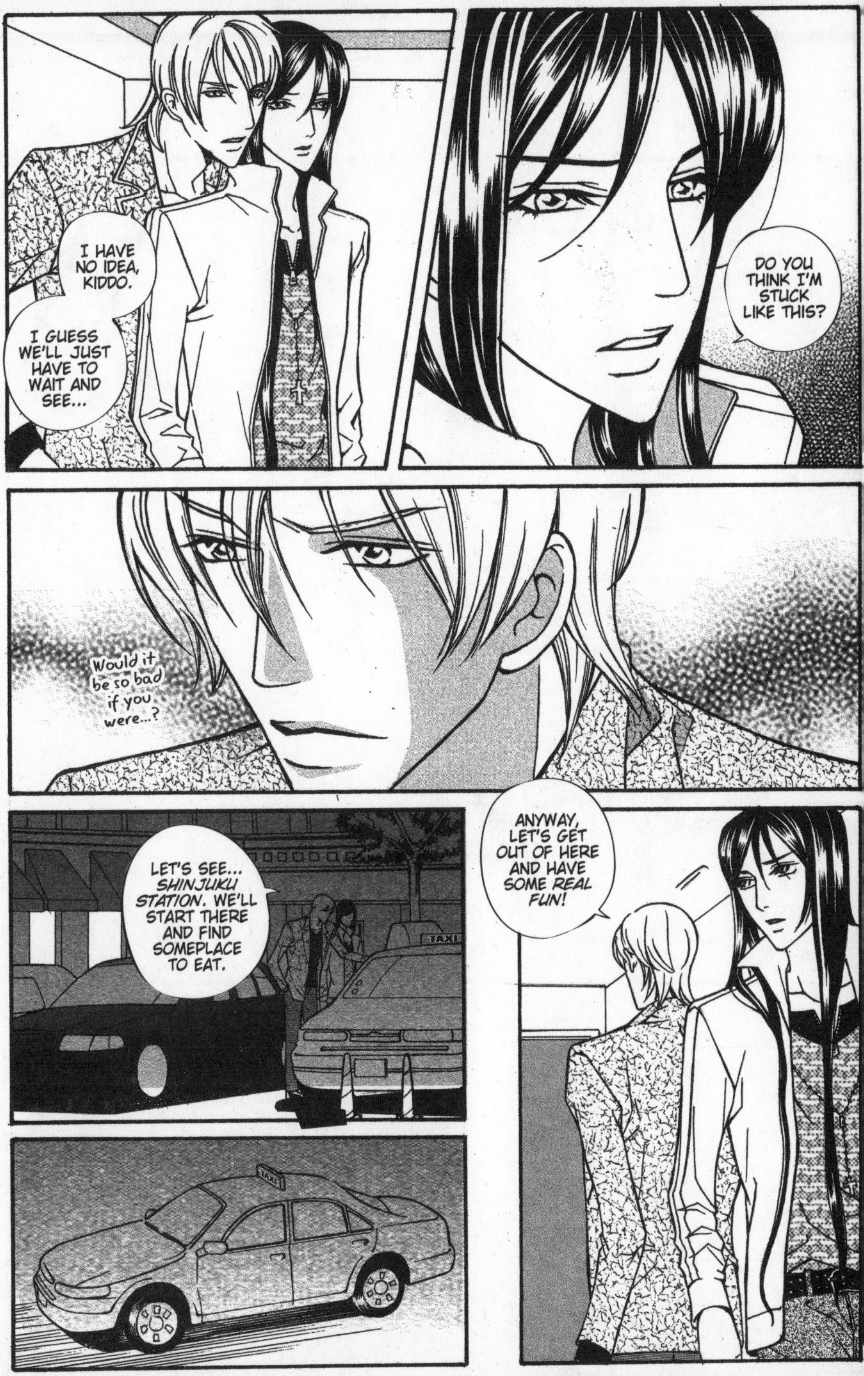
DO YOU THINK I'M STUCK LIKE THIS?
I HAVE NO IDEA, KIDDO.
I GUESS WE'LL JUST HAVE TO WAIT AND SEE...
Would it be so bad if you were...?
ANYWAY, LET'S GET OUT OF HERE AND HAVE SOME *REAL FUN*!
LET'S SEE... *SHINJUKU STATION*. WE'LL START THERE AND FIND SOMEPLACE TO EAT.
TAXI
TAXI

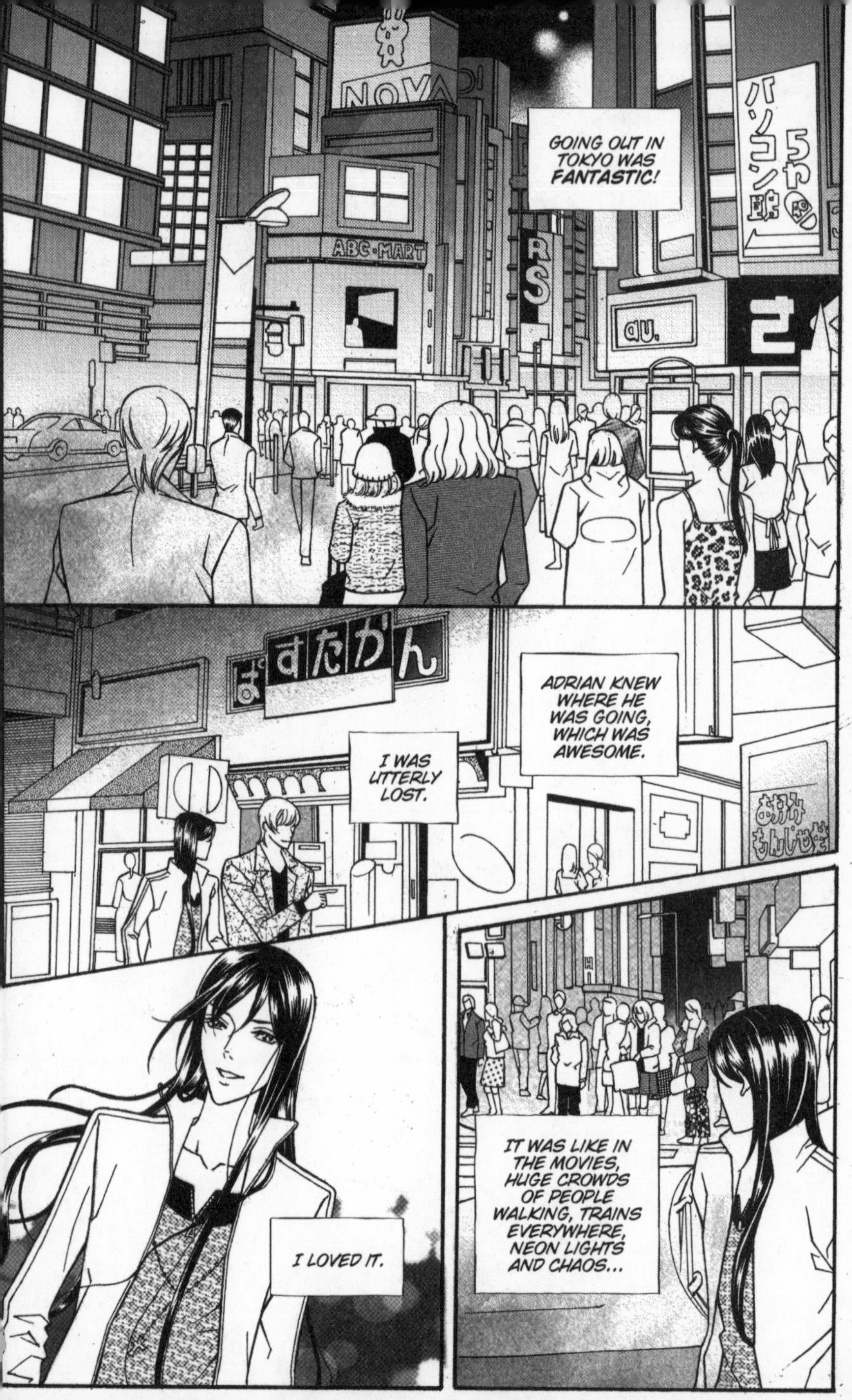
GOING OUT IN TOKYO WAS FANTASTIC!
NOVA
ABC-MART
au.
ADRIAN KNEW WHERE HE WAS GOING, WHICH WAS AWESOME.
I WAS UTTERLY LOST.
ぱすたかん
IT WAS LIKE IN THE MOVIES, HUGE CROWDS OF PEOPLE WALKING, TRAINS EVERYWHERE, NEON LIGHTS AND CHAOS...
I LOVED IT.

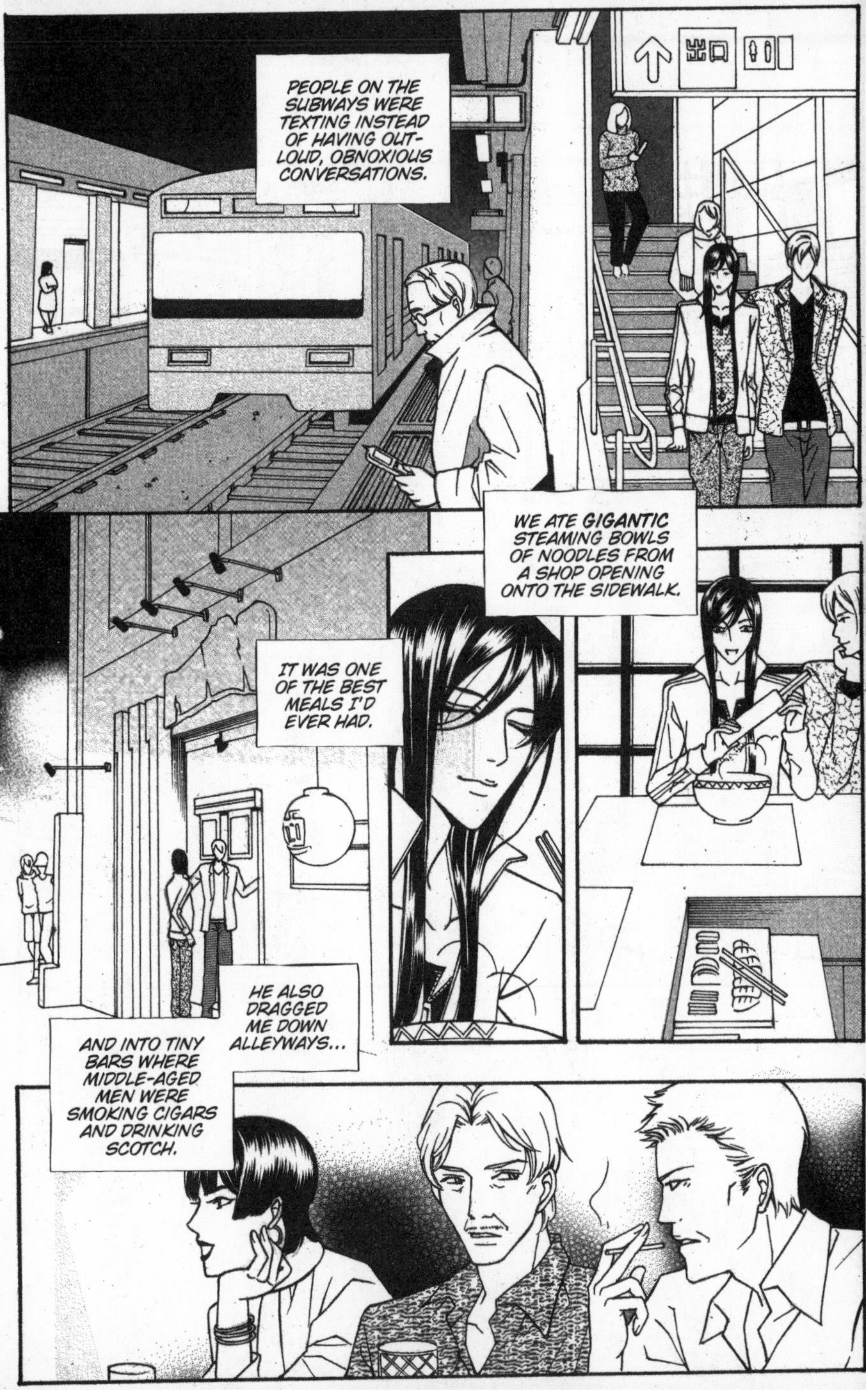
出口
PEOPLE ON THE SUBWAYS WERE TEXTING INSTEAD OF HAVING OUT-LOUD, OBNOXIOUS CONVERSATIONS.
WE ATE **GIGANTIC** STEAMING BOWLS OF NOODLES FROM A SHOP OPENING ONTO THE SIDEWALK.
IT WAS ONE OF THE BEST MEALS I'D EVER HAD.
HE ALSO DRAGGED ME DOWN ALLEYWAYS...
AND INTO TINY BARS WHERE MIDDLE-AGED MEN WERE SMOKING CIGARS AND DRINKING SCOTCH.

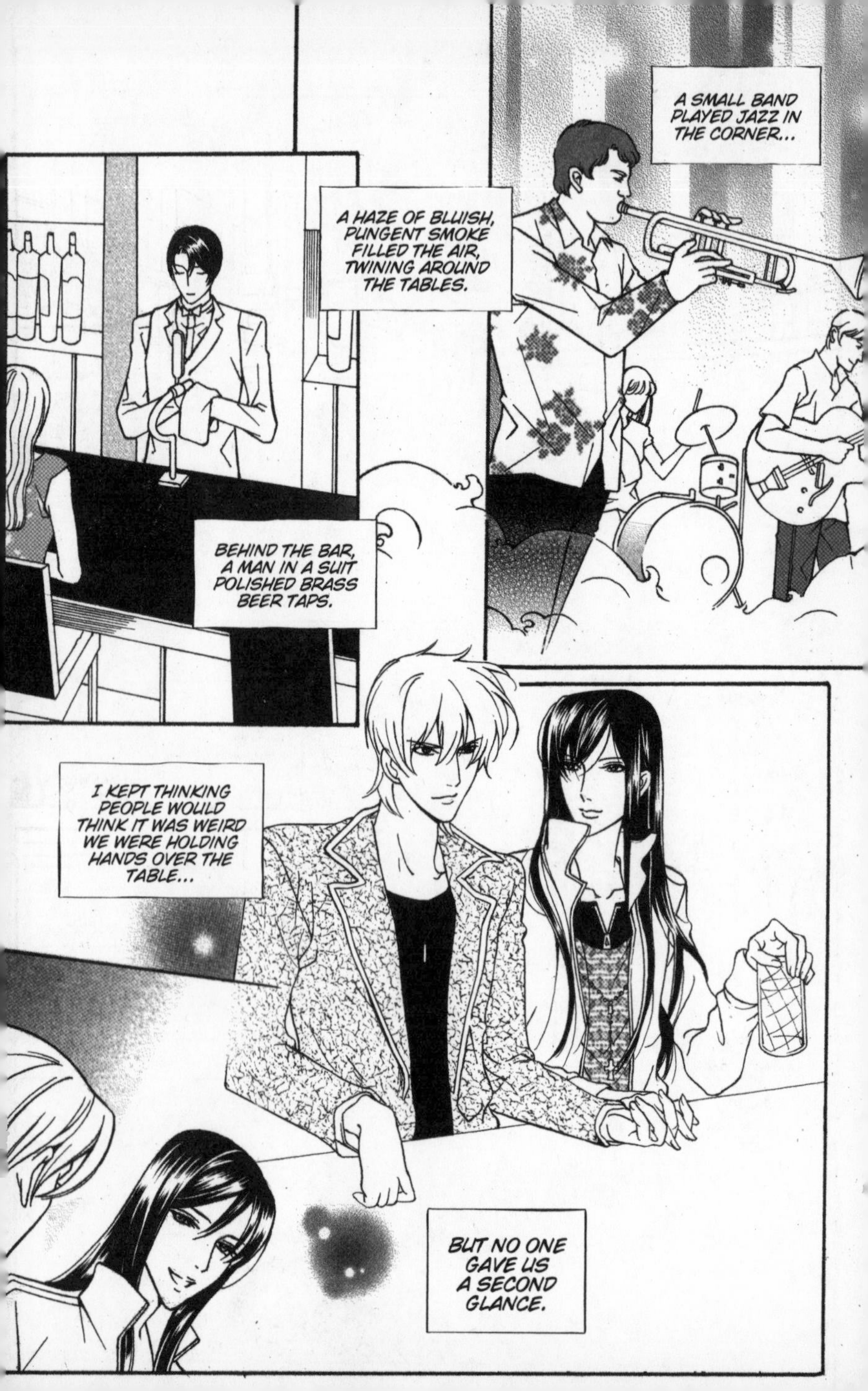
A SMALL BAND PLAYED JAZZ IN THE CORNER...
A HAZE OF BLUISH, PUNGENT SMOKE FILLED THE AIR, TWINING AROUND THE TABLES.
BEHIND THE BAR, A MAN IN A SUIT POLISHED BRASS BEER TAPS.
I KEPT THINKING PEOPLE WOULD THINK IT WAS WEIRD WE WERE HOLDING HANDS OVER THE TABLE...
BUT NO ONE GAVE US A SECOND GLANCE.

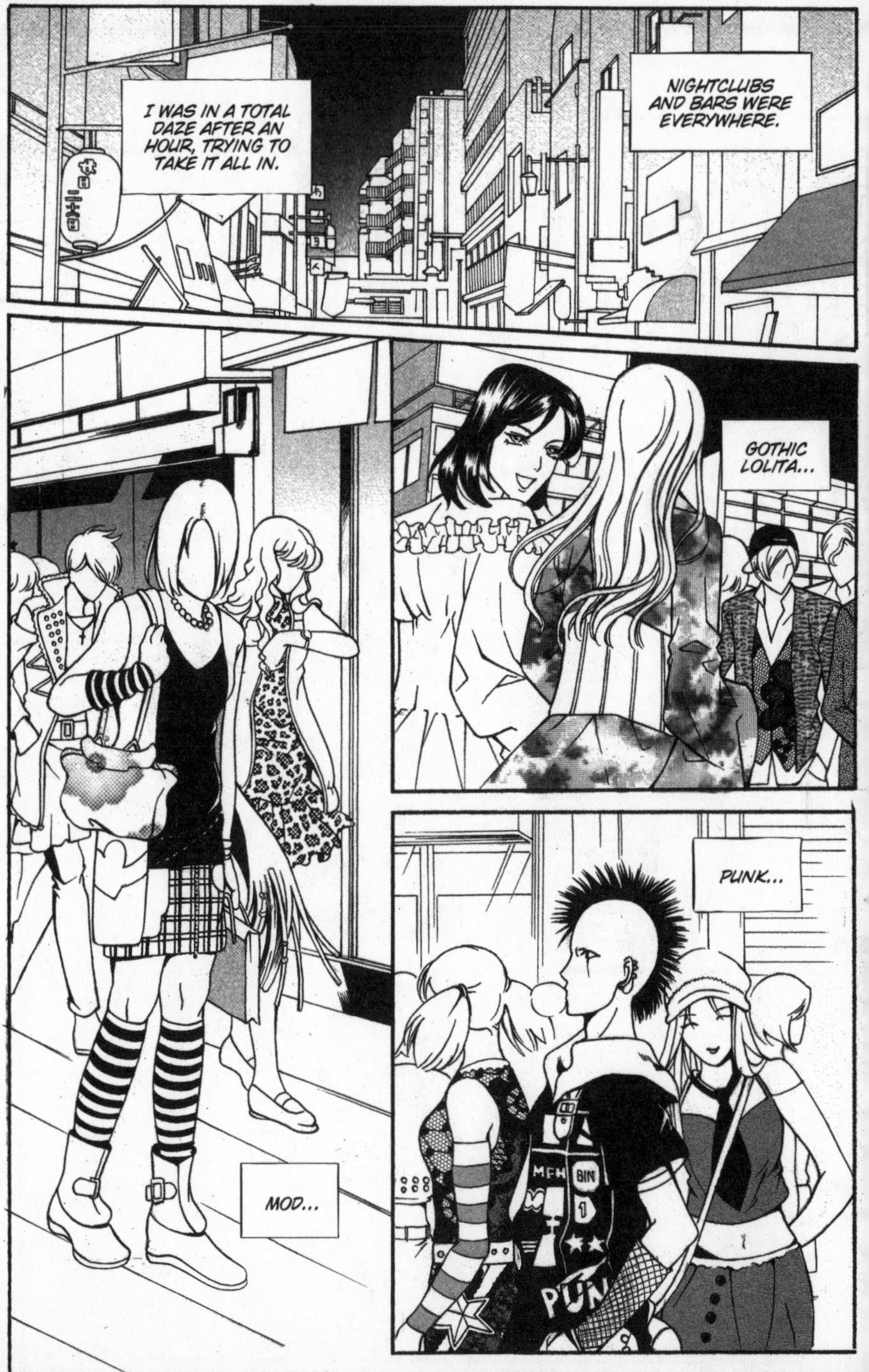
NIGHTCLUBS AND BARS WERE EVERYWHERE.
I WAS IN A TOTAL DAZE AFTER AN HOUR, TRYING TO TAKE IT ALL IN.
GOTHIC LOLITA...
PUNK...
MOD...

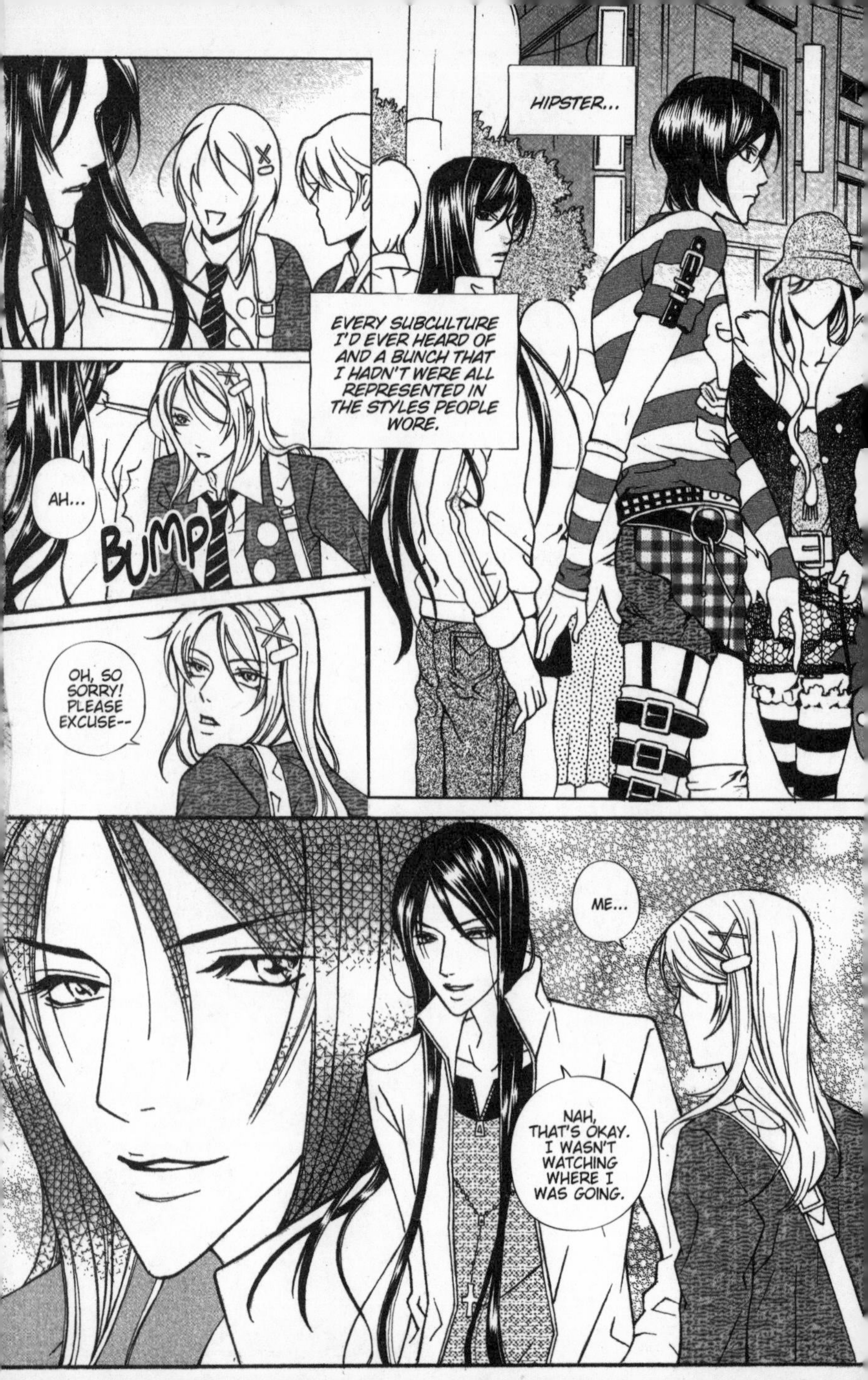
HIPSTER...
EVERY SUBCULTURE I'D EVER HEARD OF AND A BUNCH THAT I HADN'T WERE ALL REPRESENTED IN THE STYLES PEOPLE WORE.
AH...
BUMP
OH, SO SORRY! PLEASE EXCUSE--
ME...
NAH, THAT'S OKAY. I WASN'T WATCHING WHERE I WAS GOING.

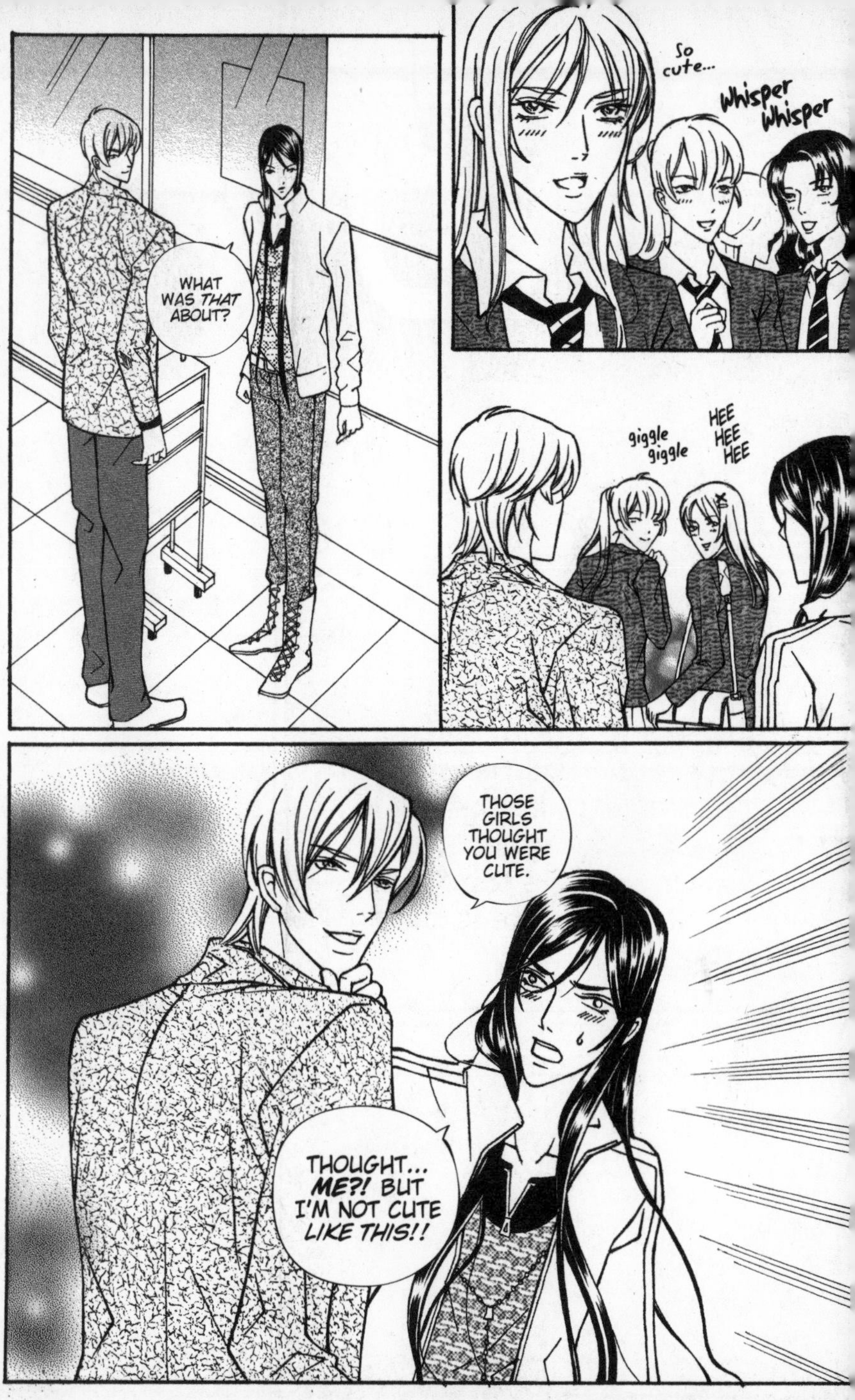
So cute...
Whisper Whisper
HEE HEE HEE
giggle giggle
WHAT WAS *THAT* ABOUT?
THOSE GIRLS THOUGHT YOU WERE CUTE.
THOUGHT... ***ME?!*** BUT I'M NOT CUTE *LIKE THIS!!*

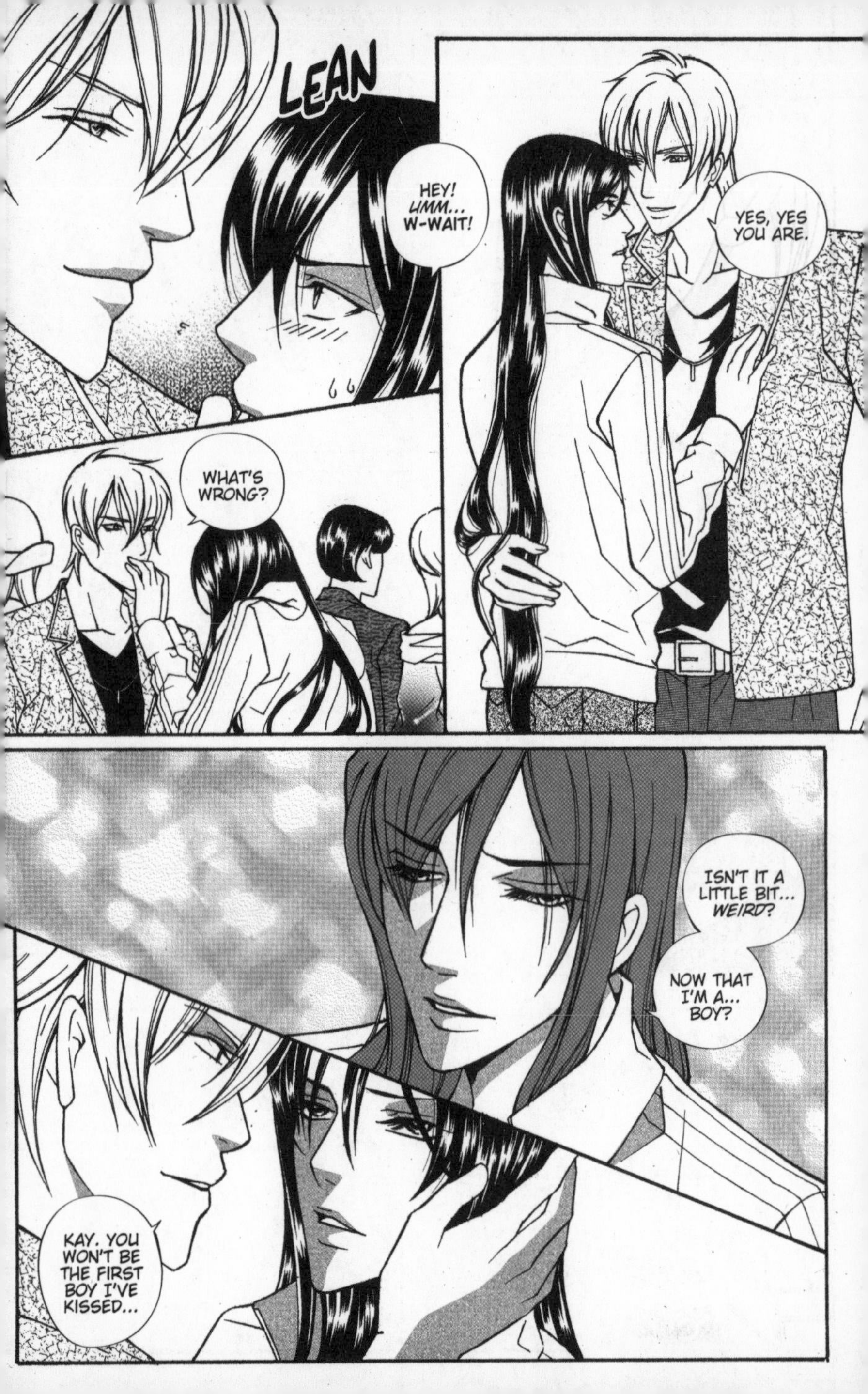
YES, YES YOU ARE.
LEAN
HEY! UMM... W-WAIT!
WHAT'S WRONG?
ISN'T IT A LITTLE BIT... WEIRD?
NOW THAT I'M A... BOY?
KAY. YOU WON'T BE THE FIRST BOY I'VE KISSED...

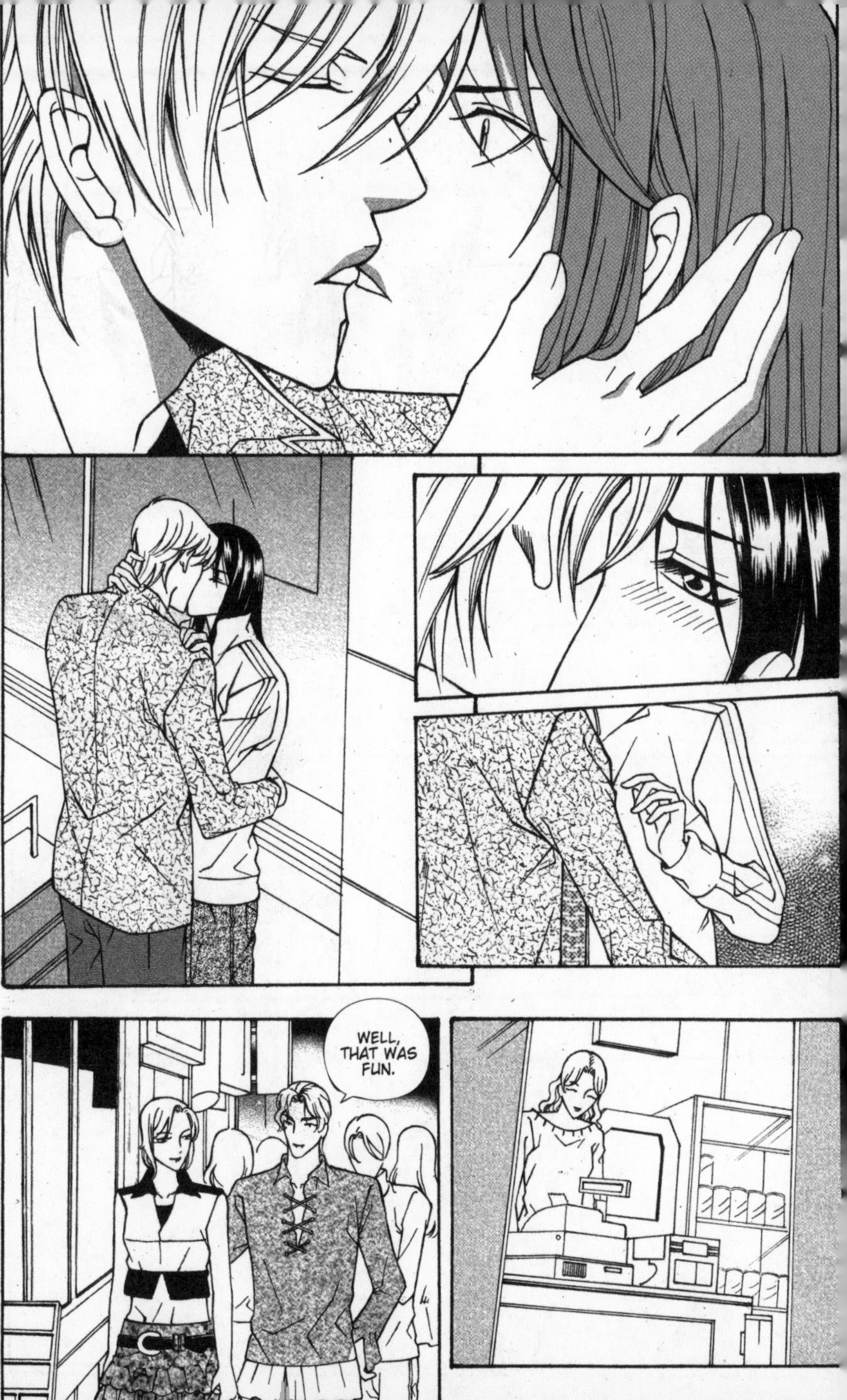
WELL, THAT WAS FUN.

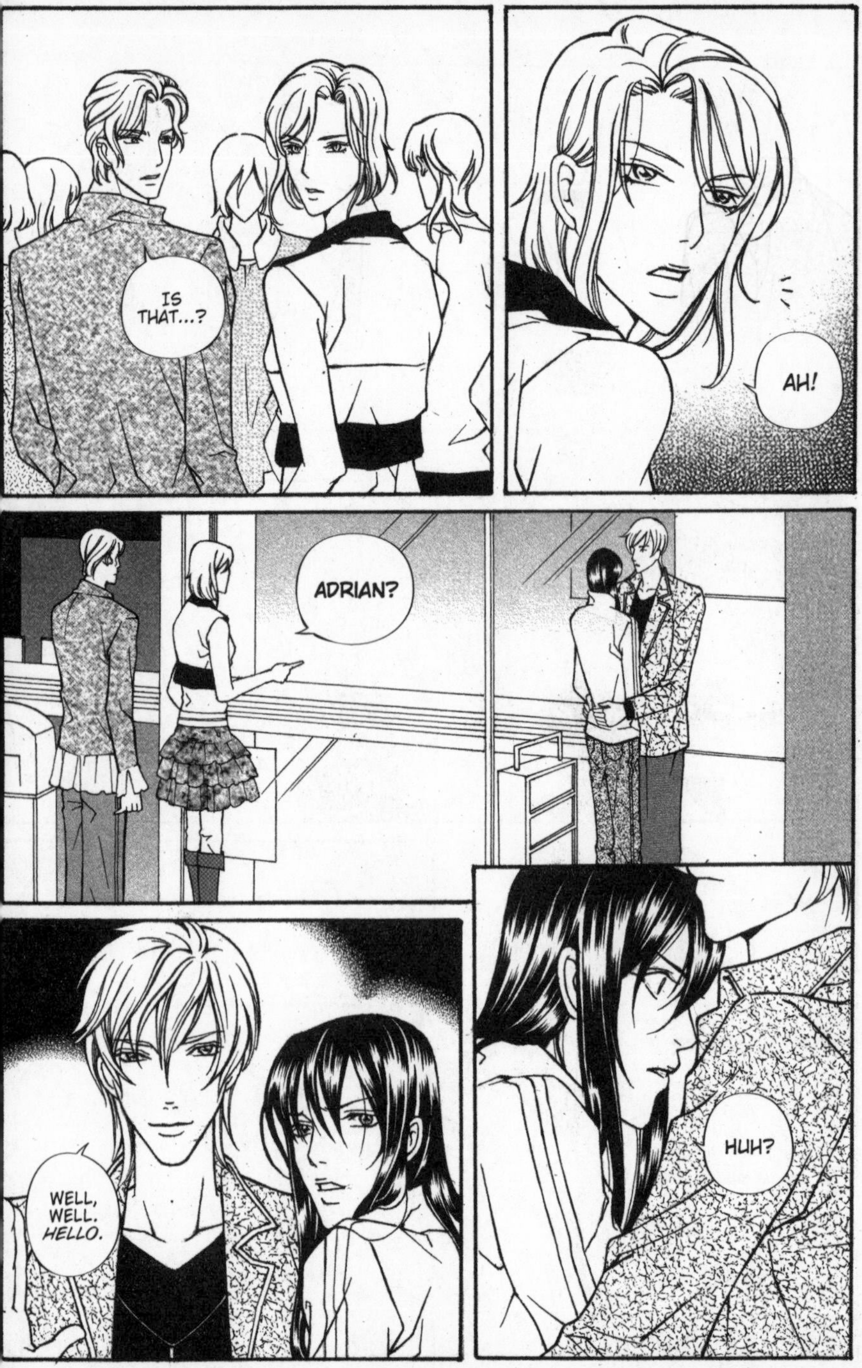
AH!
IS THAT...?
ADRIAN?
HUH?
WELL, WELL. *HELLO.*

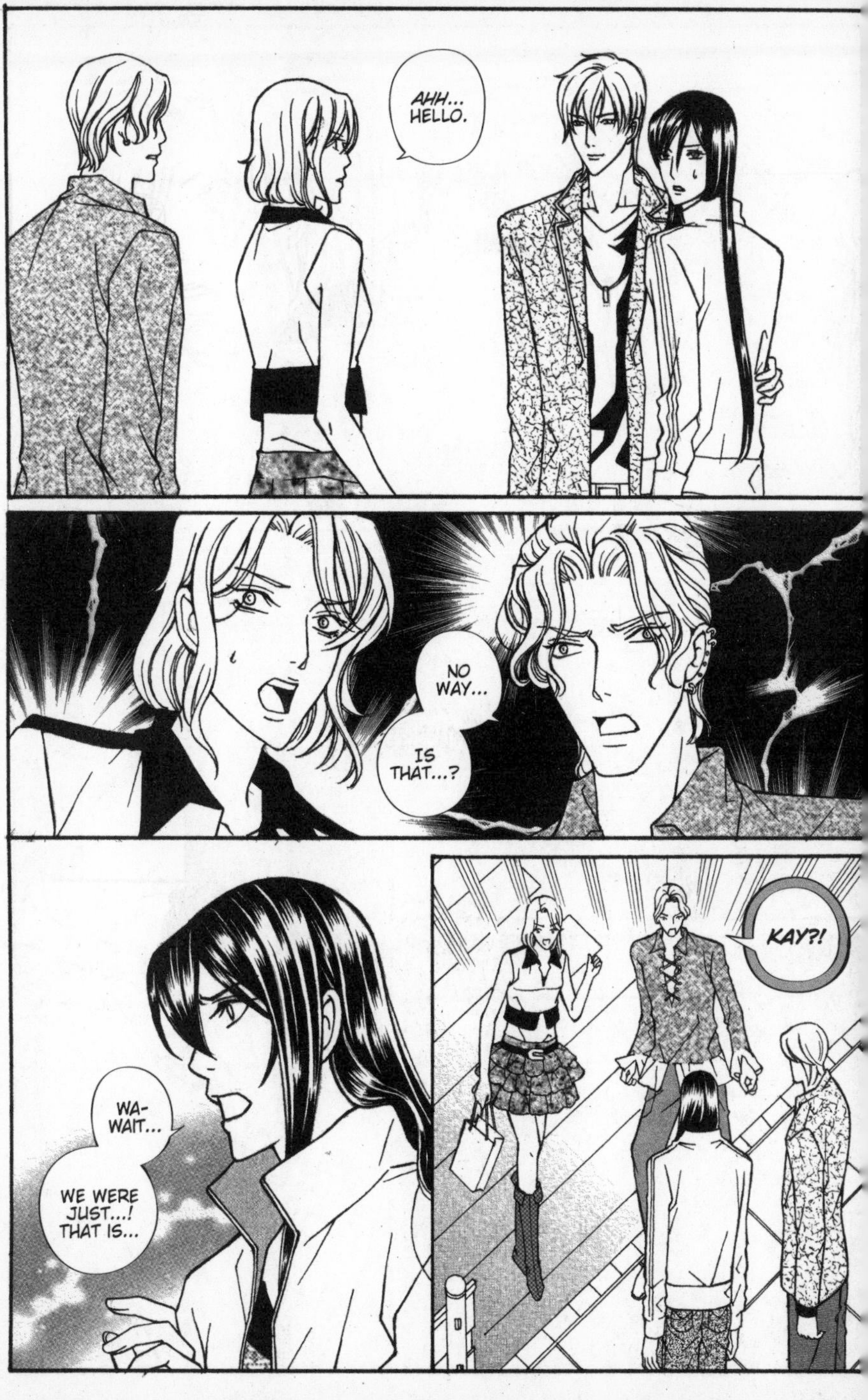
AHH... HELLO.
NO WAY...
IS THAT...?
KAY?!
WA-WAIT...
WE WERE JUST...! THAT IS...

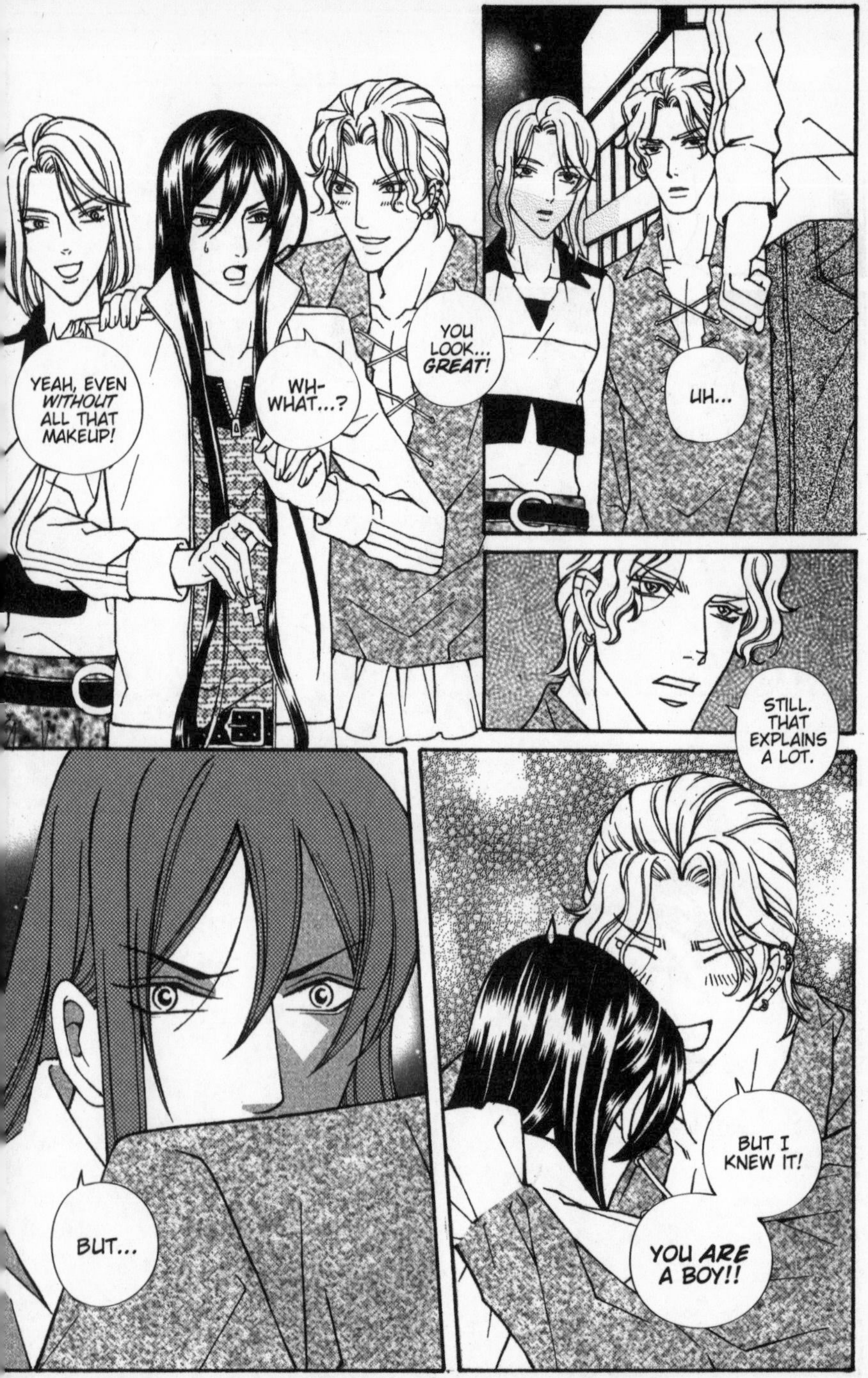
UH...
STILL. THAT EXPLAINS A LOT.
YOU LOOK... *GREAT*!
WH-WHAT...?
YEAH, EVEN *WITHOUT* ALL THAT MAKEUP!
BUT I KNEW IT!
YOU *ARE* A BOY!!
BUT...

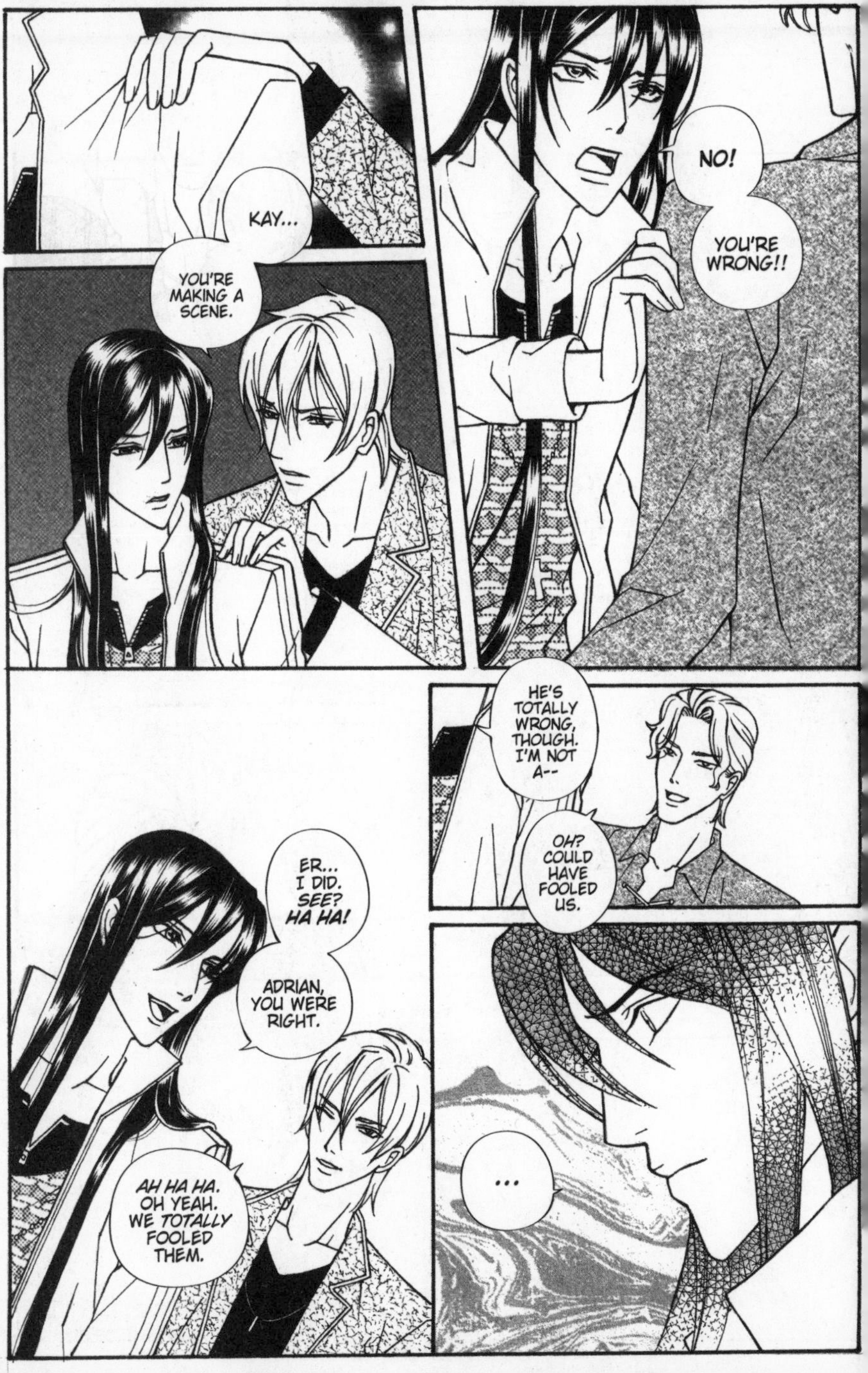
NO!
YOU'RE WRONG!!
KAY...
YOU'RE MAKING A SCENE.
HE'S TOTALLY WRONG, THOUGH. I'M NOT A--
OH? COULD HAVE FOOLED US.
...
ER... I DID. SEE? *HA HA!*
ADRIAN, YOU WERE RIGHT.
AH HA HA. OH YEAH. WE *TOTALLY* FOOLED THEM.

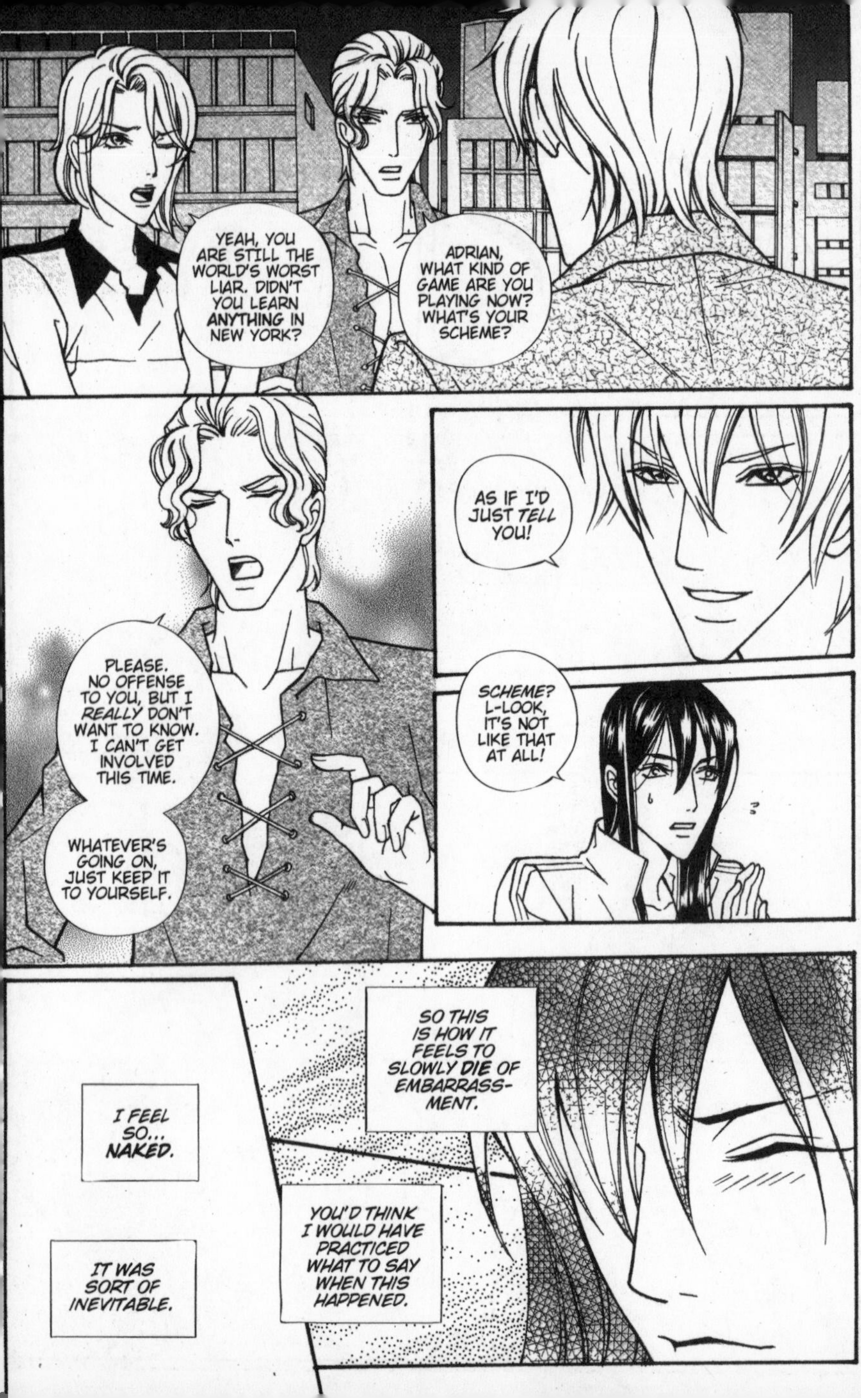
ADRIAN, WHAT KIND OF GAME ARE YOU PLAYING NOW? WHAT'S YOUR SCHEME?
YEAH, YOU ARE STILL THE WORLD'S WORST LIAR. DIDN'T YOU LEARN **ANYTHING** IN NEW YORK?
AS IF I'D JUST *TELL* YOU!
SCHEME? L-LOOK, IT'S NOT LIKE THAT AT ALL!
PLEASE. NO OFFENSE TO YOU, BUT I *REALLY* DON'T WANT TO KNOW. I CAN'T GET INVOLVED THIS TIME.
WHATEVER'S GOING ON, JUST KEEP IT TO YOURSELF.
*SO THIS IS HOW IT FEELS TO SLOWLY **DIE** OF EMBARRASS-MENT.*
*I FEEL SO... **NAKED**.*
YOU'D THINK I WOULD HAVE PRACTICED WHAT TO SAY WHEN THIS HAPPENED.
IT WAS SORT OF INEVITABLE.

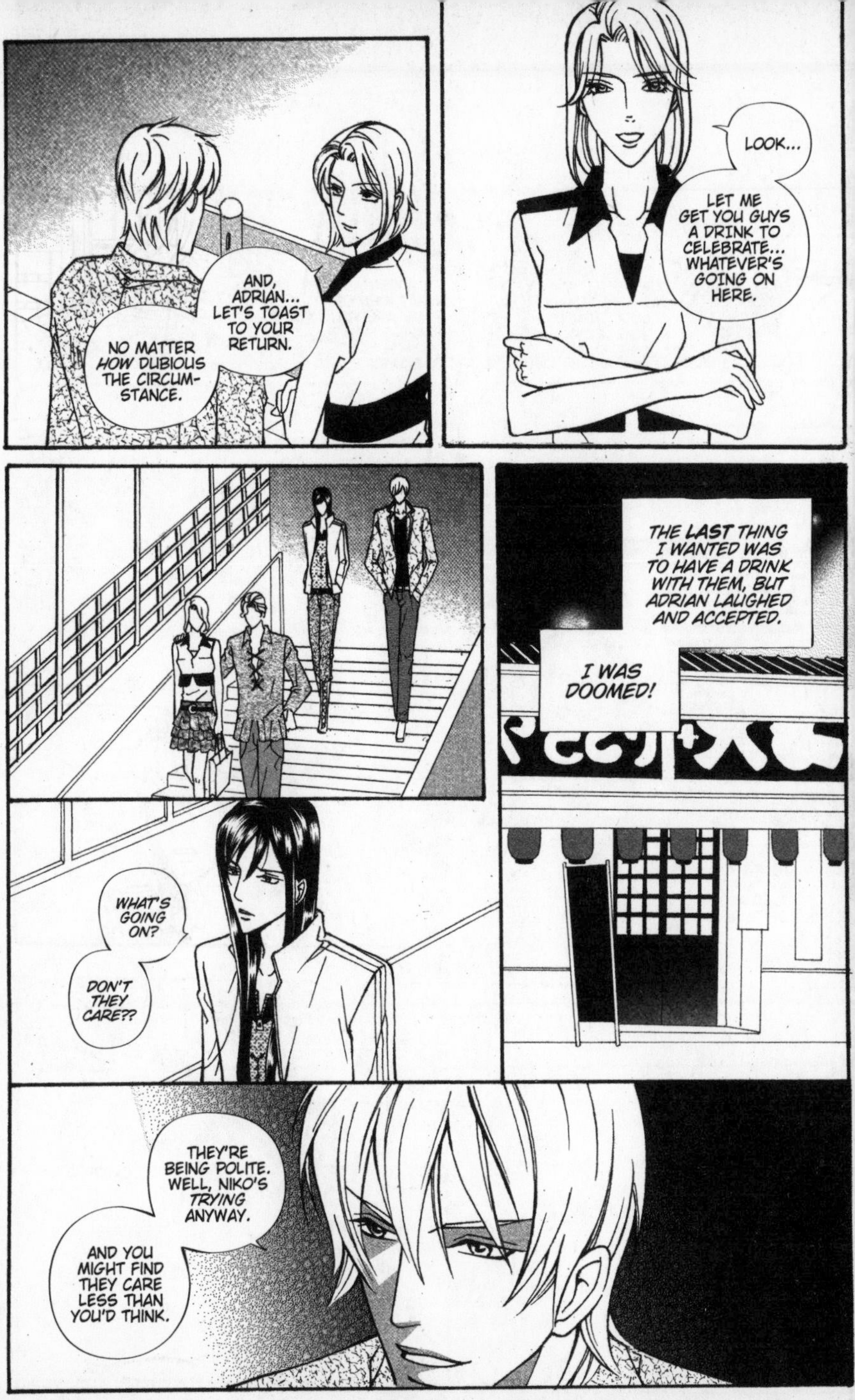
LOOK...
LET ME GET YOU GUYS A DRINK TO CELEBRATE... WHATEVER'S GOING ON HERE.
AND, ADRIAN... LET'S TOAST TO YOUR RETURN.
NO MATTER *HOW* DUBIOUS THE CIRCUM-STANCE.
*THE **LAST** THING I WANTED WAS TO HAVE A DRINK WITH THEM, BUT ADRIAN LAUGHED AND ACCEPTED.*
I WAS DOOMED!
WHAT'S GOING ON?
DON'T THEY CARE??
THEY'RE BEING POLITE. WELL, NIKO'S *TRYING* ANYWAY.
AND YOU MIGHT FIND THEY CARE LESS THAN YOU'D THINK.

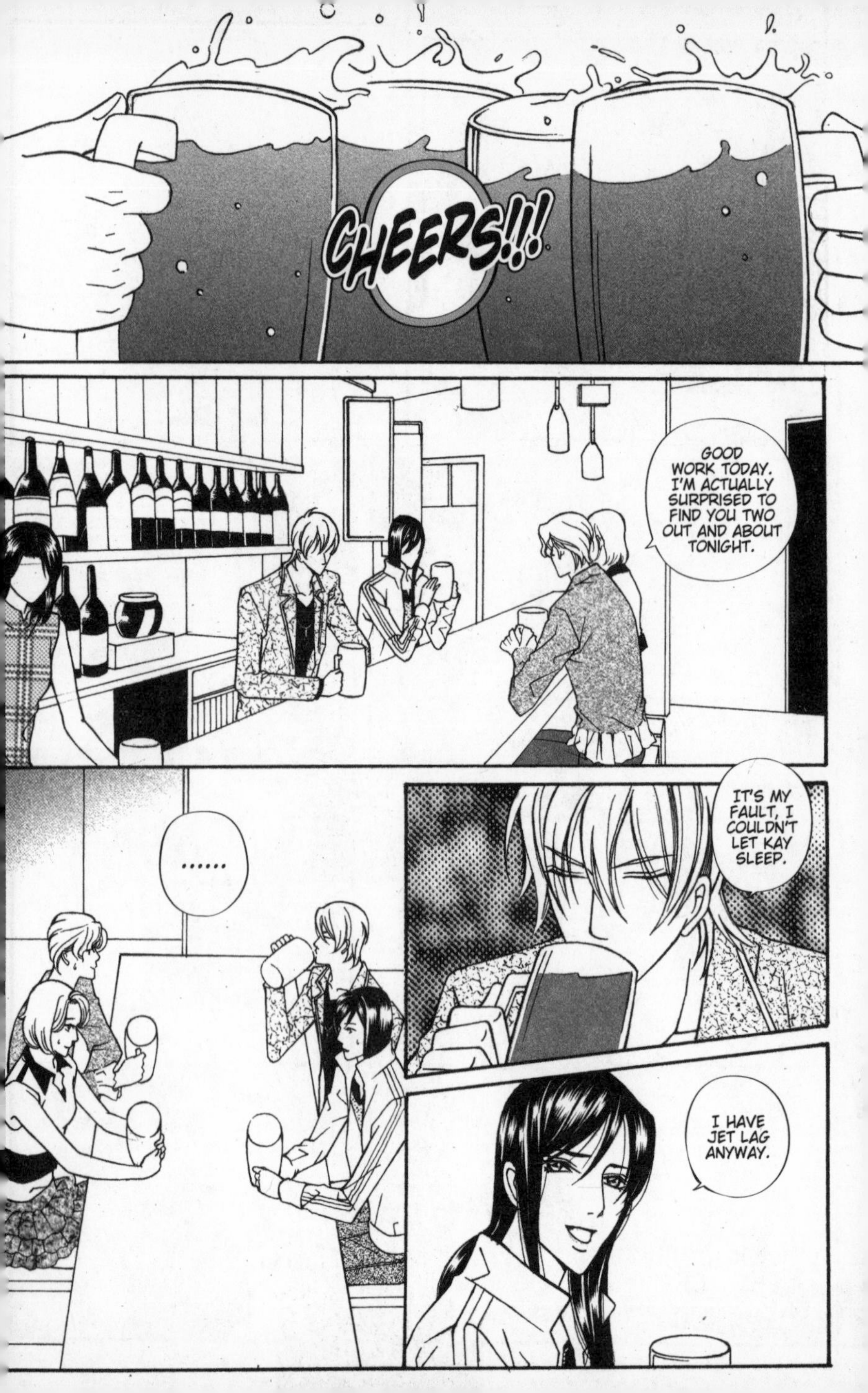
CHEERS!!!
GOOD WORK TODAY. I'M ACTUALLY SURPRISED TO FIND YOU TWO OUT AND ABOUT TONIGHT.
IT'S MY FAULT, I COULDN'T LET KAY SLEEP.
I HAVE JET LAG ANYWAY.
......

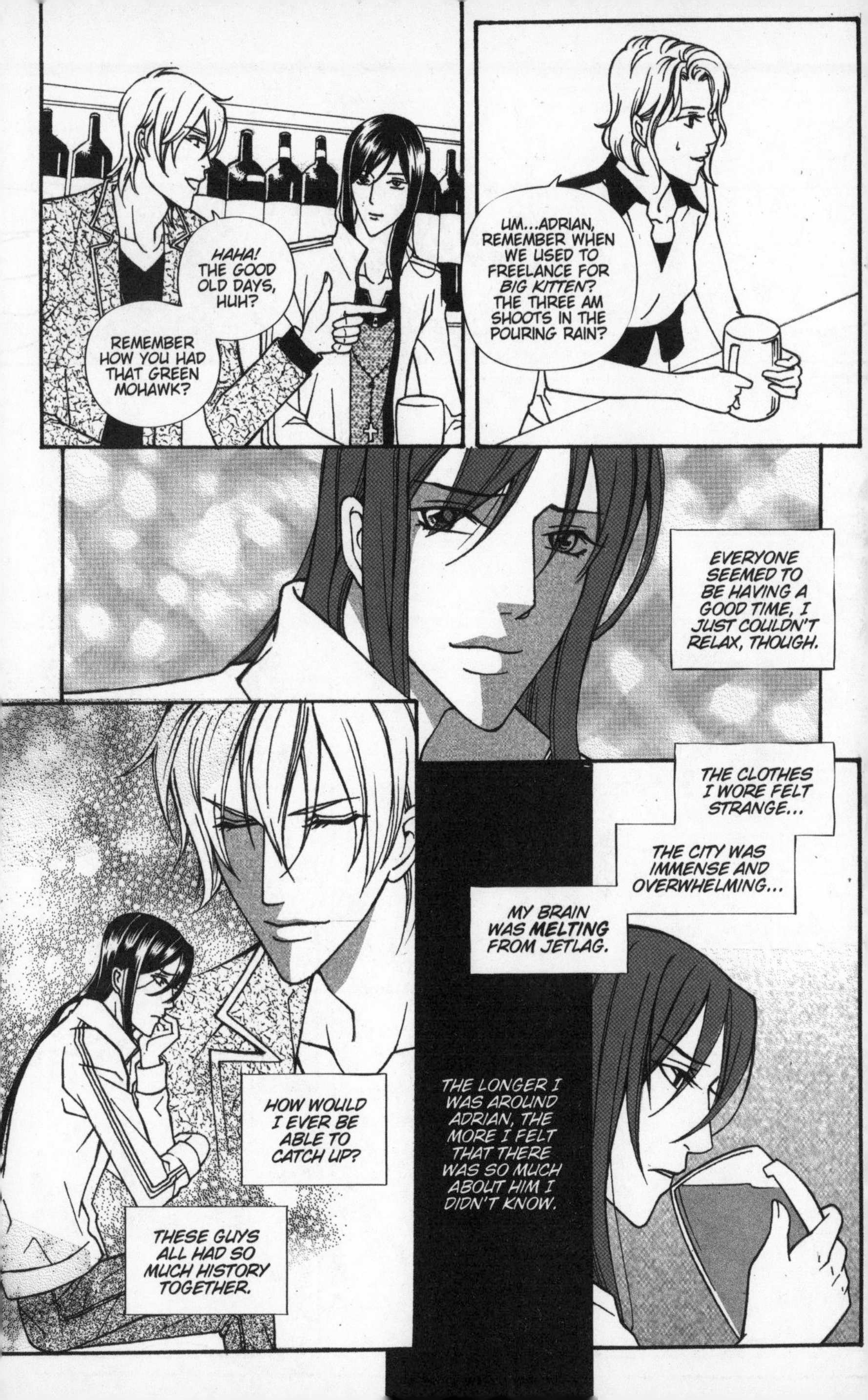
UM...ADRIAN, REMEMBER WHEN WE USED TO FREELANCE FOR *BIG KITTEN*? THE THREE AM SHOOTS IN THE POURING RAIN?
HAHA! THE GOOD OLD DAYS, HUH?
REMEMBER HOW YOU HAD THAT GREEN MOHAWK?
EVERYONE SEEMED TO BE HAVING A GOOD TIME, I JUST COULDN'T RELAX, THOUGH.
THE CLOTHES I WORE FELT STRANGE...
THE CITY WAS IMMENSE AND OVERWHELMING...
MY BRAIN WAS **MELTING** *FROM JETLAG.*
THE LONGER I WAS AROUND ADRIAN, THE MORE I FELT THAT THERE WAS SO MUCH ABOUT HIM I DIDN'T KNOW.
HOW WOULD I EVER BE ABLE TO CATCH UP?
THESE GUYS ALL HAD SO MUCH HISTORY TOGETHER.

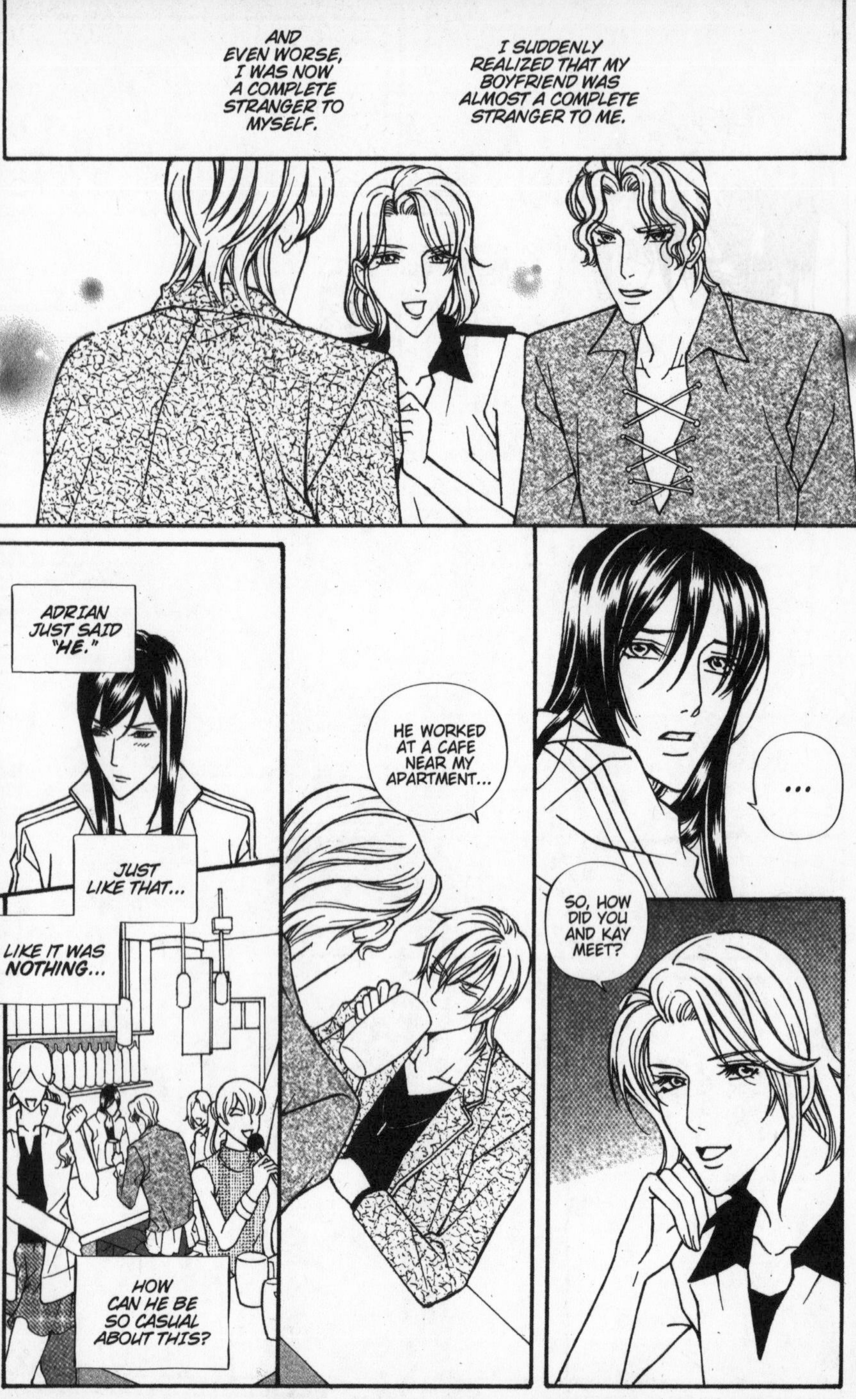
I SUDDENLY REALIZED THAT MY BOYFRIEND WAS ALMOST A COMPLETE STRANGER TO ME.
AND EVEN WORSE, I WAS NOW A COMPLETE STRANGER TO MYSELF.
...
SO, HOW DID YOU AND KAY MEET?
HE WORKED AT A CAFE NEAR MY APARTMENT...
ADRIAN JUST SAID "HE."
JUST LIKE THAT...
LIKE IT WAS NOTHING...
HOW CAN HE BE SO CASUAL ABOUT THIS?

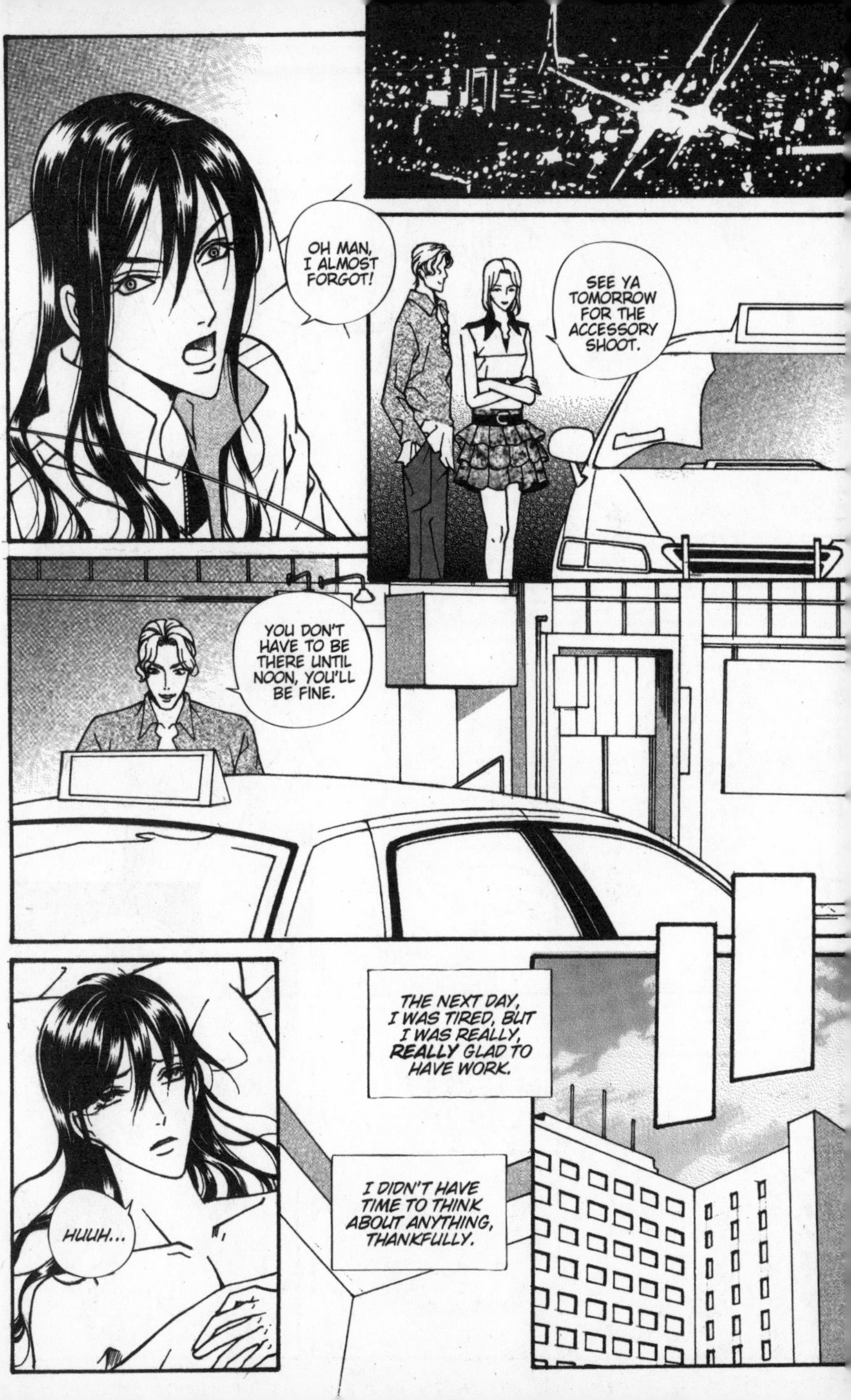
SEE YA TOMORROW FOR THE ACCESSORY SHOOT.
OH MAN, I ALMOST FORGOT!
YOU DON'T HAVE TO BE THERE UNTIL NOON, YOU'LL BE FINE.
THE NEXT DAY, I WAS TIRED, BUT I WAS REALLY, **REALLY** GLAD TO HAVE WORK.
I DIDN'T HAVE TIME TO THINK ABOUT ANYTHING, THANKFULLY.
HUUH...

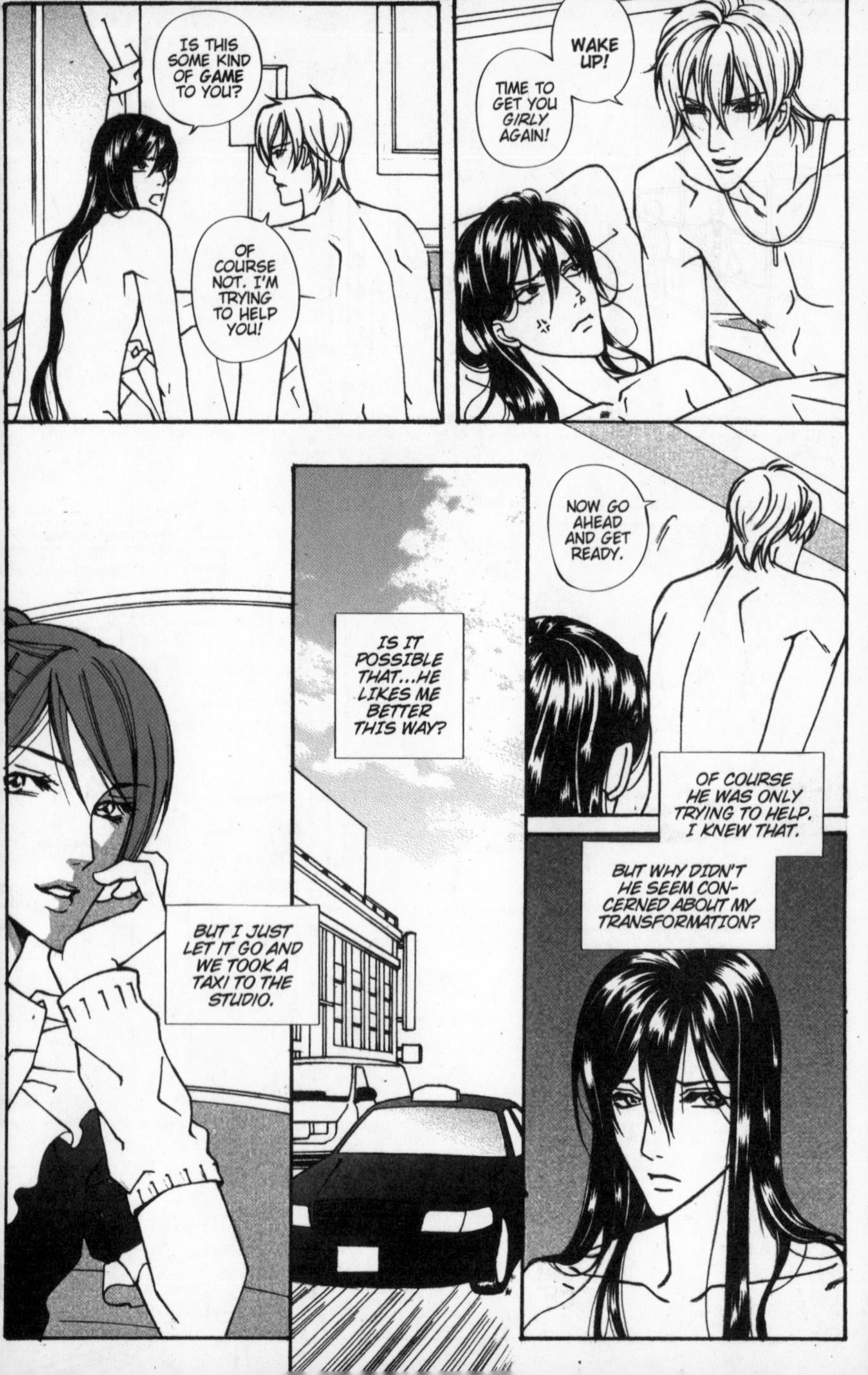
WAKE UP!
TIME TO GET YOU GIRLY AGAIN!
IS THIS SOME KIND OF GAME TO YOU?
OF COURSE NOT. I'M TRYING TO HELP YOU!
NOW GO AHEAD AND GET READY.
OF COURSE HE WAS ONLY TRYING TO HELP. I KNEW THAT.
BUT WHY DIDN'T HE SEEM CON-CERNED ABOUT MY TRANSFORMATION?
IS IT POSSIBLE THAT...HE LIKES ME BETTER THIS WAY?
BUT I JUST LET IT GO AND WE TOOK A TAXI TO THE STUDIO.

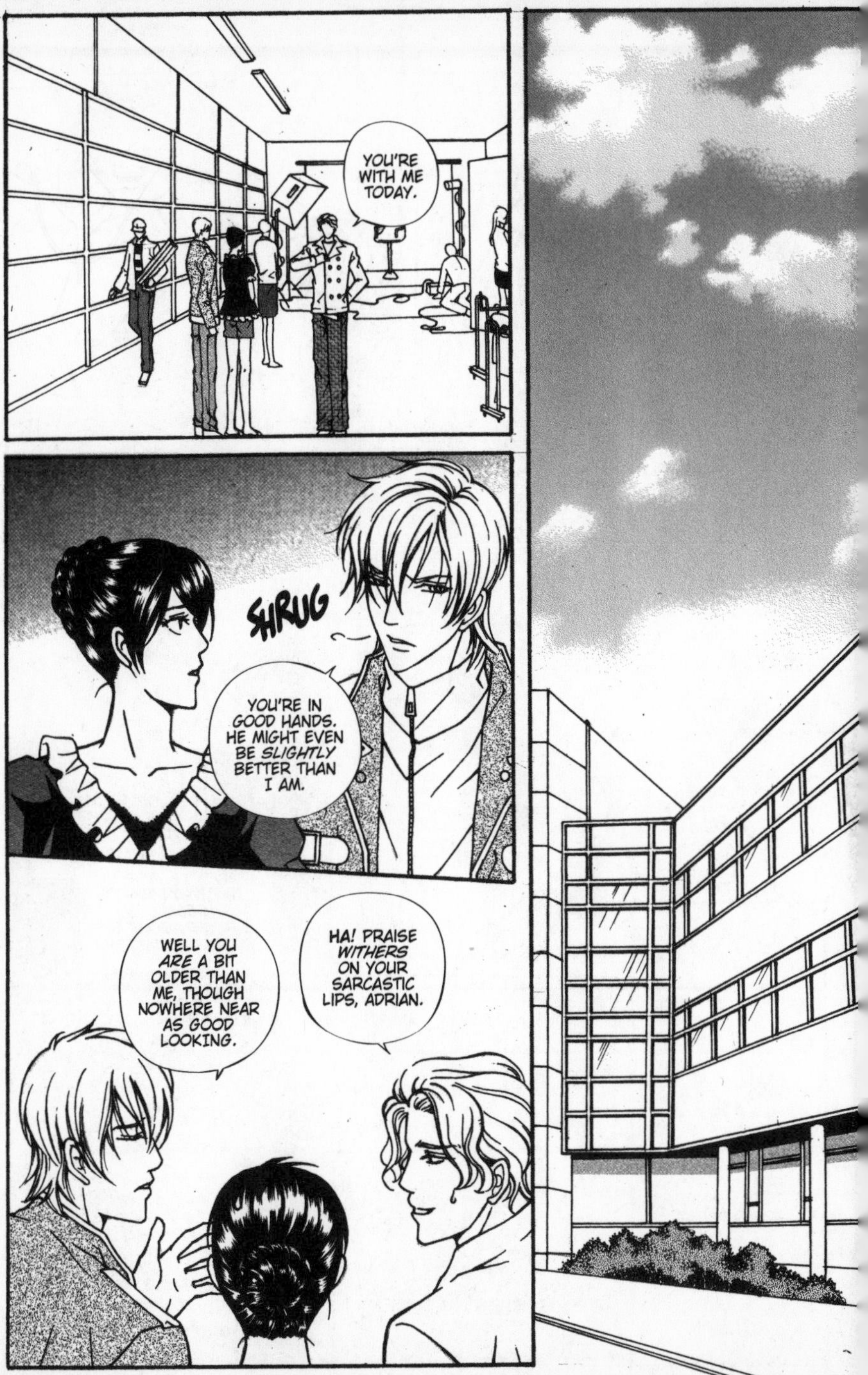
YOU'RE WITH ME TODAY.
SHRUG
YOU'RE IN GOOD HANDS. HE MIGHT EVEN BE *SLIGHTLY* BETTER THAN I AM.
HA! PRAISE *WITHERS* ON YOUR SARCASTIC LIPS, ADRIAN.
WELL YOU *ARE* A BIT OLDER THAN ME, THOUGH NOWHERE NEAR AS GOOD LOOKING.

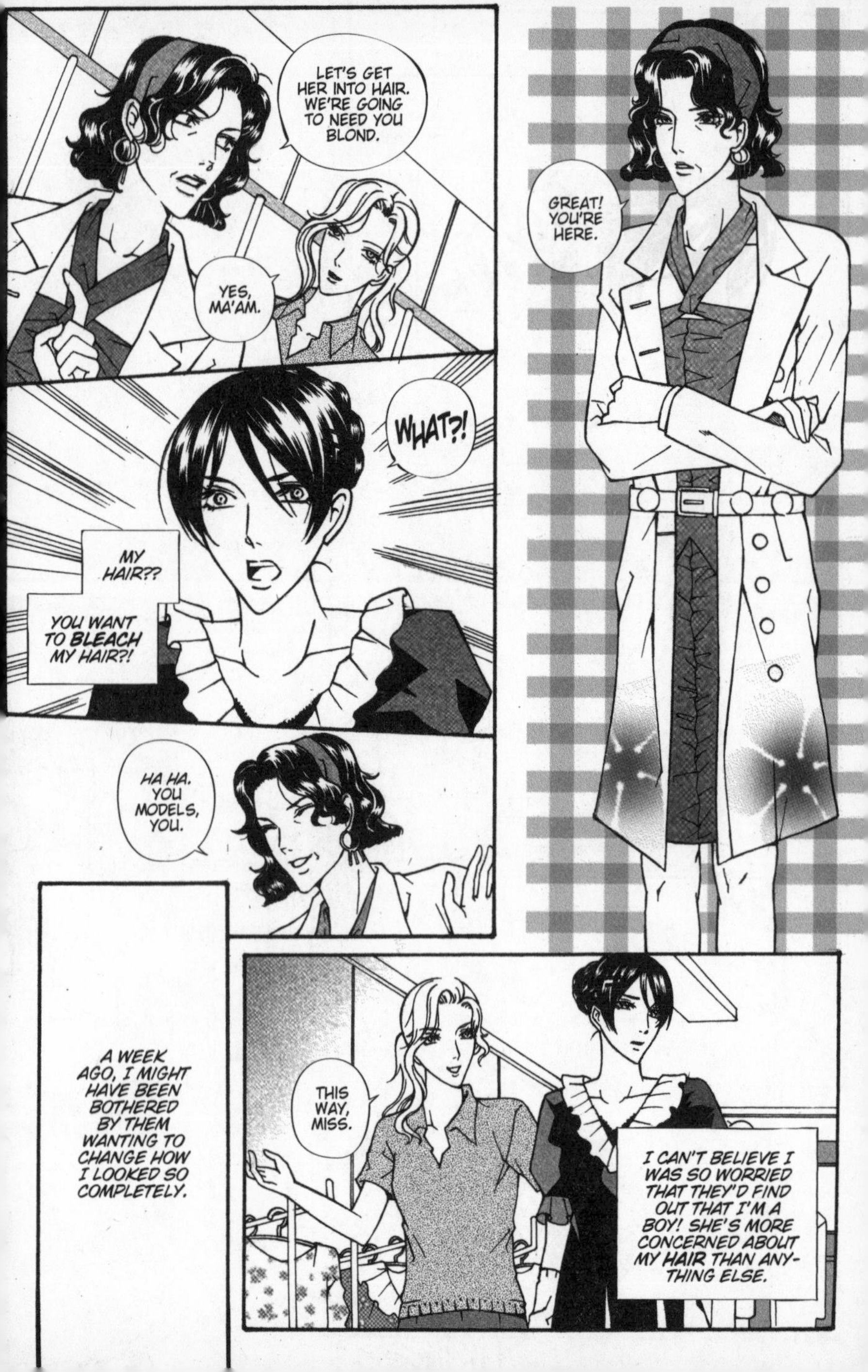
GREAT! YOU'RE HERE.
LET'S GET HER INTO HAIR. WE'RE GOING TO NEED YOU BLOND.
YES, MA'AM.
WHAT?!
MY HAIR??
YOU WANT TO **BLEACH** MY HAIR?!
HA HA. YOU MODELS, YOU.
THIS WAY, MISS.
I CAN'T BELIEVE I WAS SO WORRIED THAT THEY'D FIND OUT THAT I'M A BOY! SHE'S MORE CONCERNED ABOUT MY **HAIR** THAN ANY-THING ELSE.
A WEEK AGO, I MIGHT HAVE BEEN BOTHERED BY THEM WANTING TO CHANGE HOW I LOOKED SO COMPLETELY.

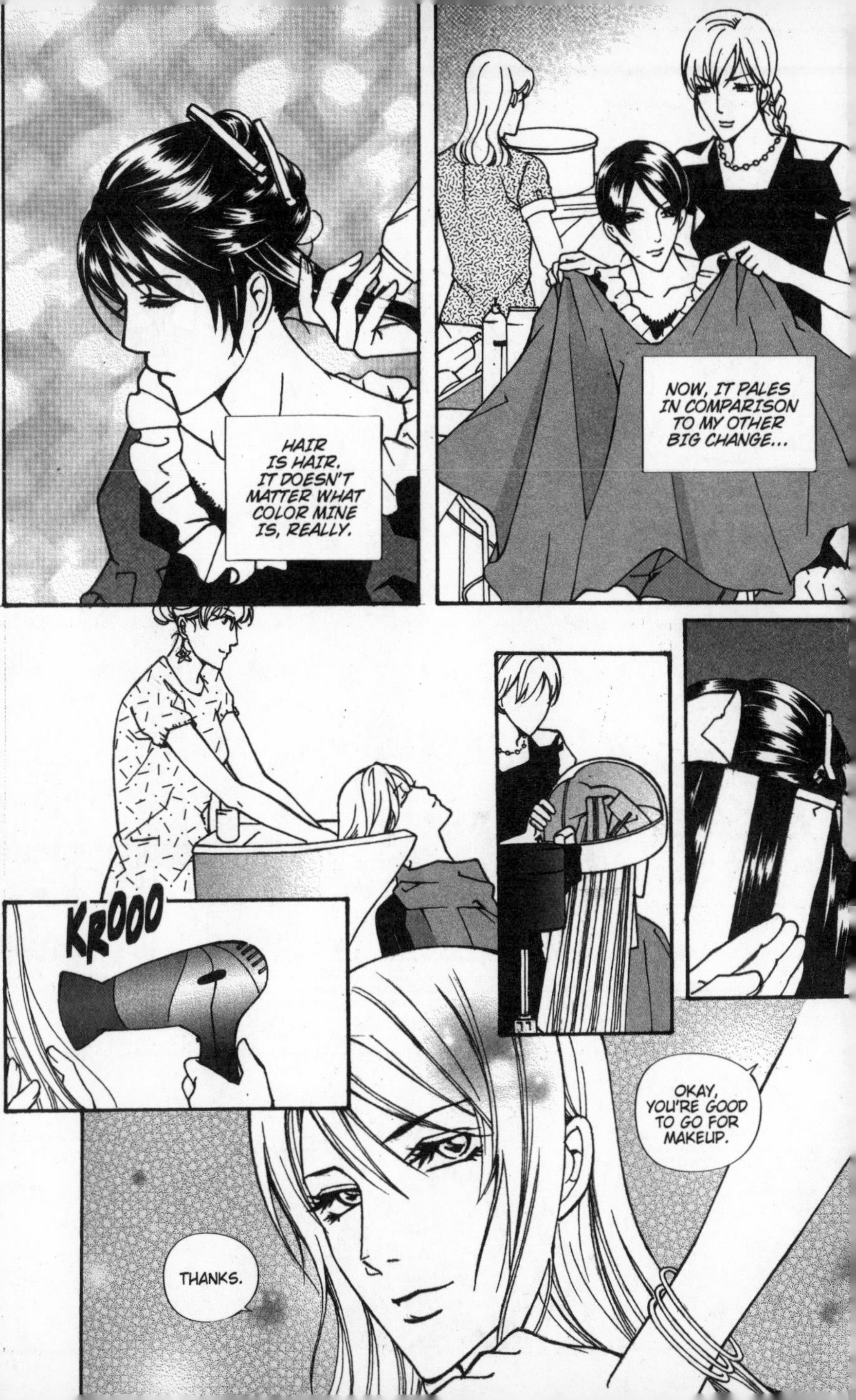
NOW, IT PALES IN COMPARISON TO MY OTHER BIG CHANGE...
HAIR IS HAIR. IT DOESN'T MATTER WHAT COLOR MINE IS, REALLY.
KROOO
OKAY, YOU'RE GOOD TO GO FOR MAKEUP.
THANKS.

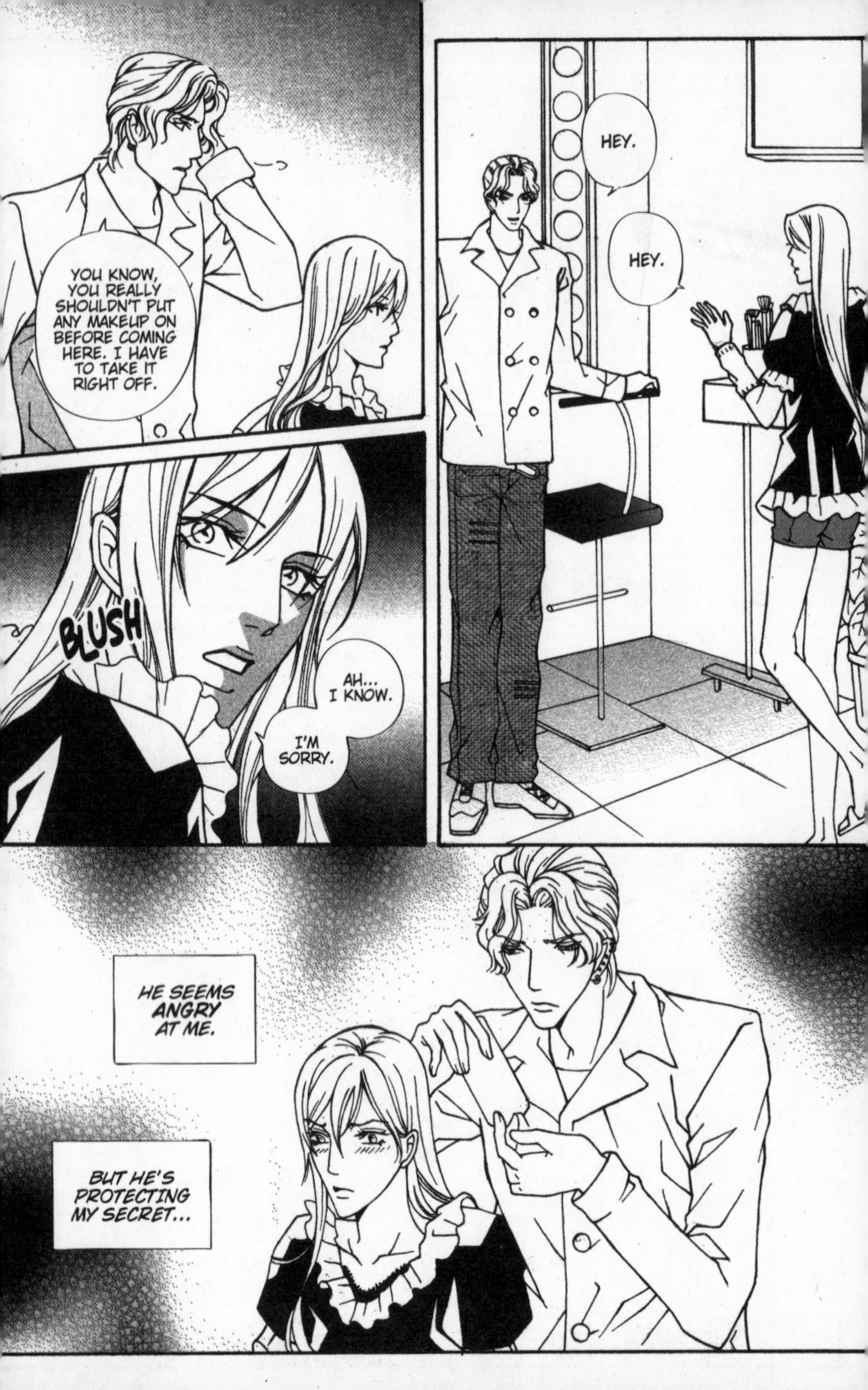
HEY.
HEY.
YOU KNOW, YOU REALLY SHOULDN'T PUT ANY MAKEUP ON BEFORE COMING HERE. I HAVE TO TAKE IT RIGHT OFF.
BLUSH
AH... I KNOW.
I'M SORRY.
HE SEEMS ANGRY AT ME.
BUT HE'S PROTECTING MY SECRET...

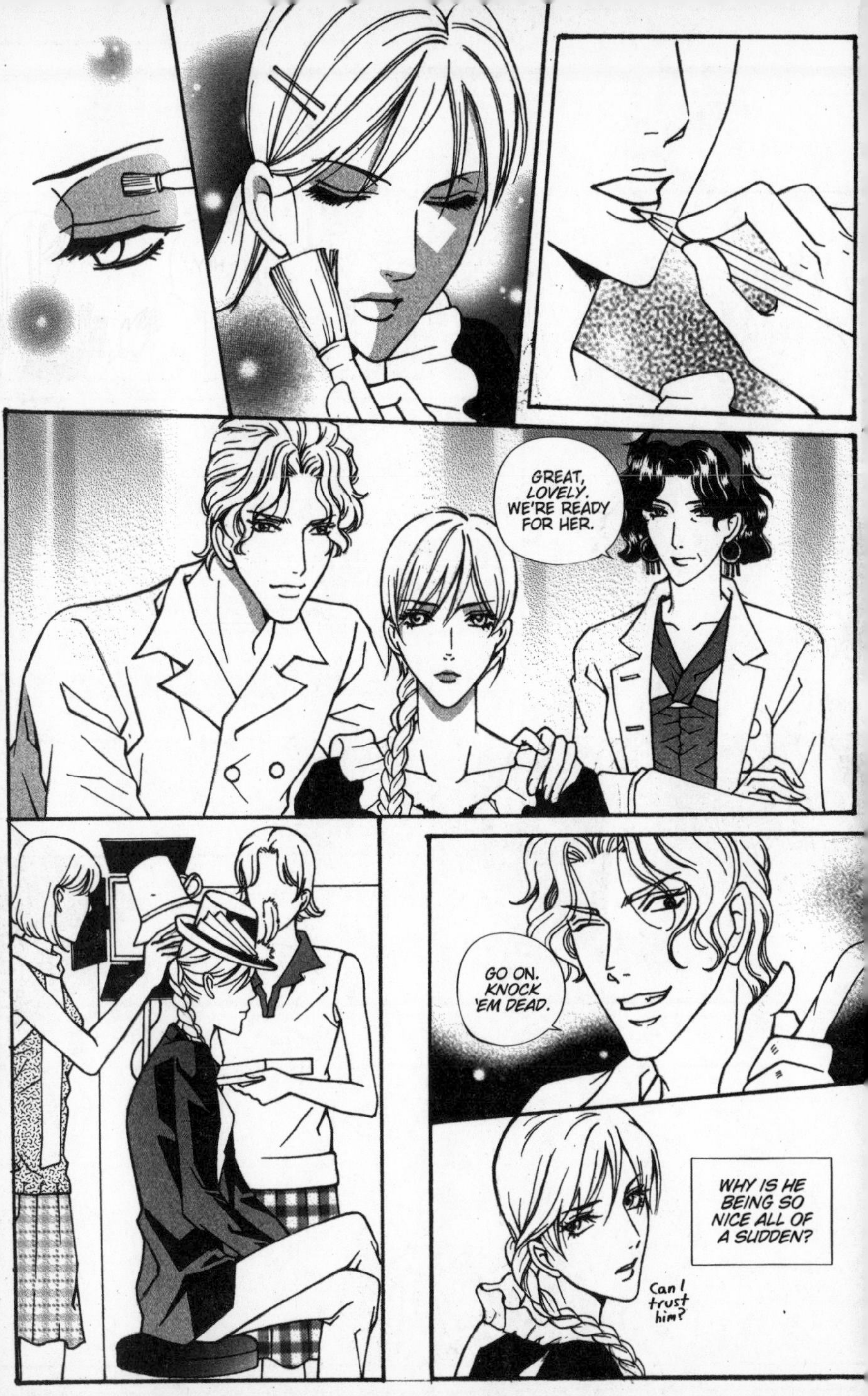
GREAT, LOVELY. WE'RE READY FOR HER.
GO ON. KNOCK 'EM DEAD.
WHY IS HE BEING SO NICE ALL OF A SUDDEN?
Can I trust him?

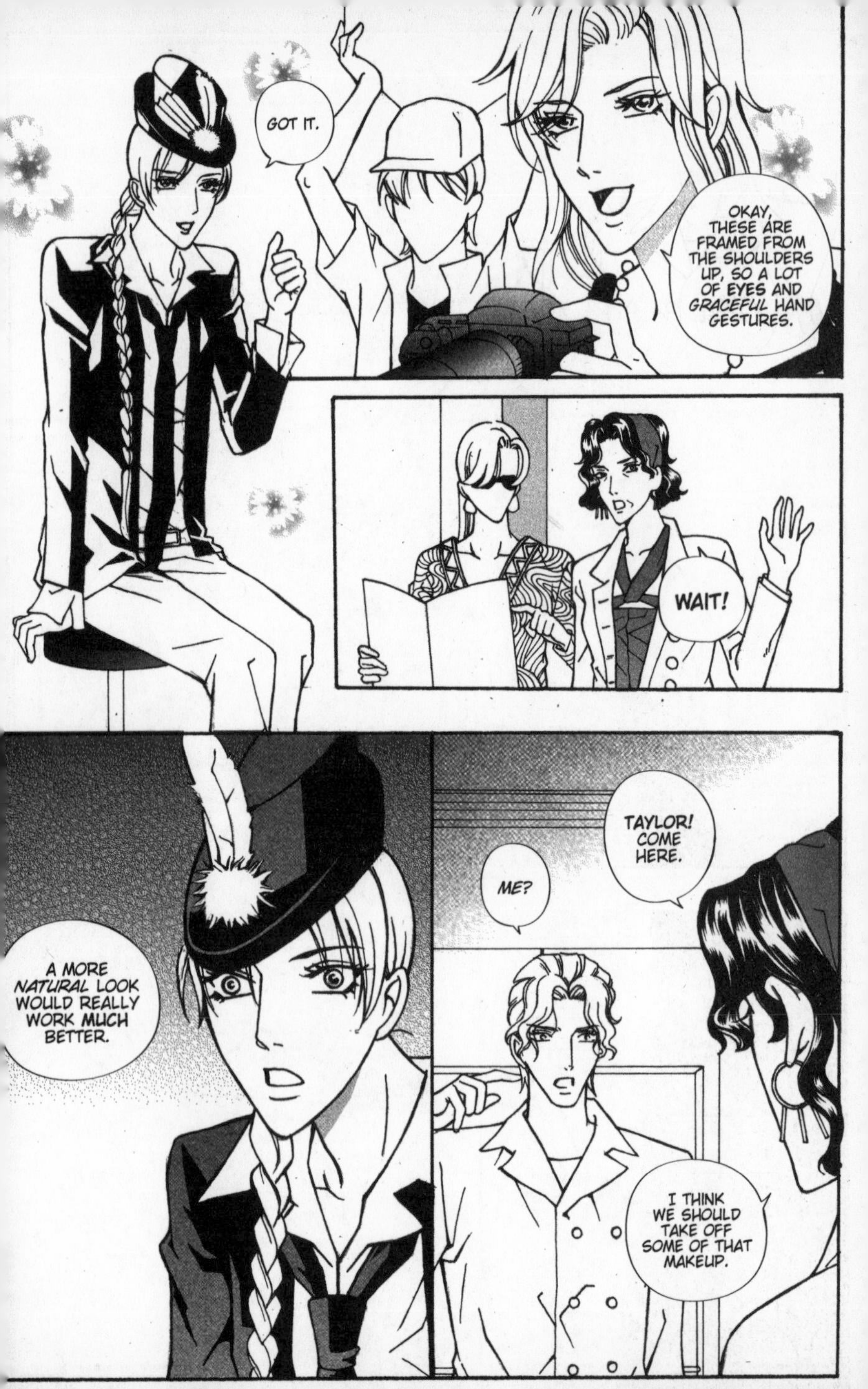

OKAY, THESE ARE FRAMED FROM THE SHOULDERS UP, SO A LOT OF EYES AND *GRACEFUL* HAND GESTURES.
GOT IT.
WAIT!
TAYLOR! COME HERE.
ME?
I THINK WE SHOULD TAKE OFF SOME OF THAT MAKEUP.
A MORE *NATURAL* LOOK WOULD REALLY WORK MUCH BETTER.

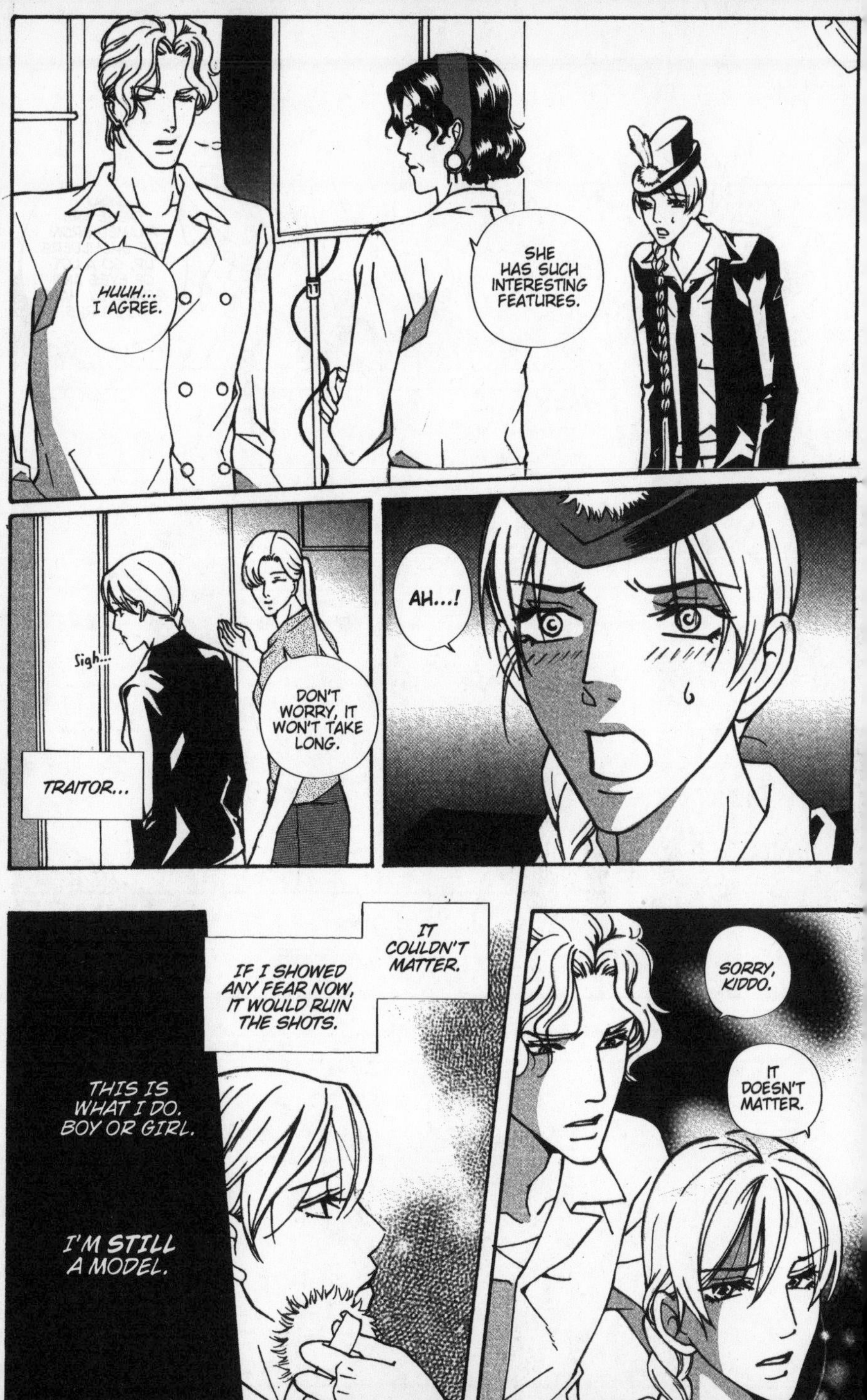
SHE HAS SUCH INTERESTING FEATURES.
HUUH... I AGREE.
AH...!
DON'T WORRY, IT WON'T TAKE LONG.
Sigh...
TRAITOR...
SORRY, KIDDO.
IT DOESN'T MATTER.
IT COULDN'T MATTER.
IF I SHOWED ANY FEAR NOW, IT WOULD RUIN THE SHOTS.
THIS IS WHAT I DO. BOY OR GIRL.
I'M STILL A MODEL.

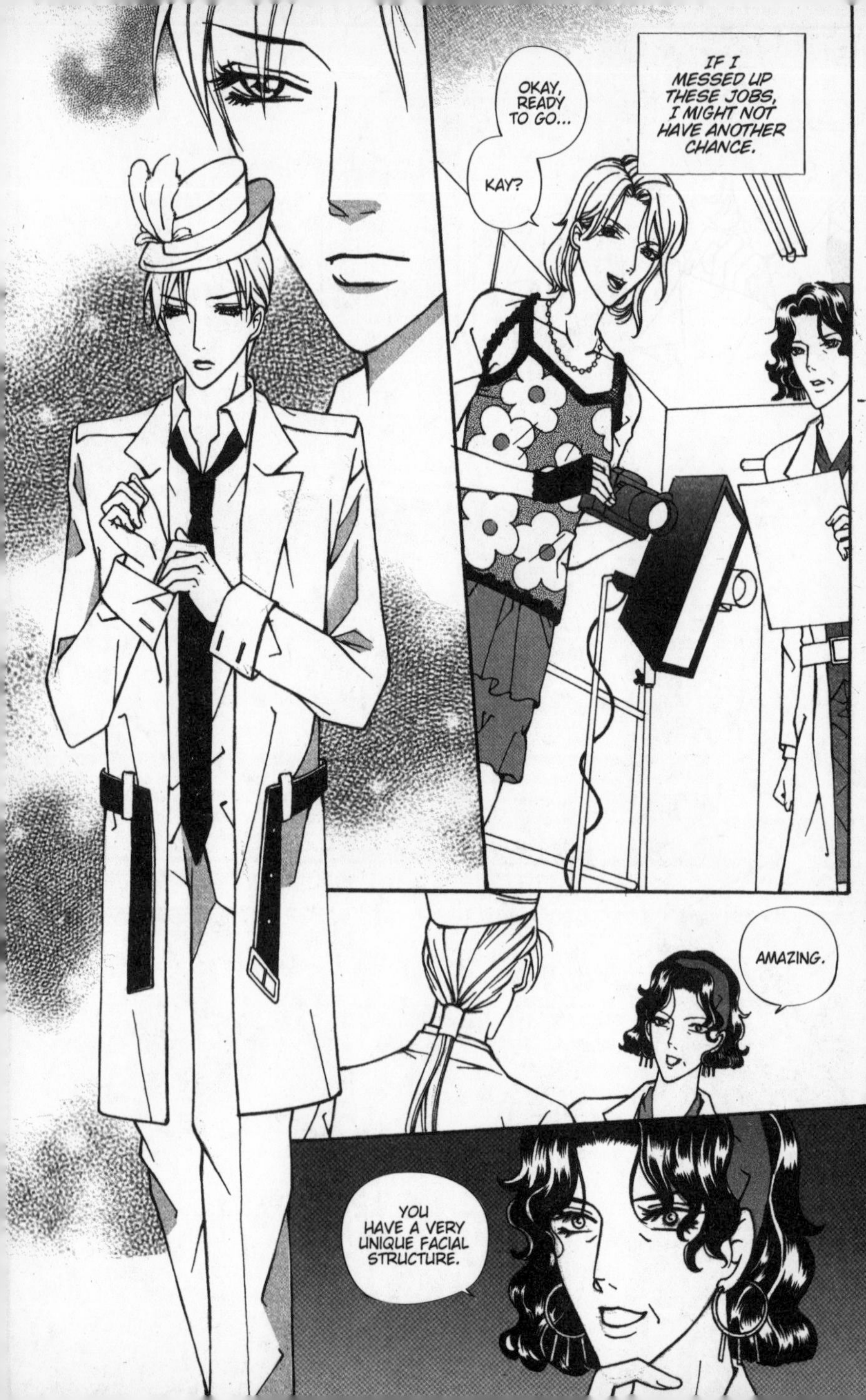
IF I MESSED UP THESE JOBS, I MIGHT NOT HAVE ANOTHER CHANCE.
OKAY, READY TO GO...
KAY?
AMAZING.
YOU HAVE A VERY UNIQUE FACIAL STRUCTURE.

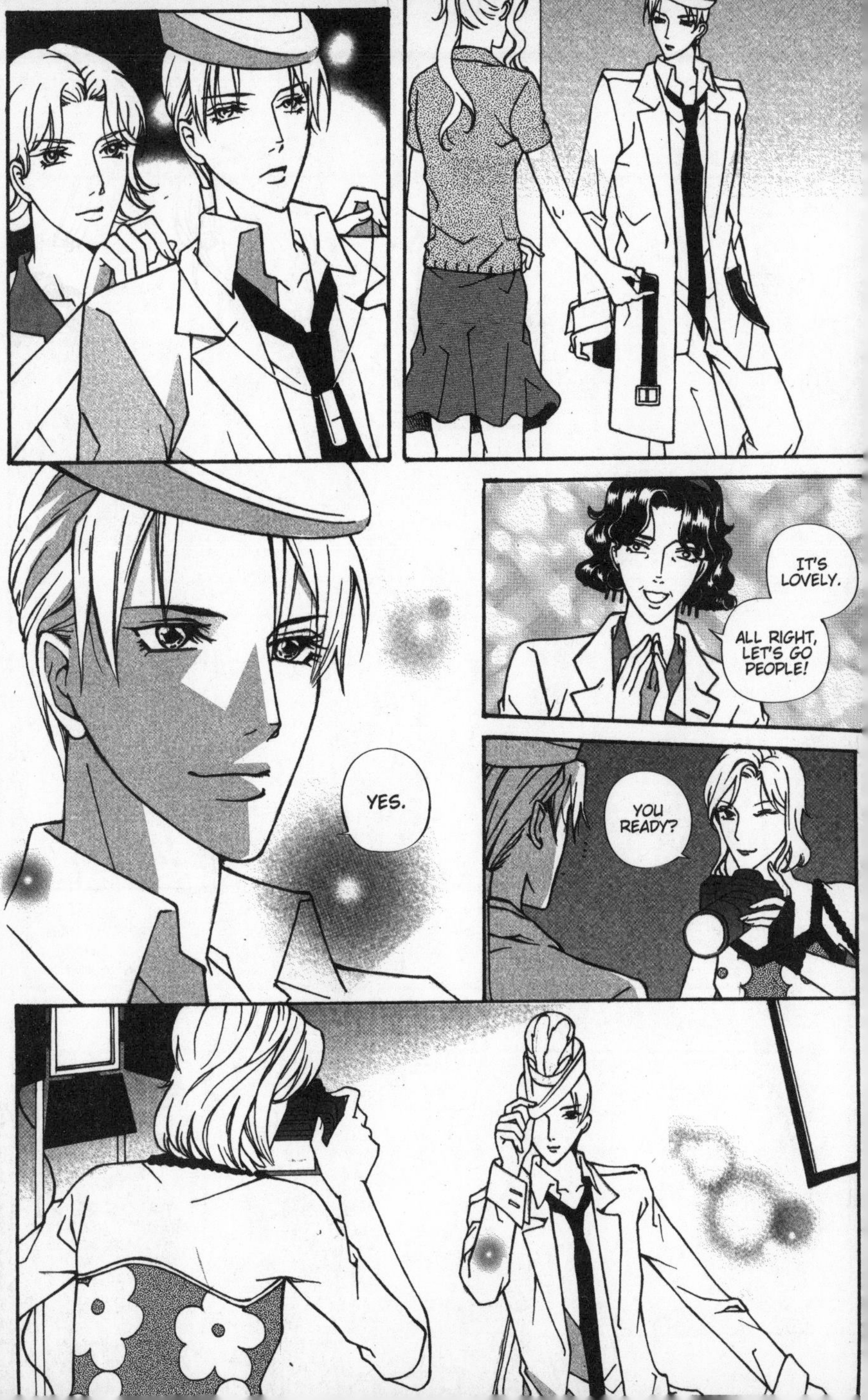
IT'S LOVELY.
ALL RIGHT, LET'S GO PEOPLE!
YOU READY?
YES.

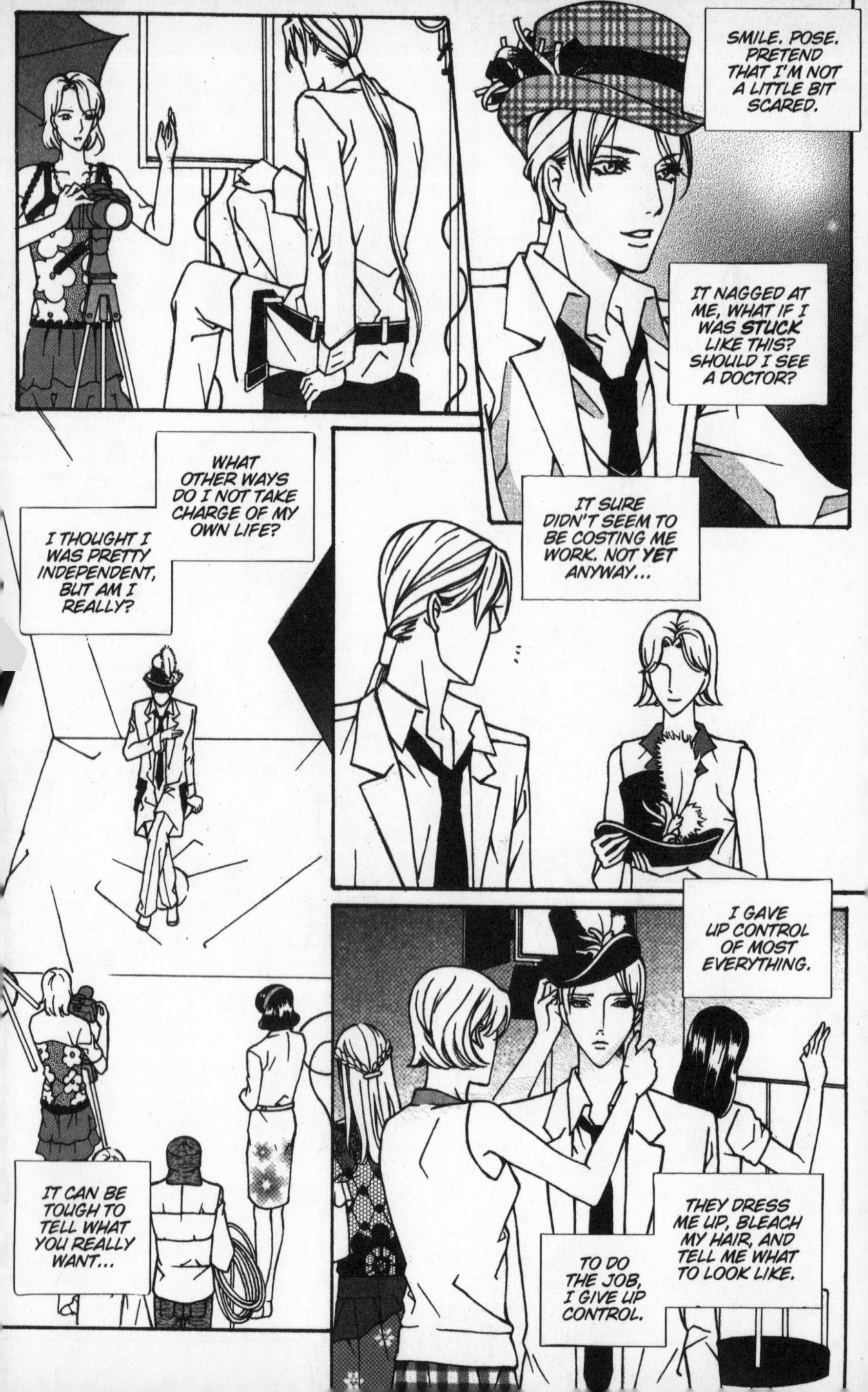
SMILE. POSE. PRETEND THAT I'M NOT A LITTLE BIT SCARED.
IT NAGGED AT ME, WHAT IF I WAS STUCK LIKE THIS? SHOULD I SEE A DOCTOR?
IT SURE DIDN'T SEEM TO BE COSTING ME WORK. NOT YET ANYWAY...
WHAT OTHER WAYS DO I NOT TAKE CHARGE OF MY OWN LIFE?
I THOUGHT I WAS PRETTY INDEPENDENT, BUT AM I REALLY?
I GAVE UP CONTROL OF MOST EVERYTHING.
THEY DRESS ME UP, BLEACH MY HAIR, AND TELL ME WHAT TO LOOK LIKE.
TO DO THE JOB, I GIVE UP CONTROL.
IT CAN BE TOUGH TO TELL WHAT YOU REALLY WANT...

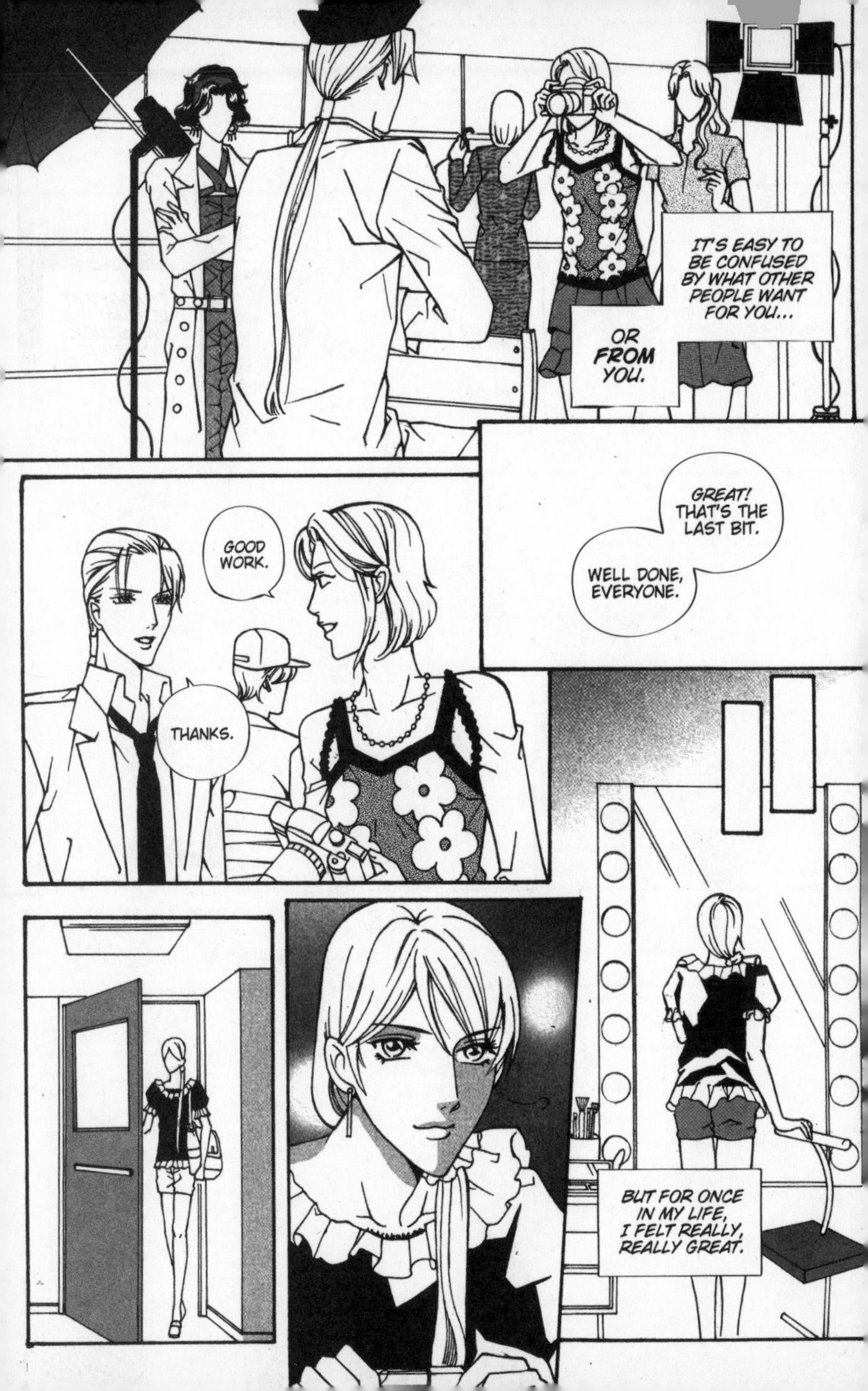
IT'S EASY TO BE CONFUSED BY WHAT OTHER PEOPLE WANT FOR YOU...
OR FROM YOU.
GREAT! THAT'S THE LAST BIT.
WELL DONE, EVERYONE.
GOOD WORK.
THANKS.
BUT FOR ONCE IN MY LIFE, I FELT REALLY, REALLY GREAT.

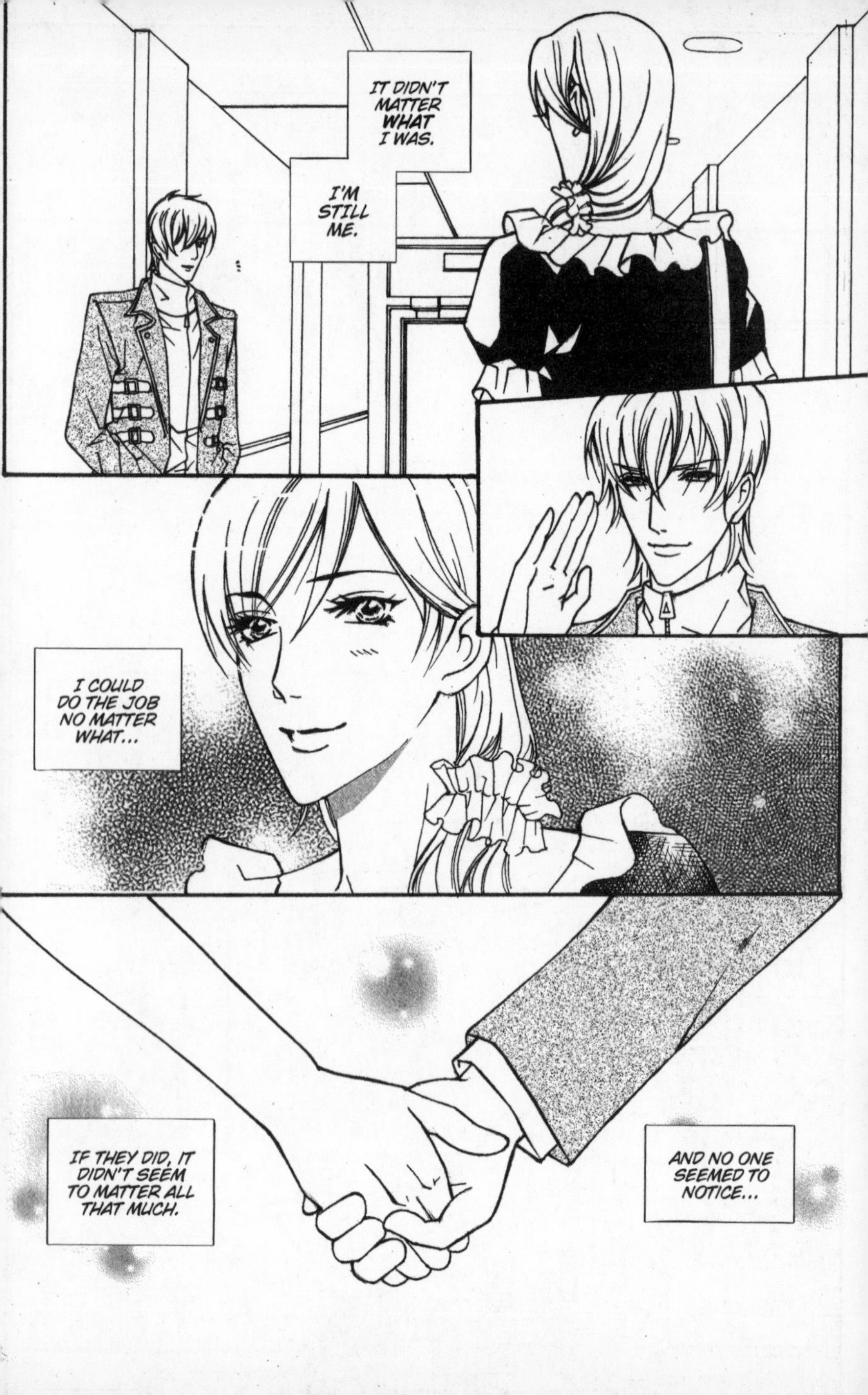
IT DIDN'T MATTER **WHAT** I WAS.
I'M STILL ME.
I COULD DO THE JOB NO MATTER WHAT...
AND NO ONE SEEMED TO NOTICE...
IF THEY DID, IT DIDN'T SEEM TO MATTER ALL THAT MUCH.

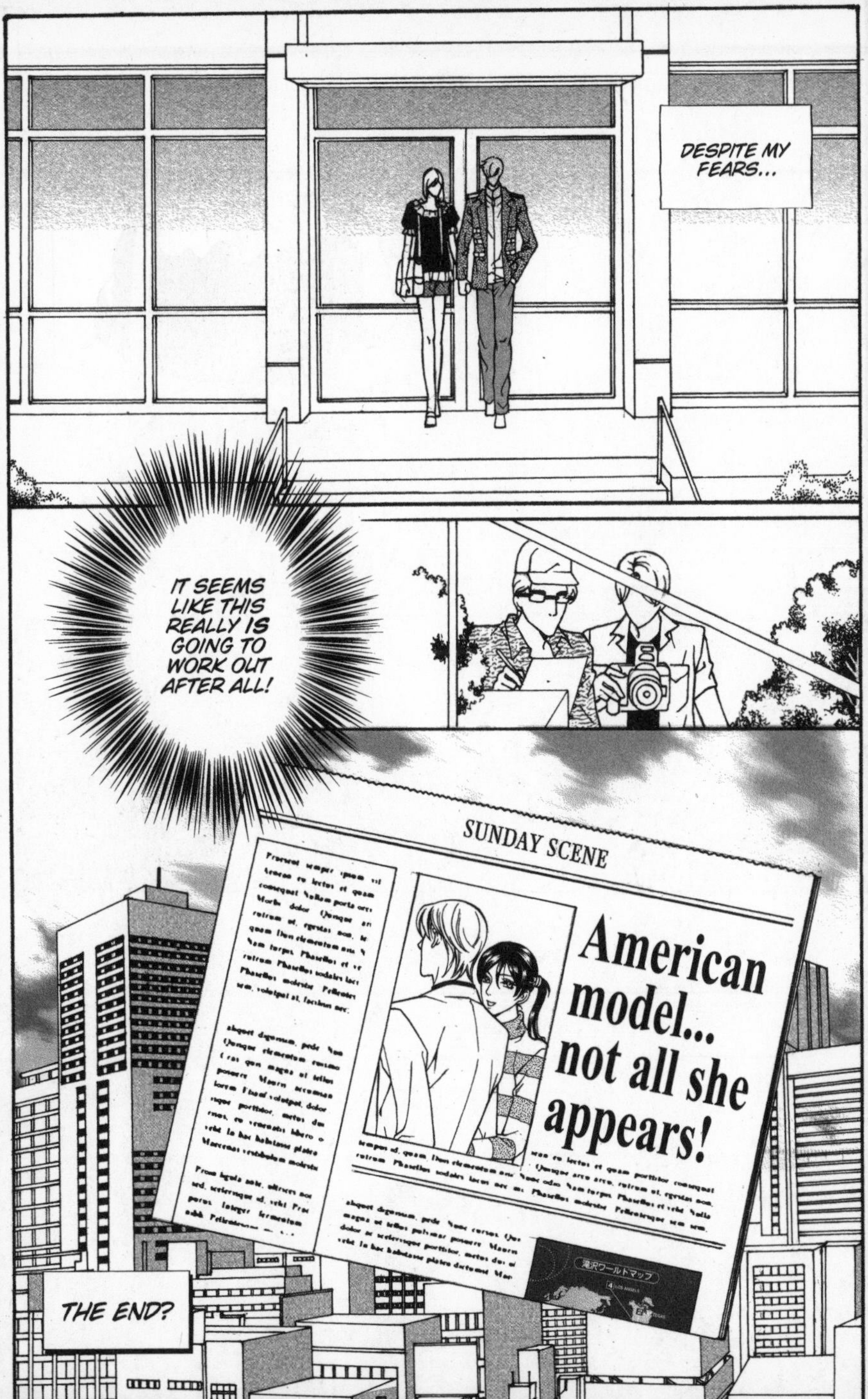
DESPITE MY FEARS...
IT SEEMS LIKE THIS REALLY IS GOING TO WORK OUT AFTER ALL!
SUNDAY SCENE
American model... not all she appears!
THE END?

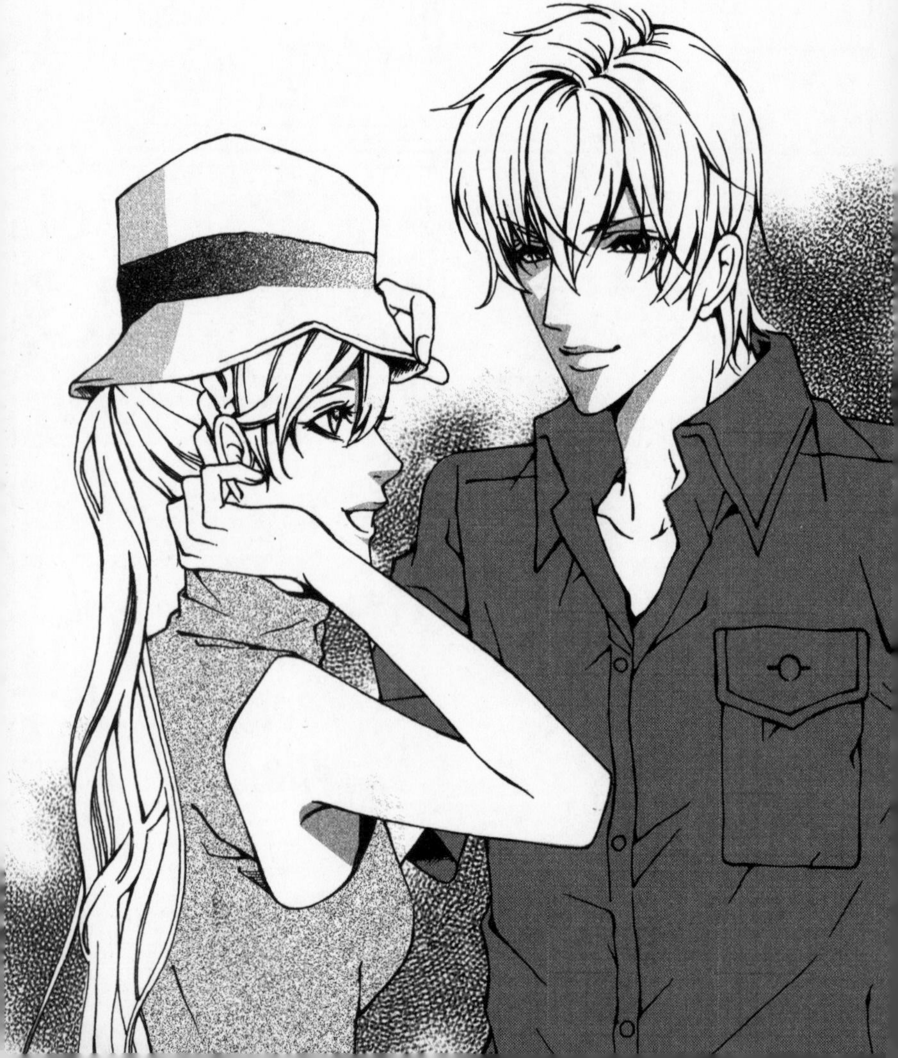

InVisible

[CHARACTER DESIGN PORTFOLIO]

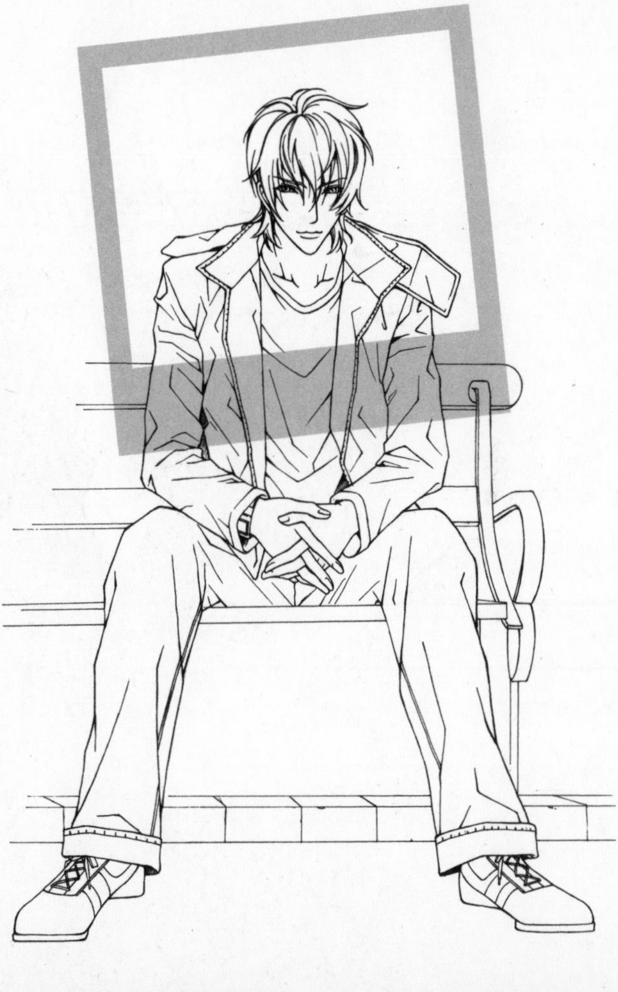

InVisible

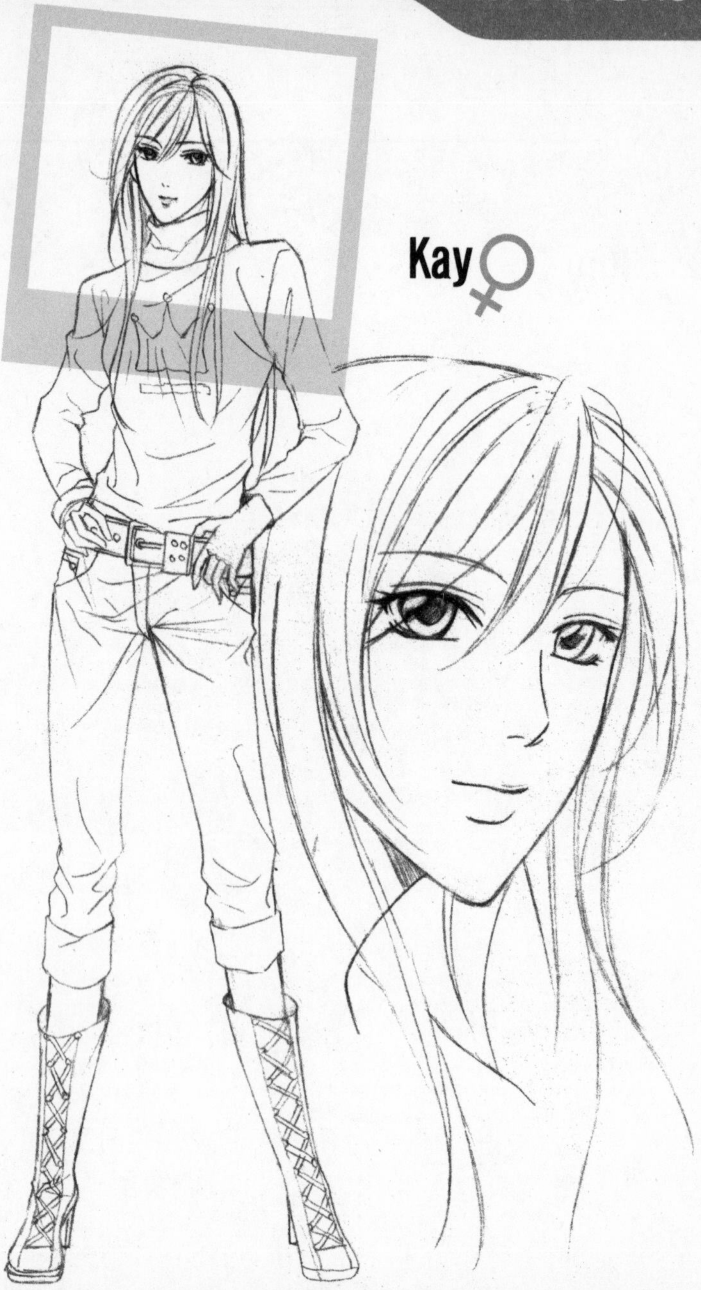
Kay ♀

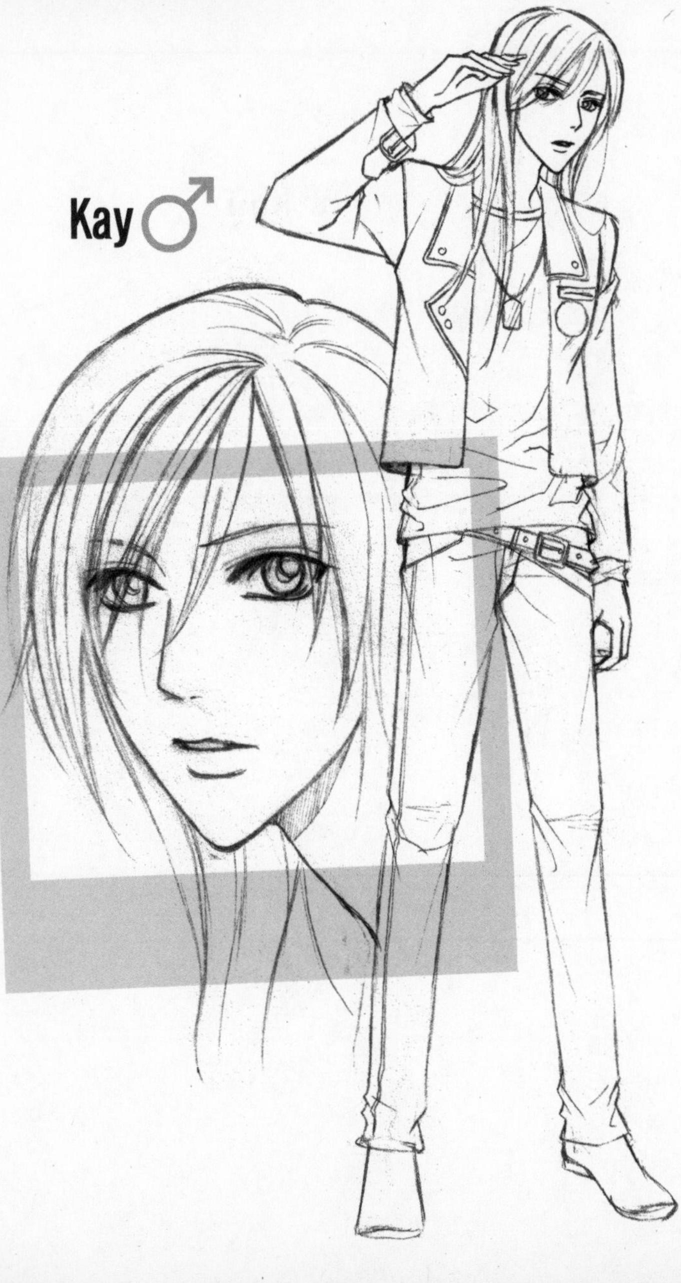
Kay ♂

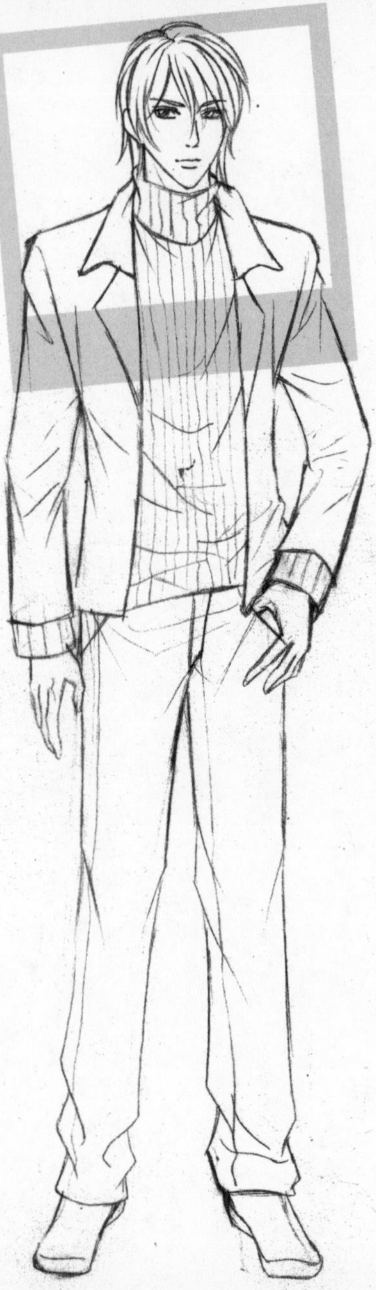

Adrian

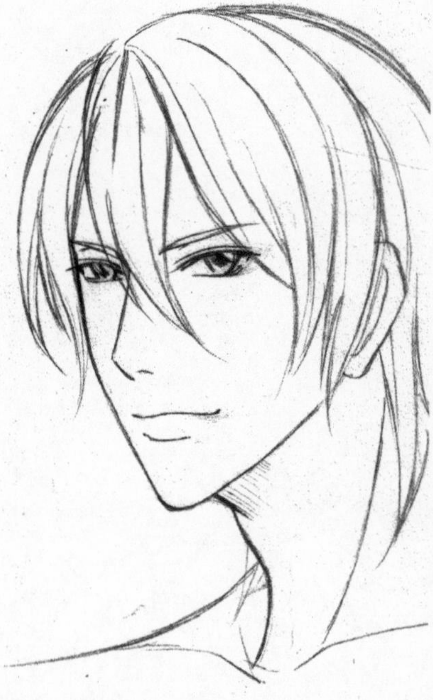

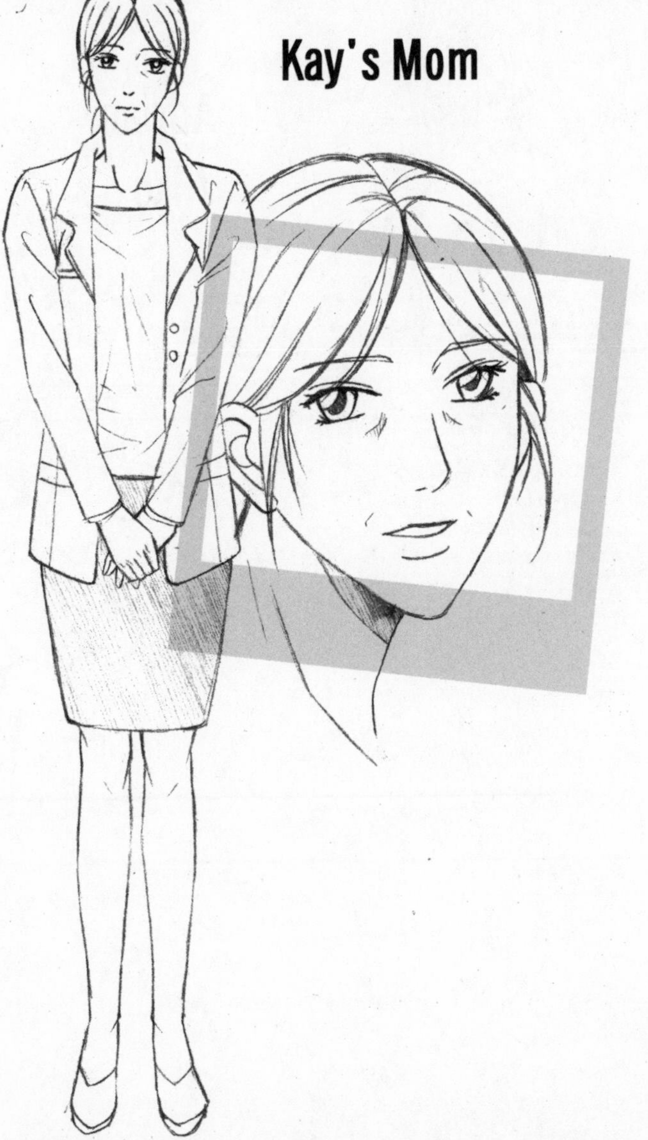
Kay's Mom

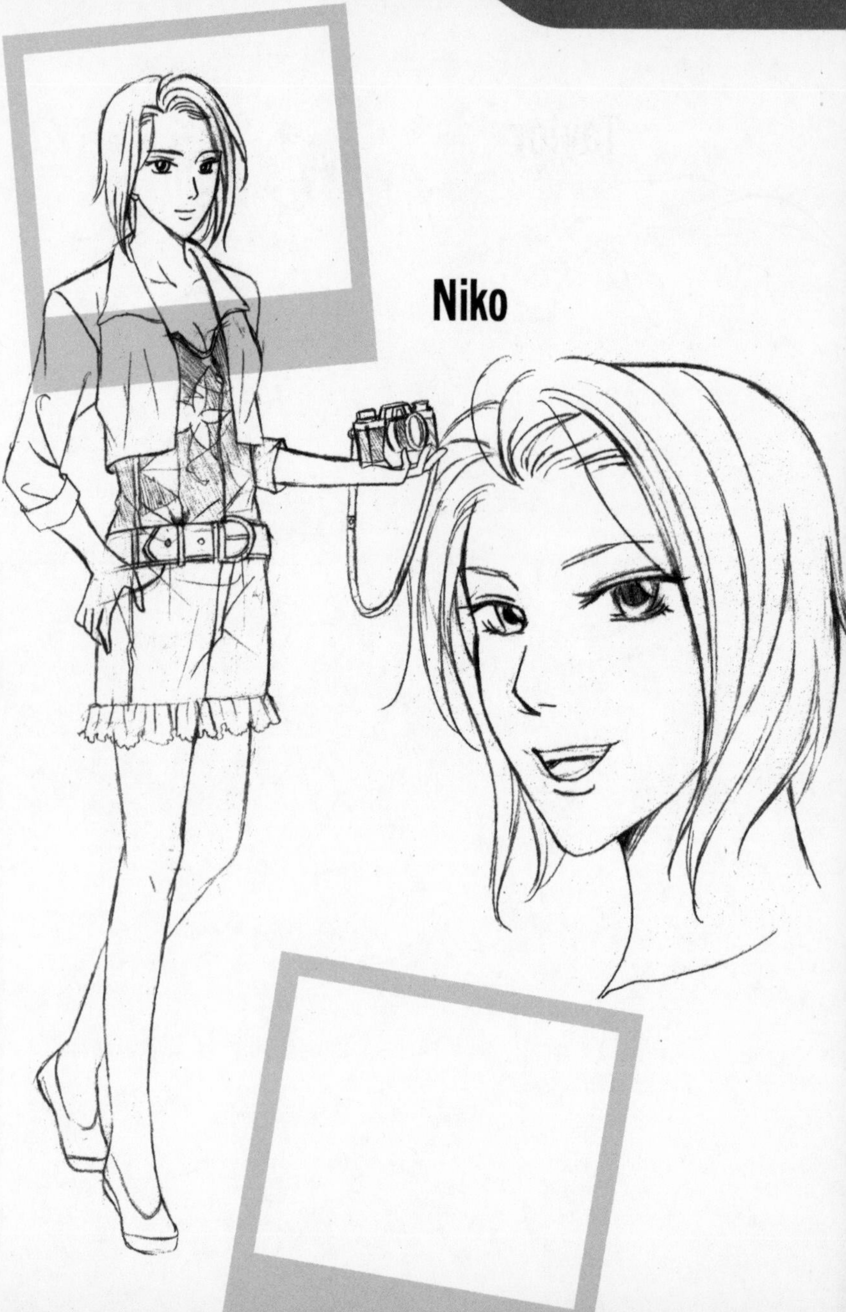
Niko

Taylor

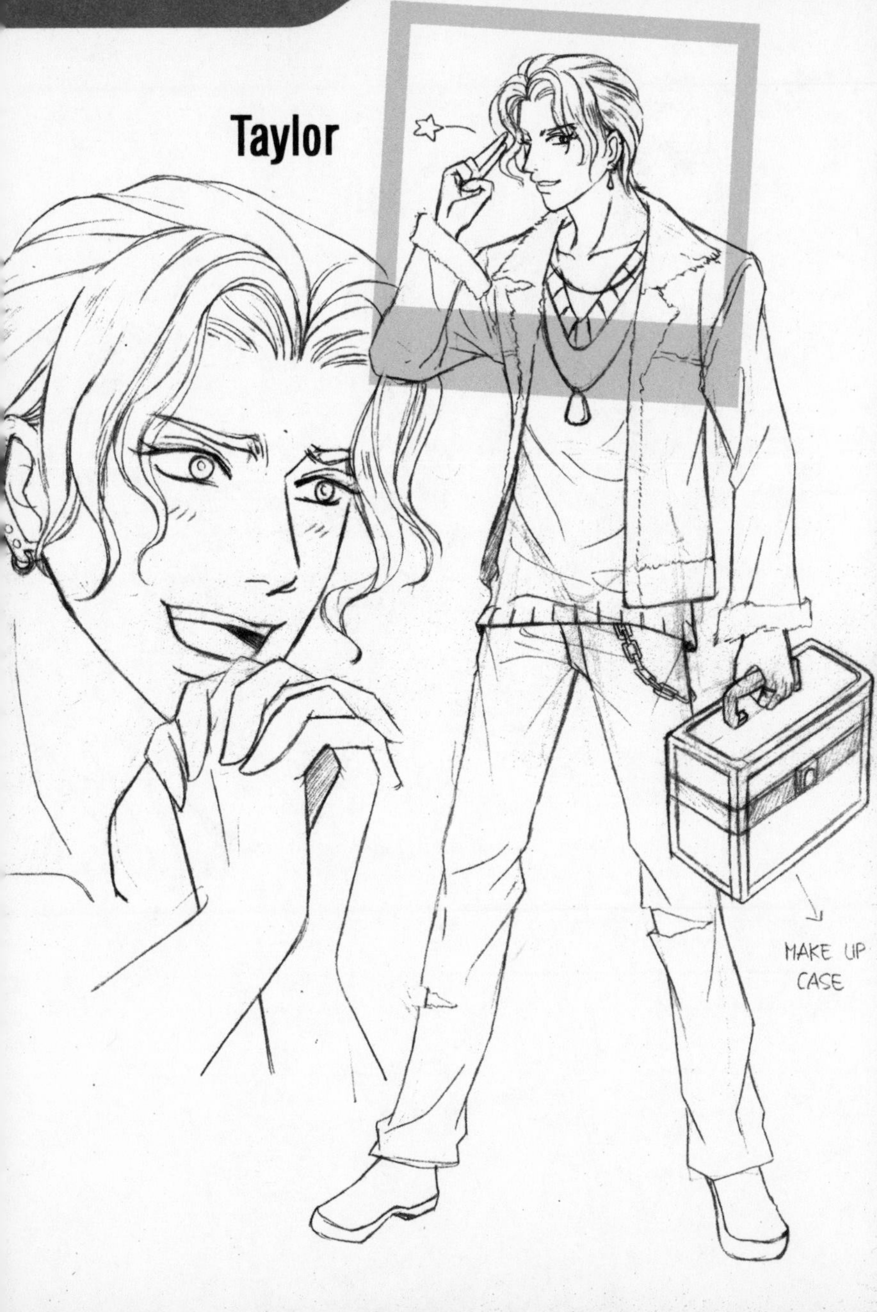
MAKE UP
CASE

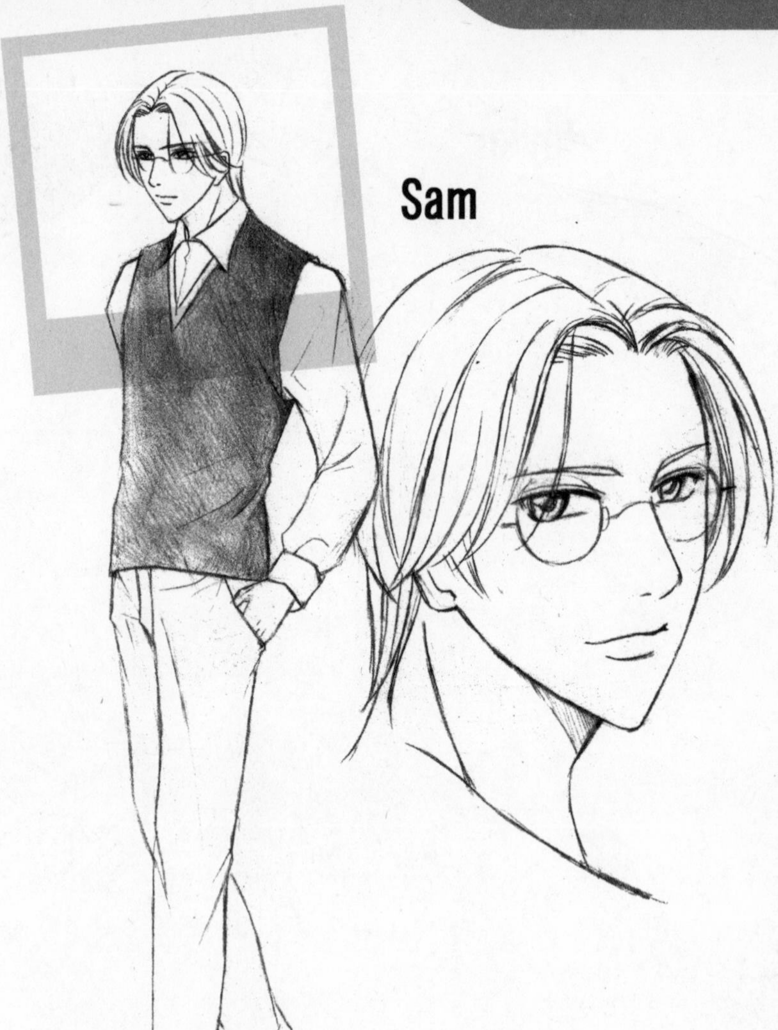
Sam

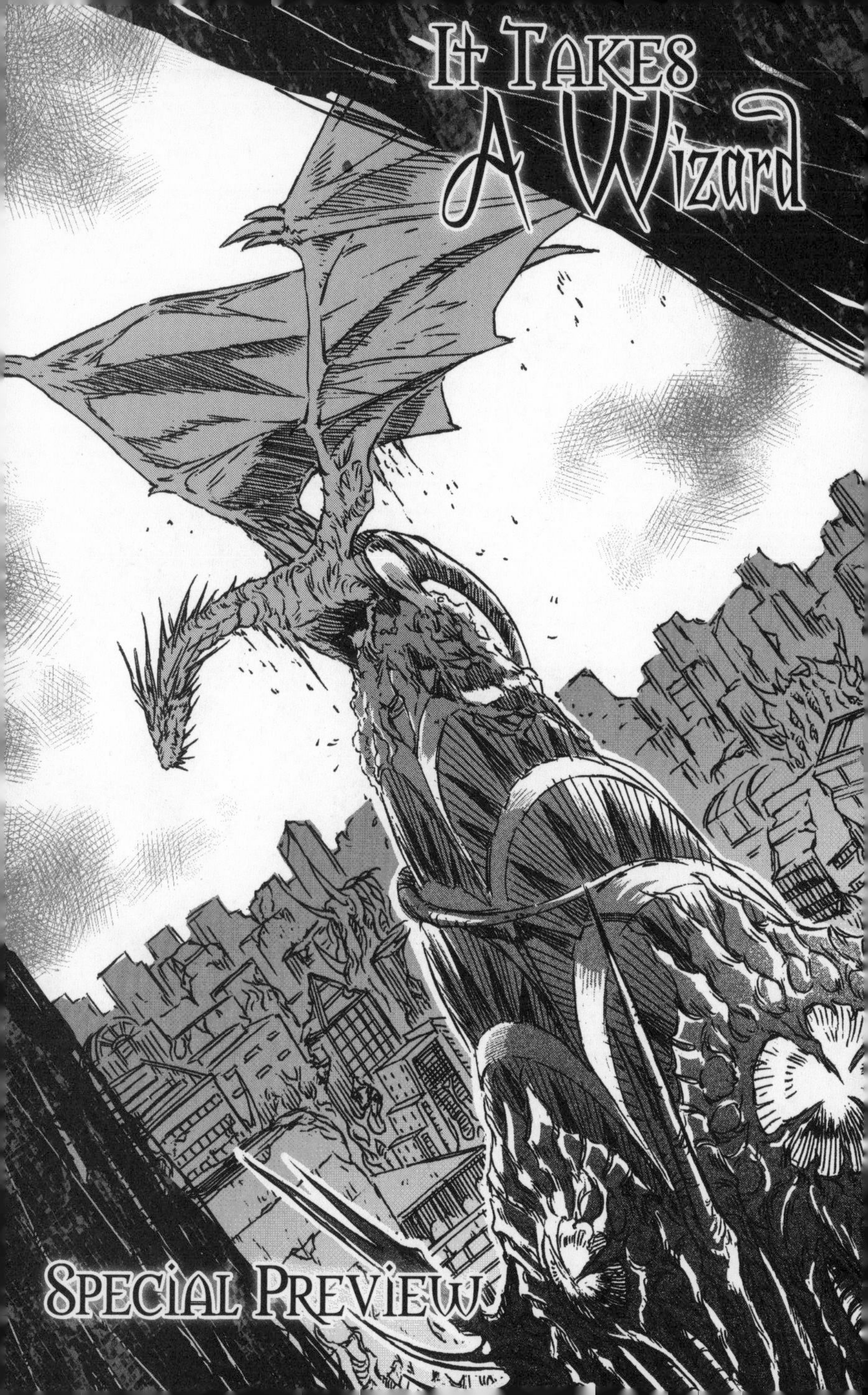
It Takes
A Wizard
Special Preview

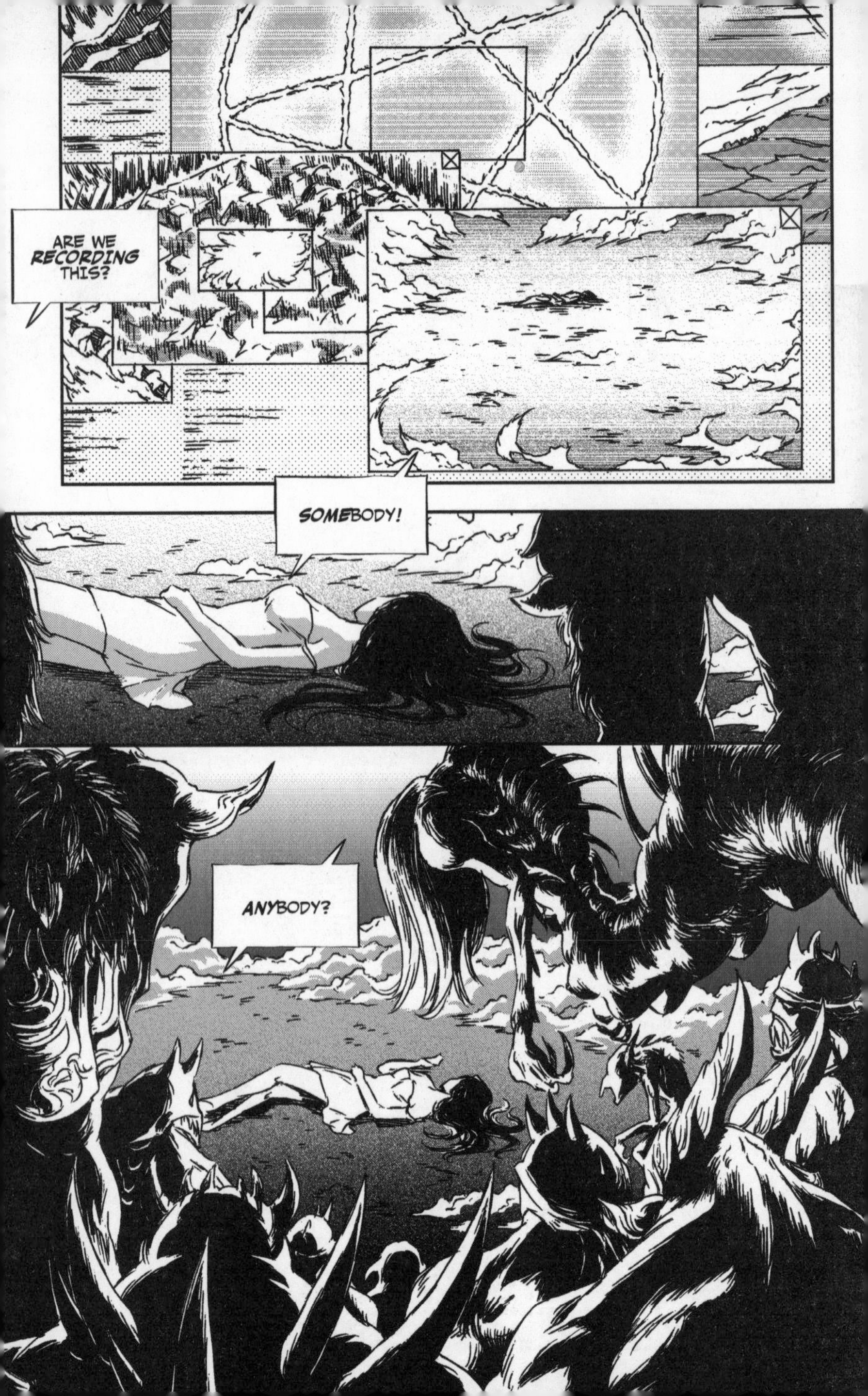
ARE WE RECORDING THIS?
SOMEBODY!
ANYBODY?

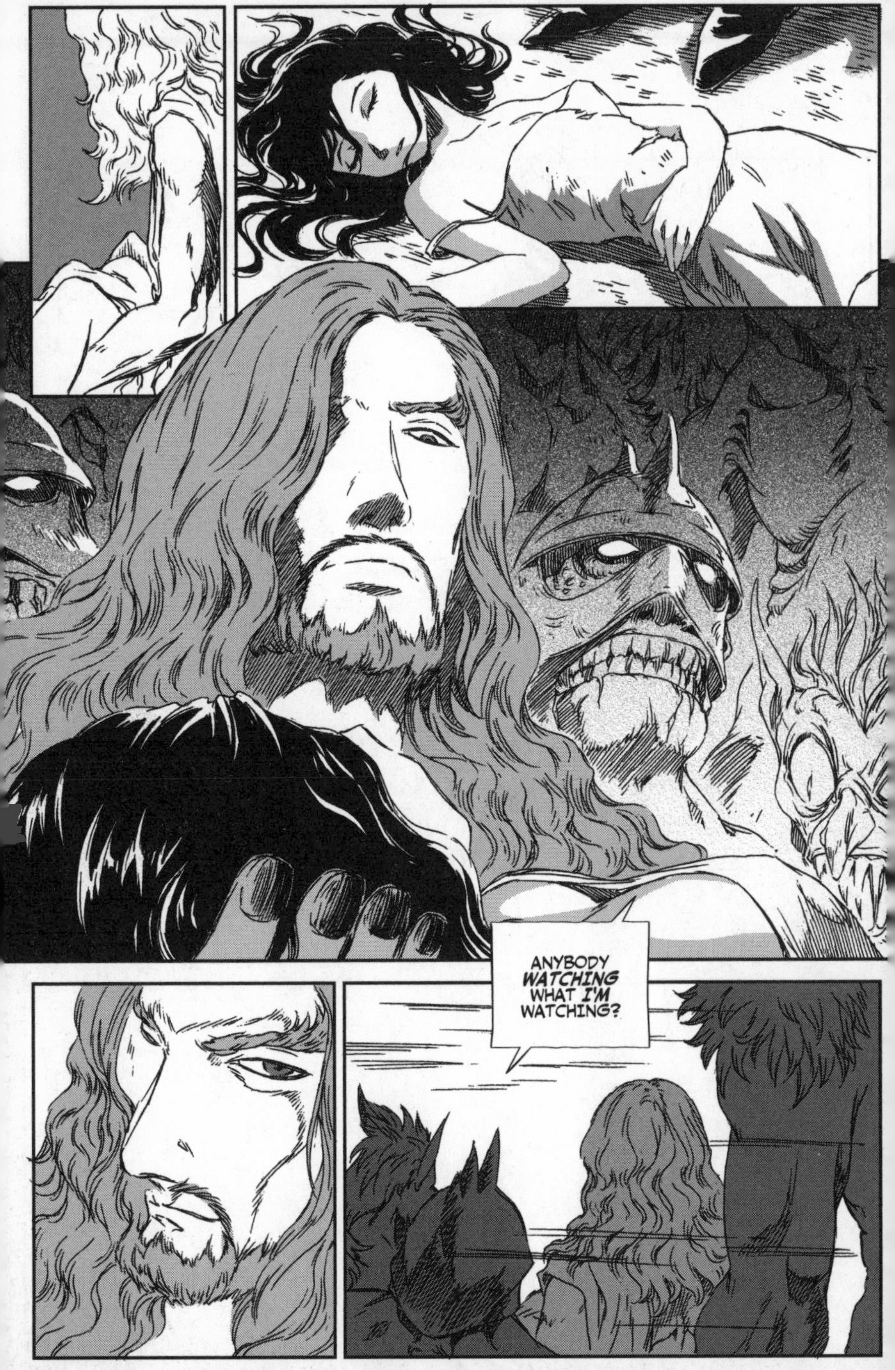
ANYBODY WATCHING WHAT I'M WATCHING?

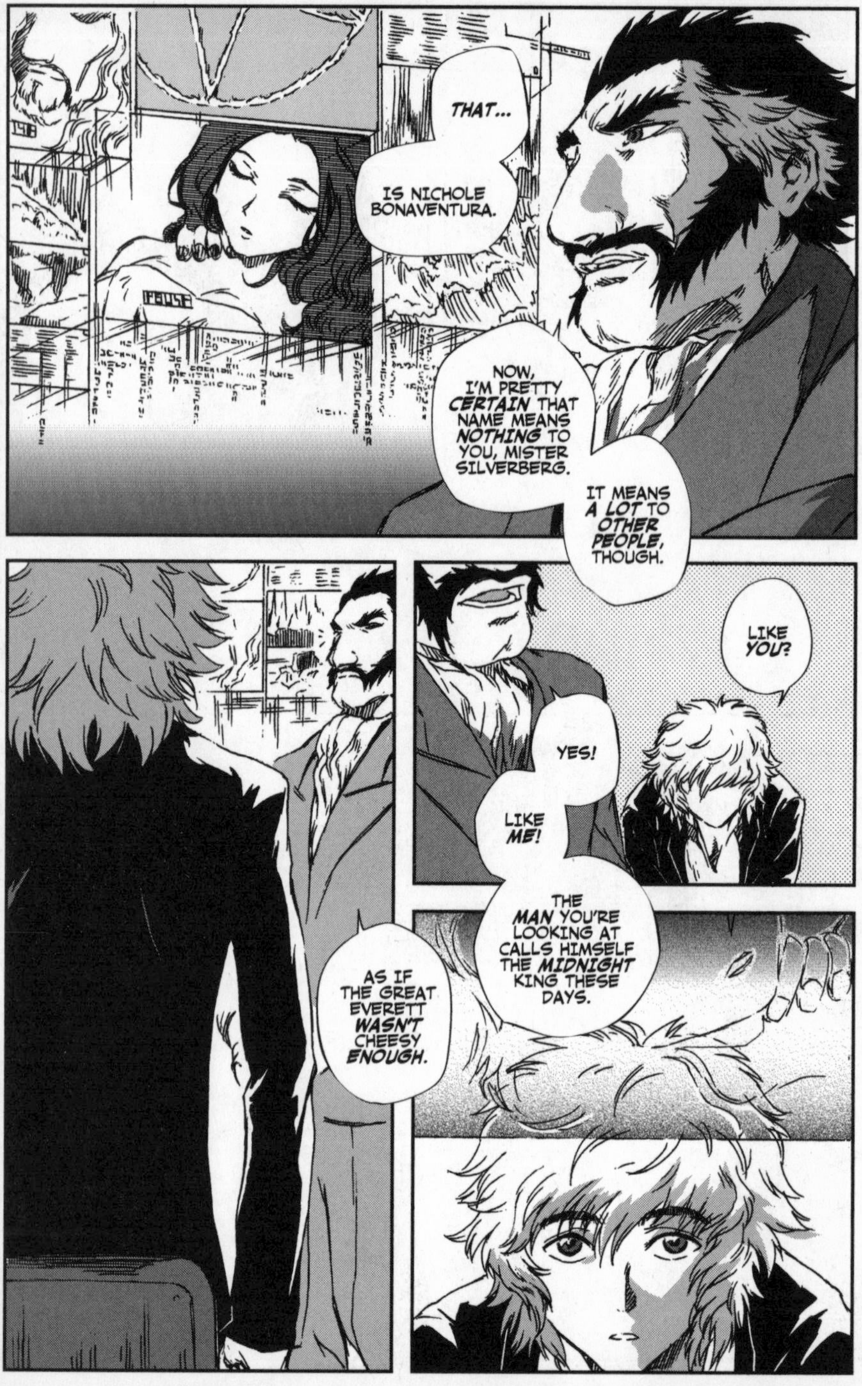
THAT...
IS NICHOLE BONAVENTURA.
NOW, I'M PRETTY CERTAIN THAT NAME MEANS NOTHING TO YOU, MISTER SILVERBERG.
IT MEANS A LOT TO OTHER PEOPLE, THOUGH.
LIKE YOU?
YES!
LIKE ME!
THE MAN YOU'RE LOOKING AT CALLS HIMSELF THE MIDNIGHT KING THESE DAYS.
AS IF THE GREAT EVERETT WASN'T CHEESY ENOUGH.

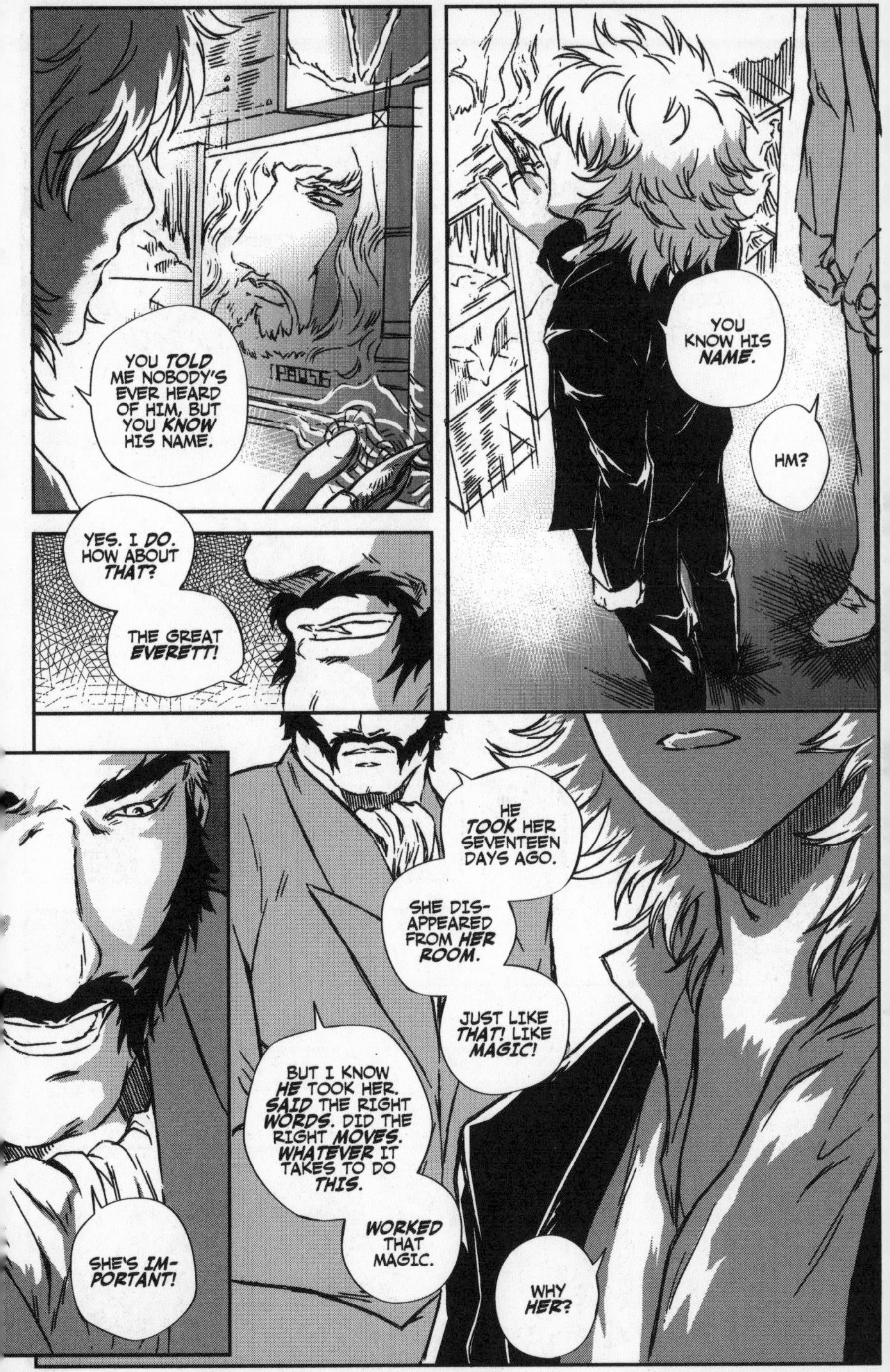
YOU KNOW HIS NAME.
HM?
PAUSE
YOU TOLD ME NOBODY'S EVER HEARD OF HIM, BUT YOU KNOW HIS NAME.
YES. I DO. HOW ABOUT THAT?
THE GREAT EVERETT!
HE TOOK HER SEVENTEEN DAYS AGO.
SHE DIS-APPEARED FROM HER ROOM.
JUST LIKE THAT! LIKE MAGIC!
BUT I KNOW HE TOOK HER. SAID THE RIGHT WORDS. DID THE RIGHT MOVES. WHATEVER IT TAKES TO DO THIS.
WORKED THAT MAGIC.
WHY HER?
SHE'S IM-PORTANT!

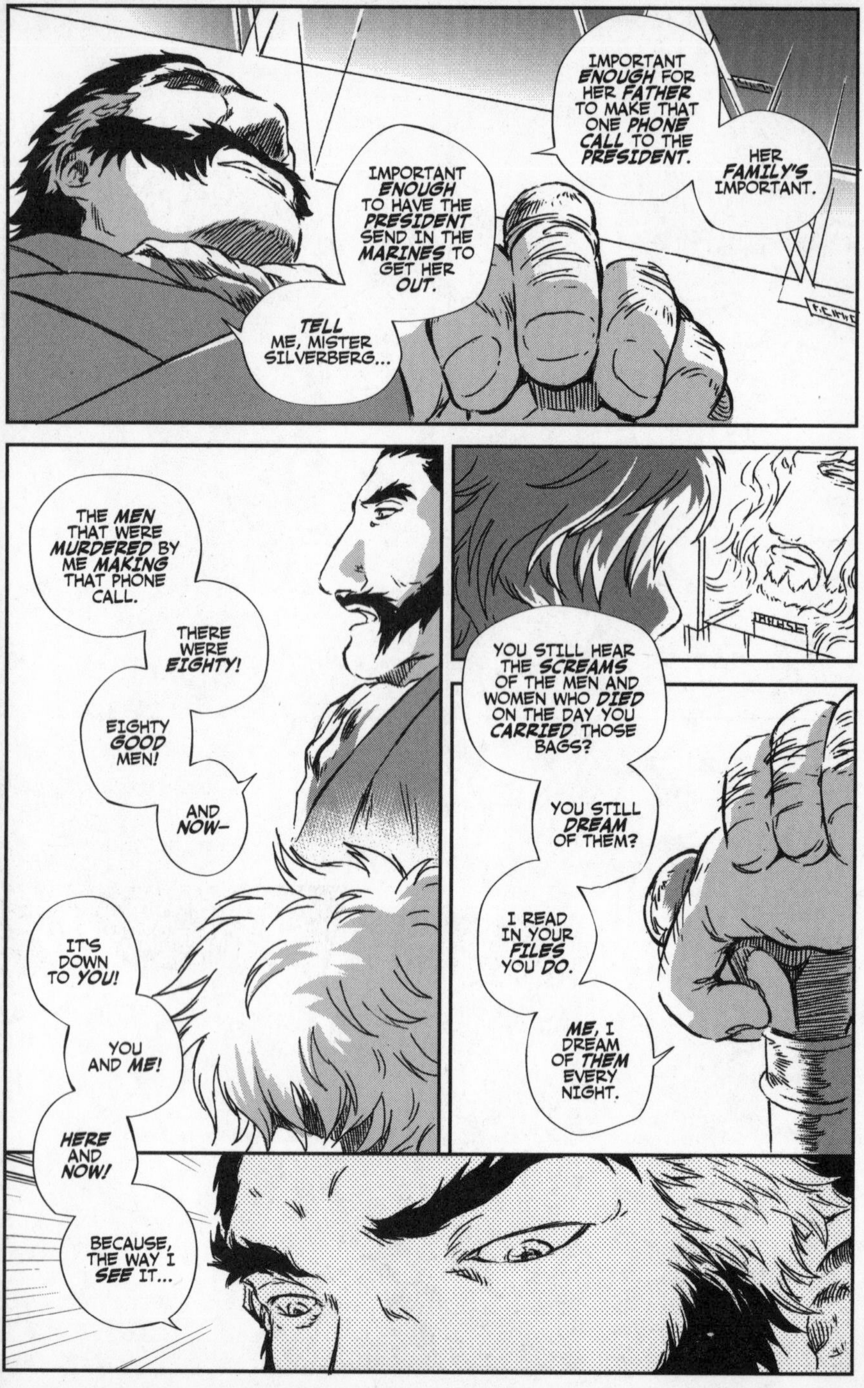
HER FAMILY'S IMPORTANT.
IMPORTANT ENOUGH FOR HER FATHER TO MAKE THAT ONE PHONE CALL TO THE PRESIDENT.
IMPORTANT ENOUGH TO HAVE THE PRESIDENT SEND IN THE MARINES TO GET HER OUT.
TELL ME, MISTER SILVERBERG...
YOU STILL HEAR THE SCREAMS OF THE MEN AND WOMEN WHO DIED ON THE DAY YOU CARRIED THOSE BAGS?
YOU STILL DREAM OF THEM?
I READ IN YOUR FILES YOU DO.
ME, I DREAM OF THEM EVERY NIGHT.
THE MEN THAT WERE MURDERED BY ME MAKING THAT PHONE CALL.
THERE WERE EIGHTY!
EIGHTY GOOD MEN!
AND NOW-
IT'S DOWN TO YOU!
YOU AND ME!
HERE AND NOW!
BECAUSE, THE WAY I SEE IT...

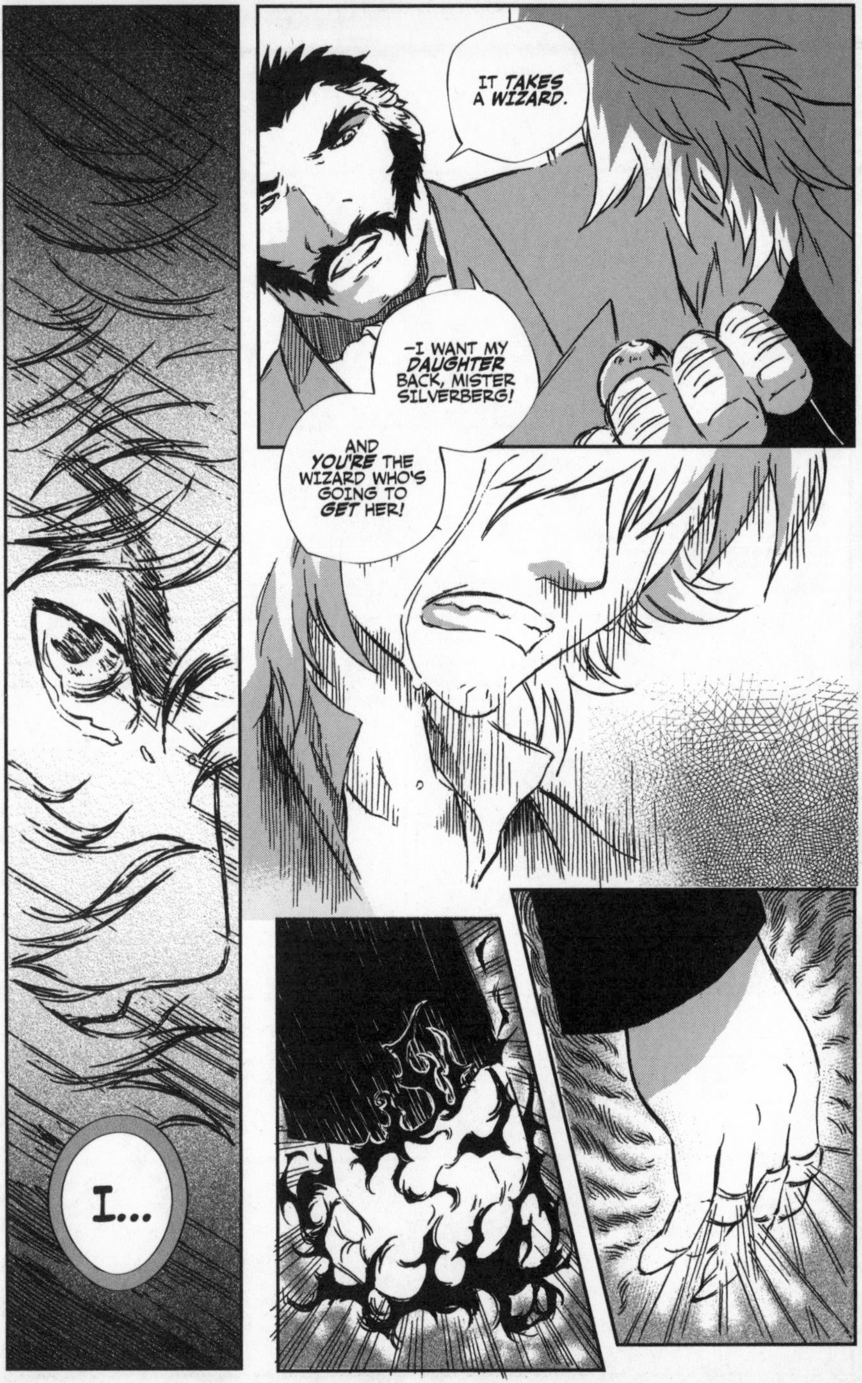
IT *TAKES* A *WIZARD*.
–I WANT MY ***DAUGHTER*** BACK, MISTER SILVERBERG!
AND ***YOU'RE*** THE WIZARD WHO'S GOING TO ***GET*** HER!
I...

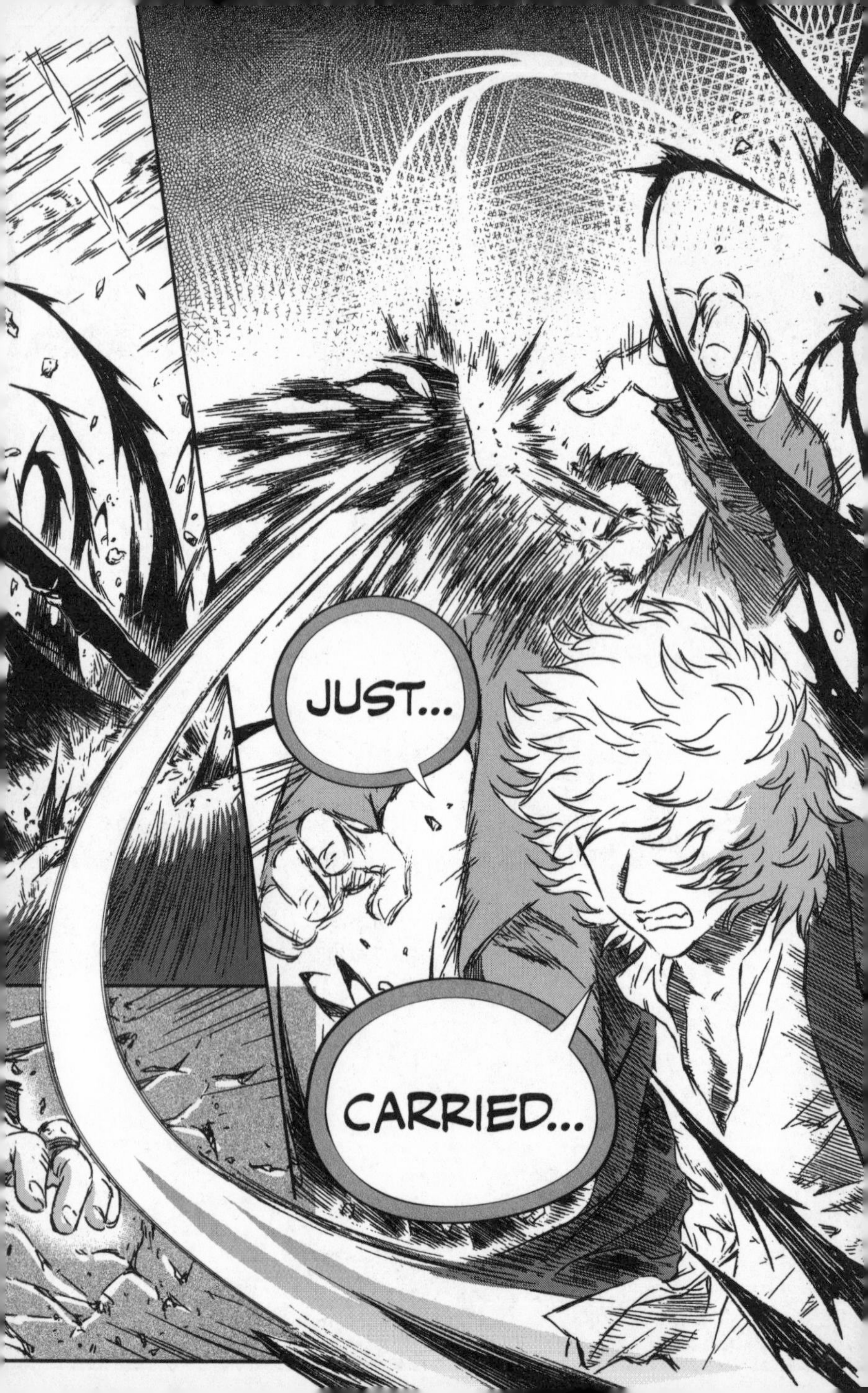
JUST...
CARRIED...

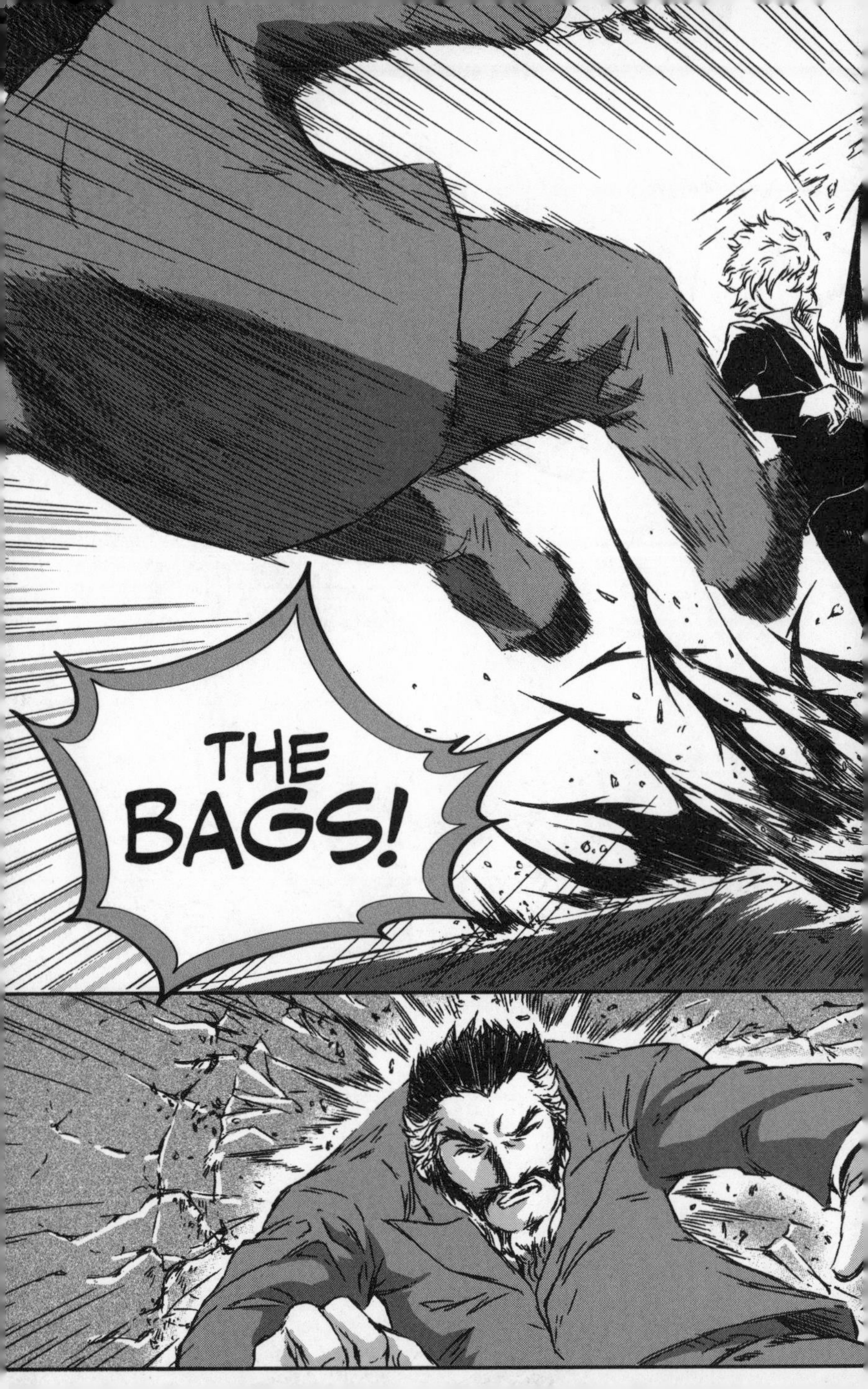
THE BAGS!

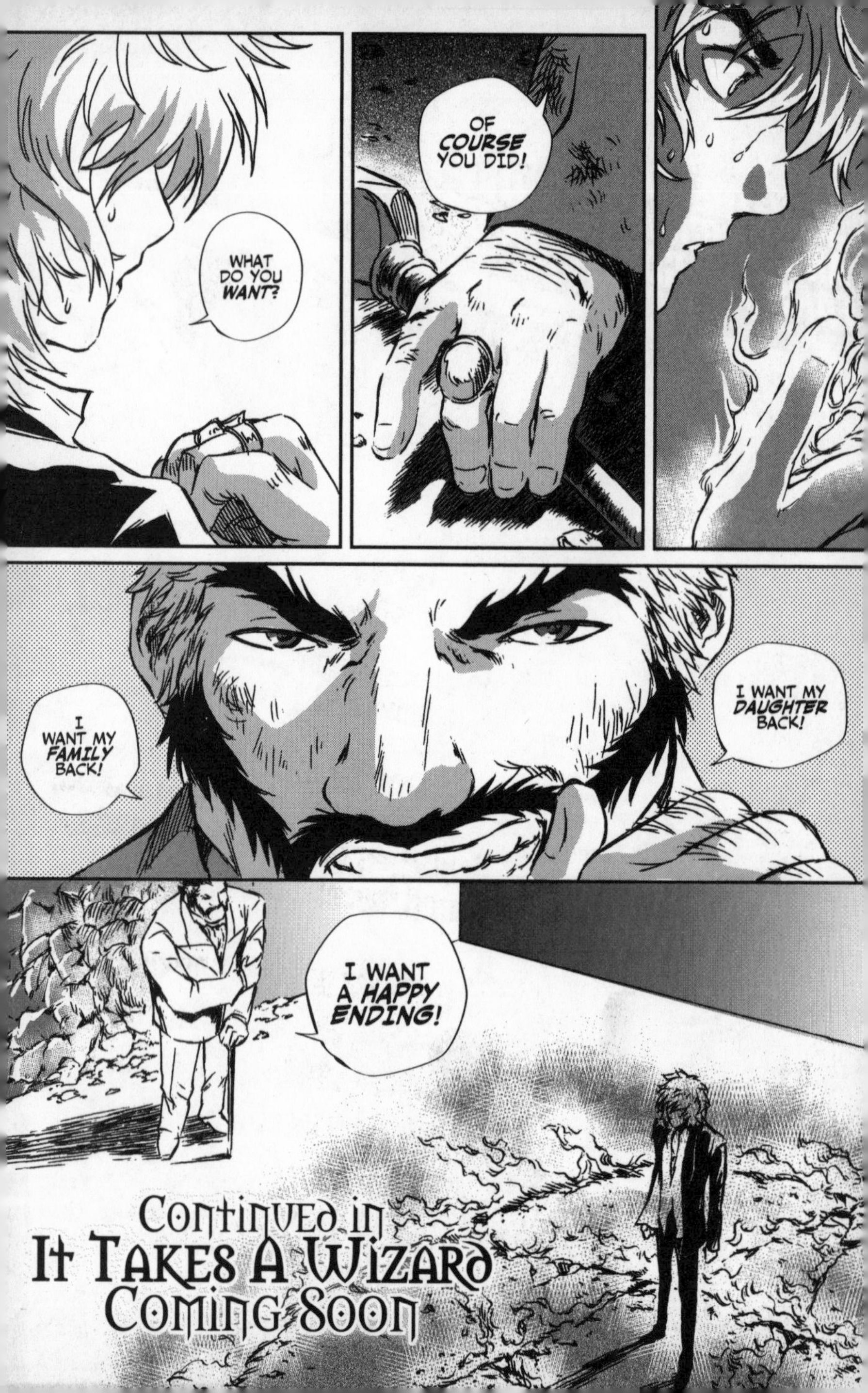
OF COURSE YOU DID!
WHAT DO YOU WANT?
I WANT MY DAUGHTER BACK!
I WANT MY FAMILY BACK!
I WANT A HAPPY ENDING!
Continued in
It Takes A Wizard
Coming Soon